THE
STOPWATCH GANG

THE
STOPWATCH GANG

Greg Weston

Macmillan Canada
Toronto

Canadian Cataloguing in Publication Data

Weston, Greg
    The stopwatch gang

ISBN 0-7715-9136-5

1. Stopwatch Gang. 2. Bank robberies - Canada. 3. Bank robberies - United States. 4. Criminals - Canada - Biography. 5. Criminals - United States - Biography. I. Title.

HV666.C32S8   1992   364.1'552'0971   C92-094315-2

Macmillan Canada wishes to thank the Canada Council for supporting its publishing program.

Macmillan Canada
A Division of Canada Publishing Corporation
Toronto, Canada

1 2 3 4 5   JD   96 95 94 93 92

Printed in Canada

In memory
of
John Anthony David Weston
who left us
to chase the wind

ACKNOWLEDGEMENTS

Naturally, a project of this scope and duration has required the time, effort and cooperation of literally dozens of people. To all of them, I owe my gratitude.

I owe my most profound thanks to Stephen Reid and his wife Susan Musgrave. Their generosity of time, absolute frankness and warm hospitality—even as I repeatedly invaded their lives—occasionally made it difficult to maintain a comfortable journalistic distance from my subjects.

To my editor and good friend Hubert Bauch, there is the overwhelming gratitude of an author rescued from the bottom of a deep well.

To my publisher Denise Schon, I remain awed by her patience and honored by her friendship throughout the past two years.

I am also greatly indebted to Gordon Fisher and Graham Parley of the Ottawa *Citizen* for their support and encouragement of the project since it began twelve years ago; and to Editor Jim Travers and Photo Director Richard Starnes who more recently gave me free use of the newspaper's files and photographs, many of which appear in the book.

I am grateful to the librarians and research staffs of the *Citizen,* the *Los Angeles Times,* the *San Diego Union* and the *Tribune* (now one paper), the *Arizona Republic,* and the Associated Press.

Others who have made special contributions over the past decade to the print and photographic material in these pages:

In Canada: the families of Paddy Mitchell, Lionel Wright, and Stephen Reid; former Ottawa *Citizen* reporter Neil Macdonald (now with the CBC) whose reports on the capture of Paddy Mitchell were of exceptional value; Crown prosecutor Mac Lindsay; defense attorneys Colin McKinnon, David Wake and Leonard Shore; Oleh Rumak and Bob McKeown (now with NBC) of the CBC, and the staffs of the Federal Department of Justice, the Ontario Court of Appeals, and Millhaven Penitentiary.

In California: FBI agents James Bird, Jack Kelly, Ron Orrantia, and particularly their former boss, Norman A. Zigrossi; Harlen Hudson and officials of the Loomis Armored Car Co.; Assistant U.S. Attorney Jack Robinson; defense attorneys Barton Sheela, Michael McCabe, Michael Aguirre, and Ralph Larsen; and my good friends Sylvie and Andre who shared their home with me during my research in San Diego.

In Arizona: Jack and Judy Seely for their hospitality; FBI special agent Stephen Chenoweth who provided me with some of the best-available photo material on Paddy Mitchell; Mike Arra of the Arizona Department of Corrections; Warden Joe C. Martinez at the time Arizona State pen; Larry Troutt of the Arizona State Police; and particularly detectives Jim Thomas and George Harden (since retired) of the Phoenix Police Department.

On a final personal note, there probably would have been no book—and likely not much left of its author, either—without the unswerving kindness, encouragement and good humor of a wonderful mother, a caring Sis (Jo Bennett-Weston), my good friends Tom Van Dusen, Glen and Joan—and, of course, the dreaded Wyches.

Then, there's that fellow Paddy Mitchell...

INTRODUCTION

Like most good news stories, it all started with a ringing phone. A reporter at the *Los Angeles Times* was calling the Ottawa *Citizen* looking for home-town file material on three crooks named Patrick Mitchell, Stephen Reid, and Lionel Wright. I happened to take the call. Life would never be quite the same

There was plenty of Canadian file material, all right—the nation's largest-ever gold robbery, a totally off-the-wall drug smuggling scheme, wild prison escapes. One of them used to work for my own newspaper, for heavenssake. But no one had ever connected all the players and events. And now the three Canadians had made bad in the U.S. as the "Stopwatch Gang." It sounded like a pretty good yarn.

The next afternoon, I was en route to Arizona and the Maricopa County Jail for interviews with Wright and Reid, who had been arrested two days before. (Actually, I was probably the first person ever to sneak *into* the jail, but that's another story.)

Whatever I imagined two of America's most-hunted bank robbers might be like, these guys didn't even come close—witty, intelligent, refined, and generally likeable characters.

Their story was even more of a surprise—I had hardly expected to laugh through most of a three-hour interview with two men described on the FBI's Most Wanted posters as "Armed and Extremely Dangerous!!!"

The only question they wouldn't answer was where I might find Paddy Mitchell, the affable family man from suburbia turned criminal mastermind. Reid suggested I might try the Yellow Pages under "Wanted, Ten Most." Had I known then what I know now about these characters, I wouldn't have been so quick to laugh off the remark.

As I left Maricopa County lock-up that day, I knew I had stumbled upon an extraordinary story. But nothing seemed to fit: the engaging individuals I had just met didn't match their record-setting crimes. As I would soon discover, I had joined a substantial crowd of law-abiding citizens across North America who had similarly been left shaking their heads— and usually smiling—at the same thought: Naw, it can't be true. These guys can't be bank robbers.

That was twelve years ago. Since then I have continued to be both amazed and amused (and even arrested once, but that's another story, too) as the research for this book has unearthed one bizarre tale after another. Even to this day, the story continues to evolve as one of America's great unsolved mysteries.

The Stopwatch Gang may very well be the last of America's legendary bank robbing gangs, routinely grabbing more loot in ninety seconds than most others in their business would steal in a lifetime. Thankfully, the advent of automated-teller machines and long-overdue security precautions have all but shut down the big times of bank robbery. There likely never will be another Stopwatch Gang.

The story that follows is a reconstruction of events based on hundreds of hours of interviews and more than 10,000 pages of official documents, including transcripts of police wiretaps and other legal voice interceptions on which much of the early dialogue is based. Wherever possible, I have insisted that interview material be backed with official records.

Much of the material is based on the personal recollections of the bandits themselves, and the many other people whose paths they crossed. Perhaps more than anything, I have benefitted from the lively, colorful, and remarkably accurate story-telling of Stephen Reid, whose ability to recall minute detail is every journalist's dream.

No one has been paid for any information in this book, nor was anyone afforded any rights of review in return for their cooperation. The names of certain individuals have been changed to protect their privacy. The following names are fictitious and any similarity to actual persons of the same name, living or dead, is purely coincidental: Barbara and Johnny Mitchell; Aunt Molly Somerville; Chuck Hogan; Howard J. Hoover III; Gerda Ottinger; Sam Stone. In some other cases, last names have been deleted and/or nicknames invented for the same reasons of privacy. The Dollar Motel and the Shamrock Bar have also been fictionalized in name only to protect the identities of some individuals. The book *Stopping Theft* is not its true title. The aliases used by the gang members were either borrowed from dead people or invented.

Certain details such as police radio communication codes have been altered at the request of law enforcement agencies. Some dates and the precise locations of certain crimes have been changed.

Finally, much of the dialogue has been reconstructed from interviews and best recollections, and therefore should not be construed as having absolute verbatim accuracy.

PROLOGUE

San Diego, California,
September 23, 1980

"Don't try to be a hero or I'll make you a dead one..."

It wasn't supposed to happen this way. Not him. Not like this. It was supposed to start with some whacked-out druggie in a ski mask. It was supposed to end with a .38-caliber Smith & Wesson flashing from hip holster to eye level, and blowing a new hole in the balaclava. That's how it happened in all those bulletproof daydreams, anyway. He always won; the punks always lost. He always lived; they always died. No one was going to fuck with this ex-Marine and live to brag about it.

It wasn't supposed to happen this way, but it was—a gun barrel jabbed into his ribs, his own weapon dangling useless as bagged milk on his belt.

His eyes darted from the bandit's neatly trimmed beard to the silk tie to the pinstriped suit. A businessman sticking up an armored-truck guard? In the middle of a crowded bank? Even the warning about fatal heroics had sounded more like a casual greeting than a death threat.

It definitely wasn't supposed to happen this way...

Harlen Lee Hudson—Ray to his friends—lit another cigarette as the armored truck swung on to Garnet Avenue. He didn't usually admit it at the Legion, but his nine years with the Loomis Armored Car Service in San Diego had been pretty boring stuff. Day after day, alone on a jump seat welded to the floor of the rear cargo compartment. Smoking, sipping coffee. Sixty stops a day. Sometimes more. Loading, unloading. Backbreaking work, even for a burly guy of forty-two. The contract called for three minutes per bank. No time to get to know

1

names, much less people. Usually just a hello, lousy weather, maybe a bad joke while someone filled out the delivery sheet. The faster he could make the day's rounds, the sooner he could go home. Same pay every day.

He stared at the money sacks piled across from him. He guessed maybe two million dollars, perhaps three. He didn't much care. Some guys couldn't handle being around that much cash all the time and quit after a few weeks on the job. But they were all just packages to him, and he was a courier who happened to carry a Smith & Wesson .38 on his right hip. Not that he minded the danger. It added some excitement to the life of a delivery boy. Besides, after three tours of duty with the Marines in Nam, this was chickenshit. His wife hated his job.

He liked his driver Henry Koppen, even though they didn't talk much. It was hard to hear anything up front through the thick steel wall and three-by-five plexiglass window that separated them. He had tried screeching small-talk from the back when he first came on the job. But that had just made him hoarse. Now he didn't bother. Actually, he kind of enjoyed the solitude. No one pushing him around, telling him what to do.

The engine growled as the truck swung into the parking lot beside the Bank of America at 912 Garnet in the Pacific Beach area of northern San Diego. The branch had moved there only recently after a string of five armed robberies at its old location up the street. The last time it had been hit by a gang that was knocking off banks all over California and a dozen other states. Once they'd hit two in the same morning. All big hauls. Precision stuff. Front-page news every time. One of them usually wore a stopwatch around his neck. Always in and out in less than ninety seconds. Then, poof, they'd vanish. No leads. No suspects. Obviously pros. They were sure driving the cops crazy. They were driving Ray Hudson's wife crazy, too.

The truck began its loud warning beeps as it backed into the handicapped parking spot. That always got people pissed at them. But the drivers did it anyway, as a favor to the backseat hoppers like Ray Hudson who had to do all the heavy physical stuff. The wheelchair spaces at least put them close to the doors, and there was always a ramp for their carts.

Ray Hudson checked his watch and scowled. It was 10:47 already and they had made only a dozen stops. Twenty-eight minutes late. There had been delays all morning, mostly shipments that weren't ready to go when the truck arrived. These were the same customers who insisted the armored pickups and deliveries be made at the same time on the same days every week. As far as he was concerned, that was just an asinine invitation to armed robbery. But the company wanted to please the customers. And what did the banks care? If he was held up, Loomis paid. To hell with the guards.

Hudson climbed out the rear door of his truck and began loading boxes of coin onto his trolley. Sixty-five of them. Forty-seven pounds apiece. Three trips at least. Damn. Not going to make up any time at this stop.

The balloon tires on the cart made a low hiss as they rolled across the freshly waxed tile floor. The long customer counter was on the right, the loans department on the left, a rather sumptuously furnished area of deep carpets, plush couches, and oak desks where clients could at least plunge themselves into debt comfortably.

He scanned the customers. Four of them were talking to tellers at the long counter. A businessman in a blue suit was sitting at a table at the edge of the loans department. Another fellow was filling out a with-drawal slip at the far end of the bank, standing at a desk just inside the main doors on to Garnet Avenue. Kind of lean-looking, light tan suit, black belt, black shoes, freshly styled blond hair parted on the left, horn-rimmed glasses, and some weird Vandyke beard. Hadn't seen one of those in years. Must be a musician or something.

He unloaded the boxes of coin at the vault and a man signed for them as Hudson began piling his cart with the outbound bags of unwrapped change. He thought it all a big waste of time—shipping coin in bags all the way to the Federal Reserve in Los Angeles so it could be put in boxes and shipped all the way back to the banks in San Diego. There was a lot about this business that didn't make any sense to Harlen Lee Hudson.

He headed back towards the truck, towards the businessman writing some kind of application form at the round table in the loans depart-ment. Sure looked like he already had enough money. The three-piece pinstriped blue suit. Definitely expensive. Nice yellow silk tie, light blue shirt, probably monogrammed on the pocket. The guy liked hair, all right, his face reduced to a nose, lips, and a pair of glasses protruding from a mat of curly charcoal fuzz. He also had bandages on the thumb and first two fingers of his right hand, but Ray Hudson didn't notice.

The businessman flipped a brown Samsonite briefcase onto the desk and snapped the locks as the cart approached. He kept his hand on the case, but didn't open it. Without looking up, he went back to his paperwork.

Another load of coin boxes came back into the bank. Another signature on the delivery sheet. Another load of bagged change to the truck. Finally, Hudson piled the last twenty-five boxes of coin onto the trolley and headed one last time to the vault. The customers who had been at the tellers' counter had left and new ones were arriving. But the businessman was still at his desk in the loans department. The musician was still struggling with his withdrawal slip.

The last time Ray Hudson checked his watch in the vault it was 10:54. He frowned. They'd be lucky to finish their rounds before dark.

He began piling his cart with the locked bags of paper currency bound for the Bank of America main branch downtown. He always left them until the last. Get all the heavy loads done first, then a light one, then back into the truck for a smoke, a coffee, and a rest before the next stop.

There were three canvas sacks, each about thirty inches high, roughly ten pounds apiece. He checked the tags: $200,000 in the first; $75,000 in the second; $8,000 in the third. Just more packages.

"Have a nice day," he said to the man signing the delivery slips.

"Uh-huh," he mumbled.

The glance at his watch and the light load made him step up his pace as he headed for the doors at the far end of the bank. A lanky blonde was striding towards him, her red silk dress pasted to her thighs. His head twisted slightly to the left, the mirrored sunglasses on lock. In the same instant, something moved on his right.

It all happened so fast—the businessman at the loans table reached into his briefcase, slid something under the pile of papers, picked them up with his left hand, and stepped directly into the oncoming path of $283,000 on a handcart.

"Hold it or I'll kill you."

Another goddam prankster, Hudson thought. Like the twit who asked if he had change for a million, or the woman who wanted him to mail a letter...Dammit, not today...I'm already running late.

He swerved the cart to the left to dodge the unexpected nuisance in his path. Then the jab of the gun barrel in his ribs, the sound of a revolver being cocked. Another message from the bearded businessman, something about becoming a dead hero.

The message suddenly registered. Hudson froze.

The businessman was still holding his loan application in his left hand as he reached to the guard's hip, flipped the snap on the thin holster strap and pulled out the Smith & Wesson. The revolver in the assailant's right hand gave a final poke to the guard's ribs, an unspoken signal for Hudson to unwrap his white knuckles from the cart handles, shuffle back two paces, and reach for the air above his head.

"Okay, folks, this is a holdup," the businessman boomed, his gun aimed squarely at the mirrored sun glasses three feet from his outstretched arm. "Everyone get down on the floor and let's not have any heroes today."

The words sounded calm, casual, commanding but almost polite, more like a fireman directing an evacuation than someone threatening a bloodbath. There was a moment of stillness, another dozen people frozen in fear, their minds racing to reconcile a natty three-piece suit with the two loaded revolvers and a preamble to death. There was a rustle of movement. Then nothing.

Ray Hudson had landed facefirst on the carpet of the loans department, his head turned away from his assailant, the mirrored sunglasses grinding into the bridge of his nose. He pulled off the shades and listened. Footsteps moved quickly towards him from the far end of the bank. Closer. Faster. Suddenly they stopped. Something touched the crook of his neck, something cold and hard. A gun. He closed his eyes tight.

"Move and I'll kill you," said a new voice.

"Let's go!" the businessman whispered. "Let's get out of here."

A teller behind the customer counter had dropped to the floor on command and now clawed herself across the carpet until she was under her desk. She reached up and hit the silent-alarm button under the center drawer. The security cameras began snapping thirty-five-millimeter photographs, one every second.

Click. The businessman is standing with a raised revolver in his right hand, a large sack of cash slung over his left shoulder.

Click. The musician with the weird Vandyke beard is standing beside the trolley with a gun at Hudson's head. He tucks the revolver into the waistband of his suit pants. There is another gun over his right hip in a belt holster. He is holding the other two money bags, one in each hand.

Click. The two gentlemen bandits are walking towards the Garnet Avenue doors near the opposite end of the bank from the parking lot where Loomis driver Hank Koppen is checking his watch and cursing.

Click. The musician has dropped his two sacks of loot and is running back towards Ray Hudson. The businessman is casually scratching the side of his nose with the back of his .38.

Click. The musician has gone back to the round table for the businessman's briefcase. He is leaning hard on the lid of the attaché case, struggling with the snap locks. One of them won't catch.

Click. The musician is back and has picked up both bags with his left hand, the briefcase dangling from his right. The two men are again heading towards the door.

Click. The briefcase has fallen open an inch. Click. Now six inches. Click. Now halfway. Click. Now completely. Click. Papers and a weapon—looks like an Uzi submachine-gun—are spilling from the briefcase onto the floor.

Click. The musician is on his knees frantically trying to scoop everything back into the briefcase. He can't get it closed again. The businessman is holding his forehead. His eyes are rolled upwards.

Click. The musician has the two money bags in one hand, the briefcase tucked under his other arm. It is still open an inch. They turn their backs to the cameras and wheel for the door. A gun barrel is protruding from the back of the briefcase.

Click. They have stopped at the door and turned, the loaded .38 once again aimed at a Loomis guard sprawled on the carpet of a Bank of America loans department…

As soon as the two bandits started to leave the bank, Ray Hudson twisted his head to watch. No one had ever threatened his life, not in a bank, not in Nam, nowhere. No sonofabitch had ever stood over Harlen Lee Hudson and made him smell dirty carpet. His fingertips curled in a growing rage—I hate that prick in the fancy suit, more than I've ever hated anyone…I'm going to get a hunk of that motherfucker's ass…He's got a gun, my gun, and I don't. But I know where there's another one and I'm going for it…That fucker's goin' down…

"Okay, everyone stay on the floor and no one will get hurt," the businessman shouted in his everything's-going-to-be-just-fine tone. "No heroes today, please."

He turned for the door, paused, and turned back towards the customer counter: "There's someone outside with a shotgun and anyone who sticks a head out there is going to get it blown off."

All very matter-of-fact. Then they were gone.

The entire holdup had taken one minute and thirty-three seconds.

Hudson was now on his feet and barreling towards the doors to the parking lot, to his truck, to the loaded 12-gauge shotgun. The thrity-foot dash seemed like a marathon—limbs pumping, eyes bulging, pulse throbbing in his ears. He imagined the .38 being lowered, cocked, aimed at his back...His own gun...Killed by his own revolver...How embarrassing...

The guard was still waiting for the crack of his Smith & Wesson when his two hundred pounds crashed against the steel-and-glass doors. He lunged to his right towards the Loomis armored truck where his driver was still placidly oblivious to the holdup.

"We've been fucking hit," he screamed, scrambling through one side door of the cargo compartment and out the other, barely pausing to grab the pump-action shotgun off the wall rack. Hank Koppen turned in his seat and pressed his face against the plexiglass peephole.

"I said, we've been fucking *hit*..."

The biggest bank robbery in San Diego's history had suddenly thrown the local FBI operations into pandemonium. Someone had called the bank to confirm the alarm. The news crackled across the city from one agent's walkie-talkie to another: "A big one in progress at the B of A, Pacific Beach...Three hundred grand...Armored-truck job...Two males in business suits...More of them outside...Lots of artillery...Guard in pursuit with a shotgun...Sounds like our Stopwatch boys..."

Hudson moved quickly along the front of the bank, body turned sideways, leg over leg, his back always to the wall, shotgun vertical, finger beside the trigger, just like they did it in Nam. He heard the roar of the armored-truck engine as Hank Koppen wheeled onto the street and turned to block traffic away from the shootout. Hudson knew his partner would stay in the truck. Company regulations. Protect the load first.

He reached the corner of the building. They had said there was someone with a shotgun outside the bank. He stopped...Never come around a corner blind...That's what they always said in Nam...Come around a corner blind and you're dead...

Hudson flattened himself against the rough brick. His mouth was dry. His lungs were heaving. He lowered the gun to firing position, stroked the trigger with his index finger, and dug his right foot into the dirt.

He gulped for air. Count of three and he was going for it. He wanted to kill them. All of them. Those bastards were dead meat.

This was how it was supposed to happen.

"One...Two...Three..."

CHAPTER ONE

Ottawa, Canada

Psychologist's Report: Patrick Michael Mitchell has been described as a gentle, overly generous, and thoughtful person well loved by his family and friends. He is the product of a stable family background, and is reported to be a devoted son, husband, and father. Mr. Mitchell describes himself as a leader and has been known to influence others in positive ways. He presents himself as an articulate, amiable, and intelligent person. Mr. Mitchell possesses the strengths of personality that could lead him into successful and lawful enterprises—should he determine to do so...

Paddy Mitchell grabbed the rifle and snapped it over his knee. It wasn't often anyone saw him in a temper, but on this summer's eve there was no mistaking his rage. Minutes before, his young son had rushed into the kitchen, wailing something about murder and bullets and the kid next door. Sure enough, Dad found it all in the field behind their suburban home—the gun and the neighbor's kid and one hapless songbird dispatched to eternity. Paddy disarmed the adolescent assailant and came straight to the point: the next shot in the neighborhood would draw return fire from the birds' side.

That evening, Barbara Mitchell watched her husband and their little boy make a cross out of twigs and string and bury the bird's remains in their suburban back yard. Hunting anything with a gun is the sport of heartless cowards, Paddy was always telling his son. The strong who prey on the weak are scum.

"The strange thing is there was nothing at all strange about that kind of behavior," she would recall years later. "Pat was the most gentle,

9

easygoing and kind-hearted soul you could ever meet. It's the rest of the story that's weird."

Even Paddy Mitchell could never have imagined back then just how weird the story could get—how a bright and likeable family man from the suburbs would become one of the FBI's notorious Ten Most Wanted; how the apparently devoted son, husband, and father who abhorred violence would become one of America's most successful armed bandits; how a fun-loving guy in search of the Good Life would wind up in the shotgun sights of a San Diego armored-truck guard named Harlen Lee Hudson.

Barbara Mitchell's part of the story began on a drizzly April morning at a bus stop. She couldn't help staring at the handsome fellow with the mischievous smile and seductive Irish eyes. He was bright and charming. Mature for his age. Quite the young gentleman, she thought. Not a rough edge anywhere—except, maybe, the crudely lettered tattoo on his left arm. She did wonder what kind of guy inscribes his body with "Fat and Heller." (Apparently a schoolmate with a nib pen and too much beer in his belly was responsible for the permanent typographical error; it should have read Pat and Helen, a high-school sweetheart.) Paddy promised to have it removed, but he never got around to it.

Barbara didn't bother to ask about the other nib-pen inscription on his body—a crucifix on his chest. That one was self-inflicted. An altar boy educated entirely at local Roman Catholic schools, Paddy had swallowed church dogma the way other kids devour ice cream. He was particularly moved by the part about the Lord forgiving the sins of all who truly believe. It seemed a nominal price to pay for the liberty to do whatever the hell he wanted. This blind faith would guide him down many a path in the years to come—unfortunately, righteousness was not one of them.

After the bus ride that day, the tattoo was the last trace of the Pat-and-Helen romance. Paddy was instantly drawn to Barbara's quiet self-confidence and pleasant self-deprecating humor. She was an aspiring singer on her way to some acclaim as a song-writer. Couldn't read or write a note of music. Usually composed her words on the bus, and hummed the tune into a pocket tape recorder. Paddy envied anyone with her kind of talent.

It was 1958. He was sixteen. She was nineteen. He was a high-school drop-out pumping gas for Shell. She was a high-school grad pushing paper for the federal government. Three years later, they became man and wife; a year after that, father and mother.

For the next nine years, the couple and their son John lived happily with Paddy's parents in rural Stittsville, about twenty miles from the national capital. The arrangement wasn't as odd as some might have thought—Paddy had always been close to his three brothers, three sisters, and especially to his doting mother. His father worked for the E.B. Eddy paper company, and other than drinking a little too much, was rather ordinary. He and his youngest son had never been really close.

The baby of the clan, Paddy had grown up the undisputed favorite, a considerate kid with a sunny disposition and a dedication to being liked by everyone—except in the boxing ring. The gloves turned him into a bulldog and the champ of the local Boys and Girls Club.

For the most part, their Stittsville years were good times. Jean Mitchell took care of the baby while her son and daughter-in-law worked. Paddy completed his final two years of high school with an 83 percent average, including marks in the nineties in math. He enrolled in a college accounting program, but dropped out after the first semester. By then, he was a husband and father and he figured good husbands and fathers were supposed to be good providers.

He quickly landed a job as a salesman for the Pure Spring soft-drink company. The position wasn't going to make him a millionaire, but it paid the bills. He insisted that Barbara put all of her government income into the bank; he would provide for the family's daily needs. In their ninth year of marriage, they used Barbara's savings to buy their first home in Hazeldean, a middle-class suburban neighborhood. It wasn't the mansion of their dreams, but she was a talented decorator and he proved to be an able handyman. Father and son spent almost a year building a new recreation room from scratch, an achievement proudly displayed to all who attended the Mitchells' regular parties and backyard barbecues.

Paddy wasn't the perfect husband—he spent too much time out with the boys, too much money at the race track, and never hesitated to give away the family's last twenty dollars to some pal with a hard-luck story. There certainly wasn't much to spare—a man from the finance company even showed up one evening and tried to repossess the family car. Dad wasn't too happy about that. Caught the guy in the driveway trying to hot-wire the ignition. Sent him packing with a broken nose and ten bucks for cab fare.

Barbara took it all in stride. At least Paddy wasn't heavily into drink or drugs like a lot of other husbands she knew—he couldn't handle much of either without falling asleep. And she had to admit he was a dedicated father. He drove his son to hockey practice, treated him to centerfield seats at pro football games, and regularly took young Johnny on fishing and camping weekends. Dad could sit for a whole day in one spot waiting for a nibble. Gives a man time to think, he told his son. Paddy always seemed to have a lot to think about.

As the Mitchells celebrated their tenth anniversary in the early 1970s, they were outwardly no different from millions of other young middle-class families in suburbia: two working parents; a house with a barely manageable mortgage; two cars in the driveway; one son in school; and an English setter named Shiska, trained by Dad to do just about everything but run to the corner for smokes. Johnny was growing up like his father—intelligent, articulate, and thoughtful. When he stole a beachball from a local store, Dad blew his stack. Made the kid return the beachball and apologize to the store owner. Never steal, Dad was always telling his son. Ordinary folk work hard for their money.

Ambitious and determined, Paddy Mitchell eventually quit Pure Spring for a better job at Pepsi-Cola, then negotiated an even better position back at Pure Spring. At both places he attracted a following of fellow workers imploring him to take positions of union leadership. At the same time, Barbara had been steadily climbing the bureaucratic ladder, while her song-writing was starting to attract the attention of big-name performers and more than one record company.

Still, Paddy Mitchell was discovering that wage-earning was definitely no fast-track to the good life that seemed to be growing ever more elusive as time went by. All that busting his butt for big business never seemed to cover the mountain of monthly bills. There had to be an easier way.

Then, in fall 1971, a strike at the Pure Spring soft-drink company turned ugly, in part because union leader Patrick Michael Mitchell wasn't about to be intimidated by his corporate bosses nor, for that matter, by the police called in to quell a near-riot at the plant gate. When it was all over, the corporate bosses suggested the union leader might want to practice his firebrand leadership style elsewhere. Six months before his thirtieth birthday, Paddy Mitchell's determination to be a model provider had suddenly come to nothing.

It was a curious thing, his wife thought, but being out of work for the first time in his adult life didn't seem to bother her husband all that much. In fact, before a month was out, he arrived home one evening with flowers and champagne and great news. He had been granted the franchise for an aluminum-siding company. He'd finally be his own boss, he said, and the hefty commissions would put an end to the family's financial woes. He opened a thick briefcase jammed with glossy brochures. Think of the potential, Dad said. Just slap the stuff on the side of your house and never look at another paint brush. Barbara and Johnny agreed it sounded pretty exciting.

And so, for the next four years, Paddy Mitchell would put on a suit and tie and a freshly starched shirt in the morning, grab his briefcase, and head off on his salesman's mission to cover the world in aluminum siding. Gotta dress for success, he was always telling his son. Johnny agreed his dad certainly looked successful.

He was evidently good at his job. There was never big money in the bank, but usually enough to keep the bill collectors at bay, and the couple never missed a mortgage payment on the house. There were lots of good times at first: parties in Hazeldean, weekends with the whole Mitchell clan at the family cottage on a lake in the picturesque Gatineau Hills. Paddy always bought the beer and the steaks.

There were even plenty of festive family evenings at the race track to watch the latest addition to the Mitchell household thunder down to the wire. Paddy said he won old Fireball Express in a card game, pretty well the nag's only significant payoff. No matter, the outings were exciting, and Dad always seemed to come away from the betting windows with cash in his pocket—or so he claimed. Paddy Mitchell wouldn't admit to losing the penny from his loafer.

"If our horse wins, will you buy me a bike?" eleven-year-old Johnny asked his father one evening at the track.

"If our horse wins, I'll buy you a Cadillac," his dad promised.

Fireball lost, as usual, but Johnny got his new bike the next day anyway. Dad was like that, generous to a fault.

Mom was starting to wonder where Dad was getting the money. Must be great stuff that aluminum siding...

In the shadow of the stately Parliament Buildings in a capital known for faceless bureaucrats, safe streets and cold winters, the Belle Claire tavern was the Cheers of the town's seamier set. Over the years, a ragtag assortment of rounders, thieves, hookers, and hoods had shared the draft kegs and pickled eggs with an assortment of politicos and policemen, judges and journalists, lawyers and other liars. It all made for an interesting kind of demilitarized zone: half the place had done time in jail; the other half had helped put them there. No matter, the two sides of the law largely ignored each other as long as the beer taps were flowing.

In the far corner of the tavern was a ten-place round table, a seat at which was generally considered something of an honor among thieves. It was there that the Man held court and generally attended to matters of current criminal concern. Brilliant guy. Could figure out the most complex problems. Mostly how to steal things.

The Man certainly stood out among the rather seedy crowd on the lawless side of the Belle Claire. Every inch a gentleman. Always wore a suit, silk tie, and crisp shirt. Never just said goodbye, always, "God bless." He loved to laugh and joke and tell lies, but never allowed swearing at the table with ladies present. A real charmer. Never seemed to lose his temper. For someone who seemed to spend half his life in the tavern, he didn't drink much, either. Just talked. And when he talked, people usually listened.

It was a curious thing about the Man, how someone so bright and so pleasant could be so feared by so many otherwise fearless thugs. Local police chief Ken Duncan probably had it right when he told the newspapers that the Man wasn't really dangerous. "But some of his friends sure are."

The Man had a lot of friends, all right. A vast network of contacts both high and low, mostly low. They had all grown up together in the same Preston Street area of the capital, a community where it was said the lower the house number, the tougher the residents. The Man was raised in the single-digit block. As time went on, some of his pals became businessmen and lawyers and judges and cops. The rest became crooks. The Man never really saw much of a distinction between the two groups.

His three sisters had all married well and gone straight, as had two of his three brothers, one of whom became a respected businessman and pillar of the Rotary Club. His third brother, Bobby, became a high-class "pleasure consultant" to a coterie of judges, lawyers, police officers and business types. Nice guy on the outside; nails on the inside. Once took on a whole motorcycle gang who had roughed up his chauffeur. Found them all in a small town outside the capital one night, pulled a gun and blew their Harleys into spare parts. Thereafter they called him sir. A lot of the townsfolk wanted to make him mayor.

For years, the Man had hung out with his pals at the Belle Claire. He had a home and a family and a rather ordinary life in the suburbs. For years, he also had a regular nine-to-five job—until he gave up on the work ethic to become chief crime consultant to the crooks of the Round Table. He certainly saw no contradiction between the two sides of his life.

His mother had taught him to be kind and generous and gentlemanly, to get his way using his mind, not his muscle. But like many kids from hardscrabble neighborhoods, he had grown up with no love for the banks or big corporations that made people miserable over money, nor for the cigarette and liquor barons who made money out of people's misery. He was only too happy to use his mind to help out his old friends who were stealing from banks and big corporations and the barons of the cigarette and liquor trades.

The Man never thought he was doing anything terribly wrong. He figured the world was a lot safer place because of him. Criminals were always going to be committing crimes, he reckoned, but at least he was bringing a sense of decorum to the game. His rules were clear: stealing from Big Business was okay—just crooks stealing from crooks, as far as he was concerned. But purse-snatching or mugging innocent folk was out. They work hard for their money.

Gunplay was also discouraged. Use your brains and no one has to get hurt, the Man was always saying. Unfortunately, most of the Belle Claire bandits didn't have a lot of brains. There was Nitro, who blew himself to bits in the bathtub. Freddie Fingers lost four of them trying to rob a night depository. Limpy the safe-cracker broke into a movie house by lowering himself through the ceiling with a twelve-foot rope—unfortunately, he was at the fifty-foot end of the theater. Even the great butter heist went sour when the hijacker hired to steal a whole truckload of the stuff neglected to turn on the refrigeration unit. Left a hundred-mile slick on the highway.

The cops called them the Keystone Krooks.

Such was life at the Round Table. Throughout the first half of the 1970s, nothing much of substance was likely to go missing in the nation's capital without the hand of the don of disorganized crime. Mention something that needed stealing and the Man would have figured out a way to lift it by lunchtime the next day: booze, cigarettes, televisions, open airline tickets, blank travelers' checks, even the truckload of butter. Good rate of return from a truckload of butter.

Not that the Man himself had ever boosted so much as yesterday's newspaper. He was just the brains and the one with the connections to make things happen. Worked on commission, like any respectable consultant. The brawn was entirely the business of others.

Over time, most of the Keystone Krooks went to jail, got out, went back to the Round Table and, ultimately, back to jail again. Class reunions at the lockup, they used to call them. The Man had never been charged with anything; there wasn't even a traffic ticket on his record. The cops suspected he was up to no good, but could never catch him in the act because there was never an act to catch him in.

It was almost as though the guy was untouchable...

Late in November 1973, the Man convened the historic meeting at the Belle Claire. He checked his watch and scowled. Almost midnight. He wouldn't be able to explain this one to his wife, how the meeting hour had been necessary to accommodate a scruffy freelance gunslinger named Stephen Reid, an escaped convict none too keen to yuk it up with the regular daytime bar crowd of police detectives.

The other special guest at the Round Table was a local fence with a profitable line in Air Canada cargo "diverted" by enterprising baggage handlers. One day he would be flogging a hundred gold Dunhill lighters, the next a few dozen designer shirts. This week's special was a shipment of pocket calculators originally destined for Sears.

"So these guys at the airport unload the planes and load up their cars, just like that?" the Man asked dubiously.

"Yeah, happens all the time," the hot-calculator salesman said-."The airline just tells the customer the shipment got lost and some insurance company gets dinged for the damage."

"I can't believe there's no security at the airport," the Man scoffed. "The feds are all over that place."

"Security's a joke," the salesman shrugged. "Even really valuable stuff like gold and shit like that just sits around the warehouse. Anyway, you got someone who wants the calculators?"

The Man and the escaped convict at the table looked at each other.

"Did you say gold?" the Man whispered to the calculator salesman.

"Yeah, like these shipments of gold bricks going from the mines up north to the Royal Mint here. Come in all the time. They just pile it in this wire cage thing till Brinks takes it away. And, like, sometimes they forget to pick it up and it just sits there overnight with a rent-a-cop. Anyway, 'bout them calculators—"

"These gold shipments can't be worth a helluva lot if there's no security," the Man said, hoping he was wrong.

"Well, gold's not exactly my line of work, but the guys at the airport tell me something like a half-dozen bricks come in at a time. Apparently, stuff weighs a ton. Must be worth millions. So you maybe want to see one of them calculators?"

The disposal of the calculators was hurriedly arranged and the fence left after a final "God bless" from the Man who then turned and smiled across the table at Stephen Reid.

"A few million in gold sounds like it might be an interesting little project for us," the Man said to the escaped convict.

"I'm not sure I like the word *us*," Reid said hesitantly.

"Think about it," the Man said in a loud whisper. "One good haul and we can all retire."

Christmas 1973 wasn't particularly merry at the Mitchell house. Barbara had been growing disenchanted with their marriage. Her husband had become remote and unromantic, treating their home like a hotel stop between the race track and parties elsewhere with people unknown. He stayed out late at night with the boys, and didn't seem to care if she worried. One Saturday morning, he left the house for a haircut and returned at 6 a.m. the next day. As always, he had an innocent smile and another excuse.

"Just playing cards with the boys," he said. "Fell asleep. Relax, Princess. No big deal."

"Like hell," Barbara retorted, flinging an alarm clock that hit him squarely between the eyes, a permanently scarring reminder of his untimely behavior.

Just when it seemed their bus-stop romance was heading for the end of the line, the Mitchells decided to give it one more try. Everything was going to work out just fine, Paddy promised. Had a few big deals coming down in the aluminum-siding business that would put them all on easy street. Not to worry, he told Barbara. Everything would change.

Everything was about to change, all right. But the big deals coming down weren't in the aluminum-siding biz.

In fact, there was no siding biz. Never had been. Just a lot of elaborate lies.

And a round table in a tavern.

And a gentlemanly mastermind they called the Man, a.k.a. Patrick Michael Mitchell, reportedly devoted son, husband, and father, unwittingly destined for continent-wide criminal notoriety and the enactment of Harlen Lee Hudson's worst nightmare.

But first, there was the matter of six gold bricks...

CHAPTER TWO

Ottawa, Canada

Psychologist's Report: Various tests have revealed Stephen Douglas Reid to be an intelligent person, well adjusted psychologically, and someone who seems to display good insight into his own personality. He comes from a tight-knit family and was considered a good student with high potential. However, shortly after beginning his secondary school education the subject stated he started to experiment with drugs and align himself with the "hippie" crowd, supporting his drug habit by a string of illegal activities...He is a strong personality and may at times appear *threatening to others, but this is so neither in fact nor intention...*

At first, Paddy Mitchell didn't know quite what to make of the rather wilted former flower-child. Stephen Reid had been living in a basement apartment after escaping from prison when the Man dropped by to give him a job interview. Paddy didn't have a lot of time for druggies, and the three long scars carved into Reid's cheek from a knife attack weren't particularly endearing, either. At twenty-three, he even dressed like a hood who'd seen better days—ratty T-shirt, shoes that looked like army boots with three-inch heels, jeans with a back pocket patched over one knee-hole. Reid called them his lucky Levis. Said he wore them for special occasions. Like prison escapes.

But the more the two men talked, the more Mitchell became intrigued with the newcomer. There was something about the sparkle in those hangdog eyes, the roguish smile beneath the droopy moustache, the quick wit, the refined manners, the articulate speech peppered with Shakespearean references—clearly this was no average down-and-out thug.

Like Paddy Mitchell in his early years, Stephen Douglas Reid had grown up with the blessings of intelligence, wit, charm, good looks, and a caring family. Born in the small northern Ontario mining town of Massey, Reid was the second of eight children. His accountant father was the office manager of the local mining company, his mother a teacher's aide at the elementary school. There wasn't much money to throw around, but always plenty of love. In short, a pretty ordinary bunch.

At school, Stephen kept up an A-average without much studying and excelled at sports without much practice. His room was cluttered with medals and trophies for swimming, hockey, and track. "He was so bright and such a naturally gifted athlete that he seemed to get bored quickly with everything he did," his father reflects. "At first, he became mischievous. Then he became rebellious."

Like the Mitchell siblings, Reid's older brother and six younger sisters all went on to lead conventional adult lives. But not Stephen.

At sixteen, in the heyday of the psychedelic '60s, he joined the mass-migration of flower children hitchhiking to Vancouver for a summer of free love and bountiful drugs in Haight Ashbury North. And, like thousands of otherwise lawful teens, Stephen Reid ran afoul of the law with a half-smoked joint of marijuana.

By the time the courts threw out the charges, Reid had missed his first term of studies back home. He went to work in the mine to pass the time until the beginning of the next school year, but it didn't take long to decide that back-breaking work in a filthy underground tunnel was no life for a flower child.

Within a year, Reid had become just another one of the drop-outs and druggies inhabiting the hippie havens of Toronto. As often happens, one thing led to another—soft drugs led to hard drugs; a corner-store stickup led to armed bank robbery in support of the lifestyle to which he had become addicted.

In 1972, at the age of twenty-two, Stephen Douglas Reid told a judge that the banks he had been robbing were evil institutions forever tormenting hard-working folk like his father. He also pointed out that he hadn't hurt anyone important in the course of criminal misadventures that would have done the Keystone Krooks proud. Reid confessed that he'd accidentally shot himself in the foot during one robbery, and blown a partner's ear off before another. But that was all.

The judge was unimpressed. He sentenced Reid to ten years in federal penitentiary.

***

Without a gun in his hand or drugs in his blood, Stephen Reid impressed his jailers at Warkworth Penitentiary. They thought him bright, friendly, respectful and not the least bit dangerous. Frankly, they quite liked the guy. He became the prison sports director, developing new athletic programs for the institution.

On October 19, 1973, eighteen months after Reid had been sent to jail, he was allowed out on a day-pass with two guards for a government crash course on fitness programing. On the way back that evening, he convinced his escorts to stop for Chinese food. It was a major violation of the rules, but Steve Reid was no ordinary con. In fact, even as he was munching his egg-rolls, his social worker was back at the pen filing a glowing inmate assessment: "He has good attitudes toward his work, is co-operative, and even shows some concern for rehabilitation. He accepts advice gracefully, and shows respect for authority..."

Sometime between the chow mein and the fortune cookies, Reid put down his chopsticks, excused himself from the table, and walked alone to the washroom. The guards thought nothing of it.

The next morning, Reid's prison social worker added a footnote to his report: "Trustworthiness: okay until he escaped."

After scrambling out the bathroom window of the Chinese restaurant, Reid didn't have far to go for a getaway car—a friend was waiting with his motor running. Everything had been planned to the minute without raising the slightest suspicion. The authorities were duly embarrassed.

Paddy Mitchell was duly impressed as the tale quickly filtered along the criminal grapevine to the Round Table. If nothing else, he figured he could use a guy with moxy and—who knows?—maybe even some brains. For his part, Reid was immediately in awe of the Man.

"Beautiful leather jacket you're wearing," Reid remarked during their first meeting in his basement hideout.

"It should be," Mitchell chuckled, as he usually did to preface a lie. "Got it at Saks Fifth Avenue in New York. Cost me two grand."

"I used to have one just like it," Reid said. "Got it at the Bay store. Cost me thirty days."

Mitchell laughed and tossed the jacket to Reid. "I've got a whole closet full of them at home," Paddy lied.

Reid said he was looking for work. Mitchell said he had plenty of that. The two men shook hands and unknowingly forged a partnership and friendship that would eventually put their faces on police bulletin boards from Montreal to Miami.

Paddy Mitchell was true to his reputation. The calculator salesman's off-handed reference to gold shipments through the airport hatched a scheme for grand larceny by lunch time the next day. It was a plan fraught with danger and difficulties, but most of all it needed someone on the inside. Brinks and the airline didn't always leave the gold bricks lying around overnight, and Paddy Mitchell wasn't about to lead a raid on an empty warehouse.

Mitchell was apprehensive about involving strangers in any of his operations, much less the theft of gold bullion. But he didn't have much choice. He knew only one of the three airport cargo runners with regular night shifts around the freight shed, and the man wasn't interested. The other two had been involved in the theft of the calculators and other miscellaneous cargo. One of them had been described as the more "reliable," meaning he was less likely to go running to the police.

Shortly after noon one day in the first week of December, 1973, Mitchell strolled into the Broken Cue poolhall and asked for a regular named Gary Coutanche. The manager pointed to a scrawny guy at one of the far tables.

Coutanche was twenty-three with a new wife and big dreams and not a hope in hell of materially satisfying either with his limited prospects. Paddy Mitchell smelled the perfect mark.

"How would you like to make a lot of money with a simple phone call?" Mitchell asked as the two men huddled in a far corner of the pool hall.

"What kind of phone call and why me?" Coutanche asked cautiously.

"All of that will become clear to you at an appropriate time."

"I don't even know who you are," Coutanche protested.

"You don't need to know that, either, Gary."

"Well, Mr. Whoever-You-Are, when you have a few answers to my questions, maybe I'll answer your question. In the meantime, I'm not interested."

"All right, Gary," Mitchell said calmly, "I want you to think about this overnight and meet me at eleven o'clock tomorrow morning at the Alexander Hotel."

"Why should I meet you anywhere?"

"Because, Gary," Mitchell said with a wry smile, "I know all about the calculators."

The next morning, Gary Coutanche was at the Alexander Hotel at eleven sharp. The two went for a long drive in Paddy's yellow Cadillac.

This time, Mitchell introduced himself by name and asked a lot of questions about the handling and storage of airline cargo in general, and the gold shipments in particular.

"What do you want me to do?" Coutanche asked.

"Call me when the gold is there overnight," Mitchell said.

"What's it worth to you?" Coutanche asked.

Mitchell stopped the car. "Thousands, Gary. Cash."

Two months and more than a dozen similar meetings later, Gary Robert Coutanche finally agreed. Mitchell would call him at work and ask how he was doing. Coutanche would answer "fine" if a shipment of gold was there. Otherwise, he would answer "terrible."

Coutanche's services, however, did not come cheap. He insisted on $100,000 from the proceeds of the stolen gold. Cash.

Mitchell agreed, figuring that he'd deal with the consequences later.

In the meantime, he had a million other things on his mind—all those angles to cover, all those dozens of details that had to be arranged. Details, details—Paddy Mitchell hated details. Fortunately, he didn't have to take care of them personally. That was the Ghost's job. The Ghost loved details.

Psychologist's Report: Lionel James Wright feels his childhood was happy and he had adequate love and material support. He spends most of his evenings at the family residence watching television or reading. He has never been known to abuse alcohol or any drug. One of his previous employers described him as fast, reliable, and always to work on time. He also displayed an unusual memory. He has always been considered neat, meticulous, patient and even-tempered. He shows no evidence of any emotional disturbance. He is considered shy and introverted. He is considered a loner...

The Mitchells' pre-Christmas party of 1972 had been a gala affair. The sizable gathering of family and friends included a assortment of prominent businessmen, lawyers, bureaucrats, fellow salesmen—even a local judge and his wife. Paddy Mitchell seemed to know just about everyone in town. Then there was that rather homely little fellow Lionel Wright. He always looked sad, his lifeless eyes downturned and sunk into dark sockets as though in fearful retreat from daylight. At five-seven and 140 pounds, he had a nerd's physique. He even dressed as if he shopped at the Sears boys' department—a white shirt buttoned to the neck with no tie; wide-wale corduroy bellbottoms with no belt; heavy, black-laced shoes and white socks. Didn't smoke or touch a drop of booze, just downed Coca-Cola by the gallon.

No one paid Lionel much attention at the party. Didn't seem to bother him, though. He spent the entire time playing with the dog, disposing of empties, and running errands for mix, ice, and other essentials. Very polite and obliging. Also very quiet. Rarely spoke to anyone. Slipped away early without so much as a Merry Christmas.

Barbara Mitchell never could make any sense of the relationship between her bon-vivant husband and his barely-vivant friend. She guessed there was probably something paternal between them, the way Lionel always seemed to be catering to Paddy. But it was only a guess— Barbara's attempts to pry answers from Lionel were like talking to the dog.

Whatever anyone might have suspected of Paddy's silent sidekick, no one would ever have cast Lionel Wright as another candidate for the FBI's Most Wanted list. A wallflower, yes. But a desperado?

Even Wright's family had long given up asking Lionel to explain himself. From the day he could talk, he rarely did. His mom and everyone else simply got used to answering their own questions. He seemed lost in a world of his own. The youngest of five children, he never knew his dad who passed away before Lionel was born.

Other than acute introversion, there was nothing particularly re-markable about Lionel James Wright's plodding shuffle into adult-hood. His single-parent family was close and caring and supportive of one another and managed to maintain a modest house in a nondescript blue-collar Ottawa neighborhood. Lionel had above-average marks in school, never caused any trouble, and rarely missed a class. At twelve, he got a paper route so he could help out his mom like all the other kids in the family. Didn't have a lot of school chums, though. Wouldn't talk to them, either.

At sixteen, he finished Grade Ten, quit school, and exchanged his Ottawa *Citizen* paper route for a job as an office boy in the newspaper's business department. His take-home pay was sixty-eight dollars a week. He gave twenty-five to his mom for room and board.

For the next five years, Lionel Wright was regarded as the best darn office boy the newspaper had ever hired—"fast, reliable, and always to work on time." He was still reticent to a fault, but universally well liked. He missed only one day of work—the day before Christmas when he was told he had to sing carols to everyone. The secretaries jokingly insisted it was tradition. Lionel booked off sick.

Wright never touched drugs and didn't drink or smoke—except the one night he was found sitting in his boss's office, feet on the desk, smoking a cigar and reading *Playboy*. Everyone thought that was pretty cute. The next time he was in that office, however, was to be shown the door. The Boss said Lionel had been doing a wonderful job for the past five years, but there was nowhere for him to go at the newspaper without having to deal with the public. And Lionel was just too doggone shy for that, said the Boss.

The secretaries cried the day Lionel left.

A month later, Wright became chief night clerk for the Kingsway Transport Company. The firm quickly came to regard him as dependable, punctual, and remarkably capable in his work. In fact, he became something of a clerical celebrity. Seems Lionel had a photographic memory that could recall entire truckloads of cargo details, waybill numbers and billings to different clients. Not that he boasted about his talents. Rarely spoke to anyone there, either.

By fall 1972, Lionel was twenty-seven years old and had no girlfriend, no hobbies, no vices, and no apparent friends. He was still living at home with his mother and older brother, and passed his free time alone in his room, watching TV or reading obscure history books.

Suddenly, he quit his job at the transport company. No explanations to anyone. Three months later, the company begged him to return, in part because most of the company's records were stored in his head. Wright went back to his job, but people noticed there had been a startling change in the timid clerk. He'd started wearing flashy clothes. Always seemed to have money to lend fellow employees on a no-interest, pay-me-when-you-can plan. Told his boss he frankly didn't give a damn about the job.

Even Lionel's mother and brother remarked upon the sudden make-over of their otherwise reclusive kin. One day he showed up driving a Lincoln Continental, for chrissakes.

There didn't seem to be any explanation, least of all from Lionel. Certainly, no one imagined he could ever get mixed up with someone like the Man...

***

It was early in 1972 when Lionel Wright was first introduced to Paddy Mitchell, who had an understandably keen interest in the trucking business. The Man treated Lionel to steaks and new clothes and introduced him to a circle of strange people. He was invited to sit with the crooks of the Round Table, primarily so he could be dispatched down the street for newspapers, cigarettes, and other menial errands. Lionel didn't mind. Every day, he would go to work at the Kingsway Transport Company from four o'clock until midnight, then be on call to the Man by ten the next morning as chief chauffeur and all-purpose gofer.

Most of the crowd called him the Ghost, though never to his face. People like the Keystone Krooks tended to figure anyone that mysterious must be dangerous. The silent type.

Finally, Lionel Wright quit his job at Kingsway Transport for the second and last time. As usual, there were no discussions, no explanations. By now he was working as full-time chauffeur for the Man, taking care of all the time-consuming chores and annoying details of the crime consulting biz. Lionel was good with detail. Very well organized. Never wrote anything down. Stored everything in that amazing memory of his.

Paddy Mitchell and Stephen Reid were delighted to have Wright's services at their disposal. Planning the Great Gold Robbery involved a morass of intricate detail that would strain even Lionel's filing-drawer mind.

Though none of them knew it at the time, the Stopwatch Gang had been born—a gregarious family man, an ex-hippie, and a self-effacing clerk bound for infamy no one could have imagined.

April 17, 1974: A light morning mist was rolling across the runways of Ottawa International Airport when in-bound Air Canada flight 444 pulled up to the main terminal building at exactly 10:32 a.m.

The freight manager was expecting the flight. Shortly after five o'clock the previous afternoon, a message had clacked across his teletype: "RQR PRO GUARD ITEM 1—5/368 LBS—DEST YOW FLT444/17." Translation: Request protective guard for shipment of gold bullion—five boxes weighing 368 pounds—destination Ottawa, Flight 444, arriving April 17.

The manager had left the message on his desk overnight as a reminder to get someone to call the Brinks Armored Transport Co. the next morning before the flight arrived. Probably have to call again in the afternoon, he grumbled. Brinks wasn't always that swift with the gold pick-ups.

A few minutes after the DC-9 came in, a ramp attendant was dispatched in a Jeep to retrieve the shipment of gold and transport it to the freight shed, a cavernous warehouse with an office at the front and an adjoining vehicle-repair shop.

The cargo was exactly as expected: five wooden boxes, each four inches square, a foot long, and weighing about seventy pounds. Four of them contained single bricks of gold packed in sawdust. The fifth held two smaller bars. The paperwork said the shipment was coming from Campbell Red Lake Mines in northern Ontario, en route to the Royal Canadian Mint. Total weight of gold: 5,167 ounces. Estimated value: $700,000 (about $1.8 million at 1992 prices).

The ramp attendant took the boxes from the Jeep in front of the freight building, piled them on to a metal handcart, and rolled them into the ten-by-sixteen chain-link security cage at the rear of the warehouse.

At five o'clock, the gold shipment was still sitting on the handcart where the cargo attendant had left it that morning. No Brinks today. The manager called the Universal Security Co. and asked for a guard to be posted in the warehouse overnight.

6:10 p.m. Cargo attendant Gary Robert Coutanche had been at work just over three hours when he was summoned to the phone.

"How ya doing tonight, Gary?" the caller asked.

Coutanche sounded harried.

"Um, ah, yea, for sure, ah—"

"How are you feeling tonight, Gary?"

"Ah, fine, just fine," Coutanche sputtered. "Yea, just great, ah, I mean, fine."

"Talk to you tomorrow," the caller said.

Paddy Mitchell hung up the phone.

8:30 p.m. Stephen Reid was face-down on a friend's sofa with a near-coma hangover. The phone rang for more than a minute before any sign of life stirred on the couch. Reid finally groaned into the receiver.

So far, plans for the nation's largest-ever gold robbery were not going well. Mitchell was not amused. "Dammit, man, I've been looking for you for two hours," he shouted. "Where the hell have you been?"

"Not even sure where I am," Reid mumbled.

"Tonight's the night, you understand? A car will be around to pick you up in one hour. Be ready."

"Ah, man, gimme a break," Reid protested. "Like not tonight—"

"One hour. Be ready."

The phone went dead.

Reid pulled on his lucky Levis and began packing a blue carry-all, checking off a neatly printed reminder list he had been handed the week before. He laughed at the last item: "Bullets." The Ghost loved details.

At precisely 9:30 p.m., a car pulled into the driveway.

11:14 p.m. A Universal Security guard arrived at the Air Canada cargo shed. He was packing a .38-caliber Smith & Wesson and wasn't afraid to use it. Four years in the U.S. Marines had taught him that much.

11:25 p.m. Gary Coutanche punched out from the evening shift along with two fellow Air Canada workers. The security guard was alone in the warehouse when he called his office to say all was quiet.

11:50 p.m. The phone rang.

"This is the ramp superintendent," the caller said with some agitation. "I sent a man over there twenty minutes ago to pick up two cans of varsol from the repair depot and he hasn't come back yet. Is he there?"

"No, sir," the guard replied. "I'm alone on guard duty here and no one has been by for anything like that in the past half hour or so."

"Goddammit," the ramp superintendent hollered, "you tell that lazy sonofabitch to call me from there the minute he arrives. If he's not back here in five minutes, he's going to be looking for another job."

"With all due respect, sir," the guard said, "my orders are not to allow anyone in here. I would have to call the duty manager in the main terminal to get that kind of authorization. I—"

"I know you're just trying to do your job," the super said with some exasperation, "but I was just talking to the duty manager and he's gone on break for the next hour. I need those cans of varsol now. Anyway, you'll recognize that idiot who works for me. He's wearing Air Canada coveralls and a blue company parka. He's driving one of our green stationwagons. Just check his security pass. Now—"

There was a knock at the front door. From where he was sitting, the guard could see a man in a blue Air Canada parka and white coveralls with a red security pass dangling from the lapel of the overcoat. He couldn't see the man's face, which was turned away from the light.

"Hang on a minute," the guard said. "Looks like your man's just arrived."

The guard opened the door. "Your boss is on the phone in the office. He's some pissed at you, pal."

The man followed the guard into the office and picked up the phone. "Yea...Right...Uh huh...Yea, for sure...Right away." The cargo attendant hung up the phone. His back was turned to the guard.

"Sounds like you better get your ass moving or you're going to be looking for work by tomorrow morning, pal," the guard said, turning to lead the way to the store room.

"Actually, you're probably the one who's going to be looking for a career change, pal," Stephen Reid said cheerfully, jabbing the barrel of a silver revolver into the guard's neck. "And if you don't do exactly as you're told, you'll be job-hunting without your head."

Paddy Mitchell had arranged everything—the counterfeit security pass, the coveralls, the Air Canada parka, the revolver. From the moment Reid finished his phone call, the heist was timed to the second: Take down the guard (one minute); use his keys to open the security cage (thirty seconds); remove the gold (two minutes, in case there was a lot of it); and beat it.

Allowing for the unexpected, the nation's largest-ever gold heist was supposed to take five minutes max.

Reid reached forward and pulled the .38 from the guard's hip holster.

"Who are you expecting in here?" Reid asked.

"Ah, well, the cleaning staff and my supervisor," the guard sputtered.

"When?"

"Any minute."

"In that case, we'd better get moving," Reid said casually.

The guard had his hands on his head and his own gun at his back as they marched out of the freight office, into the warehouse, and over to the security lock-up. Reid and his hangover staggered along behind.

"Okay," Reid said as they reached the cage, "slowly lower your right hand to your keys and open the padlock."

"I—I don't have the key," the guard stammered.

Reid was speechless as he struggled with this unsettling news. "Don't lie to me——."

"I—I'm telling you the truth," the terrified guard pleaded. "The key for the padlock is kept in the main air terminal at night."

Reid took the loop of three keys from the guard's belt and tried them all in the lock. None worked.

"Jesus Christ, now what?" Reid exclaimed, as though the guard might have some helpful hints. There was a long pause. "Let's go to the repair shop, partner."

Inside the repair shop, Reid found a pick-hammer, a crowbar, and a hacksaw. First he dropped one, then another. Finally, he told the guard to grab everything, then thought better of arming his hostage, and gathered them all up again.

The five minutes Mitchell had allocated for the robbery had already passed. The man outside in the green stationwagon was checking his watch.

11:57 p.m. Reid threw the tools on the floor in front of the security cage and took three steps back, out of reach of an ex-Marine about to be armed with a pick-hammer.

"Pick up the hammer with your right hand and pry that lock open," Reid ordered.

The guard looped the pick through the padlock and leaned hard on the handle. The shaft bent like a kitchen fork. The lock didn't budge.

"Pick up the hacksaw and cut the goddam thing," Reid growled. "I want to be home for Christmas."

It took the guard five minutes to saw through one side of the steel loop on the government-issue padlock. Reid checked his watch: 12:04. Twenty-four minutes since it all began. He wondered when the cleaners and the supervisor would walk in on the robbery-in-marginal-progress. He wondered if the green stationwagon was still outside.

Reid ordered the guard to lie face-down in a nearby baggage cart, and covered him with empty cardboard boxes.

He tugged on the half-cut lock. It didn't budge. He banged it with the twisted hammer. Still nothing. The guard had cut the wrong side of the loop.

"Our Father, who art in Heaven," Reid muttered, "why the fuck are you doing this to me?" He attacked the troublesome lock with the hacksaw.

12:10 a.m. Half an hour after Paddy Mitchell's five-minute precision gold robbery began, the lock finally bounced on the cement floor. The guard heard the security cage rattle, then a door open, then a second set of footsteps and a door closing.

Reid ordered the guard out of the cart and told him to kneel facing the wall at the far end of the security cage.

The guard felt his handcuffs being lifted from his belt and clamped to his left wrist.

"Ever been in a pair of these before?" Reid asked casually, as he snapped the other handcuff to the wire cage.

"N-n-no, sir, I-I haven't," the guard sputtered, certain he was about to be executed.

"Well, there you go," the bandit said cheerfully, "there's a first time for everything."

12:14 a.m. The guard heard receding footsteps. They stopped. A door opened. And for a moment, there was an eerie silence.

"Bye for now, mon ami," a voice boomed from somewhere in the stillness. "Have a good night..."

CHAPTER THREE

Ottawa, Canada

Immediately after Stephen Reid's departure from the scene of the precision five-minute gold robbery which had taken precisely thirty-five minutes, the airport cleaners arrived to find one rather hysterical security guard handcuffed to the inside of the security cage.

"Call the police!" the guard shrieked. "Get me out of here! Call the cops! There's been a robbery! They got the gold! Call the police!"

The two cleaners looked at the frenzied character in the cage and exchanged words in their native Portuguese. One of them finally shuffled toward the guard and asked if he wanted the security cage cleaned.

"No! No!" the guard wailed. "For godssakes, call the police! The police! Tell them there's been a robbery! Get me out of here!"

By the time the guard communicated enough sign language with his free hand to get a call placed to the federal constabulary, Stephen Reid and his getaway driver were miles away. Five minutes later, several RCMP officers converged on the freight shed, freed the prisoner, and calmed him enough to get a brief statement. They concluded there appeared to have been a robbery of some sort.

Unfortunately, although airports are the property of the federal government and therefore under the proper authority of the RCMP, the armed robbery of gold bricks falls under the jurisdiction of the local municipality in which the crime scene is located—in this case, the suburban township of Gloucester.

By the time the guard had got his message through to the cleaners and they had conveyed it to the emergency operator and she had contacted the RCMP and they called their dispatch to contact the Gloucester PD, the first roadblocks barely missed the fleeing bandits by no more than forty-five minutes.

Throughout the night, police buzzed around the cargo warehouse. Several huddled with the security guard, taking notes and trying to make some sense of his excited babble. Another sat in the office with a groggy Air Canada official, sifting through the mountains of waybills and shipping invoices, each with eleven carbon copies, trying to establish that the missing gold was officially missing. The identification team was busy—one officer spent hours taking sharp black-and-white photographs of the vacant security cage and equally empty hand cart. The fingerprint guys did more dusting than the cleaners, but came up with only one suspicious smudge. Found it on the guard's handcuffs. Alas, it belonged to one of the RCMP officers.

As dawn broke over the capital, Air Canada was screaming at Brinks for not picking up the shipment, Brinks was screaming at Air Canada for not calling and the police were screaming at both companies for leaving $700,000 in gold bricks lying around.

Over the next forty-eight hours, officers from five separate police forces descended on every ex-con, two-bit hood, deadbeat, junkie, and street snitch within a hundred-mile radius—somebody had to know something. No one did.

The guard was taken to police headquarters to pore over mugshots. Somehow not included in the photo albums of undesirables, however, was the face of one Stephen Douglas Reid, convicted armed robber and recent prison escapee. Needless to say, the exercise was fruitless.

The trail of the Great Gold Robbers was growing colder by the minute.

Gloucester Police Chief Kenneth Duncan was an ex-military type who insisted all constables under his command snap to attention and salute in his presence. The morning after the Great Gold Robbery, the entire police station was snapping and saluting as the Chief stormed around the place in a rage. Publicly, he was blasting Air Canada for not heeding his department's previous warnings about lax security for the gold shipments. Privately, he was blasting his own department for not heeding an even more explicit warning that someone was about to steal one of those shipments.

It was all there on the Chief's desk—a sworn statement that had been gathering dust in the department files for more than three months. It was signed by one Gary Robert Coutanche.

Three weeks after his first encounter with Paddy Mitchell, Coutanche had marched into the Gloucester police station and announced that some guy was planning to steal a gold shipment from the airport. The duty officer dutifully took down all the details. Coutanche's sense of civic duty, however, did not extend to identifying Mitchell by name. Claimed he had never seen the guy before or since.

The officer who took the statement promised to call Coutanche in a few days to look at the mugshot files. That was the last Gary Coutanche heard from the Gloucester Police Department until four months later when the unidentified individual allegedly planning to steal the gold did, in fact, steal the gold with the help of Gary Coutanche, who was obviously none too impressed with the Gloucester PD.

No wonder regimental Police Chief Kenneth Duncan was picking ceiling tiles out of his hair. It was bad enough that he was surrounded by nitwits. But he had also grown up with the Mitchell brothers, and had no doubt the youngest of them was behind the gold robbery. That Paddy had just triumphed over police incompetence was the ultimate insult.

The Chief summoned Archie and the Winch.

Detective Sergeant Robert Archambault and Detective Gary Wincherook were two of Gloucester's toughest cops. Archie was generally regarded by the criminal element as one with whom it was not wise to mess without a world heavyweight title or a loaded bazooka. Preferably both. The Winch had less experience and a lower rank but proved a quick study in Archie's methods.

Archie and the Winch understood their marching orders perfectly: Get the gold and get Mitchell and not necessarily in that order.

Every Air Canada employee remotely connected with the airport freight operations was questioned at length, but the two detectives had an understandably keen interest in Gary Coutanche. Under interrogation at the station, he gave them a solid alibi for the night of the robbery. Besides, why would anyone planning the nation's largest-ever gold robbery warn the cops about it first?

After more than two hours of questioning, one of the interrogating officers dropped an eight-by-ten photograph of their prime suspect on the table in front of Coutanche and asked him if he recognized the face. He immediately shook his head.

"Nope. Who is it?"

The detective bent down almost nose to nose with the inside-man of the Great Gold Robbery. "Does the name Paddy Mitchell ring any bells?"

"Nope. Never heard of him."

Archie and the Winch exchanged glances. Coutanche's reaction had been just a little too emphatic, a little too fast.

Lunchtime at the Belle Claire tavern the day after the Great Gold Robbery had a distinctly festive atmosphere. Even those in the lawful section of the bar could barely contain their amusement at the master rascal in their midst. Not that anyone had a single scrap of evidence linking the Man to the gold caper. After all, he was downtown having a late-night pint with some folks from the Prime Minister's Office when the whole thing went down. But there was no doubt in anyone's mind, either—only Paddy Mitchell could mastermind something that big.

The police had the same feeling, but that's all they had. Six weeks after the heist Paddy Mitchell was a mile from the American border at Windsor-Detroit, merrily selling the gold to a couple of old pals doing odd jobs for the California mob. That evening, he drove home with a briefcase stuffed with $200,000 in U.S. currency. It was less than he had hoped to get, but such was the cutthroat world of fencing numbered gold bricks.

Over the following week, Mitchell paid off most of his partners in crime. Even then, with what he had left he could have paid off the mortgage on the cherished family home, put his son through university, and never again have had to punch out some guy trying to repossess his car. But fulfilling the family duties of the devoted son, husband, and father was not exactly the lifestyle to which Paddy Mitchell wished to become accustomed. Three months after the robbery, he owned three more racehorses (which gave him three times as many chances to lose three times as much money at the track), and opened an illegal gambling parlor in Cartier Towers, a highrise apartment complex in the trendy part of town (which gave him a thrice-weekly opportunity to fritter away even more cash). The flat was also a convenient place for him to charm a steady queue of young lovelies, the latest of whom happened to work in the Prime Minister's Office. Paddy called her Princess. She was almost as expensive as the ponies and poker games combined.

In no time at all, Mitchell was down to his last $40,000 without having spent a nickel on anything but his own amusement.

Not that he was publicly flaunting his good fortune. He knew the cops would be watching for any sign of new-found wealth. Nothing was deposited in bank accounts, the illegal gaming apartment was rented to a fictitious Byrnes Investments, and even the racehorses were registered in Lionel Wright's name.

Stephen Reid did not have the option of throwing his money anywhere but under the bed in his basement hideout. He was, after all, an escaped convict, and assumed that the gold robbery now had every police department in the country actively looking for someone matching his description.

After almost two months of hiding in his basement, Reid finally decided to take his money and run. With $60,000 in his pocket and a doctor's daughter on his arm, he partied his way across the United States until both the cash and girlfriend ran out.

Lionel Wright seemed to have come into some money as well, but just didn't have much on which to spend it. He was still living at home, and still didn't drink, smoke, or do drugs. A gourmet meal was a hot turkey sandwich, hold the gravy and vegetables. The part-owner of the four racehorses, he wouldn't bet a dime on any of them. Even the white Lincoln Continental he acquired with a finance company loan—just in case the cops wanted to know where he found the money for it.

He did buy himself a nice new gold watch; his clerical mind, it seems, had a fascination with clocks. He was forever telling people the exact time, even if they didn't ask. But that little luxury didn't burn up more than five hundred bucks.

The one member of the gold heist gang who most wanted to flaunt his money, but had the least to flaunt, was Gary Coutanche.

Reid had warned Mitchell that shortchanging Coutanche on the promised hundred-thou payoff was asking for trouble. But Paddy just laughed—he had no intention of turning over half the proceeds for answering a lousy phone call.

Two weeks after the heist, Mitchell and Coutanche met at an Italian restaurant for what the inside-man had assumed would be his big payoff. Instead, he got a lousy thousand bucks and a long story about the problems of trying to sell numbered gold bricks. Just be patient, Mitchell implored him.

"You'll have your money by the end of next month," Mitchell lied. "In the meantime, how would you like to make a quick five grand?"

Other than smoking the occasional joint, Paddy Mitchell had never had much interest in the drug trade. But the airport gold robbery had given him a business tool that just seemed a crime to waste—a freight runner whose job put him between incoming aircraft cargo and Canada Customs. If Gary Coutanche could steal crates of calculators, why could he not swipe, say, a suitcase the owner actually wanted stolen?

Two of Mitchell's friends apparently had the same thought. Not long after the gold robbery, Tommy Harrigan and Chris Clarkson had taken a little trip to the Caribbean island of Curaçao, a place renowned for its tacky casinos and booming trade in South American drugs.

Harrigan had a long gray beard, a penchant for serious gambling, and a high-class drug business. In 1974, cocaine was nouveau and expensive and a popular status symbol among his otherwise respectable, upper-crust clientele. He was rarely short of cash.

Clarkson was twenty-six, with degrees in philosophy and journalism, no criminal record, and a budding career as a drama series producer for the Canadian Broadcasting Corporation. He just wanted to make a fast buck.

On May 6, two hours after Clarkson and Harrigan checked out of the Curaçao Intercontinental Hotel and headed back to Canada, a green suitcase packed with cocaine was consigned air freight from Curaçao to Toronto aboard KLM Royal Dutch Airlines, thence to Ottawa by Air Canada. The attached waybill No. 074-77486-360 indicated that the shipper, one Anthony Young, was sending home a bag full of his own clothes.

Paddy Mitchell called Gary Coutanche with a waybill number and a description of the suitcase. "The easiest five grand you'll ever make, Gary my boy," Mitchell said. All Coutanche had to do was intercept the suitcase before it got to customs. No one would notice it missing. No one would complain. No one would investigate. The perfect crime.

For his part, Mitchell saw this job as no different from fencing a truckload of butter. Stolen butter, illegal drugs—they were all just commodities to Paddy Mitchell. They were also big money. A hundred grand in Paddy's pocket just for getting Gary Coutanche to swipe some dumb suitcase. The fast lane to retirement.

Two days later, Mitchell called Coutanche, who said the suitcase had not arrived, but he could sure use his end of the gold money. Mitchell scolded him for being a nag, and promised to pay him another $20,000 at the end of the month.

The calls continued every night for the next week. Finally, Coutanche had some news: "Well, ah, the suitcase came in but, um—"

"But, what?" Mitchell exploded.

"Like, uh, well, I missed it."

During Mitchell's tantrum, Coutanche came up with Plan B. The suitcase, he said, was being held in bond at the Canadian National (CN) customs warehouse about five miles from the airport.

"If someone wrote them a letter asking that it be shipped on Air Canada to Toronto again," Coutanche said, "I could grab it on the way back through the airport here."

On May 21, CN shipping agent Joe O'Brien received a letter from one Tony Young asking that the suitcase be forwarded to Toronto.

A week later, the suitcase was transferred from the CN customs warehouse to the Ottawa air cargo terminal to be flown by Air Canada to Toronto International Airport. Feeling that perhaps Coutanche needed a little motivation, Mitchell had given him another $5,000.

Coutanche thanked Mitchell for the cash, and promptly missed the suitcase again.

So far, the entire exercise had moved the suitcase from Curaçao to customs in Toronto to customs in Ottawa and now back to customs in Toronto again.

"Listen, I know this guy who works at the shed in Toronto," Coutanche said through Mitchell's lengthy blast of profanities. "I'll get him to send the suitcase back here again."

"So you can miss it again?" Mitchell snarled.

Stephen Reid had been right about one thing: Mitchell's rash promise to pay Coutanche $100,000 for the gold robbery would lead to nothing but hassles.

Three weeks after selling the gold in Detroit-Windsor, Mitchell promised Coutanche another $10,000, "but only when the cops stop watching us. We can't afford to have someone spreading a lot of bread around right now."

"Oh, I'm not goin' to throw money around," Coutanche assured him. "I want to invest in this apartment building that my uncle's buying, and it will be in his name so no one will know I've got anything to do with it."

Mitchell agreed the plan sounded safe enough and coughed up the ten grand.

Coutanche promptly bought a used Harley-Davidson motorcycle for $3,300; a boat, motor, and trailer for $4,000; and gave his latest girlfriend a spiffy new $500 ring.

The spending spree did not go unnoticed by Archie and the Winch.

One day in June, the two detectives did exactly what Paddy Mitchell most feared they would do—they followed Gary Coutanche to his new $4,000 boat, motor, and trailer. Not bad for a young fella taking home a hundred bucks a week. Then they followed him around on his new Harley. Finally they followed him to the Broken Cue poolhall, where he met with Paddy Mitchell, whom he had supposedly never seen before.

All of which amounted to a lot of excitement around the station house, but not much more. Truth was, two months of investigation hadn't given them enough solid evidence against Paddy Mitchell to fill a half-page in their notebooks.

They did notice Mitchell was eating a lot of T-bones, and that he seemed to split his days between the Belle Claire tavern and the race track with no visible means of support. But that wouldn't get them an arrest warrant, either—hell, the guy had been drinking with the up-pity-ups from the Prime Minister's Office when the gold was taken.

Lionel Wright's new Lincoln Continental got them all excited until they discovered the finance company loan on it—hardly grounds there to go digging for gold under the guy's bed.

No matter, on July 7, eighty-five days into the largely fruitless investigation, Archie and the Winch told a magistrate they had reliable information that the missing gold bars were stashed at the homes of Patrick Mitchell, Lionel Wright and Gary Coutanche. The judge bought the story and signed the search warrants.

Three days later, police raided Lionel Wright's house and told him he was under arrest for conspiracy to commit armed robbery. If anyone was going to crack, they reckoned it would be the shy little fellow everyone called the Ghost. Bad guess.

According to Wright, Archie and the Winch drove him into the backwoods and told him he could either finger Mitchell or dig his own grave. Lionel started digging. The official version was that the suspect was taken in for questioning and left in jail overnight because he was too cheap to call a lawyer to get him out sooner. One way or another, he was released without indictment.

At 2:30 the following afternoon, the detectives repeated the exercise at Paddy Mitchell's house, and took him into custody. He told the arresting officers: "Nice try, fellas. Now, if you don't mind, I'd like to call my lawyer." He was released within the hour.

That evening, Coutanche was nabbed outside his parents' highrise and told he was being arrested on the same charges. His father intervened and Gary was home again by ten.

Mitchell called Coutanche in a panic. "What happened when they grabbed you?"

"Well, they grabbed me," Coutanche said blithely.

"I know that," Mitchell snapped. "What happened?"

"They picked me up and said I was under arrest and grabbed me by the arm and said they were going to put the cuffs on me or I could just get in the cop car, so I said, well no sense putting up a scene for nothing. So, you haven't got no more money for me yet? Did you get—"

"No, no," Mitchell interrupted. "Keep telling me the rest. I wanna hear it all."

"Oh yeah, then driving down to the cop shop, this detective says, 'You think you're so smart,' and on and on. And I just didn't bother answering."

"You denied everything?"

"Oh yeah, I denied everything," Coutanche said.

"Tell them to go fuck themselves."

"Well, I mean, this never happened to me before," Coutanche whined.

"You're doing all right, Gary," Mitchell said soothingly. "I'm proud of you."

Paddy Mitchell's instincts sensed danger but his mind wasn't paying attention. All he wanted was that one big score. Then he could retire. If only he could get his hands on that damn green suitcase...

The elusive green suitcase had been sitting at Toronto customs for so long it was eventually transferred to the department of unclaimed goods. For six weeks, Coutanche had been saying that another of his pals in the Toronto warehouse was sending it back to Ottawa. Promise.

Lionel Wright had been calling Coutanche every day for progress reports. Now, it seemed, there had been another change of plan.

"Well, the guy says, you know, paperwork and all that, like he'll do it," Coutanche sputtered, "but well—"

"I'm listening," Wright said sourly.

"Well, uh, um," Coutanche began, "I think Pat's going to have to write the guy in Toronto a letter, you know, like the last one you wrote the last time, and ask them to send it back here to Ottawa again. And then my friend here at customs says he'd steal it, which should be no problem. Heard anything about the money that's coming to me?"

There was a long silence. Then a heartfelt sigh from Lionel.
"I don't believe this..."

On August 6, the following letter was sent to CN customs at Toronto International Airport:

Dear Sir,
I am writing to you in another attempt to retrieve a small green suitcase of personal belongings I had shipped air freight from Curaçao on May 6, 1974. I had asked that the suitcase be held at Ottawa airport for pickup as I would be staying a short while in the city. There were some delays, the suitcase did not show up, so I asked that it be sent down to me in Toronto. This was in June.

My company has since transferred me to Ottawa and I have at last received notice that my suitcase is in Toronto and I am unfortunately in Ottawa.

I am therefore writing to you to have my belongings sent *back* to Ottawa. Please notify me of its arrival at the following address...

Thank you for your help.

Tony Young

Ten days later, the Toronto *Star* ran a story about the seizure of a certain green suitcase full of drugs at Toronto International Airport. "RCMP dog sniffs out $1.8 million in cocaine," read the banner headline. Unfortunately, neither Mitchell nor Wright nor drug smugglers Clarkson and Harrigan bought a newspaper that day, and didn't find out their green suitcase had been seized by a Mountie's mutt until three months later when Paddy spotted a photo of it in a *Reader's Digest* article on drug-sniffing dogs.

Paddy Mitchell was beginning to wonder if God was trying to tell him something. So far, the green suitcase had gone to the RCMP in Toronto, the last of the gold money had gone down the drain, and Gary Coutanche had run his Harley up a telephone pole and been fired from Air Canada.

Life was no better on the home front. Barbara Mitchell's latest song sounded conspicuously like a dirge for her marriage, and even the faithful family bowser was starting to growl at the late-night intruder returning home from one more round with the boys.

Finally she told him to take a hike.

Paddy was devastated, and blamed his recent lack of bread-winning for putting their marriage on the rocks. He'd solve that problem in a hurry, he vowed, and then everything would be fine again. All he needed was one big score...

On November 15, Mitchell convened a meeting at the Cartier Towers apartment. The discussion concerned sending Coutanche to Peru on a shopping trip for drugs. "Now, the first time down, there will be about $100,000 made," Mitchell began. "Then we take out $30,000 and reinvest the other $70,000. Now, the next load may be worth a half-million and the load after that may be worth millions. Then we retire..." He turned to Coutanche. "Gary, you know you're on your own if you get pinched."

"I know," Coutanche said. "If I go down, I go down by myself."

Among all the mistakes Stephen Reid had made in life, fooling around with a friend's ex-wife proved particularly costly. When police subsequently busted the jealous ex-husband for trafficking in narcotics, he merrily volunteered Reid's whereabouts in return for immunity from the drug charges.

On December 10, 1974, fourteen months after he'd climbed out the bathroom window of the Chinese restaurant, Stephen Douglas Reid was arrested peacefully in Kingston, Ontario, and thrown back in prison, conveniently located only two miles away.

Paddy Mitchell waited for the axe to fall on all of them, but it didn't happen. Reid was charged with escaping custody, but no mention was made of the gold robbery.

Ten months after the gold robbery, Paddy Mitchell was back in suburbia with Barbara, the couple having decided to give their ailing marriage yet one more last try. It was about all Paddy had left.

In the end, no one had gone to Peru. Mitchell had run out of money to send anyone anywhere. He did manage to borrow $3,500 to send Coutanche to India to meet another dope dealer so the two of them could smuggle some hashish back into the country. The accomplice flew to Bombay and waited, but Coutanche got no further than Toronto.

Three days after he was supposed to have left, Coutanche called Mitchell from Toronto to say the airfare was more than expected and if he paid for the ticket and then a hotel and meals and stuff in

Bombay, well, darn, he wouldn't have enough left to buy much hash to smuggle—

The line went dead with the loud click of a phone being slammed.

Gary Robert Coutanche turned to the two police narcotics agents in the room.

"That's it. I'm not doing this no more."

CHAPTER FOUR

Ottawa, Canada

Gary Coutanche was at least true to his word. He was going down alone, if he was going down at all—which he wasn't.

Every crook's worst nightmare had started the day Archie and the Winch conducted their police raids and brief arrests at the homes of Mitchell, Reid, and Coutanche three months after the Great Gold Robbery.

"It's kinda too bad you're going down like this," Archie told Coutanche after they had hauled him down to the police station. "We know you're just a small fish in the operation. The guys we wanted were Mitchell and Wright, but Lionel already decided he'd rather finger you than spend the rest of his life in prison."

The detectives had already tried the same skit on Mitchell and Wright with a notable lack of success. Coutanche just shrugged and said nothing.

"By the way," Archie continued, "for a guy who's never met Mitchell, it's kinda strange you were talking to him at the pool hall. And then today we find your phone number at his place and his number in your address book."

Coutanche was starting to shake, but still said nothing.

"Geez, Mitchell must be one helluva friend for you to be throwing away the rest of your life like this."

In fact, at that point, Gary Coutanche wasn't inclined to throw away the day's garbage for the man who was trying to cheat him out of his fair share of the gold money.

Archie and the Winch finally looked at each other and shrugged.

"Okay, let's go," Archie said, meaning Coutanche was free to go home.

Gary Coutanche thought he was going to jail.

"Let's go for a drive," Coutanche said out of the blue. "I wanna talk..."

The ensuing two-hour drive was every detective's dream tour of the countryside. Coutanche confessed to everything from his role as the inside man for the gold heist to his part in the calculator thefts and other missing Air Canada cargo. He also fingered Paddy Mitchell as the mastermind of the Great Gold Robbery.

In return, Coutanche was promised immunity from all prosecution and was allowed to keep everything gained thus far from the avails of crime—the boat, the Harley, his girlfriend's ring, the stolen Air Canada merchandise, and whatever other cash Mitchell had already given him from the sale of the gold.

"Oh yeah, there's one other thing," Coutanche said. "Mitchell and Wright are real interested in some dumb green suitcase..."

The morning after Coutanche turned informant, the RCMP narcotics boys in Toronto were given a waybill number and advised to look for the corresponding green suitcase thus far shipped from Curaçao to Toronto to Ottawa and back to Toronto. The suitcase was quickly located and shoved in the snout of a canine drug-sniffer named Duke who got one whiff of the contents and went nuts.

Among all of Coutanche's supposed friends working inside the customs warehouses, only one actually existed—undercover narcotics agent Tim Anstis. Mitchell never suspected as much, but he certainly had plenty of misgivings about the dozens of other short haircuts and chromeless cars that seemed to appear everywhere he went. Most of the time, he probably had good reason. Never before had the combined police forces of the nation's capital devoted so much time and manpower to putting one man behind bars.

Shortly after Coutanche's drive in the country, he had agreed to carry a concealed transmitter and have his phones tapped for all conversations with Paddy Mitchell, Lionel Wright, and related criminal associates. (The RCMP had promised him 10 percent of the value of any seized drug shipments, which was an even bigger joke than Mitchell promising $100,000 from the gold robbery.)

In eight months, Archie and the Winch and their pals in the narcotics squad were able to electronically intercept more than sixty hours of Mitchell and friends discussing the gold robbery, chasing the green suitcase, and plotting an assortment of other equally ill-fated get-rich-quick schemes.

Sometimes the eavesdropping officers got more than they bargained for—a tapped phone left off the receiver during one of Mitchell's noisier dates; a senior justice of the court asking that a hooker be delivered to his chambers.

A lot of the time, they got nothing at all. On nine separate occasions, the electronics malfunctioned or the batteries died in mid-sentence. Twice the phone bugs fell off the phones. Umpteen times the listeners got an earful of static when Coutanche scratched the transmitter taped to his crotch. And on one memorable day, the entire police surveillance team got their wires crossed and went to lunch while their informant was meeting with Mitchell.

The grand finale was Coutanche's Bombay hash-buying venture that never got past Toronto airport, supposedly because the airfare was more than expected. In fact, the mission was aborted at the last minute when the RCMP's plan to send along a few undercover agents was scuttled by the Department of External Affairs who went berserk at the mere thought of the notoriously stonehanded federal cops running amok on foreign turf.

At that point Gary Coutanche threw up his hands and said enough is enough.

Five days later, Archie and the Winch and the Chief were all smiles as Paddy Mitchell's life as the apparently devoted suburban husband, father, and son came to an abrupt end.

March 4, 1975: Paddy Mitchell was asleep in bed with Barbara three days before they were due to leave on a two-week vacation in the Bahamas. He called it their second honeymoon. She called it their first.

At 5:30 a.m. there was a loud banging on the front door. Barbara was still half-asleep when her husband got out of bed and went downstairs. "Ah, c'mon guys, it's the middle of the night," she heard him say.

Barbara pulled on her housecoat and went downstairs. She got as far as the doorway to the kitchen, where Paddy was making coffee for the early-morning guests. Her hands suddenly clamped over her mouth. "Oh, my God..."

At the same moment, other squads of police were rounding up the rest of the co-conspirators. Lionel Wright was arrested at home. So were Tommy Harrigan and Chris Clarkson.

Stephen Reid was handed his gold-robbery indictment through the bars of the prison cell he had been occupying since his recapture three months earlier.

As Paddy Mitchell was being led from his suburban home in handcuffs, he stopped at the door and kissed his wife goodbye.

"Don't worry, Princess," he said. "I'll be home for dinner. God bless..."

A week after their arrests, Harrigan and Clarkson were released on bail. Since they had no prior convictions, Mitchell and Wright were all but guaranteed similar treatment.

But now that the police had Paddy Mitchell where they wanted him, they had no intention of letting him go. The morning of his bail hearing, he was suddenly charged with a particularly vicious bank robbery in which a lone gunman had taken a hostage and opened fire on a pursuing police officer. Charges of armed robbery, attempted murder, and kidnapping were enough to convince the presiding judge to keep Mitchell behind bars. The same fate was dealt to Lionel Wright—just to be fair.

That afternoon, a teacher found young Johnny Mitchell crying in the school washroom, clutching a note from his mother. It said Dad would not be coming home for dinner as promised, and maybe not for quite a long while.

As it happened, never.

Shortly after Paddy's arrest, the Mitchell clan gathered for its regular Sunday evening supper at the Stittsville farmhouse. The elderly Jean Mitchell took one look at the empty chair at the table and burst into tears. Unwilling to accept that her favorite kid was a crook, she passed most of the evening reminiscing about all the wonderful things he was always doing for her. "This is the week he would have been here to turn over my garden," she sobbed.

Eventually, the conversation turned to all the dreadful things the police had been doing to the entire family in the ongoing hunt for the six missing gold bricks—things like tapping their phones, for heavenssakes.

One of the Mitchell brothers left dinner that evening with an interesting idea. Two days later, Paddy called from the jail.

"How are things going?" Paddy asked.

"Ah geez, I'm flat broke," his brother said.

"Well, I guess you'd better do some digging in mom's garden," said Paddy.

"Yeah, we really don't have much choice," said his brother.

That afternoon, a small army of shovel-toting police officers turned over Mrs. Mitchell's garden in search of the gold which, needless to say, was not to be found.

As proud as Archie and the Winch were of their handiwork in nailing Mitchell, they also knew there would be no end of snapping to attention and saluting in the Chief's office until they had found those wretched gold bricks.

It wasn't for lack of trying. All of Gary Coutanche's incessant whining about not being paid his share of the gold proceeds was inspired by the police hoping to get Mitchell to reveal the exact whereabouts of the missing merchandise. Problem was, Paddy was lying so much to Coutanche that no one could separate fact from fiction.

Mitchell, meanwhile, couldn't resist telling a number of people the remarkable story of getting five of the gold bricks from the Air Canada warehouse to the Windsor-Detroit area where they had been sold to the California mobsters.

"Actually, we didn't really steal the gold at all," he explained. "Air Canada stole its own gold. All we did was repackage it and retag it and park it all in the regular cargo area and that nice airline flew it to Windsor for pick-up. The getaway car never left the airport. It was a rental..."

The eventual recovery of some gold bricks in California was a banner day for the Chief, but did not exactly enhance his department's reputation among certain other police agencies. The Ottawa police department had put a tap on the pay phone at the Belle Claire in an attempt to trace $1 million in stolen American Express travelers' checks. Three weeks after the gold heist, Paddy Mitchell unluckily chose that telephone to call his chums in the California mob to discuss the sale of the gold bricks.

The information was passed along to the Gloucester PD which neglected to convey it to the Federal Bureau of Investigation. The FBI accidentally stumbled on the numbered gold bricks at a California refinery fifteen months later.

Well, some of them anyway.

By then, three of the bricks had been sold and turned into jewelry. Only two were recovered at the precious-metals refinery. That left one gold brick weighing more than a thousand ounces on the missing list. It was never found.

With Paddy Mitchell in jail and five of the six gold bricks accounted for, the Chief should have been content. But a funny thing happened on the way to the jury.

Three months after Mitchell's arrest, a judge conducted a preliminary hearing to determine if there was sufficient evidence to proceed to trial on one of the drug-conspiracy charges. At the end of three weeks of testimony, the judge wondered why the charges had ever been laid. Case dismissed.

A month later, another judge concluded that whatever conspiracy there might have been to import hash from Bombay was mainly inspired by police informant Gary Coutanche and his narcotics-squad handlers. Case dismissed.

Shortly thereafter, Mitchell bumped into a fellow in jail who mentioned the nasty bank heist and consequent charges of armed robbery, attempted murder, and kidnapping laid against Paddy the morning of his first bail hearing. "Well, you remember there was only one guy involved in the shoot-out with the cop, right?" the man said to Mitchell. "And guess what they've got me in here for?"

Two days later, Mitchell's lawyer was angrily pointing out to the prosecutor's office that the police now had two men charged with the same one-man crime. Case dismissed.

Paddy Mitchell and Lionel Wright were elated. If their luck held through the remaining cocaine conspiracy and gold robbery cases, they would both be free men.

The same thought had evidently occurred to the police, who went to the federal prosecutor who went to the officials in the Department of Justice who went to the federal Minister of Justice, who said not to worry, he'd take care of everything.

On the evening of August 26, 1975, police informant and key prosecution witness Gary Coutanche answered a knock at his front door to find a masked man with a gun in his hand. The would-be assassin fired a shot into the ceiling and left.

Whereupon the federal justice minister signed a cabinet decree overturning the two preliminary court decisions exonerating Mitchell and Wright. At the same time, he scrapped the pre-trial process altogether for the remaining cases. The unprecedented move was necessary, the government claimed, to speed up the process because obviously the life of key witness Gary Coutanche was in danger.

Paddy Mitchell claimed the ceiling-shooter at Coutanche's house was just a police set-up to give the Justice Minister grounds to subvert justice. Not that Mitchell wouldn't have liked to throttle Coutanche. But murder wasn't Paddy's style. Instead, he wrote to the taxman.

Dear Sir,

I wish to report a fraud which has taken place against your Tax Department. The fraud in question is for not filing a return for approximately $20,000 in taxable income. The person in question is Gary Robert Coutanche...I have proof that Mr. Coutanche received this amount of money from different sources and neglected to pay tax on his 1974 Income Tax Return. If you require further information regarding this fraud, you may either call me or write me at this address...

The letter was signed by Patrick Mitchell. The tax investigator didn't know that the address given was the local jail until he walked through the front doors of the place. His surprises were just starting. Mitchell promptly told the stunned taxman all about the gold robbery and the $20,000 in payoffs made to Coutanche.

The Tax Department never did go after Coutanche, but the information taken from Mitchell sure put smiles on the faces of Archie and the Winch and the Chief.

Then Mitchell got a note from his lawyer saying he was quitting unless Mitchell coughed up a $10,000 retainer. Since neither Paddy nor his wife had that kind of cash lying around, he called the folks at legal aid who told him he didn't qualify for a public defender because he owned a home.

At that point, Barbara Mitchell had a husband in jail, a son being constantly taunted at school, friends who were treating her as though she were the criminal in the family, and a government employer denying her a promotion because the RCMP deemed her a security risk, given her association with "a known criminal" who hadn't been convicted of anything yet. Now she had to sell her home so her jailed husband could get legal aid. She couldn't imagine how life could get any worse. Nor could Paddy Mitchell.

But it did.

On January 7, 1976, the cocaine-conspiracy trial of Patrick Mitchell, Lionel Wright, Tommy Harrigan, and Chris Clarkson was convened before His Honor Frank Donnelley, who could never be accused of treating criminals lightly.

The trial opened with an attempt by the prosecutor to remind the judge that Harrigan and Clarkson were on bail on other lower-court charges which, if dismissed, would mean neither accused was being held on anything. His Honor cut the prosecutor off in mid-sentence and demanded that his own show begin immediately.

Halfway through the cocaine trial, the lower-court charges were indeed dismissed. Clarkson and Harrigan immediately threw an impromptu party at a local tavern, thanked their lawyers for all they had tried to do, and promptly disappeared. The next day, His Honor demanded to know why no one had told him the two weren't being held on bail.

After several days of legal arguments, His Honor decreed the two accused would damn well be tried in absentia. That had never been done before, but His Honor didn't seem to care.

In the early morning hours of February 21, after thirteen hours of deliberations, His Honor made no attempt to hide his pleasure as the jury foreman read the verdicts: Patrick Mitchell, Lionel Wright, Tommy Harrigan, Chris Clarkson—all guilty as charged.

Sixteen days later, Mitchell and Wright were marched back into the court of Mr. Justice Frank Donnelley to be sentenced in the case of the peripatetic green suitcase.

The psychologists' reports on both of the accused were unusually positive. The one on Mitchell described him as a "gentle, overly generous, and thoughtful person...he is reported to be a devoted son, husband, and father..."

The psychologist trying to interview Lionel Wright, on the other hand, had trouble getting him to say enough to fill a one-page report. Nonetheless, it was noted he had been a quiet, law-abiding clerk up until the time he met Paddy Mitchell.

Both accused, the psychologists concluded, were definitely to be considered "salvageable."

With these reports in their favor and having no previous criminal records, Mitchell and Wright were advised by their lawyers to expect sentences of seven to ten years. Max. With good behavior, they could probably get parole in three.

The court having been called to order, His Honor noted that a doctor testifying for the prosecution had had some pretty dreadful things to say about the effects of heroin which wasn't what the accused were accused of conspiring to import, but His Honor wasn't about to sweat the fine points. As for all the glowing comments in the psychologists' reports, His Honor concluded that Mitchell and Wright obviously had the brains to know better.

"Parties who conspire to import narcotics thereby show no mercy or compassion for the ultimate users, and they deprive themselves of a right to compassion and mercy," His Honor thundered.

Paddy Mitchell was suddenly mopping a torrent of sweat off his face. Lionel Wright, as usual, was staring impassively at his shoes.

Chris Clarkson and Tommy Harrigan were sentenced in absentia to twenty years in federal penitentiary—if, of course, they were ever located.

His Honor then ordered Mitchell to stand.

"You have not been admitted to bail and I propose to take that into consideration in sentencing you," His Honor began as Mitchell felt a moment of relief.

"You will be imprisoned for a period of seventeen years."

Seventeen years. Mitchell's knees buckled.

Wright was ordered to stand and asked if he had anything to say. Lionel continued to examine his shoes.

"I see no reason you should be treated any differently than Mitchell," His Honor concluded. "You will be imprisoned for a period of seventeen years..."

On April 18, 1977, Mitchell got another three years for possession of the stolen gold. That made twenty altogether. It would be almost the turn of the century before he would be a free man. His son would be thirty-five. His wife would be fifty-eight. He might get parole in a decade, if he was lucky.

Two months later, Stephen Douglas Reid was convicted of armed robbery for the gold heist and sentenced to another ten years in federal penitentiary. The presiding judge noted that while Reid had not harmed anyone physically, the crime was "well planned and well executed with considerable aplomb and cool."

Well-executed. Aplomb. Reid wanted to laugh, but thought better of it—the judge was already mad at him for falling asleep and snoring through half the trial.

By the age of twenty-seven, Reid had accumulated a criminal record that now overflowed on to a second page of one-line entries. But, unlike Mitchell's sentences, the clock had been ticking on Reid's time since his original incarceration in 1972. That meant he would be eligible for parole at least five years ahead of Mitchell and Wright.

Lionel, however, did not intend to stick around for Reid's parole party.

The year in jail before their trials had been bad enough for an experienced con like Stephen Reid and an ex-boxer like Mitchell, who wound up running the joint as though the Round Table had been moved to a new location with different decor and no beer.

But for a timid ex-clerk, life amidst so much violence and ugly humanity was a neverending nightmare. The whole time he was behind bars, the Ghost rarely spoke to anyone or left his cell.

A month before the cocaine trial began, Wright decided he had endured enough pain and suffering for one lifetime. Through no fault of his own, the entire detention center suddenly erupted into a mini-riot one morning. Lionel was in the visiting room when someone conveniently smashed the bullet-proof partition where he was sitting.

The Ghost excused himself, climbed through the hole in the glass, and walked out the front door.

A week later, however, Wright and five others who had similarly released themselves from the jail were recaptured at a nearby motel. The police officer who drove him back to jail offered the novice escapee a bit of unsolicited advice: "Geez, Lionel, the next time you decide to make a run for it, for godsake don't hang around with a whole crowd of other guys who are all on the most-wanted list."

Ten months later, seventeen years of hard time ahead of him, Wright went for an unusually long stroll in the exercise yard.

On the afternoon of Sunday, October 3, 1976, a car pulled alongside the jail's perimeter fence and a man casually tossed a shotgun and pair of wire-cutters into the exercise yard. A minute later, Lionel Wright again followed six others to freedom.

As before, it didn't take police long to locate the crowd of criminals trying to hide out in the same house. Six of the escapees were arrested on the spot.

But Lionel had apparently taken the helpful police officer's advice to heart.

The Ghost had vanished.

CHAPTER FIVE

Millhaven Penitentiary

Paddy Mitchell cursed the July heat wave as he snapped the letters on to the Scrabble board and smiled triumphantly at the convicted killer across the picnic table. Gumball soured his face into bulldog furrows of disgust, muttering something obscene. Reid and the others laughed. As always, Paddy was winning, not a huge feat in a penitentiary where half the population could barely read a stop sign. But no one in the group much cared who won or lost the daily contests in the yard. The real game was under their feet.

As Mitchell had originally explained it, if the East Germans could burrow their way to freedom under the Berlin Wall—he'd seen it in the movies—a bunch of inmates with twenty years to kill should be able to tunnel under a couple of wire fences. As usual, he had a plan.

The old recreation shack at the north end of the yard would provide the perfect cover. The shed, originally built to store sports equipment, had been sealed after one inmate had used its seclusion for batting practice on another con's head. Since then, the guards never bothered to check the place. The hut was also conveniently stocked with old hockey sticks, baseball bats and other materials that could be used as makeshift shoring.

As soon as the frost had left the ground, the picnic table was moved in front of the shed and work began. A hacksaw blade unsealed the door. Tools and extra shoring materials were smuggled out of the prison workshops. Every day, as the same group gathered for a friendly game of Scrabble, one of them would drop under the table out of the guards' view, slip into the shack, and start digging. The tedious part was getting rid of the dirt, which was stuffed into plastic bags concealed in bulkier-than-usual prison garb, then dumped during casual walks around the jogging track.

After three months, they had burrowed their way across the yard and under the tennis courts. Another twenty feet and they would be past the first perimeter fence.

The long drug sentence imposed on Mitchell, and Reid's previous escape record had condemned both of them to Canada's worst penitentiary at the height of its worst-ever period of prison violence. In the previous twelve months, there had been more murders, stabbings, and riots in the country's penal institutions than in the previous five years. Millhaven had been the most heinous of them all, a concrete crucible for the outcasts and the downright deranged. The fifth warden in as many years conceded that at least a third of his clientele belonged in a mental asylum.

Ever since an ignominious ribbon cutting in 1971, the place had been a fermentation tank for frustration and bloodletting. The opening ceremonies included three hundred arriving inmates in handcuffs and leg irons being forced to shuffle through a welcoming-committee gauntlet of guards who beat them with clubs. Every inmate owned a shiv—anything sharp enough to puncture skin and long enough to reach vital organs. Stabbings were a weekly event.

Mitchell and Reid had been reunited in the Mill in the fall of 1976, just in time to watch a young convict stumble around the prison yard for a full three minutes, gagging out shrieks for help, the five-inch steel blade protruding from his back like the broken key to some macabre wind-up doll. It was the third stabbing in as many weeks. The second victim had died with forty-two holes in his body.

The day after the young con had performed his grotesque death dance in the prison yard, a guard with a loudhailer and no sense of timing ended the daily exercise period by hollering: "Okay girls, hike up your skirts. No stabbings today; the blood bank is running low."

The lid blew off the pressure cooker. In the twenty-four-hour riot that ensued, inmates redecorated the institution in post-A-bomb motif, prompting yet another government inquiry. It concluded that life in Millhaven was "marked by the use of gas, shackles, clubs and dogs...let loose on inmates in the yard and in their cells. Inmates who were first shackled, sometimes hands and feet together, were then beaten with clubs, made to crawl on the floor and finally gassed...Now all that remains is abuse and harassment."

Paddy Mitchell didn't need the government to tell him he had landed in hell's half-acre. The only thing more certain was that he wanted out of there the fastest possible way—*any* way.

Ronald J. Fairley had barely a year's experience as a classification officer at Millhaven when he first met Mitchell. Armed only with a BA in psychology, he found his job description straightforward enough— "to counsel inmates with problems and attempt to motivate them through prison rehabilitation programs."

In practice, Fairley's task verged on the absurd. Most of the inmates at the Mill had enough serious psychiatric problems to wear a hole in a shrink's couch, and motivation does not come easily to those doing two decades of time, or more. As the graffiti on the cell-block wall said: "Notice to lifers: Learn a trade. You too can be a retired welder when you get out."

But Inmate No. 2212 was different. Ronald J. Fairley had never met—and would never again meet—a convict quite like Paddy Mitchell. The psychologist later wrote: "Patrick Mitchell is an extremely charming, personable person. I find he is very friendly, easy going, very relaxed...Since he has been in the institution, he has posed absolutely no disciplinary problem...He is very salvageable..."

Over time, the two men looked forward to their regular encounters. Unlike most of the other inmates, Mitchell never swore and never threatened to kill his adviser. For Paddy, Fairley's gentle nature and intelligence were a welcome relief from the goon-squad mentality of the guards and the unrelenting rage of the prison population.

The one question that nagged Mitchell most was why he was doing more time than half the convicted murderers in the place.

"I just don't get it," he told Fairley. "I've never hurt anyone, much less killed anyone. It's not like I'm some big mean threat to society. It just doesn't make sense."

Mitchell was certain that God was just working in His usual mysterious ways and would communicate the meaning of it all in due course. He began reading the Bible and praying a lot in the hope the Message would be delivered sooner rather than later.

Meanwhile, when he wasn't waiting for a sign from Above, Mitchell could be found hard at work in the prison print shop where his ability to motivate a garden slug into a marathon, created an efficient, commercial-scale operation for government publications. The administration was duly impressed.

Mitchell had always regretted not finishing his college degree in accounting. Now that he had enough time on his hands to complete every degree a university could offer, he enrolled in a chartered accountancy correspondence course. His gameplan was to appeal his cocaine sentence and get it reduced to ten years. In four years he could be out on parole, back with his family, and earning a good living as a chartered accountant. Those guys always seemed to have ingenious ways of making money and beating the tax department. Besides, he reckoned his big weakness hadn't been making money, just losing it.

A month later he received a letter from the official governing body of chartered accountants. He was welcome to take all the correspondence courses and get his diploma, they said, but he could not be licensed unless he got a pardon. And that couldn't even be considered until after his sentence had expired. Twenty years down the road. *Notice to lifers: Learn a trade. Become a retired accountant when you get out.* The governing body of accountants wished Paddy Mitchell well in his endeavors.

Mitchell was becoming withdrawn and despondent when the administration decided to allow him his first open visit with Barbara. It had been three years since he was led away from his home in handcuffs, promising to be home for supper. Three years since they had touched.

The huge steel door banged shut behind them like the crack of a starter's pistol. For a moment, they just stood and stared, all those dreams of falling into each other's arms suddenly frozen. They were trembling. Tears began to stream down Barbara's cheeks. Paddy bit hard on the corner of his lip. Then they were both sobbing. Separated. Speechless.

Later, as they sat at the bare wooden table, it became clear to both that there was no joy in their tears. Distance had only made the heart grow colder. The magic that had brought them together at a bus stop sixteen years before was gone.

He suggested she get a divorce. She promised to wait. Both of them knew she was lying—their life together was all over but for the formalities.

Barbara climbed aboard the prison bus heading back home and looked around at the other wives and mothers. She wondered how each coped with the misery. The day had been one of the most painful of her life.

Mitchell called Barbara the next evening, but the phone went dead in mid-sentence, just after he told her how much he would always love her. Another inmate had overheard the conversation and tried to strangle Mitchell, convinced the woman on the other end of the phone was his own wife.

A few weeks after Barbara's ill-fated visit, Paddy's favorite Scrabble opponent dropped by.

"Afraid, ah, well, I, I got some bad news," Gumball stuttered.

"They've decided to let you loose on society?" Mitchell quipped without looking up from his book.

"Well, see I got word from a pretty reliable source about your pal Lionel Wright," the con said. "Well, um, I'm not sure I should be telling you this. Like I don't know how—"

"What happened to him?" Mitchell demanded. "Did he get pinched?"

"Well, ah, sort of, yeah," Gumball began. "Well, ah, not exactly got him, no, not really like, you know—"

"Tell me, you crazy bastard," Mitchell said angrily. "What happened?"

Gumball took a deep breath. Word had it, he said, that a few months after Wright's escape, Lionel had fallen sick in a cabin somewhere in central Florida.

"Been shot by some guy. Musta been a case of mistaken identity or somethin'. Anyway, poor little prick got a real bad fever, ya know? But he wouldn't go to hospital, they say. Stupid fucker was too shy to ask for help, know what I mean? Wouldn't even call a damn doctor." Gumball paused. "Well, word has it, your buddy's, like, well, gone, ya know? But for sure they buried him real nice."

Reid and Mitchell had seen little of each other during their respective trials. In the summer of 1977, Reid returned to Millhaven to find his once bon-vivant pal in danger of sliding into a black hole of anxiety and depression. The cons called the all-too-familiar condition "acute Mill-dew"—rotting of the soul, a fungus of frustration, fear, and hopelessness grown in an atmosphere of hostility and degradation. As Reid wrote to a friend: "This is the place where the cure becomes the sickness. It's sad."

The first day of their reunion in the Mill, Reid and Mitchell were having lunch in the dining hall. Mitchell leaned across the table.

"Steve, I've been thinking—"

"That's always a bad sign," Reid chortled.

"No, I'm serious," Mitchell pleaded. "I've been thinking a lot about this and I've reached the conclusion that we've just got to get the hell out of here. Five years, maybe ten, I could have stuck it out. But not twenty. I won't make it. So we've just gotta go."

"Well, if we hurry and pack," Reid said around a mouthful of food, "we could probably catch the six o'clock flight to Vegas."

Mitchell didn't laugh. "Listen, asshole, I've got a plan..."

There are only so many ways out of a prison and Paddy Mitchell would ultimately think of just about every one of them, short of beaming up to the Starship Enterprise.

The perils of being nabbed in the act were pretty simple. At worst the guards would fire a "warning shot" that might just blow the escapee's head off (a lot of cons considered that a best-case scenario). Or the foiled inmate could spend the ensuing years trapped in a hideous corner of the institution known as the Special Handling Unit or SHU— "the Shoo," in prison parlance—home of the most rabid of the rabid.

Residents of this psychological torture chamber were locked in their cells up to twenty-three and a half hours a day, and even then were allowed no contact with anyone. Each cell was a windowless, concrete tomb—a solid steel door with a five-inch peephole; a foam mattress on the floor; a toilet that was merely a hole in the cement. A light burned overhead twenty-four hours a day, dimmed at night from a hundred watts to twenty-five. Too bright to sleep. Too dim to read. Guards banged on the cell doors at hourly intervals throughout the night.

Some inmates were stripped naked for weeks at a time. There was no hot water. Food was passed under the door. Everyone shared the same razor; skin infections were the norm. The daily exercise period was a solitary shuffle along the range corridor, between two wire-mesh guard cages manned with loaded and pointed shotguns. A handwritten sign on one of the gun turrets read: "Psychologist." Radio was piped through an intercom in each cell. The guards left it tuned to the static between channels.

Beatings were routine. Suicides were expected.

One of Mitchell's first encounters with a graduate of the Shoo was a con with lifeless eyes. The guards, apparently proud of their dehumanizing handiwork, had nicknamed their latest zombie "Sparkey." He was handy to have around— whenever someone smeared excrement all over the walls, Sparkey was enlisted to clean up the mess. Sparkey didn't mind. He washed his hands twenty-five times a day anyway—in a toilet-bowl full of his own urine. At night he would spend hours trying to rip open his abdomen, gouging at the flesh with his finger-nails, convinced there was a sewer rat living in his bowels. He smiled a lot, even when he was ordered to do all the dirty work. Sparkey didn't mind. Sparkey didn't have a mind.

He hadn't always been mad. By most accounts, he was relatively normal when he was first thrown into the Shoo for disciplinary prob-lems no one could quite remember.

Sparkey had fought it for a while—the beatings; the isolation; the perpetual overhead light burning a hole in his mind. Then one day they locked him in a cell where another inmate had slashed his wrists and turned the walls into a bloody portrait of death. Sparkey was given a wash cloth and told to clean up the mess—not once, but three times in the same week, in three different cells, after three separate suicides.

Sparkey had tried to hang on. He knew what they were attempting to do to him. He loved books and had tried to encase himself in their fantasies. But now he could only read one sentence at a time, chasing it around the page until he forgot he had read it. Eventually he tried to hang himself. Ultimately, he forgot he was alive.

By the time they let Sparkey out of the Shoo, he had become a robot. In short, he had become precisely what the administration defined as "rehabilitated."

But what they had created was a man-made alien with no respect for life—neither his nor anyone else's.

The last time Mitchell saw Sparkey was in the showers, clawing at the sewer rat in his gut, the blood from his slit wrists mixing with the soap suds swirling around the drain. Sparkey was humming the national anthem.

Paddy Mitchell spent a lot of time thinking about Sparkey, and about the Shoo, weighing the dismal life that lay ahead against the conse-quences of being caught trying to escape. What he clearly hadn't considered, however, were the consequences of not being caught.

"You know that if we do hit the road, you'll never be able to see Barb or Johnny or your mother or the rest of your family again," Reid said one afternoon as they were walking in the yard.

Mitchell looked puzzled. Why else would he try to escape?

"You know those are the first places they'll go hunting for you," Reid continued. "They'll tap their phones, sit on their houses. Christ, they'll hide in their goddam bathrooms until you show up for a piss."

"Let me worry about that," Mitchell said with a sigh. "I'll find a way—"

"No, I can't just let you worry about that," Reid said firmly. "Barb is never going to go on the run with you; she's not that kind of lady. You know that. And if you try to go home, you're going to get pinched. And if you get pinched, I get pinched. That makes this whole thing as much my business as yours. So I want a promise from you that you'll never try to pull one of your wild schemes to get together with Barb."

Mitchell told Reid about his one and only open visit with Barbara, and how they had decided not to try it again for a long time.

"I suppose if I can't get together with my family in here," Mitchell concluded, "and I can't get together with them on the outside, I'd rather be missing them out there than in this rat-hole."

In fall 1977 Patrick Mitchell and Stephen Reid declared an unholy war on the fences of Millhaven Penitentiary. Over them, through them, even under them. They would try everything. There had to be a way.

With a million tons of concrete, two twenty-foot-high fences joined by eight gun towers, and more floodlights than Yankee Stadium, Millhaven was built to be an escape-proof fortress. Instead, it had become what one report called "an unlikely solution to prison over-crowding."

On one occasion, fourteen inmates had simply cut the chain-link fences and walked away from the place. A dozen others were found wandering back and forth through the gaping hole, trying to decide whether to stay or leave. Another time two of Mitchell's pals had gone over the fences on a foggy day in what became known as the Vapor Caper. They later told a judge they had been jogging in the prison yard and just sort of got lost in the mist.

But the word was out that the fences were about to be equipped with new high-tech sensory devices. In the meantime, to Mitchell's way of thinking, that meant the high wire barriers were still vulnerable.

It was just before nightfall when Tiny Tim, the pipsqueak bandit, dove off the jogging track and rolled up to the first fence. The shears smuggled in pieces out of the tinsmithing shop made easy work of the wire strands. He crawled through the tear and wriggled on his belly to the second fence. Mitchell, Reid, and four others began loping around the track towards the hole.

But something was wrong. The nut on the shears had fallen off into the grass. And by the time Tiny Tim found it, he had four shotguns at his head and a two-year ticket to the Shoo.

The Hollywood archives are crammed with fictional footage of convicts exporting themselves to freedom in food carts, garbage pails, or laundry hampers. But in real life, escapes via the shipping and receiving department were rare. At Millhaven all deliveries and pick-ups were intentionally made at night when inmates were locked in their cells. But Paddy Mitchell believed that for every precaution there was an equal and opposite way around it.

One evening before lockdown Mitchell stuffed a dummy in his bed and hid in a cart piled with repaired mailbags, scheduled for pickup by the Post Office that night. Unfortunately, one of the crazies had chosen that same day to avenge his wasted life of stitching canvas mail sacks— he dumped the entire load into the trash shredder and compactor.

Among all the ways Mitchell had thought of leaving Millhaven, in compacted strips was not one of them. He was, however, spared the Shoo after convincing the authorities he had jumped into the garbage disposal in an attempt to commit suicide.

Then there was the tunnel.

As the summer heat wave hit, Mitchell figured there couldn't be more than a month of burrowing left to connect the old sports equipment shack with the outside of the fences. He couldn't wait to see the headlines about this one, a classic among prison escapes, for sure.

Mitchell wiped another stream of sweat off his face and scanned the drab Millhaven scenery, waiting for Gumball to come up with something better than "bote" for the Scrabble board. The high, chain-link fences with their odious razor wire fringes quivered beyond the smoldering heat rising from the prison yard. The daily hubbub of two hundred and fifty convicts in an outdoor playpen had been stilled by the swelter; bodies sprawled lazily in the shade like cattle before a storm. The man on the radio had said the mercury was headed for a record ninety-six. The guard on the loud hailer had said there'd be no riots today. Just too damn hot. No one had felt like digging in the tunnel that day, either.

Suddenly, Mitchell gripped the edge of the picnic table and shot up off the bench. "Holy shit!" he yelped, his jaw clenched, eyes bulging. The others turned on their benches and stared towards the tennis courts. The asphalt surface had seemed like the perfect roof for an escape tunnel. Except in a heat wave.

The tennis net had suddenly been swallowed by the earth.

Thwarted in their attempts to go through the fences or under them, Millhaven's dogged deserters were left with only one alternative: over the top.

Shortly before 8 p.m. Mitchell, Reid, Gumball and three others gathered in Glen Landers's cell which looked out over the south fences. It had taken almost two months to saw through the bolts that fastened the window bars and steel frame to the concrete. Now it was time to move. Landers and two others would go first, part of the original deal for the use of his cell.

Mitchell and Reid watched as the first wave crawled out the window. From there, they moved along the roof on their haunches to the administration building and dropped to the ground directly below one of the gun towers. Inmates were never allowed in that area. No one would be looking for them.

A woman shrieked.

One of the infirmary nurses had been going off shift the moment the first would-be escapee hit the ground a few feet away. Startled and frightened, she lunged back inside the building, screaming for the guards.

Landers ran along the ground back in the direction of his cell window. Now he was scrambling up the first fence, hand over hand, his feet slipping, then catching a link, then slipping again.

There was the crack of a rifle in the blackness somewhere beyond the glare of the floodlights. The back of Landers's shirt erupted in a bloody hole, his life spattered into the night before he hit the ground.

Mitchell ran back to his cell and began vomiting. There must be an easier way...

Aside from the aborted mailbag caper, neither Mitchell nor Reid had been caught at any of their escape attempts. For the most part they were considered model prisoners, a couple of personable inmates just trying to do their time without killing anyone or starting a riot. Part of that was earnest—neither had any inclination to spend a lot of time in the Shoo for the sheer pleasure of redesigning a guard's face. But both of them also knew the next best thing to an escape was a transfer. That meant convincing the Department of Corrections that they were indeed being corrected.

No inmate, least of all Patrick Mitchell or Stephen Reid, honestly believed that anything remotely beneficial happened to a person locked up in a place like the Mill. But doing good time meant doing a third less time. It also meant a quicker transfer to a less gruesome—and less secure—institution. And if they couldn't escape from Millhaven, the only alternative was to try somewhere else.

Mitchell and Reid joined every self-improvement group in the place and began bombarding the warden's office with helpful hints on how to reduce prison tensions.

At the same time Mitchell was unfailingly courteous to the guards and talked a lot about God and Jesus. He never fought with other inmates and kept his cell tidy. The printing shop was humming and saving the government a bundle. Everyone in the administration knew Mitchell was no saint in convict's clothing, but they liked him anyway.

The model-inmate image came easily to Mitchell. It meant following prison routines, obeying the guards, and abstaining from unauthorized activities such as sticking sharp objects into other prisoners. For the most part, he was happy minding his own business anyway. He had little in common with the other inmates intellectually, and regarded most of them as unpredictable psychos.

Mitchell also became a compulsive fitness freak. In a sequestered world where material possessions are not allowed, physical prowess is an alternative form of status, power, and self-esteem—not to mention a useful deterrent to unprovoked attacks. Mitchell even became a vociferous anti-smoking campaigner, though his own efforts to quit were notably unsuccessful.

"Whatever you do," he wrote to his teenage son, "don't ever start smoking. It will ruin your life. And once you start that first pack, you'll never be able to quit. If you have to smoke something, a bit of grass is okay..."

The boy's mother was horrified.

While Mitchell was waiting for a message from God, he became a born-again something—although it was never exactly clear into which religion he had been reborn. In a series of long letters to his son, the otherwise devout materialist fervently preached the virtues of just about every known spiritual concoction from raw Catholic dogma to Eastern mysticism. Not surprisingly, "God's will" was a recurrent theme in the epistles according to Paddy Mitchell—no one could possibly fuck up his life that badly without guidance from Above.

"I did some things that were wrong," he confessed in a letter to his son, "and I have to accept some punishment. But not twenty years..."

Reid was also busy trying to sprout his own halo, organizing recreational and sports activities, including a softball tournament at which the warden threw out the first ball. Reid had escorted him into the yard, the first time a senior administration official and inmates had ever shared that space without tear gas. The warden was impressed.

That winter Reid joined the in-house hockey league, only to find the skating and stick-handling talents that had brought him teenage stardom mattered little in a face-off with convicted murderers. "Hockey in Millhaven is played along the same lines as rollerball," he wrote to a friend at the end of his first season with the Ravin' Havens. "The meanest enforcers in the NHL are sniveling wimps compared to this gang...I'm a solid mass of welts, bruises, cracked bones, torn ligaments and broken skin. To say the least, I'm relieved it's over."

Reid's entertaining letters prompted one of his friends to suggest he consider putting his talent to serious use, a vocation that would indeed be cultivated many years later. In the meantime, he had other plans.

One day over lunch Reid announced he had enrolled in a prison program to become a professional hairdresser. Mitchell blew the soup off his spoon.

"What a great idea, Stevie!" Mitchell bellowed. "I'm sure the drag queens around this place will be absolutely delighted by the news."

Reid smiled. "It happens that the final phase of the course can only be completed at Joyceville. Still sound stupid?"

Joyceville Penitentiary was a nearby medium-security lockup that ranked just next to Nirvana compared with Millhaven. Its escape record had also prompted more than one critic to wonder why the authorities didn't install turnstiles in the fences—at least they could keep an accurate count of unscheduled departures.

On April 6, 1978, Reid wrote the following letter to the Millhaven administration:

> I have spoken to my shop instructor in reference to my continuation of training as a barber. He foresees no problem—if I were to be approved for a transfer to Joyceville...I would very much like to be transferred out of Millhaven at this time. I find it very difficult to sustain a healthy mental approach to my life within the general attitudes of the population here...
>
> I have the support of my family and friends and my primary interest, my only interest, is to prepare for parole as best I can and to go home as soon as possible...

Even Reid's hairdressing instructor sent a note to the warden: "Stephen has excelled at the barbering course...and would fit very nicely into a medium [security] setting... As far as a change of attitude is concerned, I have never seen Reid when he didn't project sincerity..."

Exactly six months later, Stephen Douglas Reid received a notice that his move to Joyceville had been approved. The last line of the document stated: "Reason for transfer: To facilitate correctional treatment."

Stephen Reid and Paddy Mitchell had a good hoot about that one.

CHAPTER SIX

Joyceville Penitentiary

Paddy Mitchell took one look at the straight razor and jammed himself into the barber's chair like a passenger on a crashing jet. He had waited eight months to get out of Millhaven and join Stephen Reid in the relative luxury of Joyceville Penitentiary. Now he was half wishing he hadn't bothered. More precisely, he was regretting having blithely volunteered to play guinea pig for one of Reid's hairdressing and barbering classes. The two had just spent the weekend in front of the television, watching baseball and popping six-packs of Valium pills— the prison equivalent of pretzels and beer. Now the razor in Reid's hand was shaking like a jackhammer as it moved towards Mitchell's foam-covered neck.

"Just sit still and read this," Reid grunted as he handed a letter to his squirming victim.

The memo to Stephen Douglas Reid from the National Parole Board said there had been a regrettable error. The earliest date he would be eligible to apply for parole was not three years away as previously stated.

"Upon further review of your file, it has come to our attention that your parole review date has in fact passed. Should you wish to submit an application, you may do so at any time… Your case will be reviewed within five months of receipt of your application…"

Mitchell read and reread the five-line letter in disbelief. "This has gotta be a joke," he sputtered. "The only way your parole date passed was in some former life."

"Oh, gee, Patrick," Reid said as he scraped another swath of foam off Mitchell's face, "I'll be sure to call right away and tell them there must be some mistake."

Despite the convenient error in the parole board's counting department, Reid knew the road between a parole application and approval could be as long and complicated as the most intricate escape plan. The halo Reid had sprouted to get out of Millhaven might be of marginal consequence to those who would now consider letting him loose on society. They would want proof he would be heading to a job and a stable home. They would want to know he had the support of his family to help him go straight. More than anything, they would have to be convinced he had the means and inclination to pursue a life of something other than armed robbery. In short, Stephen Reid would have to prove he had somehow been rehabilitated in prison. Not surprisingly, the vast majority of first-time parole applications are denied.

On June 11, 1979, Stephen Douglas Reid formally applied for parole. The first line of the one-page form asked him to give reasons for making the request. He wrote: "To be allowed to serve the remaining portion of my sentence in the community. A parole would afford me the opportunity to re-establish myself as a productive member of the community and would serve to reunite me with my family."

The model-inmate image Reid had begun to polish at the Mill had continued virtually untarnished at Joyceville. He had completed most of his hairstyling courses and was captain of the hockey team (considerably less of a gladiator's sport than in Millhaven). He had volunteered for the general inmate committee, the sports committee, and the entertainment committee. One evening in early June he was even allowed out—albeit under constant guard—to present a local junior hockey league with a trophy donated by the inmates. (A photograph in the next day's paper showed him at the banquet looking so perfectly respectable in a suit and tie that the caption wrongly identified him as the president of the Rotary Club. The cons got a big laugh out of that one.)

One of Reid's relatives agreed to offer him a job and a place to live in the northern Ontario town of Sault Ste. Marie. He even applied for admission to the community college there. He collected written references from his family and the few respectable friends from his past.

In the first week of August Reid's father and mother visited their son at Joyceville to hear the good news firsthand. Despite all the grief, anxiety, and embarrassment his criminal activities and imprisonment had inflicted on the family, his parents had remained steadfastly supportive and hopeful. Douglas Reid had already buried prison authorities in letters of concern for his son's safety at Millhaven. Now he would inundate the parole board with letters of support for his son's early release.

Reid's careful groundwork began to pay off in mid-August when the administration granted him a day pass under the escort of Joyceville guard Andy Houston. As stated on the application, it was "part of an overall resocialization program." Attached to the form was a detailed itinerary for his day on the outside. They would visit a local halfway house where Reid might stay if granted day parole. Also arranged was an interview with the owner of a hairdressing salon to explore the possibility of becoming a trainee after his release. Finally, they planned to visit Houston's prized woodworking shop, a barn-like building where a hobby group practiced carpentry without nails or screws. Andy Houston was totally absorbed by his carpentry pastime, and was thrilled when Reid took an interest. For months they had talked about little else.

Andy Houston finally wrote to the administration: "Stephen Reid's institutional behavior over the past three years has been exemplary... Nothwithstanding the above, the writer is aware of the risk factor involved in an escorted temporary absence, but believes the benefits to be derived will greatly benefit the subject..."

The warden was clearly impressed with Reid's itinerary for his first day pass. Reid had run into him the day before the escorted leave of absence was granted.

"Glad to see you're not going to be spending your day lying around on the beach," the warden said to Reid.

"No, sir," Reid said politely. "I wanted to make the best of my time. Besides, I look like hell in a bikini."

They both laughed and parted with the warden's wishes of good luck in the interviews.

A light drizzle was falling the morning of August 23, 1979, as Houston and Reid drove through the high wire fences around Joyceville Pen and headed for the city, thirteen miles away. The morning went pretty much as planned. Reid seemed genuinely excited by his visit to the wood-working shop. He wanted to know everything about the process, the place and the people there. He couldn't wait to join the club when he got out.

The two then headed to the beauty salon for Reid's hairdressing interview. The owner had said in her letter that she could only spare about fifteen minutes, and now opened the conversation by saying she didn't anticipate any job openings for quite some time. Translation: she wasn't about to hire an ex-con.

An hour later, she was chatting and laughing with Reid as though they were old friends. Sure, Reid could have a job there anytime; he had certainly changed her opinion of inmates. She just couldn't seem to get enough of his wit and charm. Reid began checking his watch.

It was a few minutes before noon when Reid and Houston finally said goodbye to the chatty hairstylist and climbed back into the car. They were due at their next appointment at the halfway house in just over an hour.

"Hey, Andy, I'd kill for fish and chips right about now," Reid said casually. "Murphy's is just up the street. Best seafood in the world. How 'bout it, ol' buddy?"

"Oh, no, no," Houston said. "We're not going to get into that kind of stuff. It's not on the itinerary. And besides, I have to go to City Hall and pay a parking ticket."

"Ah, fuck that, Andy. You can pay it anytime. But me, I've been eating prison garbage every day for four years and now I got one hour to have some fish and chips and you say a goddam ticket is more important. Thanks, pal."

"Ah, what the hell," Houston relented. "But we don't have much time."

Reid promised it would be the fastest lunch the guard had ever seen.

City Hall was only a few blocks from Murphy's Seafood, and Houston stopped to pay his parking ticket anyway. Reid was annoyed as he checked his watch again. Ten past twelve. They didn't have much time.

Reid was first through the door of Murphy's when he almost collided with a waitress and a tray of dinners. He was still apologizing when Houston reached the table and headed for the far seat, facing into the restaurant.

"Hey man, this is my only chance to check out the T and A in this place," Reid said, slithering past Houston into the seat with a view into the crowded eatery.

"Geez, you complain a lot, Reid," Houston said, shaking his head in feigned disgust.

Reid slung his jean jacket over the back of the chair and checked his watch again.

"Order me fish and chips and a large Pepsi," he told Houston. "And tell them to make it fast. We've got fifteen minutes to be out of here. I'm going for a quick piss."

The waitress took the rush order seriously and was back at the table within a few minutes with Houston's dinner.

"I'll keep your friend's order hot till he gets back," she said.

"Naw, you better bring it now," Houston said. "We're in a big rush. He's just gone to the washroom."

"Whatever you want. He was the one who told me to keep his dinner hot. Said he might be a while. Rushed off down the street somewhere."

Stephen Reid had no way of knowing if his head start was three minutes or three seconds. He wanted to run faster, but held back. That's what Houston would be watching for—someone in a pair of Lucky Levis, rushing among the crowds on the street.

Reid turned left one block, then south two more. His chest was aching. Now he could see the red brick tower of the Holiday Inn. The man with the getaway car had been told to be there from ten o'clock till noon. It was almost one.

His pace quickened. A siren was shrieking behind him...

Andy Houston stared at the waitress and asked her to repeat what she had said. His heart stopped. Damn. He wasn't supposed to let escorted prisoners out of his sight for a second. But Reid was different. He was smart. Likeable. No need to worry about the guy. Not like the other cons. Or so it had seemed.

He scrambled down the restaurant stairs onto the crowded street.

Reid bounded over the sagging steel wire roping off the Holiday Inn parking lot. He wheeled towards the main doors, scanning frantically for the green Pontiac...Where the hell was it?...Suddenly, he froze.

The hotel chain that promises no surprises certainly had one for the frenzied fugitive staring at the huge billboard: "Welcome: Police Association."

CHAPTER SEVEN

Joyceville Penitentiary

The media had a field day with Stephen Reid's escape. "The inmate, serving a lengthy term for one of Canada's biggest armed robberies, was not only allowed an escorted day pass, but also an unescorted trip to the bathroom. Apparently, he did not specify which washroom and was last seen fleeing from the restaurant while his guard munched on fish and chips...Reid is considered armed and extremely dangerous."

Reporters also seemed to take great delight in pointing out the caper was not the first time the escapee had chosen to eat and run. "Reid had pulled precisely the same stunt on an escorted pass in 1973 when he escaped through the bathroom window of a restaurant less than three blocks from the scene of yesterday's vanishing act. Only the menu had changed—the first time he had convinced his guards to stop for Chinese food..."

Paddy Mitchell read the stories and laughed for days. Everything had gone as planned, more or less, from the moment of their reunion at Joyceville two months before the escape. Reid's model-inmate disguise, and the myriad arrangements he was making for parole, were all part of an intricate blueprint for escape. The guard's woodworking hobby had bored Reid to the point of considering other less agonizing means of escape. He had no interest in hairdressing. Even the trophy presentation at the hockey banquet had been orchestrated to lull authorities into thinking he could be trusted with a full day's leave of absence. The unexpected miscalculation in his parole eligibility date had simply made the whole scheme easier to execute.

Reid and Mitchell had spent hours poring over maps of the city, honing every detail of the escape. Don't try anything in the morning— that's when Andy Houston would be most alert to signs of trouble.

Don't have the getaway car outside the restaurant—it would be easier to outrun the guard in a foot race than the police in a car chase. And whatever happened, Reid couldn't let Houston sit facing the restaurant door.

Mitchell had no way of knowing how perilously close the master plan had come to failure; how it had almost run out of time over a parking ticket; how Houston had nearly landed in the wrong seat after Reid's near collision with the waitress; and how the green Pontiac and its driver had finally been located in the midst of a police detectives' convention. It didn't much matter to Mitchell, though. One way or another, his friend was free again.

The thing that had puzzled Mitchell was why Reid wouldn't hang around until his parole hearing, why he chose the uncertain life of a fugitive on the eve of possible release with society's blessings.

"In the first place, you know the chances of the parole board cutting me loose the first time around are almost nil," Reid had said one day as they paced the prison yard. "And even if they did, there's no way I'd make six years of it. My ass would be kicked back in here—or worse, some hellhole like the Mill—in no time. Those poor folks in the parole offices are so overworked they'd do anything to get someone off their caseloads. Just look around this place. It's full of guys who've been around the revolving door. Besides, you know me—I'd give them plenty of good reasons to pull the plug."

Forever saddened by what he had done to his own family, Mitchell had reminded Reid that escaping would also disappoint and hurt his parents.

"Yeah, that's about the only thing that's ever held me back," Reid said reflectively. "You know, my dad is a good, intelligent, law-abiding guy who thinks I have learned the big lesson and will be Mr. Upstanding Citizen when I get out. And I really don't want to cause him any more grief. But I can't go back to all that suffocation of working in a mine somewhere."

Mitchell began to understand that his own dream of simply going home to his family was not shared by his friend. Clearly, Reid was going to leave prison with his professional ambitions intact—namely, to become rich and infamous.

Reid had finally put a hand on Mitchell's shoulder and smiled. "Besides, one of us has got to get that dream score organized. Then we can all retire."

Paddy Mitchell had first stumbled across the Dream Score back in the days of planning the airport gold heist. He had heard through the vine that the Brinks Armored Transport Company routinely flew tens of millions of dollars in currency, securities, precious metals and other valuables from New York to various Canadian cities and back to the United States. The only trick was stealing it from the heavily armed guards on board the aircraft and the armored-truck escorts who retrieved the loot on the tarmac. Clearly, a holdup with anything less than Leopard tanks was going to be messy. As usual, Mitchell had a plan...

The smug euphoria of achievement that Mitchell felt in the days following Reid's disappearance seemed to fade into despondency. Unless the parole board used its faulty calculator on his sentence, too, Mitchell wouldn't be eligible to apply even for a day pass for another four years. That he should remain behind bars while a hardened crook like Reid was free only heightened Mitchell's sense of unfairness and desperation.

Barbara's visits to Joyceville were more relaxed than they had been at Millhaven, but the encounters nonetheless exacerbated his anxiety over so much life and love lost.

Meanwhile, the prison authorities were trying to have him shipped back to maximum security in Millhaven on the rather astute suspicion that he might try to follow Reid out the door. He would fight it. His social workers were already fighting it. Anything but Millhaven.

By early fall Mitchell was showing symptoms of what appeared to be severe depression. Then he began complaining of headaches, chest pains, and sporadic numbness in his left arm. Hospital tests found nothing. The prison doctors passed it off as acute anxiety.

The evening of November 15, 1979, Mitchell went for his routine jog around the inside perimeter of the Joyceville yard. It was shortly before six o'clock, the early nightfall shrouded in soggy melancholy. The chain-link fences rippled and rattled in the wind, rain wafting across the halogen floodlights like waves of tiny bombs pounding his face. The sound of strained breathing mixed with the metronomic slapping of running shoes pounding the ooze.

He squinted at his watch. His time was up. He thought about his last visit with Barbara two weeks before. He imagined himself scaling the wire fences and falling into her arms. He would probably be killed, but he didn't care much anymore. His legs were pumping faster, splashing through the puddles, lunging towards the darkness. Barbara would understand.

Mitchell's chest was heaving as he jogged back towards the concrete cell block at the end of his four-mile run. He reached for his plastic water bottle, drained it, and took one last sprint the length of the prison yard. He tugged on the steel door and flung it open.

Suddenly, his stomach lurched. He staggered forward, then sideways, a few more steps ahead, sideways again, weaving down the corridor like a drunkard. The walls began twisting and spinning out of focus, gawking faces melting into foggy distortions.

Mitchell was barely conscious when he clutched at his chest and collapsed headfirst into a pile of aluminum garbage cans outside the inmate common room.

The nurse on duty in the infirmary pressed a stethoscope to Mitchell's ribcage. His heart sounded like a fish flapping in a dry pail. He was pouring sweat. Her fingers groped for a pulse. He seemed confused, barely conscious, agitated. He muttered something about pain in his chest, numbness in his left arm. His eyes were glazed.

"Call an ambulance and tell them to move it," she yelled at the orderly as she slipped a nitroglycerine pill under Mitchell's tongue and frantically tried to pump Demerol into a collapsing vein. He was writhing.

"Tell them we've got a cardiac."

By the time the ambulance paramedics arrived, the nurse had checked Mitchell's file. Repeated complaints of chest pains, numbness. Why hadn't they sent him to hospital? Acute anxiety? It was acute, all right.

"My heart?" Mitchell gurgled as he rolled his head towards the ambulance attendant. "The big one? Am I going to die?"

"We don't know what has happened to you," the attendant said softly. "The important thing now is to get you to hospital as fast as we can."

Mitchell lapsed back into unconsciousness.

Guard Dennis Bowen was standing on the opposite side of the stretcher and gave the attendant a raised-eyebrow look that asked what the paramedic really thought of the patient's condition. The answer came back in a slow, hopeless shake of a bowed head.

A minute later Paddy Mitchell was being loaded into the back of the ambulance, strapped to the stretcher, in handcuffs, leg irons, and an oxygen mask. Bowen climbed in with him. Another two guards followed in an escort car. No one was taking any chances, even with a motionless corpse. The siren and flashing lights sped off into the rainy darkness.

"What the hell is going on here?" the ambulance driver sputtered as he pulled to a stop on the street in front of the hospital. He leaned forward, straining to see beyond the slapping windshield wipers. Everywhere there were mounds of earth and amber flashing lights. The road construction had been going on all week, but now there were barricades across the ramp to the emergency department.

"Over there," the other paramedic shouted, pointing to a makeshift emergency entrance sign. The arrow pointed to a semi-circular drive leading to the main administration doors at the front of the hospital.

The guard glanced at his watch and then at Mitchell as the ambulance lurched into the driveway. Five minutes after seven. He wondered if it was already too late.

The hospital had been alerted to expect an incoming cardiac victim. Two attendants in white uniforms were walking in the direction of the ambulance.

"Hey, you two," Bowen hollered at the attendants. "Over here. Give us a hand. Hurry up, for godssake. We've got a heart attack..."

Bowen turned to watch the paramedics unload the stretcher. As his head twisted back again, he was staring down the long barrel of a .357 magnum.

"Hurry up, yourself, asshole," the armed hospital attendant hissed through his medical mask. "All of you, into the back of the ambulance. Move it!"

A black Chevy van pulled onto the lawn alongside the ambulance. The two hospital attendants cut the stretcher straps, dragged Mitchell to the truck, and pitched him onto the floor in the back. The van's engine raced as its wheels spun on the wet grass.

"That you?" Mitchell moaned as the van bumped through the potholed road construction and made a skidding right turn down a side street.

"Right here, my boy," said a voice beside him.

A familiar chuckle came from the front seat. "All present and accounted for, sir."

Paddy Mitchell smiled and let his eyelids fall, just as the headlights began closing in on them from behind.

"Looks like we got company," Lionel Wright shouted from the front seat.

Stephen Reid reached for his shotgun.

CHAPTER EIGHT

Somewhere in Vermont

Stephen Reid gazed blankly at the passing countryside, his mind gently tranquilized by the monotonous sway and clacking of the Amtrak coach. Maybe just get off at the next stop, he mused as the glass of Remy Martin spilled its warmth into his throat. Just evaporate into the calm of some sleepy New England town with its white clapboard church and tidy homes amid the postcard beauty of Vermont's pine-laden valleys and rolling mountains. Neon is banned. Quaint is everything. A nice place to settle down, all right. Maybe someday.

But not now. The well-meaning folk in these tiny perfect villages would ask too many questions. A gang on the run would have too few answers. And for the time being, at least, Stephen Reid couldn't run far enough fast enough.

At first, Reid had wanted the gang to flee to Europe. Wright had argued for South America. But Mitchell had persuaded them that three fugitives trying to pass themselves off as natives of a strange country with a strange language and culture was not going to be easy. Americans, on the other hand, were just Canadians with twangy accents, too many guns, and a big problem with crime. Three bandits would fit in perfectly.

Reid slumped back into his train seat and pulled JoAnne's head onto his shoulder. They had met a few weeks after his escape from Joyceville Prison. She was tending bar at a private Quebec nightclub where he could drink in relative safety—its locked doors were not readily un-locked for anyone, least of all curious police detectives. She was only twenty-three, blessed with dark good looks, and cursed with a history of lousy relationships.

77

Reid had been captivated by her mischievous eyes, girlish smile, and long slender legs beneath a tight leather mini. She had been equally drawn to his powerful build, pumped into hard contours by the years of prison barbells. More than anything, she was enchanted by his wit, charm, and gentleness. He was, she thought, the perfect gentleman. Perhaps even too perfect. Perhaps, she told a girlfriend, perhaps the guy was gay.

By the time they fell into bed after a long evening of champagne and laughter—the gay theory was forever put to rest—JoAnne figured she just might have found her mate, someone who would treat her with kindness and generosity, someone who would give her love without abuse. A man she could trust.

She didn't know what he did for a living, but that was no big deal. The nightclub was full of rich men with no visible means of support. Whenever she asked, he just called himself a businessman and changed the subject. Maybe she didn't want to know. She just wanted their affair to go on forever. And when he asked her to go to Florida with him in late November, JoAnne hoped they would be gone for a long time.

"Could I see your identification, please?"

Reid's eyes flew open in a confused panic. The Amtrak train had stopped. Uniforms. Two of them, towering over his seat, blocking the aisle. Nowhere to run.

"United States Immigration Service," one of them said. "Sorry to have to wake you. Could we see some identification and your tickets, please?"

Reid struggled to appear calm. He told the officers he and JoAnne were just going to visit his Aunt Molly Somerville at her home in Burlington, Vermont. He even had her address and phone number, randomly plucked from the Vermont directory before they boarded the train in Montreal. His driver's license and birth certificate said he was a Canadian named Walter J. Ford. (The nightclub sold that kind of stuff like draft beer.) Their tickets said they would be heading back to Canada after the weekend. That's all that really mattered to the authorities.

"Have a nice day," the officer said as he turned to move down the aisle. Reid reached for the napkin under his cognac glass and began mopping sweat.

A short while later he made his way towards the back of the train, arriving at the second-last coach just as the immigration officials were inspecting the tickets of one Daryl P. Simpson of Montreal. They could barely wedge a word into the chatter.

"Just going to Stowe for the weekend," Daryl P. bubbled. "Big reunion with some old university pals of mine. Do this every year. You know, Daryl and Bob and the boys get together over a few beers, know what I mean? Ha-ha. Last time we ended up with this whole chalet full of nurses from Boston. Wild. I mean, just wild. Ha-ha. Do you guys ski? Ever been to Stowe? Great party town. They got any snow yet? Gawd, I love that place. Wild. Just wild..."

The immigration officers couldn't get away from Daryl fast enough.

Stephen Reid was not amused. He had met a lot of liars in his life of crime, but Paddy Mitchell was in a dangerous league of his own. What if the cops had joined in the conversation? What if they had been to Stowe? Or asked which college? Or where, exactly was that chalet full of nurses? How could anyone that smart be that stupid?

Reid gulped another cognac and slumped into his seat. The worst was over. They would fly from Burlington to New York that night and then on to Florida the next morning. He just wanted to sleep in the sun for a month. Take long walks on the beach. Make love to JoAnne. He couldn't remember when he had felt so burned out.

The freeing of Paddy Mitchell had been an exhausting ordeal. Attempted escapes by prison inmates during hospital visits were about as common as fence climbs and had roughly the same success rate. Mitchell and Reid figured they had interviewed just about every con who had ever tried either stunt. That all of them were offering their valuable advice from neighboring cells was not a promising sign.

"Gotta have someone pick yuz up at the other end; that's the secret," said Porkchop, the hapless con who had won a trip to hospital by poking out both eyes with a ballpoint pen. "Reckoned I had the whole thing figured out. Just forgot to get me a guide dog, that's all. Got picked up trying to feel my way out of the fucking hospital." Mitchell dubbed him the Birdbrain of Alcatraz.

Another inmate had intentionally dropped a two-hundred-pound anvil on his leg, thoroughly pulverizing the bones. All it got him were three steel plates, a permanent limp, and a broken nose after he jumped off the hospital stretcher and fainted on his face.

Mitchell had spent hours in the penitentiary library, poring over *Gray's Anatomy* in search of a body part suitable for temporary disability. The ailment would have to be too serious for the prison infirmary to repair, but not too serious for Reid to handle after the escape. No broken bones that would need setting. No eyeballs hanging out of their sockets.

More than anything, Mitchell needed an illness of sufficient trauma to panic the prison medics into an emergency ambulance call. Timing would be everything—Reid and the others could hardly pitch a tent on the hospital lawn to await Mitchell's arrival.

Mitchell finally abandoned the library, having found no anatomical part worthy of sacrifice, even for such a good cause. Discussions turned to other possibilities.

One afternoon, an old lifer was regaling Mitchell and Reid with tales of the Shoo. Said he had been thrown into an isolation cell as punishment for knocking a guard's lights out. Had plenty of cigarettes with him, but the screws wouldn't give him matches, just to piss him off. In a final fit of nicotine desperation he soaked a pack of smokes in a glass of water, filtered it through his sock, and drank it. The next thing he knew, his ticker was going berserk and he was being rushed to the hospital cardiac unit. Sick as a dog for a day or two. Fine after that. Scared the hell out of him, though.

Reid and Mitchell were intrigued—they had found the perfect escapee's disease. They would do it in the evening when there were no doctors on duty in the infirmary, just a nurse. They hoped it would scare the hell out of her, too—at least enough to call an ambulance.

Mitchell's unscheduled addition of a four-mile run to his water bottle full of nicotine solution had come dangerously close to turning a fake heart attack into the real thing. For two days after his escape he lay on a mattress in a basement apartment, slipping out of unconsciousness only long enough to writhe in vomiting convulsions. Reid began to wonder if he'd be holed up with a dead body.

"You know you damn near killed yourself," Reid said as Mitchell finally started to rally on the third day after the escape.

"Yeah, I guess so," Mitchell said through the receding grogginess. "Frankly, I didn't really give a damn. I either wanted to wake up here or not wake up at all."

The media had had even more fun with Mitchell's escape than with his partner's dine-and-dash episode three months earlier. The stories were unanimously slanted to embarrass the authorities and left no doubt about the identities of the accomplices. The day after Mitchell vanished, the *Ottawa Citizen* bannered the headline: "Jailbreak was no surprise to prison officials."

> Penitentiary officials were aware that Joyceville inmate Patrick Mitchell would probably attempt an escape before he succeeded Thursday, but could do nothing because of his exemplary record of prison behavior...

For years, Mitchell has played penal officials for suckers. On Thursday it paid off...By the time he walked away from a prison ambulance to freedom after faking a heart attack at Joyceville, his two main former partners in crime were already unlawfully at large...

But the authorities faced a familiar dilemma, said Deputy Commissioner of Penitentiaries John Braithwaite: "We knew of the relationship between Mitchell and the two others unlawfully at large, and we knew of the implications of that relationship. But we had to judge him [Mitchell] as an individual and his prison record was good..."

Paddy Mitchell was always impressed by his own headlines. But he was less pleased with Reid's efforts to spring him. The day before his own escape, Reid had promised to return in two weeks to free Mitchell. But little had gone as planned at first, and the process had taken three months to organize.

"What took you so long?" Mitchell growled as soon as he was well enough to speak.

"I'll tell you what took so long," Reid replied angrily. "All those fucking friends of yours who had promised you they would come up with cars and guns and cash to help spring you—well, they came up with nothing after I got out. They were great bosom buddies as long as you were making them tons of dough, but—"

"Bobby told me he'd have ten grand."

"Try two hundred bucks and a chunk of hash. Maybe he thought I could just get stoned and fly in to get you out. I had to go to a lot of banks for a lot of loans..."

Police in three different cities described Reid's six-week bank-robbing spree after his escape as the worst rash of holdups they had ever seen. In total, he had withdrawn more than a hundred thousand dollars in "loans."

Once he had taken care of his financial requirements, Reid had contacted some of his old underworld buddies and placed orders for all the gear he needed to execute Mitchell's escape: guns, a stolen van, the hospital garb, fake sets of identification, a scanner to monitor the police frequencies, and a stocked apartment in which to lie low for a week until the heat died down and Mitchell recovered. Since Reid didn't dare show his face in the area, he had to hire others to take photographs of the hospital and surroundings, to time the getaway routes, and stock the hideout with a week's supply of steaks and Mouton Cadet. In all, the bills came to more than twenty thousand dollars.

The afternoon of the escape, Mitchell's brother Bobby had been dispatched to the prison with the message to Paddy to hit the garbage cans at six o'clock sharp. From that moment, Reid had calculated the time the ambulance would arrive at the hospital (he was off by only five minutes).

The road construction was an unexpected bit of luck. Reid used the barricades to block the ramp to the emergency entrance, rerouting the scene of the showdown to the dimly lit and deserted driveway that led to the main administration doors. The telltale green prison escort car was another surprise bonus—Reid's biggest nightmare had been hijacking the wrong ambulance.

Finally, the prison administration had given the plan an unintentional helping hand. Inmates had formerly been taken to any one of three area hospitals in an emergency. But the policy had been changed shortly before Mitchell's escape, ironically, as a security measure. Henceforth, all federal prisoners would be treated at the same institution where staff had been specially trained to handle dangerous inmates.

"Actually, you missed the best part of the whole show when you passed out in the van," Reid told Mitchell. "We made the corner after leaving the hospital and, sure enough, we got this set of headlights following us. So we make another turn and the guy is still with us. The next corner, the same thing. So I reach for my shotgun, and we're about to pull over—you know, just kick open the back doors and pump one into the guy's grille so he knows this ain't TV stuff."

"You didn't shoot anybody, did you?" Mitchell said with alarm.

"Well, the problem was I'd been changing out of that hospital uniform. So at this point, I'm crouching there buck naked with this shotgun in one hand, turning the door handle with the other, waiting to see what happens at the next turn. Anyway, he went straight ahead. Just some guy on his way home from work. I mean, can you imagine the scene if the poor bastard had made one more turn, eh?"

They both started to laugh: "Hi, honey, I'm home. You won't believe what just happened to me. Like, I left the office and was driving along minding my own business when suddenly this naked man with a shotgun jumped out of the back of a van and blew the front end off our new stationwagon..."

Paddy Mitchell's recovery had seemed complete by the time he and Reid checked into Montreal's downtown Queen Elizabeth Hotel a week after the escape. The Amtrak station was conveniently located in the basement where JoAnne would join them the next morning for the train trip across the border into Vermont. In the meantime Reid put his prison hairdressing lessons to work, tinting and perming Mitchell's straight brown shag into blond, curly locks. They had cleaned out the hotel minibar, joked a lot over a room-service dinner, and finally retired early for the next day's slip into the United States.

The following afternoon they left the train in Burlington, Vermont, and headed to the local airport. Then the trouble started.

By the time the commuter aircraft touched down in New York, Mitchell had lost his lunch in the lavatory and had broken into a drenching perspiration. Just a touch of the flu, he had said. Nothing serious.

But his condition continued to deteriorate on the next day's flight to Orlando, Florida. Reid's concern rapidly turned to panic. What if Mitchell's faked heart attack had done permanent damage? They could hardly just wheel him off to some Florida hospital—hello, my friend here is a fugitive from Canada and he's not feeling well.

Worse, what if Mitchell was coming unstuck? What if he couldn't handle the unrelenting tension of the fugitive's life that Reid knew lay ahead of them? Mitchell had always talked big, but planning scores for other hired gunslingers to execute took genius, not guts. Even his escape was more an act of desperation than bravery. Reid had warned him that being on the run was no picnic, that they would all need thick skins and strong stomachs. Maybe Mitchell had neither.

As they stepped into the Florida heat outside the baggage area of the Orlando airport, Reid wondered briefly whether it might have been better for everyone if he had just kept on running and left Paddy to his own fate.

"Well, if it ain't my favorite pen pals, so to speak," a familiar voice said behind them.

Lionel Wright took one look at Mitchell's condition and began to laugh. "I guess I don't have to ask if you had a good flight."

"I think we got a pretty sick puppy on our hands," Reid whispered to Wright. "Claims it's the flu, but I'm worried—"

"Yeah, yeah, it's flu, all right. Spelled F-L-E-W. Mister Big Tough Guy here is terrified of flying, that's all."

Reports of Lionel Wright's death three years before had indeed been greatly exaggerated. In the months after his escape and disappearance, the

Ghost had crisscrossed the United States to shake anyone in possible pursuit. He finally landed in Daytona Beach, a northern Florida resort town best known for epidemics of hangovers and social diseases during the annual student orgy called Spring Break. There, Wright hooked up with Chuck Hogan, one of Mitchell's old friends from their days of driving Pepsi trucks together back in Canada.

Hogan had moved to Florida a few years earlier after retirement from a motorcycle gang and a stint in prison. He bought a motel along the Daytona strip and hired Wright as his desk clerk, mainly in return for room and board and safe haven to lie low. Chuck Hogan wouldn't spend a dime to see the Second Coming.

Aside from one round-trip to Canada that lasted just long enough to help spring Mitchell from prison, Wright never strayed far from the motel. As always, the Ghost made no friends, rarely spoke to anyone, and passed his time reading Greek history. He never drank, never did drugs, never missed a day's work, never complained about extra chores, and kept meticulous books. There was never a nickel missing, nor so much as a parking ticket added to his record. On the rare occasion he treated himself to a restaurant meal, it was usually the same order: chicken sandwich. Hold the mayo, lettuce, pepper, and salt. Plain white bread. No butter.

Other than Mitchell and Reid, only one member of Wright's family and one other trusted friend had known his exact whereabouts. The friend arrived in Florida with two hundred dollars from Wright's family. Then a letter from his family confidant arrived at his post office box a week later, expressing the hope that the thousand dollars sent via his friend would help him get by. Lionel always did have trouble finding good friends.

Eventually Hogan sold the motel in Daytona and bought another one just outside the central Florida town of Dundee. Wright followed, but only after taking care of a bit of unfinished business—namely, his own death. If his only friend would rip him off for eight hundred dollars of family money, his only friend could just as easily turn him in.

Killing off the Ghost was not difficult. A hundred bucks in the pocket of a trucker headed for Canada would have delivered an entire Ludlum plot to the gossip-hungry rumor mill back home.

The news about Wright's death in a lonely cabin in the Everglades was scrawled on a one-page note, supposedly from "a friend." The handwriting would let his family know he was okay, while Mitchell got a contact on the outside to confirm the hoax with motel owner Chuck

Hogan. No one else much mattered—the death of Lionel Wright would hardly bring the nation's flags to half-mast.

The ruse worked. By the time Mitchell got the bad news from Gumball that evening in Millhaven, at least one police informant on the street had already hit the intended target. Two words were inserted into the national law enforcement computer files after the name Lionel Wright: "Deceased. Unconfirmed."

Wright knew a report of his possible murder would be forwarded in due course to the Florida state authorities. And that's where it would stop—the death of a convicted drug felon and prison escapee from another country was not likely to unleash a police manhunt through the swamps. From then on nobody anywhere was going to put a lot of effort into looking for the Ghost.

Rising again from the dead, however, was considerably more complicated. Simply introducing himself as Bob Smith did not a new identity make. He needed paper to prove it—a lot of paper. The problem is that paper begets paper. He couldn't even get a driver's license without three other pieces of identification. And he couldn't get any of those without a driver's license or some other official ID that required more paper. Bureaucracies work that way.

Most American citizens gain access to the long paper trail on the strength of their parents' identities. Governments hellbent to convert every newborn into a computer code are only too happy to wallpaper the family nursery in ID—birth certificates, hospital and medical codes, even a social security card for the tot who can't yet walk.

But for a no-name fugitive trying to start life in America at thirty-two, the almighty paper trail seemed as elusive as the road to Oz.

Wright knew that for a few hundred dollars he could buy an entire wallet full of identification, picked out of someone's jacket on the street. That was enough to get Reid and Mitchell across the border on a train—the immigration officials didn't come equipped with computers crammed with information on stolen ID. But the police did. And if Wright were going to be recaptured and sent back to prison for life, it certainly wasn't going to be for a lousy speeding ticket and license check.

One day, Lionel Wright discovered the key to reincarnation at a rather unlikely temple: the public library. The one in Orlando, like those in most major cities across the United States, had an entire shelf of how-to books on changing identities.

Wright pulled one off the shelf and read the teaser on the front cover: "Fake ID and Alternate Identities! The most comprehensive book on this little-known subject ever offered for sale! You have to read it to believe it!" God bless America and freedom of the press.

The hefty volume was a counterfeiter's dream, its pages jammed with full-color reproductions of every conceivable kind of identification papers from every state in the union—driver's permits, motor vehicle registrations, birth certificates, social security cards, press passes, welfare ID for food stamps, even police credentials—for reasons one could only imagine.

The comprehensive guide for the do-it-yourself fugitive went on to give detailed descriptions of the different numerical coding systems on each piece of identification: "The first letter of the person's surname is followed by the numeric year and month of birth; followed by the first four digits of the social security number; followed by a three-digit code for city of birth (see page 93 for full listings of city codes)." And so on, page after page, credential after credential.

Wright turned to the section called: "Building a New ID from Scratch." Step by step. Everything he needed to midwife his own rebirth. The problem was he couldn't sign out the book without a library card. That required two pieces of identification. Wright returned the next day and acquired a library card with two pieces of ID borrowed from the motel. He got the book as far as the checkout desk.

"I'm sorry, sir, but that cannot be removed from the premises," said the librarian. "Nothing personal, but books on changing identities tend to disappear along with those who borrow them. I'm sure you understand."

Wright returned to the library a week later, happy to find his chameleon's bible had not been swiped by some aficionado of another volume called *Stopping Theft*, a thinly disguised guide to successful pilfering. He scratched some notes, photocopied a dozen relevant pages, and headed to the newspapers and periodicals section.

Step One. He began spinning through the microfilmed copies of the Florida newspapers from 1951. Finally, he found what he was looking for in the obituary columns: "Scott, Ronald Peter, peacefully on his first birthday at Miami General Hospital. Beloved infant son of James Peter Scott and Diane (nee Roberts, formerly of Chicago), brother to Julie Maxeen and Carol Anne, all of Detroit, Michigan. Funeral services and internment at the Holy Cross Church, Detroit..." Perfect.

The new Ronald James Scott now knew his father's name, his mother's maiden name, and where he was born. He also knew his birth would be registered in Michigan, his death in Florida, and never would the two connect in a central file. Bureaucracies work that way.

Moreover, due to little Ronnie's untimely demise on his birthday, his successor also knew his exact date of birth. That saved him the tedium of Step Two—gaining access to the registry office to find the death certificate, or worse, going through all the 1951 birth announcements in the Detroit papers.

Wright had all the information he needed to get his birth certificate from the state of Michigan—except, of course, an official piece of identification to accompany his application. On to Step Three.

The guide to vanishing listed no fewer than eighteen pages of advertisements for mail-order baptismal certificates. Wright chose the one that offered: "Show off your pride in Jesus. Authentic replacement baptismal certificates worthy of gracing your home. Just send $25, plus $2 for postage and handling. Available in all Christian denominations. Please supply date of birth, date of baptism, name and address of church..."

Wright figured that if the infant Ronnie had been buried at Holy Cross in Detroit, chances were pretty good he had been baptized there as well—if he had been baptized at all. It probably didn't matter anyway. Odds were that the mail-order house was just a counterfeiting operation for crooks like him.

Three months after his first visit to the library, Lionel Wright was fully and officially reincarnated. Ronald Peter Scott came complete with a full set of identification: baptismal and birth certificates, a social security card, a Florida driver's license, bank account, telephone listing, and a wallet jammed with everything from oil company credit cards to memberships in the AAA and the Playboy Club.

Every piece of it was valid. And none of it would show up on a police computer as anything other than Ronald P. Scott, innocuous motel desk clerk with no police record. His new ID had even knocked a few years off his real age of thirty-four, which made him feel better already.

Finally, the late Lionel Wright could rest in peace.

"I've got a little present for you," Wright said to Reid and Mitchell as they threaded their way across the parking lot of the Orlando airport. He pulled two brown envelopes from his pocket, each one containing a complete set of identification.

Patrick Michael Mitchell, age thirty-six, had suddenly become Michael Lawrence Garrison, age thirty-two, born in Akron, Ohio, currently residing in Florida.

Stephen Douglas Reid, age twenty-nine, would henceforth be Timothy J. Pfeiffer, same age, originally of Concord, New Hampshire, now also a resident of Florida.

Mitchell showed his first sign of life after air sickness: "Thirty-two years old, eh?"

"How did I know you'd look ninety?" Wright said dryly.

Reid was equally impressed with Lionel's handiwork. "Where the hell did you get all this?"

"At the library," Wright said without further explanation.

They found Wright's car parked next to the exit from the lot, just in case there had been a uniformed welcoming party at the airport. Lionel never missed details.

"So how do you like it?" Wright asked. "I thought it kinda suited the occasion."

Mitchell and Reid stared at a black and white chromeless Chevy with bolt holes in the roof, ugly blotches of spray paint on the doors and rear trunk. It was unmistakable.

The trio that would soon become one of the most hunted holdup gangs in America couldn't stop howling as they drove away in Lionel Wright's used police car.

CHAPTER NINE

Dundee, Florida

Paddy Mitchell called her Bunny, her real name forgotten in the previous night's haze of grass and beer. Somehow he knew she was twenty-two; that much had survived the hangover. He knew she had looked better the night before than curled around him in the morning. And more than anything, he also knew that Bunny, like all the others, would soon evaporate into the haze of the endless Florida summer. It didn't matter. A fugitive's after-life was not meant to be meaningful—Bloody Marys for breakfast, seafood for lunch, lazy afternoons by the pool, siestas of champagne and sex with lanky co-eds, fancy dinners and vintage wines, long and boozy nights of howling at the local biker bar. Another day, another daze. Time meant nothing, and nothing meant anything. Paddy Mitchell figured the party would just go on forever.

The Dollar Motel in Dundee was not exactly Mitchell's dream of a Heffneresque mansion on some Caribbean island teeming with ripened fruit and riper flesh. A hundred miles south of Disneyworld, the motel's clientele included truckers running vegetables north, bikers running drugs south, and hookers making them all happy en route. No matter, it had kept Lionel Wright alive and hidden from the law for three years. And after prison, Paddy Mitchell and Stephen Reid would have been happy in a Detroit bus shelter.

Aside from motel owner Chuck Hogan, anyone who thought twice about the three escapees simply assumed the reclusive motel office clerk had some buddies in town for a visit. Most folk didn't think about them at all. Snowbirds or jailbirds—it didn't much matter around the Dollar. Asking too many questions was a dangerous pastime in the heart of Florida's cracker country, although nothing seemed to deter Paddy Mitchell from offering an abundance of answers.

The Shamrock, a bar adjacent to the Dollar Motel, is a nightly mix of tough, tougher, and toughest. The independent haulers in dirty baseball caps roll their own cigarettes and carry shotguns under the driver's seat. The motorcycle gangs in tattoos and sleeveless leathers bum their cigarettes and carry handguns wherever the hell they want. The words "Nightly Entertainment" sloppily handpainted in the front window mean two pool tables, a juke box, and the sounds of shattering glass and splintering chairs. Ladies' night is a local joke—most of the women look like they eat road gravel for breakfast. The three escaped convicts sitting at the bar feel like choirboys at a psychotic butchers' convention.

"Just passin' through?" said the voice on the barstool beside Mitchell.

Mitchell turned to the scrawny face, the eyes transplanted from a laboratory rat and jaundiced by yellow-tinted spectacles. Maybe the question was an invitation to stay. Maybe it was a warning to leave. Even Mitchell wasn't taking any chances in a place like the Shamrock.

"Not really sure," Mitchell said with a shrug. "My brother Tim here and I are just looking around for possible business opportunities. We're real estate developers."

Reid rolled his eyes and stared down at his feet, trying to avoid the conversation. Real estate developers. What if ol' Ratface had just watched the family homestead being expropriated and bulldozed for a new strip plaza? Reid chugged his beer.

"Well, now, I'd have to say yuz don't have to go lookin' much further," Ratface said, thrusting out his right hand. "Howard J. Hoover da Third's my name. An bet ya sista's panties that real estate's my game."

Reid cleared his throat and kicked the rung on Mitchell's bar stool, hoping to kill the conversation before it killed them. Paddy's once owning a suburban bungalow sold for legal fees did not exactly a real estate tycoon make.

Alas, Patrick Michael Mitchell did not come equipped with an off switch. By the end of the evening, he was talking about building multi-million-dollar condo-hotel complexes, shopping centers, and probably an airport. Yeah, for sure, gotta have an airport. Money? No problem.

"My philosophy is that the amount of money is never the primary issue in any prudent business decision," Mitchell said between gulps of draft. "A good return on a hundred million is always better than a hundred bucks lost in a poor investment."

Reid and Wright were trying not to spit their drinks across the bar. If anyone could lose a hundred bucks—or a hundred million—faster than burning it, Howard J. was talking to the master. No matter, Ratface apparently smelled a big cheese (and a pile of potential real estate commissions) sitting on the next barstool. He insisted they all be his special guests Saturday afternoon at his home for a gen-u-ine down-home corn roast. Sounded harmless enough.

Ol' Howard J. had apparently done rather well for himself. The high wrought-iron gates opened electronically—with proper identification only—onto a long tree-lined drive, manicured lawns and gardens, and a sprawling Spanish-style stucco mansion overlooking a small lake. Every inch of the place was scanned by video surveillance cameras. Mitchell was impressed. Reid didn't like his face on film anywhere.

The crowd assembled for Howie's gen-u-ine corn roast and back-yard barbecue was considerably more civilized than the gang at the Shamrock, but Reid sensed something odd about them. Maybe it was the way they talked, a meeting of minds to the right of Genghis Khan. They made a lot of disparaging references to "niggers," but that wasn't unusual. A bunch of southern rednecks, that's all. Maybe it was the concentration of middle-aged women who looked as though they had microwaved their faces once too often in the Florida sun. Maybe it was just Reid's inherent paranoia about being around so many brushcuts and fat bellies draped in floral gaudiness. Most claimed to be either local businessmen or truckers. Any one of them could have been a cop.

Reid was still scanning the gathering when Howard J. started to bellow.

"Listen up y'all," he hollered, his arm around Mitchell's shoulders. "My friend here's from up north. Says he's quite the outdoorsy type. Thinks he'd like to go fer a little water ski 'round the lake here. Now, what d'y all think o' that?"

Howie's friends erupted into a chorus of cheers, hoots, applause and laughter. An odd crowd, all right, Reid thought. Definitely not athletic.

Mitchell was in his element, the center of attention, first on two skis, then one. There were oohs and ahhs at every maneuver, more applause and laughter each time he tumbled, which was often.

"Okay, who's next?" Mitchell yelled at his audience as he landed on the dock.

"Naw, can't imagine yer goin' to find too many takers in this bunch," Howard J. said from the driver's seat of his boat.

For the next three hours, Reid and Mitchell took turns on the skis, lounging on the dock only long enough to pound back a few more beers and try to coax others into joining them. But Ratface was right. There were no other takers, just a lot of guffaws.

By the time the dinner steaks landed on the barbecue, Mitchell and ol' Howie J. were back-slapping pals. Neither was feeling any pain.

Ratface flashed his yellow teeth. "Git yer buddy over there and come with me fer a moment." It was already dark. Howie J. grabbed the flashlight and some hunks of chicken from the barbecue.

"Now, I's goin' to show ya somethin' here," he said as they reached the dock. "Ya gotta get real nice and close to the water there to see this."

Reid and Mitchell got down on hands and knees and peered intently over the edge of the dock into the still water barely inches below. Ratface tossed the pieces of chicken into the lake and pointed the flashlight where the scraps landed.

Blup. Up came a pair of eyes, bobbing to the surface like a pair of glassy golf balls released from the depths.

Blup. Another set of eyes.

Alligators.

"S-h-h-i-i-t!" Mitchell and Reid shrieked in unison as they scrambled off the dock on all fours. They were halfway up the lawn before they noticed the entire party had erupted in a roar of laughter.

Mitchell was still shaking when they walked into the Shamrock for a much-needed nightcap or six.

"What kind of sick weirdos would let us go water skiing on a lake full of goddam alligators and think it was all just a big joke?" Mitchell growled.

The barman leaned forward with a smug grin. "How 'bout the Central Florida chapter of the Ku Klux Klan?

"Ah, nothing like good service," Mitchell said as Lionel arrived at poolside with another tray of margueritas. "Must say, my boy, for someone who's supposed to be dead, you certainly make a great waiter."

"You'll make a great dead man yourself if you keep this up," Wright said sourly as he handed Mitchell his fourth drink of the morning.

As the fugitives' marathon reunion moved into its third week of brain-deadening festivities, the gang that couldn't shoot straight was beginning to target practice a lot on each other's nerves.

Reid and Wright were growing impatient to get back to work. The money Reid had boosted from banks back home to finance Mitchell's prison escape had been entrusted to Wright's clerical accounting, and his latest report to the board of directors was not glowing. "A sumptuous Christmas dinner at the Salvation Army hostel" was how he put it.

But Mitchell just wasn't interested in anything other than his next drink and Bunny's bikini. They could save money by buying booze at the store, he would say, and then order another round for every thug in the Shamrock. They could save money by not eating at restaurants, he would say, and promptly take his latest date out for the most expensive meal in town.

Finally, Reid and JoAnne drove to St. Petersburg and rented a luxurious four-bedroom house on a secluded estate overlooking the Gulf of Mexico—maybe a change of venue would bring the party animal back to earth. Instead, Mitchell celebrated the move to their new home and parsimonious lifestyle by insisting they all spend the evening at the Tampa dog-racing track. That would solve their financial problems, he promised. Christmas in the Bahamas. Just watch.

Reid and Wright watched, but all they saw was the familiar sight of Paddy Mitchell succumbing to his old addiction—sitting in the clubhouse, smoking cigars, drinking the best Chardonnay on the wine list, and throwing down hundred-dollar bets like spent matchsticks. Nothing had changed since the ponies ate through his gold-robbery money like sugar cubes.

Mitchell's checkered and largely unsuccessful career as a bettor, bookie, and finally owner of four racehorses had come to an abrupt end shortly before his arrest. After a virtually unbroken streak of losing, he eventually reached the conclusion that the winners must be cheating.

One morning, a friend named Beluga had entered the stall of Fireball Express, pulled a giant hypodermic needle from a briefcase, and pounded a full load of dope into the neck of Paddy Mitchell's prized pony.

Mitchell had already bribed two jockeys and laid off sizeable out-of-town bets on the forthcoming race. He and Beluga had agreed to split the take.

After some lunch and a few gins in the clubhouse, Beluga began to panic. Maybe the initial injection would wear off by post-time, he thought, as he headed back to the stall to give ol' Fireball a little booster shot.

In the meantime Mitchell arrived in the clubhouse and became alarmed when Beluga was nowhere to be seen. Figuring his partner-in-crime had suffered cold feet, Paddy went to the trunk of his car and pulled out another full-strength belt for Fireball's bloodstream.

By the time Mitchell and Beluga finally met up in the clubhouse and got their wires untangled, Fireball Express was doing a rabid death dance on the track. The crowd was jeering. The culprits were running for cover. And the track stewards were putting a ban on Patrick Mitchell's racing career.

Six years later Mitchell was at a different racetrack in a different city in a different country betting on different animals. But nothing had really changed. Horses or bowsers, it didn't much matter. Paddy Mitchell's propensity for losing money was undiminished by the choice of mammal.

"Okay, Lionel, give me a hundred on number two to place, another hundred on number five to win," Mitchell said to Wright before the first dog race. "No, make that two hundred on ol' fiver. Got a good feeling about that mutt."

Wright dutifully left the table to place the bets at the windows in the next room.

"It's all a science," Mitchell said to JoAnne seriously. Reid rolled his eyes.

Wright returned to the table just in time to see Mitchell's chosen bow-wows lose miserably. The exercise was repeated race after race. Mitchell had it down to a science, all right—he had picked a perfect string of losers. He was already down three thousand dollars on the evening when the last race was called.

Wright left to place the final four hundred dollars of Mitchell's bets.

Mitchell got up from the table seconds later to relieve himself. As he threaded his way through the crowd outside the betting windows, something caught his eye. He craned his neck in disbelief, then lunged through the mob.

"Holy jumpin'!" he whispered in a suppressed scream as he grabbed Wright by the shoulder. "What the hell are you doing, Weirdo?"

"Exactly what you've been doing all night," Wright replied. "Throwing your money away—only I couldn't see why anyone would stand in line to do it."

All evening, Lionel had simply been taking Mitchell's money at the table and pitching it in the nearest trash can.

***

St. Petersburg may well be the geriatric center of the universe, a sprawling colony of blue rinse and backaches, shuffleboard and shuffling feet, an entire population that raced life to the golden handshake for a chance to race death through the golden years. It is a place where the Big Band sound is pop, funeral homes are busier than beer parlors, and tippers are as rare as joggers. A trip down memory lane is a busy boulevard of myopic snowbirds in old Cadillacs making sudden left-hand turns from right-hand curbs.

Paddy Mitchell's sexual encounters with the youthful women in Dundee had made him long for his own youth. Now the aged population of St. Pete's made him dread his own aging. He had always been older than his years: at eighteen, the protector of his siblings; at twenty-eight, a husband, father, and suburban homeowner; at thirty-two, the godfather to every thief in town.

Now at thirty-eight, his alias allowed him to be anyone his imagination chose at any given moment. His name was Michael Garrison, age thirty-two. The rest was just a matter of filling in the blanks. Young and rich. Nothing else much mattered.

Prison life had significantly changed Mitchell. Physical survival had transformed his flabby, suburban lethargy into a jogging, iron-pumping fitness obsession. Boredom had given him an addiction to books. Forced introspection had made him think a lot about religion and the meaning of life.

In short, Michael Garrison was a curious mix of 1980s yuppie and traditional 1950s values. As one of the self-professed Beautiful People, he knew everything there was to know about all things trendy—at least everything he had read in *People* magazine and *Playboy*.

"This is the finest beef stroganoff that will ever grace your palate," he said proudly of his dinner fare one evening. "My *specialité de la maison*. The secret is a grating of fresh nutmeg. And heating the cream. Very important. Just below a boil."

The recipe had come directly from the *Joy of Cooking*, bought at a local bookstore that morning and consulted at every step when no one was looking. Truth was, Paddy Mitchell had spent most of his life believing the kitchen was the fastest route to the beer fridge. But Michael Garrison was going to be different. Very different.

For the most part, the others tried to be charitable. Wright's only comment about the stroganoff was that it was probably the most expensive ever served—Mitchell had bought an entire set of copper cookware for the occasion.

It was the same with wines—Mitchell would talk about a zesty Bordeaux, a lively Chianti, a fruity little number from the Loire. His pals were certain he wouldn't know a Rothschild from rotgut.

Finally, Wright had heard enough. Mitchell had been carrying on *ad nauseam* about his vast knowledge of fine wines one evening, trying to impress his latest date, a blond connoisseur of screwtop plonk.

"Gosh, you learn all this stuff at night school or somethin'?" she asked Mitchell.

"Oh, no. I grew up in a chateau in France. We had our own vineyards. My father is a count."

Wright and Reid rolled their eyes and challenged Mitchell to blind taste-test a glass of red wine. Mitchell sniffed it, swilled it on his tongue, and sniffed again. "Ah, a zappy little Beaujolais, for sure. Full body, lots of life—"

The others roared.

"Try a corner-store Gallo," Wright said, "with a dash of vanilla extract, a few drops of Tabasco, a splash of flat Diet Coke, and a pinch of dirt from the garden."

JoAnne had enjoyed the first weeks of her honeymoon, but soon tired of her role as den mother to three men and a binge. Her patience finally ran out the evening she found Mitchell riding a New Jersey cosmetician on the livingroom carpet. That the woman's husband was blithely watching it all from the sofa did not improve matters.

The next afternoon, Reid found Mitchell fishing alone under a nearby bridge.

"Now that you've laid everything but the Alaska pipeline," Reid said with no trace of humor, "it's time for all of us to get serious and do some work. Party's over, my friend."

"Ah, Stephen," Mitchell said dismissively, "you're just pissed because JoAnne is pissed. Since when did she start running our lives anyway? I thought she was just coming along for the ride to get us across the border, and then you were going to dump her. So what happened to that little plan, eh?"

That had indeed been Reid's original idea, but a lot had changed. For one thing, she was still a handy prop—the authorities would be less suspicious of a couple and a few male friends together than of a bunch of grown men on vacation. She also didn't ask a lot of questions. She had always known Reid was no encyclopedia salesman—his change of identity on the train through Vermont, and again in the parking lot of the Orlando airport, had convinced her his profession was not entirely honorable. But for the first weeks of the Florida honeymoon, at least, her inclination to pry deeper into his business affairs had been quelled by her infatuation and his terse circumspection on the issue. Moreover, Reid was not eager to send her packing back to Canada in a huff—a woman spurned could make a lot of trouble for a gang of fugitives. Most of all, Reid was enjoying JoAnne's company and the relative stability of their relationship amid the uncertainties of life on the run.

"If JoAnne's gotta go, then I guess I'll be going as well," Reid said as Mitchell threaded another worm onto the hook. "Maybe we'll head for California—"

"Naw, naw, cut the crap about leaving," Mitchell said. "I guess I'm just missing my family, and having you two love-birds around all the time doesn't help, that's all."

Reid began to understand for the first time that Mitchell's behavior since his escape had been the product of anxiety and loneliness. Paddy's promise never to risk trying to see his wife or son or brothers or mother again had seemed a tolerable alternative to prison. But freedom only made his forced separation from loved ones all the more painful.

"I understand what you're going through," Reid said after they had talked for several hours. "But you can't spend the rest of your life sitting under this bridge missing your mom and your wife, and hoping someone will toss a few million bucks into the creek."

"Okay, okay," Mitchell said finally. "Just give me a chance to throw one big score together and then we can all do whatever the hell we want..."

The way Paddy Mitchell saw the universe unfolding, the Dream Score was simply the ultimate challenge in a harmless battle of wits. If all went according to plan, no one would get hurt, except some big insurance company stung for a whopping claim. It was a high-stakes game of winner takes all—Mitchell and his partners could be set for life and quietly disappear in comfort. Alternatively, the losers would lose all—their freedom or their lives.

On one side of the contest was the Brinks Armored Transport Company and its elaborate security measures to protect routine shipments of cash and securities flown aboard chartered jets from New

York to Montreal to Toronto and other points west. On the other side was Paddy Mitchell.

His plan was simple enough in theory: the diminutive (and forever obliging) Lionel Wright would be shipped from Montreal in a large crate, along with duplicate money bags stuffed with shredded newspaper. Once in the air, he would perform a jack-in-the-box and switch the fake sacks of cash with the real ones. He and the loot would be unloaded in Toronto and long gone before anyone knew the money was missing.

They had discussed shipping Wright from New York to Montreal, convinced the biggest load of loot would probably be moving between the U.S. and Canada. But that meant the likely intervention of customs agents, and Mitchell had no inclination to tackle that department again.

Wright's propensity to find a dozen problems in every solution produced no shortage of concerns about this one. How would he breathe? What if he froze to death in the cargo hold at thirty-five thousand feet? What if the cargo area was really the passenger compartment and he popped up under the noses of the armed guards? A robbery was one thing; skyjacking was a bit out of his league.

Details, details, Mitchell had shrugged. Lionel worried a lot about details.

In mid-December, Paddy Mitchell arrived at the New York offices of the Brinks Armored Transport Company. Dressed in a three-piece suit, he handed the shipping agent a gold-embossed business card for Peter Ford, executive vice-president, International Rare Books Company.

"We have a ten-million-dollar shipment of rare manuscripts that has to be flown from Montreal to Toronto," Mitchell said to the agent.

"Why not move them by armored truck?" the agent asked. "It's only three hundred miles and a lot cheaper than air."

Mitchell hestitated, then leaned close enough to whisper: "Ever hear of the Dead Sea Scrolls?"

"No, sir. Can't say I have. But I should tell you we don't ship dead anything, so—"

"Well if you had," Mitchell said officiously, "you would know perfectly well why they must be moved by air. Now can you do the job or should we go somewhere else?"

The agent began reciting all the details of shipping by Brinks Air—loading instructions; weight allowances; insurance rates. Pages of fine print.

"How big is this container?" the agent finally asked.

"Oh, roughly six feet long, perhaps four feet wide and about the same dimension in depth," Mitchell said, quickly trying to calculate the size of a crate big enough for Wright and twenty-odd million dollars.

"I am very sorry, Mr. Ford, but no can do. New regulations. No man-sized containers on those flights. Something to do with terrorists, I think."

Mitchell argued every angle short of saying Lionel wasn't really man-sized, all to no avail. Regulations were regulations and the shipper had them in writing. Paddy Mitchell shuffled out of the Brinks offices feeling as though he had just been fired the day before retirement. The Dream Score was dead.

As he stepped onto the crowded New York sidewalk, the stark reality of his existence washed over him like the December chill. He was nothing more than an escaped convict, running from the law on borrowed time and money. Sooner or later, both would run out.

Wright left for Florida the next morning. Mitchell promised to follow in a few days. Just wanted to look up an old girlfriend on Long Island. Instead, he flew to Montreal, checked into the Queen Elizabeth Hotel, and dialed a local phone number.

Mitchell's contact arrived without police escort, but armed with some unsettling news.

"You're out of your fucking mind," the man spat at Mitchell as soon as the door was closed. "Every goddam cop in the country is hunting for you."

"Naw, relax," Mitchell said, pulling a couple of beers from the minibar. "They stopped looking for me the day after my little heart attack."

"Like hell they did. Obviously you haven't been watching TV or reading a newspaper. The cops are blaming you guys for a big Brinks job a few days ago. One of the guards got wasted with a shotgun. Forget your prison escape, man. They've got twenty-five grand on your head. They want your ass for murder."

"That's a lot of bullshit," Mitchell said angrily. "I haven't even been in the country more than three hours."

"Why don't you just trip on down to the local station house and tell the cops that?" his friend said sarcastically.

Mitchell sat on the edge of the bed, gripping his beer can and shaking his head as his friend told him about the robbery, the shootout, and the guard who had been gunned down point-blank. The third one in as many weeks. What would Barbara be thinking? What about his mom? Would his son believe his dad was a cold-blooded killer? But Mitchell's family members had been having enough problems of their own since his escape to worry about his reputation.

"Apparently," the friend continued, "your family was havin' a big reunion up at the cottage and right in the middle of dinner all these cops come chargin' in with shotguns and rifles. Wouldn't say why they were there. Warrant was in French. Turned the place upside down. Held 'em all at gunpoint for over an hour. Scared the shit out of everyone. Little kids cryin' all over the place."

Mitchell threw his beer can against the wall. "I'll show those pricks how fucking smart they are. I want to see Barbara."

The friend threw up his hands: "Forget it, Pat. They've got everyone's phones tapped and they've been tailing your wife like bloodhounds after a fox in heat. Christ, they've even got cops following Johnny to school."

Mitchell handed his friend a sheet of paper with a list of detailed instructions. "Please, just give these to her and tell her to follow them to the letter," he pleaded. "Leave the worrying to me."

"You're going to get yourself caught," the friend said slowly. "More likely, you're going to get yourself killed."

Mitchell wasn't listening. "And tell Barb if she doesn't want to see me, I'll understand. Tell her I miss her and my boy and my mom and brothers. Christ, I miss them."

The next morning, Mitchell was groggy from a sleepless night, wondering whether the new day would be his last. There was no doubt in his mind the police would just as soon blow his head off as clog the courts with another trial. But they would have to catch him first. And he just had to see Barb one last time.

The elevator was already packed when it reached his floor. He shuffled in backward with apologies, compressing a human spring that popped him like a cork into the main lobby. Straight into a wall of federal police.

They were everywhere, an army in trenchcoats with wires hanging from their ears and guns under their armpits. He turned right. More of them at every exit. Then left into the main lobby. More of them there, at the top of the stairs, the bottom of the stairs, at every doorway.

Mitchell dropped his head and tried to thread his way through the crowd to the front doors, his brain racing in panic. Why didn't they just shoot him and get it over with? Maybe they were waiting until he hit the street. There was nowhere else to go.

He was halfway across the hotel lobby when he heard it the first time. He didn't turn.

He had to keep going. He had to get out of there.

Then he heard it again, booming above the lobby din.

"Hey, Mitchell. Hey, Paddy Mitchell..."

CHAPTER TEN

St. Petersburg, Florida

Paddy Mitchell cast his line into the stream and slumped into the plastic lawn chair under the bridge. It had been the same every day for weeks since he returned to Florida. Alone with his fishing rod from dawn till dusk. Moody, irritable, withdrawn. The party was definitely over.

The trauma in the Montreal hotel crawling with federal police turned out to be nothing more than a chance encounter with a security cordon for a group of visiting dignitaries. The man shouting his name across the lobby meant no harm. Just an old school chum not easily convinced he had the wrong person. The unwanted reacquaintance was still gripping Paddy's shoulder when Mitchell jammed the fellow's arm in the revolving door and fled to an airport limousine.

But the false alarm had stretched his nerves beyond pursuing a secret rendezvous with Barbara. His friend was probably right—the police would have ensured the Mitchells' second honeymoon was brief, if not fatal.

On top of airsickness and homesickness on the plane back to Florida, Mitchell had been deeply troubled that he and his partners were being publicly linked to the rash of murder-robberies in Canada. He knew that blaming fugitives for unsolved crimes was a favorite police trick to get the media and politicians off their backs. But would his family know that? He was stricken with the misery he continued to inflict on them, even by doing nothing. First he had cost them their home. Then their marriage. Now they were to be known as kin to some gun-toting monster.

By the time Mitchell had safely returned to Florida the realities of his existence had finally hit him. The Dream Score was supposed to have put them in Rio with millions; instead, they had their backs to the wall. It was clear he could never go home. Never trust a stranger, even a lover. He could never stop running.

As their finances had dwindled, Reid and Wright spent weeks preparing to get back into business, following armored trucks, casing local banks and department stores. Paddy Mitchell passed his days sitting by the creek.

Finally, his partners grew weary of the lonesome fisherman.

"Lionel and I have got a couple of nice little scores all lined up," Reid told Mitchell one afternoon by the creek. "We figure we can move on the first one next week."

"That's great, Steve. If anyone can pull it off, it's you two—"

"Us *two*? Make that us *three*. If you think for one minute we're going to go out there and run scores while you just sit here fishing—"

"Whoa there," Mitchell said with some annoyance. "If you want to go around robbing banks, that's okay with me. You seem to enjoy that kind of stuff, and I'll gladly go over the plans with you, give 'em the ol' Paddy touch. But jumping over bank counters ain't exactly my line of work."

"And what exactly *is* your line of work these days? We're running on empty and we intend to do something about it. But let's get one thing straight: we're nobody's whores. We're not about to risk getting our asses blown off just so you can have the pleasure of cutting the cash. The old days are over, my friend. You're either with us, or you're on your own."

The argument went on for several hours. Reid was sympathetic, but unyielding in his insistence that whatever lay ahead, they were all in it together.

Finally, Paddy reeled in his fishing line, folded the plastic chair, and headed towards home with his arm around Reid's shoulders. However reluctantly, Patrick Michael Mitchell had just stepped on to a career path that would make him a member of that unique criminal club called America's Most Wanted.

"Damn," he said, as they walked home. "A whole day and not even a nibble."

The three would-be bandits gathered in the backyard of their St. Petersburg hideaway that evening, leaving JoAnne inside while they "talked business."

Their first target was a large suburban department store. Each Monday for the three previous weeks Reid and Wright had watched

Brinks pick up the weekend receipts at roughly the same time in the early afternoon. There were never fewer than two bags of paper currency. They figured a hundred grand, at least. All they had to do was make the heist just ahead of the armored-truck company.

Mitchell was scribbling a list. "Okay, we'll need guns, gloves, coveralls, disguises, a radio scanner to monitor the cop frequencies, and a set of stolen wheels. Anything else?"

"Just one thing," Wright said, his first interjection in an hour of discussion. "Where do you plan to get all this stuff?"

What had obviously occurred to Wright now dawned on Mitchell and Reid. Gone were the days back home when Paddy could wander into the Belle Claire Tavern with some cash and a shopping list and have all the paraphernalia of criminal activity home delivered in the colors of his choice. Now they were in a strange country full of strangers, some of whom were bound to be street snitches, if not undercover agents.

"We can buy the clothes and disguises anywhere," Mitchell shrugged. "Any electronics shop sells cop scanners, and you gotta be able to buy guns somewhere around here."

Reid produced two hand-scrawled advertisements he had found on the laundromat bulletin board among the notices for stray cats and babysitters. Welcome to the United States of Armageddon.

"Winchester 12-gauge shotgun. Plenty of ammo. Clean. Best Offer." The phone number was written a dozen times over on tear-off strips along the bottom.

The other ad was a bit ominous: "Smith and Wesson .357 Magnum, very good condition. Hardly used."

"So there we go, my boys," Mitchell said. "No problem. Just steal a set of wheels and—"

"*Who* steals a set of wheels?" Wright asked.

Wright had never stolen so much as a bicycle. Mitchell had been lucky if a month passed without his having to call the motor league to get the keys out of his own locked car.

Reid raised his hands. "Don't look at me. A buddy and I tried to hotwire a Mustang once. Took us two days to get the thing going, and then it caught fire in the middle of the freeway."

The idea of renting or even buying a getaway car was discarded. Both would leave behind paper trails—registrations, driver's license numbers, credit card slips, bank drafts. Even if all their identification were phony, they couldn't risk its falling into the hands of some detective.

The next morning Wright drove to Tampa and returned later in the day with a solution—another library book, this one among a dozen dandy how-to volumes on stealing cars. The guide to grand-theft-auto professed no evil intent, of course. Just the lively memoirs (complete with detailed technical instructions) of some guy who had made a living repossessing cars for finance companies—which is to say, he stole them back from people's driveways.

Wright photocopied the entire book and arrived home with it all neatly organized in a blue, three-ring binder.

"This slim volume contains explicit information on how to break into and drive a motor vehicle without the key," said the promotion page. "The author covers basic locksmithing, including lock-picking, and the use of the slim-jim and slide hammer. There's also a lot of information listed by specific make of vehicle, such as tumbler dimensions of Ford and Chrysler locks, and wafer types in General Motors locks."

Mitchell laughed as he read the disclaimer on the title page: "Neither the author nor the publisher assumes any responsibility for the use or misuse of information contained in this book. It is sold for informational purposes only. Be Warned!"

The next afternoon, Wright was sent shopping for the tools of the trade: two screwdrivers, one pair of pliers with wirecutters, one roll of electrical tape, a flashlight, a long thin metal slat for opening car doors, and a handy little gadget called a "puller," used by body shops to pull dents out of bashed fenders, and by car thieves to pull ignition switches out of steering columns.

Mitchell had the rest all figured out. They would switch the license plates on the stolen car with those on another similar make and model whose owner probably wouldn't notice the difference. "How often do people check their license plates?"

That would give them a hot car with clean plates. A policeman punching the numbers into his cruiser computer would come up with nothing amiss.

It sounded simple. Too simple.

Reid was cursing a rusted license plate screw as he crouched behind a Buick in the underground parking garage of a southside St. Petersburg apartment building. Wright was holding the flashlight and blue binder full of car-stealing instructions.

"Hey, you!"

The baritone boomed off the cement walls as a hulking superintend-ent and two meaty sidekicks began running towards the Buick. Reid glanced at the screwdriver in his hand, a toothpick to stop a tank.

The footrace had begun, up one level, down two, up one again. The pursuers weren't gaining any ground, but they weren't losing much, either. They knew the layout of the cavernous garage; Wright and Reid didn't. As they rounded another blind corner, Reid's mind was racing faster than his feet: This is insane...Half the police departments in the world are looking for us and we're going to get nabbed by Rambo and his two kids for trying to boost a license plate.

Finally, the fleeing thieves spotted the fire escape, scrambled up an iron spiral staircase, threw open the manhole cover, and raced across the lawn.

The following evening Mitchell joined them in another underground garage and decided a silver Lincoln would make a fine getaway car. Reid held the flashlight. Wright worked on the ignition. Mitchell read from the blue binder.

"What year and model is it?" Mitchell whispered.

"A Continental," Reid whispered back. "Who knows what year? They all look the same."

"Says here, you can hot-wire anything older than a seventy-six," Mitchell read out, "but do not attempt it on newer models."

"Why not?"

"Doesn't say."

Wright got the ignition out and was frantically fumbling with the spaghetti of wires as Mitchell read instructions from the blue binder: "Twist the green and the red together; white goes with orange; yellow to green stripe; touch the black to the steering column."

The engine sprang to life. They congratulated each other and scram-bled into the car. Mitchell threw the Lincoln into reverse and promptly piled the rear end into a cement pillar.

"The fucking steering wheel is locked," he shouted, as they aban-doned their crumpled handiwork.

Do not attempt it on newer models—now they understood.

In the next few weeks the trio toured the streets and parking garages of seaside communities from St. Pete's to Fort Myers in their beat-up converted police cruiser, looking for an appropriate car to steal, then consulting their blue-binder instruction manual on how to steal it.

Their mission finally came to an end in the parking lot of a condo-minium project. Mitchell was reading the blue binder as Wright was pulling the license plates off a red Oldsmobile. Reid happened to notice the car's owner had generously left the door unlocked and the keys in the ignition.

They were in business.

A light drizzle was falling as the red Oldsmobile pulled into the parking garage beneath the department store and backed into one of the handicapped spaces immediately opposite the elevators.

They had been over every conceivable angle of the plan at least a dozen times in the previous two days. The cash office was located on the second floor. An elevator from the parking garage opened immediately onto the corridor. There was a customer counter running the full length of the hall. The cash office was at the far end. One male employee would enter the cash room about thirty minutes before Loomis made its armored truck pickup.

Wright could recite every move in minute detail. He never made notes. He didn't have to—the mind that said so little could retain an entire data bank of minutiae on a dozen robberies if necessary. He knew the number of steps from the parking space to the elevator; the number of seconds needed to ride from the basement to the first floor, and from there to the second; the distance from the elevator to the back cash room; the routines of the cash clerk; and the average number of people around the customer counter during the projected robbery period. Most of the information was irrelevant; no one needed to count paces from the parking space to figure out they had reached the elevator. But so much research made them all feel better anyway—like professionals.

Reid volunteered to perform the actual stickup. Wright would take control of the elevator. Mitchell's only job was to get the customers lined up against the wall and out of the way for Reid's retreat.

"This is really important, getting those bodies out of the road," Reid said firmly to Mitchell. "I'm going to be backing out of that office into the corridor, and I don't want to run smack into some big trucker with a bad temper, or have to push my way through a crowd."

Mitchell had come up with the idea of wearing coveralls with "Otis" magic-markered on the breast pockets. As they rode the elevator towards the second-floor cash office, they stopped at the main level long enough to slap an Out-of-Service sign over the outside buttons.

The elevator announced its arrival at the second floor with two pings of a bell. Reid burst out the doors and vanished down the corridor, a .38

tucked Napoleon-style into his coveralls, his other hand toting a duffel bag for the loot. Mitchell followed Reid to the entrance of the hallway, the sweat soaking a large splotch on his coveralls. Wright pasted another out-of-service sign over the elevator buttons and held the doors.

The corridor leading to the cash room was so jammed with post-Christmas bill payers that Reid had to excuse his way through the mob to get to the scene of the crime. Mitchell pulled a plastic Richard Nixon mask over his face.

"Okay, this is a holdup," he hollered. "Everyone get back against the wall. Do as you're told and no one will get hurt."

Maybe it was his orders being reduced to an incoherent mumble by the mouthless mask. Or perhaps a Richard Nixon crook surprised no one in America. Whatever the reason, no one moved. A few people snickered. Someone told him to stand in line. Others looked puzzled by the man in the mask and Otis coveralls who seemed to be struggling with the back of his pants. Most simply continued their shuffle towards the customer counter. Mitchell screamed his orders again.

Reid came charging out of the cash room backwards as he had planned. Specifically not planned was his wheeling around and running face first into the chest of a Mr. T look-alike.

"Where yuh think yuh's goin'?" Mr. T grunted.

"I's going to blow your fucking head off if you don't get out of my way," Reid shrieked, reaching up to wave his .38 somewhere close to the giant's face.

Reid shoved his way through the throng of milling customers. Finally, he saw his partner in the Richard Nixon mask, still yelling and struggling with something behind his back. Reid didn't know whether to laugh or shoot him.

Mitchell had entered the corridor with his revolver shoved down the back of his pants. And that's where it stayed, the hammer hopelessly caught in his underwear. The more he yanked, the more tangled the gun became.

By the time Reid finally grabbed his hapless co-conspirator by the arm, Mitchell's undershorts were three inches out the top of his pants and roughly the same distance up his splitting lower anatomy. He was still trying to free his weapon when they lunged into the elevator.

Stephen Reid and Lionel Wright were laughing so hard they could barely stumble from the elevator to the waiting Oldsmobile.

The heist didn't net anything close to the hundred grand they had estimated, but forty-odd thousand wasn't bad for a day's work. There was, however, one small problem. Apparently, the crowd shopping the after-Christmas sales at the department store had been cleaning out their piggy banks for the occasion—more than a third of the entire take was in one-dollar bills.

Mitchell suggested that Wright take the two sacks of greenbacks down to the local bank and get them changed into something more sensible. Hundreds would be nice.

"You might as well take it directly to the cop shop," Reid said. "Any bank teller with half a brain is going to be on the phone the minute you walk through the door with that kind of cash. What are you going to say? Sixteen thousand people liked your singing in the mall at lunchtime?"

Wright volunteered to launder the small bills. Instead of buying two cases of beer at one outlet, he would get a six-pack at each of eight different stores. Every time, he would pay for the purchase in one-dollar bills, then ask the shopkeeper to kindly relieve him of another wad for a couple of twenties. It was the same for the groceries. A dozen different supermarkets. A dozen more bundles of greenbacks gone. Everyone obliged. No one was ever suspicious. Lionel didn't seem to mind passing his days engrossed in so much tedium.

As usual, Mitchell had neither the patience nor the inclination to spend his life driving around Florida buying six-packs. Even at the local bar, where he could safely pay for rounds of drinks with a pile of small bills, he couldn't resist the temptation to slap down a hundred-dollar bill for a beer, just to impress a cute waitress in tight Levis.

After another spree of fine dining and death-defying hangovers, Reid and Wright were anxious to get back to business at a bank they had cased in nearby Clearwater. They had even gift-wrapped a present for Paddy in anticipation of the next heist—a leather shoulder-holster they figured might save some wear and tear on his undershorts.

But Mitchell had already set sail back to his Fantasy Island, this time in pursuit of a New York banker's designer daughter. Mitchell had first met Julie at the outdoor bar of a swish haven for the Rolex crowd in nearby Sarasota. Some of his best friends were in the banking business, he claimed with a straight face, though her father likely wouldn't know them. Not yet, anyway.

Julie was twenty-four and taking a break between Harvard and Wall Street, hanging out for the winter at daddy's million-dollar condo with matching yacht. Clearly, a lifestyle worthy of her companionship was going to be a challenge even for the great pretender. No wads of one-dollar bills for this girl.

Undaunted, Michael Garrison presented himself as a fun-loving millionaire, the offspring of European aristocracy, spending a seemingly inexhaustible inheritance cruising the jet-set playpens of the world with his little brother, Timmy.

Hour after hour, he regaled her with lavish tales of opulent dining with the Aga Khan in St. Moritz; gambling alongside Princess Caroline at Monte Carlo (during the Grand Prix, of course); and wild parties at the Kennedy compound in Hyannis Port. He had been part-owner of Northern Dancer, and the Kentucky Derby was always a fun weekend. Paul McCartney really was a very nice fellow.

Julie seemed at least mildly impressed, though she wondered why a thirty-two-year-old would spend so much time hanging out with all those old folks.

"Do you ski?" she asked at one point.

"Oh, yeah, of course," Mitchell said. "My brother Tim and I have been skiing since we were two years old. Our mother was Gerda Ottinger. Ring any bells? World cup champion for Austria way back when..."

Mitchell was in the midst of boasting about his culinary skills—trained at a French cooking school in Paris, naturally—when Julie invited herself to dinner at the house. She didn't care what he cooked.

"Surprise me."

He would certainly do that.

Fat Boy couldn't remember how many banks he had robbed by the time he reached the age at which other kids graduate from college. Then again, he couldn't remember how far he had made it in school, either. He once told a judge that Grade Four "sounds about right." His only graduations had been from foster homes to detention centers, and from stealing car stereos to holding up financial institutions. A dedicated couch potato, the overweight French-Canadian was remarkable only for his ability to hurl 250 pounds of sagging flab over four-foot-high bank counters.

Shortly after Reid's escape from Joyceville pen, a friend had introduced him to Fat Boy and a partner, the Kid, as he was unaffectionately known. A lanky former athlete with the boyish good looks of a high-school all-star, the Kid had a heart roughly the same temperature as liquid nitrogen. Fat Boy and the Kid had joined Reid on the six-week bank-robbing rampage that financed Mitchell's flight to freedom. The two had also agreed to help Reid with Paddy's actual prison break on the promise they would share in the subsequent Dream Score that never happened.

Reid figured he had probably seen the last of Fat Boy and the Kid after the Dream Score project was abandoned. But the weeks of bumbling around St. Pete's trying to steal a car, coupled with the chaos during the department-store heist, clearly cried out for new blood.

Fat Boy arrived in Florida to only tepid gratitude from Mitchell for helping with the ambulance caper. Paddy thought the newcomer a consummate slob: unrefined, illiterate, unkempt, vulgar, a deadbeat perpetually stoned on grass and hooked on afternoon television.

Fat Boy wasn't exactly what Julie was expecting either, when she arrived at the house for dinner with her blue-blooded boyfriend. Before Mitchell could pour Julie her first drink, Fat Boy was hollering some tasteless locker-room joke about female orgasms. Reid tried to interrupt, but it was too late.

Julie blushed and beat a hasty retreat to the kitchen where JoAnne and Mitchell were preparing a rather ambitious dinner of Chateaubriand with Madeira sauce. He had spent all morning combing the markets for fresh everything, even the herbs and spices. He had spent all afternoon trying to figure out what to do with it all.

"How long have you known these guys?" Julie asked JoAnne.

"Oh, I met Timmy about three months ago on a holiday in Vermont," JoAnne said, reciting the answer dictated to her by Reid. "He had taken over his father's chicken business—"

"His father's what?"

Mitchell hastily interrupted. "What she means is, you, see, ah, well the family owns a big chunk of the Kentucky Fried Chicken empire, so Timmy was just taking care of a bit of business."

Julie shot a doubtful look at him. "I hear his mother was quite the skier."

"Whose mother?" JoAnne replied before Mitchell could intervene. "Timmy's or Mike's?"

Now Julie was annoyed. "I thought they were brothers—"

"Oh just a joke. Ha, ha," Mitchell chuckled, putting his arm around her. "See, JoAnne's always saying it's not possible that a sweet guy like Timmy and a jerk like me could possibly come from the same mother. Ha, ha. Just a joke, right, Jo?"

Mitchell had done it again. Keep the stories simple and boring and, above all, consistent, Reid had implored. But Paddy never learned. Partly, he had neglected to tell the others what exorbitant lies he had told Julie. Mostly, he had been too drunk to remember exactly what they were.

Mitchell was on edge, to say the least, by the time his Chateaubriand flambé was presented to the assembled dinner guests. Fat Boy took one look at the rare filet in Paddy's prized wine sauce, picked up his plate, and headed for the kitchen.

"I hain' eatin' no fuckin' raw roadkill," he said as he dumped his hulk back at the table a few minutes later, his thin slices of Chateaubriand fried to black cinders and doused in ketchup.

Mitchell wanted to throttle Fat Boy. Reid wanted to throttle Mitchell for again jeopardizing their cover. Julie couldn't leave fast enough.

The dawning of the 1980s was not a happy time for America. The news was sinister: "Moscow's decision to invade Afghanistan has deeply angered the Carter administration and seems likely to send Soviet-American relations into another period of recriminations...The United Nations Security Council approved a U.S. resolution yesterday, threatening economic sanctions against Iran unless American hostages in Tehran are freed by next Monday...The Carter administration, in a defense policy reversal, has decided to produce and deploy Navy Tomahawk cruise missiles..."

The turning of the decade similarly brought nothing but trouble to three unemployed bandits, a tag-along girlfriend, and one couch potato.

Reid couldn't understand what had happened to the Paddy Mitchell he had known, the once charismatic leader whose cunning had engineered the likes of the Great Gold Robbery, and whose caution had for years defied the investigative talents of every police detective in town.

Mitchell was getting more lethargic by the day. Pushing him into a pair of bank robberies was like coaxing a child into the dentist's chair. Both were distinctly smoother operations than the department store heist, but netted only $8,000 to be split four ways. Paddy thought it all a waste of effort. He was also terrified of getting killed.

Reid was becoming increasingly alarmed by Paddy's tall tales. Julie was gone, but she was certain to tell someone, if not everyone, about the weird people she had met. Nice house. Lots of money. Probably cocaine dealers. Reid took no comfort in the prospect of working hard to elude the FBI only to be hauled in for questioning by federal agents of the Drug Enforcement Agency.

At the same time, JoAnne was becoming edgy. Playing referee to four bickering men was not exactly what she had in mind for her Florida honeymoon. Her mood did not improve when she discovered the loaded .45 in a bag of grapefruit, stuffed in the broom closet. Reid tried to convince her they were gunrunners, which, in a country of 220 million guns, didn't seem all that dreadful. JoAnne didn't believe any of it, but she let the lie pass for the time being.

Later that evening, Reid and JoAnne retired on their own to Nicki's Bar and Grill. It was a slow night, and Maggie the barmaid was all for making small talk, including the usual bland questions asked of new acquaintances: Where are you from? What do you do? Where are you staying?

Reid spewed out the story about being in the chicken business in North Carolina. Sold it about six months ago and teamed up in a partnership with a former car dealer from Oregon. They had some investments together. At the moment they were just looking around Florida for opportunities. Maybe set up a rent-a-car franchise or something. Nothing very exciting.

Maggie didn't have to be told that the chicken business and car rentals were nothing very exciting. She was desperately trying to stifle a yawn and change the subject when Mitchell pulled up a barstool next to Reid.

"Maggie, like you to meet my friend Mike," Reid said. "He's the partner I've been telling you about."

The barmaid gave them a disapproving sneer: "Yeah, Mike and I have met. He was in here last night. Telling me all about his diamond business in New York. Said he was down here to do some sailing with his brother. And unless I'm mistaken, that would be you of the old chicken business."

Reid gave Mitchell a look that could have peeled paint. But Maggie had turned her attention to someone behind them.

"JoAnne, Mike, Tim—or whatever your names are—like you to meet my husband, Gerry."

As they swung around on their barstools to greet husband Gerry, Mitchell's half-swallowed gulp of beer shot up into his nose.

"Hello, Officer..."

CHAPTER ELEVEN

San Diego, California

April 15, 1980. FBI Special Agent Norman A. Zigrossi has called a press conference in San Diego as part of a desperate police effort to stem the recent wave of armed holdups of area banks. Authorities are certain at least four of the incidents are the work of the same bandits, but suspect the gang may be responsible for as many as twenty heists in less than two months. The following day the *Los Angeles Times* runs a dramatic bank photograph of a man in a Klingon mask with a stopwatch around his neck and a submachine gun in his right hand. The headline and story read:

Stopwatch Gang Hunted in Robberies

A gang of heavily armed men whose leader uses a stopwatch to time precision bank robberies is being sought by FBI agents in connection with four San Diego hold-ups that have netted more than $70,000, authorities said Tuesday.

The "Stopwatch Gang" members wear either ski or Halloween masks and gloves and come armed with handguns and a semi-automatic rifle. Usually striking between 10 a.m. and 11 a.m., the gunmen appear to have preassigned tasks—one guarding the customers and another the employees, while a third scoops up the cash. The leader, a stopwatch dangling from his neck, supervises the hold-up.

Seconds later, the gang members run to a waiting stolen car, possibly driven by a fifth suspect, and speed away. Authorities said the suspects may abandon their getaway vehicle for one or more cars parked some distance away, where they scatter.

Norman A. Zigrossi, special agent in charge of the San Diego FBI office, said, so far in 1980, there have been forty-two robberies in the county. That compares with only 25 during the same period last year.

Zigrossi said he has transferred additional agents to bank robbery investigations in an effort to stem the rising number of robberies. He indicated local police will do likewise...

Zigrossi said it is unusual for bank robbers to "keep coming back for more" after scoring big heists...He theorized the suspects could have costly narcotics habits to satisfy, but stressed that is only speculation.

Around 10 a.m. Tuesday, just an hour before Zigrossi discussed the robberies at a press conference, another San Diego area savings institution was held up...

Stephen Reid turned his collar to the January wind ripping spray from an angry sea. He enjoyed days like this, the monotonous crashing of the surf on a deserted California beach, the gulls straining their wings against the afternoon gale, then sweeping away in surrender to the next gust. He pulled JoAnne tight to his side as they strolled through the matinee of fury.

For the first time since his escape Reid felt at peace with his freedom, confident that his trail had been erased like footprints on the beach. The rest of the gang had been left behind in Florida. Now he and JoAnne could start a new life, a fugitive buried beneath an alias, eventually to be forgotten by the bounty hunters with more active prey to pursue.

As they closed the door on the storm and lit a fire in their beachfront cottage, the last thing on Stephen Reid's mind was spending the next three months on a bank-robbing rampage worthy of FBI press conferences and front-page headlines. All he wanted was a little peace.

The chance encounter with Officer Gerry in the St. Petersburg bar had been the last straw. There had already been an accumulation of dangerous mistakes: too many people were asking too many questions about too many conflicting stories. Sooner or later someone was going to get too few answers, and a cop with a suspicious barmaid-wife seemed a likely candidate.

By the time the two panicked fugitives had bid Officer Gerry a hasty "God bless" and slithered out the door, Reid couldn't get away from Florida fast enough. He and JoAnne were on a plane to California the next morning. Fat Boy headed back to Canada, while Wright stayed behind to babysit Mitchell at their old hideout, the Dollar Motel in Dundee.

JoAnne certainly didn't miss the rest of Reid's gang, except maybe Lionel. He had always been kind to her back in Florida, happy to run her errands, driving her anywhere she wanted to go. Every morning, he had hot coffee and fresh juice for her when she awoke. She treated him as a friend, although their conversations were one-sided. And she certainly didn't think much of the way the others seemed to use him. "Like everyone's little gofer" was how she had phrased it.

"I used to think there was this paternalistic thing between Paddy and him," Reid said thoughtfully at they walked the beach one afternoon. "And maybe there is a bit of that. But make no mistake: Lionel is very much his own person. He does more thinking than all the rest of us put together. He's like two people—very self-assured with us, and incredibly quiet and withdrawn around anyone else. Behind all that apparent weirdness, he's just shy."

Reid and JoAnne rented the best cottage they could find along the shore in Pacific Beach, a northern San Diego community largely abandoned to the winter storms by everyone but desperate snowbirds and die-hard transients. Their house came equipped with room service, bar service, maid service and any other amenities they might require from the adjacent hotel.

Their days were spent doing a lot of nothing in particular, visiting the zoo, walking for hours along the beach. In the evening the sands were dotted with flickering bonfires encircled by odd assortments of left-over hippies and lost runaways. Reid would sit for hours and chat with them over joints and jugs of Gallo plonk. They thought him not a bad guy—for an Establishment Straight.

For the first few weeks Reid and JoAnne ate well, drank a lot, and even took a jet-setters' holiday to Mexico, just for a change of scenery. The hotel-cottage was nice enough, but having the front-desk clerk calling every morning to enquire if they were checking out was not exactly JoAnne's idea of a stable home life.

JoAnne's nesting instincts were beginning to rub off on Reid. On their return from Mexico, he insisted they move into a luxury condominium, a yuppie haven complete with microwave, whirlpool, deep-pile carpets, smoked-glass coffee tables, hot-tub, exercise room, and a heated swimming pool shared with a dozen other similar units. There was a guard at the gate and a sign on the office door discouraging children and pets.

It was all very comfortable. And all very expensive. As Reid paced the beach one afternoon, he again saw the time fast approaching when his pocketbook wouldn't support the cost of robbing another bank, much less pursuing a lawful existence on his stolen savings. Finally down to his last five thousand, he placed a call to the Dollar Motel in Dundee, Florida.

"Some very interesting business possibilities in this place," Reid said. "I've already put together some preliminary plans for restoring economic health to this company...Sure, I can rent you a cottage just down the beach...Everything's dirt cheap at this time of the year...Nice place...Weather's great, if you like hurricanes...Call me back with a flight number and I'll pick you up at the airport."

Later that week Paddy Mitchell and Lionel Wright arrived in San Diego for a crime spree the likes of which California had not experienced in quite some time.

Mitchell was in no position to argue. The sale of Lionel's used police cruiser had barely provided enough cash for the two economy airline tickets on a red-eye to California. Wright confirmed that unless their coffers were replenished quickly, they would all be taking the bus to their next robbery.

By the time the others arrived, Reid had already picked a few likely targets. But there was much research yet to do as the gang's planning began to take on brushes of professionalism. As he would later recall: "We would go to work every day, Monday to Friday, for months on end. We kept banking hours. We probably knew more about banks than most bankers knew about banks."

Mitchell made a checklist. They wanted a bank with an alley or at least some curbside vegetation that would help obscure their movements from getaway car to bank and back again. They needed a main thoroughfare nearby with infrequent and relatively brief stoplights. One with rear access to the bank was a definite bonus—no one wanted to run masked and armed through a crowded shopping mall. Somewhere in the general vicinity, there would have to be an underground parking garage where they could switch to their own vehicles and ditch the getaway car.

Casing the inside of a bank was no problem. One of them would open an account; another would drop in to certify a check; another might stand in a customer queue, waiting to change a bundle of rolled quarters for twenties.

Unfortunately, Paddy's memory was not his strong suit—no matter how many times he went into a place, he would get the counter along the wrong wall, the doors in the wrong place, the vault at the wrong end of the building. Sometimes Reid and Wright wondered if their partner had been to the wrong bank.

They had to know the best time to hit a bank—more precisely, when they were most likely to get the highest possible return on their investment. They began to watch the flow of customers. The way Paddy had it figured, most ordinary folks make their deposits by check and their withdrawals in cash—the busiest afternoon of the week should require the most loot in the tills that morning.

The week before a robbery they wouldn't set foot in the place, fearing their unmasked faces would be stored on bank videos for instant-replay at FBI headquarters. (In fact, for technical and austerity reasons, most of the cameras in those days weren't activated until someone hit the alarm.)

All that remained was the usual shopping list—guns, disguises, a getaway vehicle, and a set of stolen license plates.

As it happened, California was the car-theft capital of America (Florida ranked second), and the band of expatriate Canadian felons was only too happy to contribute to the statistics. Mitchell consulted their blue binder. Wright went to a wrecking yard for a used ignition switch common to most older Pontiacs. Reid found a beat-up GTO Coupe to match.

There was one final detail. Mitchell insisted that every movement be clocked to the second. One of them, he decreed, would wear a stopwatch around his neck and yell "Time!" exactly ninety seconds into a robbery.

"I don't need a goddam stopwatch to tell me when it's time to get out of a bank," Reid protested. "You do enough of these scores and you know instinctively—"

"Screw instinct," Mitchell said. "You know damn well that someone is going to hit the alarm the second we go through the doors. This has got to be precise."

Paddy Mitchell had no idea what the perfect duration for a robbery might be. One minute? Two? Thirty seconds? No matter, he purchased the best stopwatch he could find, a Tag-Heuer. Very precise. Very expensive. And, as Reid had predicted, it would also prove to be virtually worthless to just about everyone but the headline writers at the *Los Angeles Times*. And the agents of the FBI.

Tuesday, February 19, 1980. A state of emergency has been declared in San Diego County as a gale lashes the region. Heavy rains and high winds have already claimed nineteen lives along the southern California coast. A fierce electrical storm has ripped through Pacific Beach in the early morning hours, downing telephone lines and knocking out power to much of the area. The streets are flooded. Police and fire departments are frantically trying to cope with the chaos. It is the perfect day for a bank robbery.

The decrepit GTO rattles to a stop outside the Solar Credit Union on Ketner Avenue. Wright checks his watch: 10:23 a.m. Reid and Mitchell enter the bank wearing green army-surplus jackets, sweat pants, and motorcycle helmets, the sun visors pulled down over white ski masks. No one pays them any particular attention.

As soon as Mitchell is in position about halfway along the counter, Reid flips up the visor on his helmet, unzips an Adidas gym bag, and hauls out a pump-action shotgun.

"This is a holdup," Reid booms in a fake Southern drawl. "Open your cash drawers and lie face down on the floor. Do as I say and no one will get hurt."

No one twitches a muscle. Reid has seen the reaction before.

"I said everyone on the floor. Now *move* it."

Mitchell vaults the counter with a revolver in one hand, a nylon duffelbag in the other. He stuffs the gun into the holster given him by his partners, and begins scooping cash from the drawers into the satchel. Everything is happening so fast. But time seems to be passing so slowly. He glances at Reid, hoping for a signal to leave. Three more cash drawers to go. Now two...

Reid hasn't bothered to look at the stopwatch around his neck. He is too intent on scanning every corner of the bank, watching for a sudden movement, maybe an off-duty policeman with a snubnosed .38 strapped under a pant cuff.

"Time!"

Reid's instincts are as good as he had boasted: exactly one minute, twenty-eight seconds. The stopwatch is still sitting at zero.

Mitchell has never been happier to leave behind a drawer stuffed with cash. He retreats over the counter with such enthusiasm that he almost lands on his face. He races towards the door, stumbling, dropping the money sack, picking it up again, running.

The rusted GTO pulls away from the curb and chases traffic for two blocks. Reid and Mitchell are flat on the back seat and floor, yanking off their helmets, masks, jackets and sweatpants like a couple of strippers with a ten-second act. Wright is straining to see through the slapping wipers.

The car skids into a right-hand turn down a narrow side-street—sadly, one of the many thoroughfares otherwise closed due to flooding...

Stephen Reid dove into the heated swimming pool and let the warm water soothe his knotted muscles. The $24,661 from the credit union heist wasn't bad for a morning's work. And the gang sure didn't have to worry about disposing of the getaway car—hell, the FBI would need a diving team to dust it for prints. All things considered, it was a pretty good score. A little damp maybe, but—

Reid's hand grasped the lip of the pool just as his head broke the surface of the water. He shook the chlorine from his eyes and was staring at two hairy legs and a set of dirty yellow toenails.

"Hey, Reid. Steve Reid," said the raspy voice above him.

Reid froze. No one had called him by his real name since his escape.

"I'm terribly sorry, but you must have the wrong—"

Reid fell silent as his eyes moved slowly upwards. The word "Suck" was tattooed in blue script on the intruder's left kneecap; the word "Me" on the right one. If this was a cop, he ought to be reported.

"Hey, Stevie, how ya doin'?" the man continued. "Hey, man, like, don't sweat it. Like we're both on the same day pass, you know. Remember me? Joe. Like I'm AWOL from the joint, too. Just hangin' out here for a few weeks. Relax, man."

Reid recognized the man from his earliest days in the Mill. One did not readily forget that kind of physical misfortune—the deep scar as though someone had been weeding his cheek with a garden trowel; the hideous smile of black stubs and empty spaces; the bulbous, crooked nose apparently broken with fists and reset with boots. And those eyes: hollow, cold, glassy, like a dead cat.

Wacko Joe, as he was known in the pen, had been doing time for armed robbery and other felonies when he was transferred out of Millhaven to another institution from which he subsequently escaped. He and Reid hadn't been close buddies. Reid had no inclination to befriend someone who looked as though he could just as easily slit a throat as pass the salt, but he wasn't eager to antagonize a possible psychopath, either. Prison relationships are like that.

Reid was not enthusiastic about welcoming Wacko to the gang. But what the hell—they had another five scores ready to go and could certainly use an extra body. No point leaving behind tills stuffed with cash just because they didn't have enough hands to grab it all. Besides,

Joe was an experienced armed robber, though evidently none too bright—lately, he had been holding up banks for boxes of blank travelers' checks.

Mitchell wanted nothing to do with Wacko. He figured anyone stealing numbered travelers' checks must be related to the robber in Tampa who had scribbled his holdup note on the back of a personalized check.

Wacko terrified JoAnne. There was something in those eyes, the way they sneered at her. She imagined he would like to beat her, rape her, even torture and kill her. Reid only half dismissed her fears as paranoia. The ugly newcomer made him uncomfortable as well. Something about Joe's criminal record rang a faint bell, something about sex offenses. Reid couldn't remember.

The branch of the California First Bank looked more like a Chinese restaurant than a bank with its Pagoda-style architecture and tile roof. But the gang's reconnaissance had indicated a consistently booming business that required half a dozen tellers every morning. Unfortunately, they locked their cash drawers after each transaction; crowbars would be required to reopen them in a rush. Otherwise, the score seemed straightforward enough—a relatively secluded rear entrance across from the Pacific Plaza parking lot; a side street exit, and underground parking at another nearby bank to switch cars. But Mitchell had a little surprise for them even before the robbery had started.

Tired of trying to steal cars, they had decided to buy one. In the three months they had been together in the U.S., Wright had made a hobby of acquiring phony identification. Now that they had more than a dozen full sets, spending one alias on a getaway car seemed a small price for the pleasure of retiring the blue binder and all the hassles that went with its instructions. They could safely drive to the bank with the real plates, then use two-sided tape to slap on a set of stolen ones for the getaway.

Mitchell had insisted he was by far the best qualified to go shopping for a new set of wheels. No used-car salesman was going to pull anything on him. No sirree. He knew every trick in the book.

"What do you call that?" Reid asked when Mitchell arrived home with his prized acquisition.

"I call it a deal, that's what I call it," Mitchell said proudly. "You wouldn't believe the shyster at this place. You know, it's one of these lots with a million little plastic flags everywhere. And this guy is slipperier than the oil leaking from his cars. Anyway, he starts at twenty-five hundred bucks. Can you believe it? But ol' Paddy works this guy over. And guess what I got him down to?"

"I can't imagine," Reid said dryly.

"He paid you to tow it away?" Lionel asked.

"Six hundred," Mitchell said, puffing his chest.

Reid was still staring at the car, trying to imagine four grown men in the midst of a bank robbery scrambling in and out of a canary yellow, two-door Pinto subcompact.

"What a great deal," Reid muttered as he started to walk away. "When we're finished, we can hide it in a safety-deposit box."

The evening before their next bank job at the California First, Reid and Mitchell headed to a neighborhood beach bar for a few calming beers. Wacko showed up uninvited.

"Like, man, ya gotta see them broads up in Reno," Wacko said, his smile hanging from gums like the remnants of a napalmed picket fence. "Some o' the best lookin' broads for rent anywheres in the world, I swear. Like, man, some o' them whores would take it swingin' from the fuckin' chandelier, if ya wanted 'em to. Like, me, I pays a couple of 'em a little extra cuz they likes it rough, know what I mean...?"

Mitchell and Reid were afraid they knew exactly what Wacko meant. He was crazy, all right. And dangerous.

Thursday, February 28, 1980: Mitchell wheels the Canary towards the rear entrance of the California First Bank, the subcompact bumping and scraping pavement under its load of four cramped passengers. As always, Wright's eyes are fixed on his watch, this one a new Seiko purchased with his cut of the Solar Credit robbery nine days before.

"Okay, exactly 10:25," he announces, as though 10:30 or 10:40 would make the slightest difference to their plans.

Reid is in the front seat. He pulls on his motorcycle helmet, grabs the gym bag with a semi-automatic rifle in it, counts aloud to three and yells, "Go!" He is almost at the bank doors by the time Wright and Wacko manage to squeeze out of the back seat of the Pinto.

The three bandits with motorcycle helmets and mirrored visors look like an invasion from Mars as they storm the bank. Reid barks his usual orders, the first time to get everyone's attention, the second to jolt them from their shock. All is calm. The place is under control.

Wright's blue and white sneakers barely touch the counter as he vaults to the money drawers. Reid scans the customers, watching for the little old lady with a pistol in her purse and more ammunition than good sense. Suddenly, there is a loud crash and a woman's scream.

Wacko has gone over the counter and smashed into a teller still frozen upright, shoving her backwards across the top of a desk and onto the floor. Reid flinches. The guy really is crazy.

Amid the sound of crowbars popping open cash drawers, someone is moaning off to Reid's left. An elderly man in a tweed jacket is lying face down on the tile floor. He is hyperventilating.

"Just take it easy there, Pops," Reid murmurs, shuffling over to the man and nudging him with his foot. "Just stay calm. No one is going to hurt you. You okay? Here..."

Reid grabs the gent by the arm and helps to prop him seated against the wall.

"Let's go, Ron," Reid hollers, his instinctive timing thrown out of kilter, first by Wacko's teller-bashing, then by the unexpected medical emergency. How long has it been? Maybe too long. The stopwatch is still at zero.

Wacko soars back over the counters and starts to run for the doors. Suddenly, he stops and wheels. He draws his .44 from a hip holster, raises the weapon to shoulder level, and aims it directly at a teller. Then at a customer. Then at another employee.

"Stay in da bank one minute or we's goin' to blow yer heads off," he roars, his gun sweeping the air.

Reid is as shaken as the holdup victims. Christ almighty, what the hell is he doing? This asshole is going to shoot somebody, for sure.

"Go! Go! Go!" Reid shouts, hoping to stampede Wacko before there is bloodshed.

Seconds later the scene at the curb outside the bank is Reid's worst nightmare—three men in motorcycle helmets and a panic, trying to squash themselves, two sacks of money, and three guns into the space capsule Canary. Wacko has jumped into the front seat before the other two can get into the back. Mitchell is screaming. Reid gets jammed between the front seat and the doorpost. They hear sirens.

The Canary whines its meek four cylinders down the laneway and swerves onto a side street with a loud crash of the undercarriage gouging pavement.

Wacko jumps up and down in the front seat, waving his gun out the window, yelling, "We done it! We's rich! Yahoo!"

Reid and Wright butt heads as they struggle to get their helmets off in the tight confines of the back seat of the Pinto. Mitchell screams at Wacko to shut up. The Canary minus muffler sounds like a hundred Hell's Angels racing for cover.

The warm winds they call the Santa Ana brought a springtime afternoon to a winter's day on Pacific Beach. The Canary had been forever retired in someone's reserved parking space a few blocks from the bank, later to fall victim to one angry building superintendent and an eager towing company. The police would never be any the wiser. The guns, helmets, and gym bags had all been thrown in green garbage bags and added to the refuse of a nearby condo complex. The cash had been counted and split. Nineteen thousand was a lot better than the average American bank job, but hardly a windfall divided four ways.

Paddy Mitchell called a meeting of the Stopwatch Gang that afternoon on the beach. The topic of discussion was not whether to terminate Wacko Joe's employment, but whether to terminate Wacko altogether.

Everyone's worst suspicions about Joe had reached the point of alarm two days before the robbery. Wacko had been out all night somewhere "havin' a bit of fun," when Reid dropped by. The pungent smell was unmistakable. Burning rubber, like a pair of running shoes going up in smoke. Probably destroying evidence. But evidence of what?

There was no doubt in Mitchell's mind. "This guy is a pervert and he's going out there at night and doing God-knows-what to women," Mitchell said. "I mean the bastard isn't burning his clothes 'cause he's run out of firewood."

Reid and Wright agreed they were probably dealing with a rapist, all right, if not a murderer.

"The point is," Mitchell continued, "we can't just walk away from all this and leave some sex killer running loose."

A lengthy discussion ensued about taking Joe on a picnic in the high desert where he would suffer an acute attack of cranial lead poisoning. No one would ever know; they couldn't imagine anyone would miss him.

As usual, Lionel had been doing most of the listening and none of the talking. It was time for his inevitable judgment on the proposal. "Who's going to pull the trigger? Next idea."

Shortly before dawn the next morning, the gang quietly packed up and moved into downtown hotels. As they were leaving, they slipped a hand-written note under Wacko's door. The message said the gang was making a run for it, and would meet up with him again at the Dollar Motel in Florida. Mitchell figured the rest of the problem could be solved with a call to ol' Ratface, warning him that Wacko was raping white women connected to the Klan.

But neither the plan nor Wacko was ever executed. Within a matter of days, he was on his way back to a Canadian prison after being busted in Florida for stealing a woman's panties off her clothesline.

The first Sunday in April was a day of rest for the band of battle-weary soldiers of fortune. The banks were closed. Wacko was safely back behind bars. The gang was flush with cash after a full month of stalking tills and vaults in other states. And the thirty-day calm in San Diego County had convinced the FBI to refile their Stopwatch investigations under "Cold Trails" and pursue more pressing menaces to American society. In short, everyone from hunters to hunted could relax—albeit not for long.

While the month-long hiatus had given the California banks a break, those in Florida and Georgia had not been so fortunate. Fat Boy and The Kid had teamed up again for the first time since they helped spring Mitchell from prison, and were already cutting a notable swath across the Sunshine State by the time reinforcements arrived from San Diego. In the space of two weeks, the five bandits left their masked faces on more bank films than there were FBI agents to watch the replays.

One evening Fat Boy announced at supper that he was leaving the next day to return to Canada again "to take care of a little rap I got goin' in da courts."

"A rap?" Mitchell sputtered, choking on his linguine. "For what?"

"Ah got nabbed drivin' while ma license was suspended. My lawyer worked out a deal. Fourteen days for coppin' a plea."

The others doubled over at the thought of Fat Boy taking a break from a record-setting spree of armed robberies to go to jail for fourteen days on a traffic violation.

"Hey, look at the bright side," Reid chuckled. "If you're a real good boy in the joint, maybe they'll let you out on parole in a week so you can get back to work."

The next afternoon Fat Boy caught a flight north while the Kid and the rest of the gang headed back to San Diego for what Mitchell promised would be the slickest scores the state had ever seen.

Well, the plans were pretty slick...

Paddy Mitchell was proving a quick study in his new vocation. He learned to avoid attempted getaways through parking lots after one thoughtless shopper hemmed them in while she loaded groceries in a no-stopping zone.

He also learned a useful lesson in criminal waste management after one of the gang's discarded masks ran past them on the beach the same day it was prominently displayed in the newspapers. Henceforth, scheduled trash pickups were added to the blueprints of all robberies. Disguises, guns, gloves, bank bags—everything went straight into the garbage truck.

Mitchell studied the news reports of their escapades like a hockey coach reviewing the game films. He noticed witnesses tended to remember the unusual at the expense of the obvious. Three people had recalled seeing the letters "GTO" on the trunk of their first getaway car, but came up with three different color descriptions.

Mitchell experimented. He put a fluorescent orange hard hat in the rear window of one getaway car. He jammed a red plastic ball on the antenna of another. In both cases, witnesses remembered the decorations, but neither the make nor the color of the vehicles—not even a license number. When the decoys were removed a block from the crime scenes, the police had nothing.

By the time Fat Boy arrived in San Diego—he had served nine days behind bars and took a cab from the jail directly to the airport—the gang was ready to move back into action. Everything had been timed to the second. Nothing was left to chance. Well, almost nothing...

Monday, April 7, 1980. The Wells Fargo Bank on Balboa Avenue is covered in dark brown shingles to blend with the residential neighborhood and geographically situated to mesh with the perfect getaway plans. The secluded parking lot at the rear leads onto residential streets that dump onto a divided four-lane boulevard that connects with Interstate 805. Five blocks in all. Very convenient.

Every Monday morning an armored truck leaves bags stuffed with cash sitting on the floor of the vault. Mitchell has an account at the branch, giving him a front-row seat to study the weekly comings and goings of the armed couriers. He has reported that ninety seconds should be ample for a five-man army to clean out both the vault and the tills. A hundred thou, easy.

Shortly after ten o'clock the gang is sitting in the parking lot of the nearby Burger King, anxiously waiting for the armored truck to rumble past en route to the bank. Twenty minutes pass. Then thirty. Mitchell is getting claustrophobic behind the wheel of the Oldsmobile crammed with five sweating bandits.

At 10:40 a.m. Mitchell announces the armored truck must have made its delivery earlier than usual that day. They will hit the place anyway. He throws the car in gear, turns right onto Balboa for a hundred yards, then right again into the laneway beside the Wells Fargo Bank. They screech to a halt at the side entrance. Balaclavas are pulled over faces, guns drawn from their holsters. Mitchell counts to three.

"Go!"

Reid bolts from the front seat and sprints towards the bank. The others in the back pile out and run after him, crashing into one another as they arrive at the doors.

The four men in black ski masks are standing on the sidewalk in broad daylight, guns drawn, staring at the sign on the door. "Closed for Signature Day."

"What the fuck is Signature Day?" Reid says angrily, as though it really matters under the circumstances.

They scramble back to the car and flee, only to discover later that California considers its joining the United States a worthy excuse for an annual civic holiday.

Wednesday, April 9, 1980: The Bank of America branch on Garnet Avenue is so close to the gang's new home on the beach, it is barely worth driving to the robbery. Mitchell is back behind the wheel of the Olds. It is 10:15 a.m. when Reid hollers: "This is a holdup. Everyone get down on the floor."

For once, everything is going smoothly. The employees hit the floor without a second warning from the bandit with the Klingon mask and the stopwatch around his neck. Obviously, they have been trained to follow orders during a robbery, to avoid bloodshed at all costs. The workers in this particular bank have also had plenty of practice—this is the fifth armed holdup at the branch in as many months.

The customers, however, are a different story.

While the other three bandits are scooping cash from the bank tills, Reid turns to ensure no one comes through the doors behind him. He spots a man in natty three-piece suit and horn-rimmed glasses, leaning on a counter, legs crossed, one hand stuffed in his pants pocket, the other still clutching a check and deposit slip. He looks rather bored by the proceedings.

"Get on the floor," Reid shouts.

The man stares down the barrel of a Commando .45-caliber submachine gun with enough firepower to kill everyone in the bank and most of their relatives several times, gives Reid a sour look and a shake of the head, and waves him off with the back of his hand.

"Just do your business and get out of here so I can do mine," he says.

"I said, get on the floor," Reid growls. "Right now."

The man straightens. "Look, I don't want to get my suit dirty, okay?"

Reid is momentarily confused. One of them is definitely crazy. "You're about to get dirty, all right," he shouts. "And if you don't get on that floor right now, there won't be a piece of your fucking suit big enough to send to the cleaners."

Reluctantly, the man gets as far as his hands and knees. Reid gives up.

"Okay, time!" Reid shouts, backing towards the door. "An' if anyone steeks da head ou' da door," Reid hollers in a poor imitation of Wacko, "dey's a goin' to geet it blowed righ' fuckin' off."

When the gang flipped on the television that evening to watch themselves on the news, the defiant customer had taken his griping to the sidewalk outside the bank. He was still fuming that his busy schedule had been interrupted. His suit was dirty, he moaned. He had missed an important meeting. And the bank had immediately closed for the day before he could make his deposit.

"If you ask me, they should all hang..."

Monday, April 14, 1980. The Stopwatch Gang is back at the Wells Fargo on Balboa, one week after their first futile visit on Signature Day. At least the place is open for business this time.

They watch from the Burger King parking lot as the armored-truck rumbles by and turns into the laneway beside the bank. Wright checks his watch. The Seiko has been discarded and replaced with a Rolex. It is 10:16 a.m.

Although Reid has confessed that the stopwatch has never been used, Mitchell insists on wearing it; to hell with instincts.

The cream-colored Chevy pulls into the rear parking lot, passing the armored-truck on its way out. At 10:29 the commandos burst through the doors and begin running their not-quite-precision drill one more time.

Reid is in a particularly ugly mood: "If I see one head pop up, I'll blow it off. And don't anybody hit the alarm or you're all dead."

Fat Boy and the Kid are over the counters and cleaning out the tills. Paddy never ceases to be amazed that so much couch potato can show so much agility in a pinch.

Mitchell has his gun drawn as he runs towards the vault where three sacks stuffed with cash have been dumped on the floor by the armored-truck company. He suddenly stops halfway to the loot. He turns to watch the other two at the counter, shoveling bills into a brown muslin bag. He jumps from one foot to the other. One step forward. A step sideways. A couple of steps back towards the vault. He seems confused. Reid is equally confused.

"Let's go to the vault, hockey player," he booms at Mitchell. "Let's go to the vault."

Mitchell is still doing his odd dance and nothing at all useful.

"The vault, hockey player," Reid yells. "Let's go to the vault."

Instead, Mitchell yells "Time!" and bolts for the doors.

As the Chevy turns south on to Interstate 805, Reid turns in the front seat and glares at Mitchell. "What the fuck happened to the vault?"

"There was a plexiglass door on it, that's what. I didn't see it before. The alarm must have shut it automatically."

Mitchell's inaugural run in control of the stopwatch has also produced what would become the fastest robbery of the gang's career—just sixty-four seconds. Three tills of loot are left behind. The prized time-piece dangling from his neck, as usual, has been as useful as soap on a rope. Like Reid before him, he forgot to start it.

The FBI press conference the day after the Wells Fargo robbery put the Stopwatch Gang at the top of the evening news. As the culprits gathered around the TV set for the show—JoAnne had been sent out shopping—they felt like an Olympic team watching the first rerun of their gold-medal performance.

Paddy was pouring Mumm's champagne over Reid's head. Fat Boy was snorting cocaine through a rolled thousand-dollar bill. The Kid was looking relaxed from an afternoon of hash and beer. Lionel was sitting in the corner, sipping a can of Coke, and munching dry raisin toast.

"Hey, there's me," Mitchell said proudly as the screen filled with a bank-camera shot of a creature with a hideous Star Trek mask and a stopwatch around his neck.

"It's definitely an improvement," Wright muttered from the corner.

The cameras panned to the reporter: "Sources in the FBI say they have reason to suspect the Stopwatch Gang in as many as twenty armed robberies in the San Diego area in the past two months...Anyone with any information about these incidents or the possible identities of those responsible for this terrifying wave of armed robberies is asked to call the FBI at this number..." The telephone number of a special FBI hotline flashed across the bottom of the television screen. "A reward is being offered to anyone with information..."

Paddy Mitchell lunged for the phone.

CHAPTER TWELVE

Pacific Beach, California

The blue and white helicopter with SAN DIEGO POLICE emblazoned on its nose hovered above the surf a few hundred yards out to sea. Three blocks away a swarm of brushcuts and chromeless Chevys had invaded Pacific Beach, flashing the badge of the FBI at every tourist and transient in the place. The chopper swung towards the row of beach-front cottages and condos of Ocean Front Walk, towards the two men sunning themselves on the brick patio of the Spanish-style fourplex.

Paddy Mitchell slid off his patio chair, stepped back into the condo, and pulled the blinds. Stephen Reid raised his can of beer in mock salute to the hovering voyeurs of law and order, and went back to reading his newspaper. The helicopter turned sideways and continued its slow journey along the beach.

"Hey, listen to this," Reid shouted. "There's a story in the paper about the cops nabbing some guy working banks up in Denver."

"That makes me feel a lot better," Mitchell snarled, peering through a crack in the blinds.

"No, listen, the guy hit three banks in the same day, which wasn't too bright. But it says here that in each of the robberies, he threatened to explode a bomb to cover his getaway."

Mitchell paid no attention, dumbfounded by so much indifference to so much danger. He was convinced the gang was under constant siege on all sides. Now the cops were even hanging in the air over the hideout patio. But all that seemed to interest Reid was a new wrinkle to robbing banks.

"I wish you'd just relax," Reid pleaded. "Unless those sleuths in the chopper are expecting to find five guys in Halloween masks cutting cash on the beach, my guess is they're just checking out the bikinis."

Mitchell eventually resumed tanning on the patio. Come to think of it, the fake bomb might not be a bad twist.

The more banks they robbed, the more Reid enjoyed his line of work. It wasn't that he got any particular thrill from pointing guns at people. But there was something narcotic about the intrigue of the planning, the methodical reconnaissance, the relief of having it over, the high of counting the take, and the ego trip of so much notoriety. The Olympics of Stress, he used to call it.

For his part, Wright remained fatalistic, no matter how many banks they robbed. He preferred doing something to doing nothing, but didn't seem to much care one way or another. He was happy shopping for his expensive watches, laundering another few thousand in dollar bills, or just being left alone with his cans of Coke, a loaf of raisin bread, and some colorless treatise on the Peloponnesian War. *Que sera sera*.

Mitchell, on the other hand, still fancied himself the brains of the gang. He loathed the actual dirty work of banditry more with each job, his nerves a tattered, twitching mess. Every curious glance in his direction came from an undercover cop; every passing police cruiser was the beginning of a chase; every bank robbery a fatal shootout waiting to happen. The more times Mitchell picked up a gun, the more he never wanted to do it again. More than ever, all he wanted was that one big score. The Dream Score.

By the time the Stopwatch Gang returned to San Diego from its working holiday in Florida, the advent of spring had transformed Pacific Beach into a continuous sideshow of evolution gone amok. JoAnne had rented a spiffy new condo with an interlocking brick patio bordering Ocean Front Walk, a parade route of concrete seawall and distinctly oddball humanity: the punkers with green spikes for hair and steel spikes for earrings casually sharing a joint, their skateboard wheels clack-clacking over the breaks in the concrete pathway; the aging queens in Spandex shorts cruising on roller skates, wandering hands brushing unsuspecting bottoms; the skinhead cyclists playing dueling ghetto blasters, their shoulders supporting enough sound equipment for a stadium rock concert.

Beyond the seawall the beachboys are chasing their frisbee, the blond surfers are chasing their waves, the fat lady is chasing her

Doberman, and Paddy Mitchell is chasing a co-ed with an hourglass figure and an IQ equal to the size of her waist. He calls her Princess.

Reid and JoAnne tried hard to turn their condo at 3509 Ocean Front Walk into something resembling a home. She had spent weeks painting and decorating, furnishing it with rattan from Pier One Imports, carpets from the Indian rug shop, and framed watercolors from the trendy galleries of La Jolla and Del Mar.

Reid's housewarming present to JoAnne was an eight-hundred-dollar German shepherd pup with enough breeding credentials to wallpaper half the living room. Around its neck dangled tickets for two box seats to a Chicago concert—the band's name became the dog's. (The mutt could be thankful—the following week, they went to see *Jesus Christ Superstar*.)

The happy family made only two basic mistakes. The plug-in neon "Miller Time" sign in the window was removed after strangers began pulling up seats on the patio, looking for bar service. And Reid wrongly assumed a one-bedroom flat would be too cramped for overnight guests—namely, Paddy Mitchell.

Wright eventually took the hint and moved into his own digs, a drab apartment in a two-story walkup on Emerald Avenue, a few blocks off the beach. Fat Boy and the Kid were booked into separate motels. But Mitchell was quite content to live between his car and Reid's couch, never reluctant to invite in half the beach for a late-night bash. The endless party was starting to get on Reid's nerves.

Aside from driving the FBI crazy, the daily lifestyle of the Stopwatch Gang at first seemed remarkably unremarkable, no different from that of other snowbirds who occupied the condos and cabins along Ocean Front Walk. They had roller skates and beach bikes and walked to the corner store for beer and dog food. Their mornings were spent at work (either casing banks or robbing them), their afternoons on the beach, sunning and watching Paddy try to fly his prized Chinese kite. On their days off, they might go drinking in Tijuana, sightseeing in Beverly Hills, or window shopping the money sinks of Rodeo Drive. There were sidetrips to the desert, a weekend in Monterey, and a five-thousand-dollar Easter getaway at a luxury resort in Death Valley—Reid wanted to see the flowers.

As the loot rolled in, the champagne got colder, the Scotch got older, the cigars got longer, the drugs got purer, the dinner tabs got more outrageous, and their tips got them celebrity status wherever they went. Wright bought more expensive watches—a diamond at high noon seemed a necessary addition to his wrist. Reid's nesting promises to JoAnne became more elaborate—two kids, a dog, and a villa by the sea. And Mitchell's lies became more elaborate. By day, he was Mike Brewer, middle-aged adolescent living a Beach Boys harmony of surfer girls, hot cars, and puppy love. No one asked his age, and no one much cared as long as he was providing the party supplies. By night, he was Michael J. Brewer III, entrepreneur, connoisseur, and, above all, pretentious raconteur.

The Pisces restaurant at Rancho La Costa boasted it was the only San Diego County eatery to receive the gold medal from the Southern California Food Writers Association. "The most elegant restaurant in north county...where every dinner is a gala dinner...where guests know with ferocious exactitude what they want to eat..." As the gang ordered its way towards a thousand-dollar culinary extravaganza of gourmet delicacies and vintage French wines in honor of JoAnne's birthday, no one was quite prepared for the degree of ferocious exactitude of Fat Boy's well-worn palate.

Wright had already given Fat Boy a complete set of phony identification papers from Louisiana to account for his French-Canadian accent. He had been given a cover story that even a couch potato could not readily forget—Uncle Fat Boy had left him some money. And he had been given a hometown in the middle of nowhere that would explain his rather noticeable lack of finishing-school etiquette. But nothing could ever really explain Fat Boy.

"I wan' da poulet almandine with da wine sauce here, hokay?" Fat Boy said as the starched waiter stooped to take the menu.

"But tell da chef to hold da nuts and da booze, hokay?"

The waiter stiffened. "I, I beg your pardon, sir?"

Mitchell might have been less embarrassed if Fat Boy had blown his nose on the waiter's dinner jacket. "Oh, my friend here is only joking," Paddy chuckled to the waiter. "The chicken almandine will be just fine. And thank you very much—"

"Naw, naw, I don' need nobody orderin' my fuckin' food for me, eh? Like, when I says I don' wan' no fuckin' nuts or booze or any of that shit on my poulet, dats wha' I wan', hokay?"

Fat Boy had already provoked Mitchell's wrath that evening for making a traceable collect call to Canada; then for flaunting a pack of Canadian cigarettes at the bar. Now Mitchell just wanted to throttle the size-eighteen neck across from him.

The gathering at the next table was considerably more the kind of company Paddy Mitchell would have liked to keep. Tuxedoed gentlemen of power and influence surrounded by bejeweled ladies of charm and grace. He recognized one of the men from a photo spread in *People*, a hamburger tycoon hugging the President at some fundraiser in the Rose Garden.

"Michael J. Brewer-the-Third," Mitchell said, offering an outstretched hand. "I believe the President introduced us. Terribly sorry to interrupt your dinner."

Reid wished Mitchell were the real Michael J. Brewer, last seen on the obituary pages.

"Can I offer you a cigar?" Mitchell continued, producing a couple of twenty-dollar Monte Cristos from the inside of his suit jacket. He then proceeded to regale the burger king with an impressive disquisition on fine stogies, all of it plagiarized from a smokeshop pamphlet on the subject...Prefer a good hand-rolled Frank Correnti—George Burns gave me one at last year's Academy Awards...Happy to send along a box.

Mitchell pulled out his pocket-sized stogie cutter, neatly snipped the tip of his cigar, and offered the silver gadget to the fast-food tycoon. "Got it as a gift from a friend in London," he said casually. "Used to belong to Churchill."

The burger baron ignored both the cutter and its dubious ancestry, ripped off the end of his cigar with his teeth, spat it on to the restaurant carpet, and turned back to his dinner guests.

Rob-O, as his pals called him, was a local real estate agent and devotee of the singles circuit when he met Reid and JoAnne in a bar one evening. He subsequently introduced them to a circle of other friends who happily included the charming couple at dinner parties, cocktail parties, Trivial Pursuit parties, and frequent gatherings at one of the trendy fern bars in La Jolla.

Reid thought it all the perfect cover. Certainly at first, no one suspected the newcomers were anything but nice folk with a cute puppy and a convenient habit of always picking up the tab. Always cash.

As usual, Reid made his alias as boring as possible. He and his partner Mike Brewer had sold a string of discount auto-leasing franchises in Florida and were considering the possibility of opening similar operations in California. The intricacies of renting beat-up used cars seemed of no particular interest to Rob-O or his friends.

Unfortunately, the seating plan at Mitchell's first dinner party with Reid's new-found friends put Michael J. Brewer next to an insurance salesman. Apparently, ol' Rob-O had figured the policy on a fleet of rent-a-cars might generate some nice premium commissions for his pal.

The dinner got as far as the shrimp appetizers when the salesman started asking about collision damage waivers and contractual liability overheads.

"Well, maybe you can tell us about these kinds of details," Mitchell said as the rest of the table tuned in attentively. "This is all a new business for us. See, we're really just investors."

Rob-O turned to Reid: "I thought you and Mikey here owned a string of these franchises in Florida?"

"Oh, no, no," Reid said, filling his own mouth with food to give him time to think. "I owned the car business in Florida, not Mikey. He had a chicken processing plant, so you can understand why he's looking for something new."

Everyone laughed, and Reid quickly changed the subject, promising to get together with the insurance salesman later in the week. Rob-O was clearly not persuaded.

"So what does Mike really do for a living?" he asked Reid in the kitchen later that evening.

"Oh don't worry about it—Mike just doesn't like talking business around strangers," Reid shrugged. "Got himself some trouble with the IRS. But who doesn't, eh?"

Auto insurance returned to haunt them in a matter of days. This time, it was Wright's turn to squirm.

Lionel had just spent an afternoon arranging for coverage on their latest getaway car as a prerequisite to getting it licensed. The blue Ford was registered under the alias Stephen Kirkland. Otherwise, Lionel was known socially as Ronnie Grant. Never the two would meet—until they were accidentally introduced by the woman who had written Mr. Kirkland's auto policy. Wright spotted her at the last moment as she approached the restaurant table where the gang was dining with Rob-O and friends.

"Well, hello again, Mr. Kirkland," the woman said cheerfully, pausing on the way to join her own guests.

There were glances around the table. Then silence.

The woman hovered. "Stephen Kirkland, isn't it?"

The Ghost tried to pretend he wasn't there and said nothing.

The woman moved off, but the damage was done. If Rob-O weren't now totally convinced that something was amiss, the rejected insurance lady would surely have suspicions. Worse, she also had a name and the address of a flat on Emerald Avenue.

The morning after the FBI press conference Mitchell was pacing the beach house living room, clutching a copy of the morning paper. The string of bank robberies had already escalated his edginess to unrelenting anxiety. He couldn't sleep. His appetite was gone. And a hefty intake of booze wasn't helping his jitters much, either.

Everything seemed to be spinning out of control. FBI agents were everywhere. Rob-O had finally reached the conclusion they were all drug dealers and asked Mitchell point-blank if he had ever been in prison. Then there was the suspicious auto insurance agent out there somewhere with her damning information about Wright. And now this—a morning newspaper story with a full description of Mitchell's face. He must have pulled off his mask a few seconds too soon after their last bank heist on Balboa. An arriving customer had been close enough to remember every detail down to the blue eyes and scar between them from Mrs. Mitchell's flying alarm clock.

Fat Boy and the Kid had already made the decision not to press their luck any further. The FBI press conference had finally convinced them to grab their money and run to Los Angeles.

Mitchell's instincts told him to run, too. But where? And then what? He couldn't remember how much money he had left in bank accounts in California, Florida, and New Mexico. Maybe a hundred thousand. Maybe a bit more. Whatever the total stash, it wouldn't last long. He still needed one lucky strike. Just one major haul. Then he could retire. Then they could all retire.

A light drizzle is mixing with the eternal dusk of Los Angeles smog as the brown Buick pulls away from the Bank of America branch in suburban Long Beach. For once, everything has gone like clockwork: an armored-truck delivery of three money bags left lying on the floor of the open vault for immediate pickup by the Stopwatch Gang.

Over Mitchell's objections, the stopwatch is nowhere to be found on the bank videos. Reid has convinced them the gadget would be an invitation for the entire Los Angeles bureau of the FBI to join the posse already hunting them in San Diego.

Wright swings the Buick away from the bank and towards the exit of the plaza parking lot, a hundred yards away. Mitchell pulls off his balaclava and wonders which rendition of Murphy's Law will spoil the perfect crime this time. So far, it has not been a great week.

Tuesday, they had pulled up to an Orange County bank and were piling out of the car when Reid noticed a detail missed in their reconnaissance. A small blue and white sign over a basement door to an adjacent building, advertising a community outpost not listed in the phone book: POLICE.

Wednesday, they were awaiting the arrival of an armored truck in Hollywood when Mitchell spotted something odd at the jewelry store kitty-corner to the bank. Customers were pressing a buzzer beside the door to gain entry. Upon closer inspection he discovered patrons of the exclusive diamond shop were being scrutinized by two armed guards with a full view of the street. Would they leave their post long enough to shoot a couple of masked bandits fleeing the bank next door? No one was betting against it.

Now it is Thursday and the Buick moves away from the latest victim bank and rolls slowly towards the parking lot exit, trying not to attract attention. Mitchell is sweating. Reid is struggling to change clothes in the back. Wright is checking his Rolex.

They are still fifty yards from the street. Doomsday dawns.

"Oh my god have mercy," Mitchell whispers in a low growl. "J-e-e-s-u-s..."

The black and white police cruiser is coming directly at them.

"Stay cool, eyes straight ahead," Reid says as he slides across the back seat. There is the electric whirring of the rear window dropping. Then the chuck-chuck of a pump-action shotgun being cocked. Then nothing but three bandits breathing heavily.

"I've got him," Reid murmurs.

The cruiser, manned by a single officer, is moving towards the bank as slowly as they are trying to leave. No sirens. No flashing lights.

Mitchell crosses himself.

The cruiser is close enough for Wright to lean out and touch the patrolman, close enough for the solo patrolman to jab his revolver in Reid's ear.

Reid fingers the trigger on the shotgun, watching the policeman's face.

But it is emotionless, a pair of eyes stuck in forward lock, a crashtest dummy in a constable's uniform, unable—or unwilling—to see the three most-wanted bandits in all of California, their getaway car having passed like some ghost ship in the morning drizzle.

The close shave with the law left Paddy Mitchell close to asylum material. He shook all the way back to San Diego and refused to talk. Despite the sizeable bank haul, he shrugged off the usual celebration of cutting the cash and headed for the beach.

All afternoon he sat alone, gazing at the sea. All evening he lay on the cold sand, gazing at the stars. All through the night he walked and sat and walked some more until dawn cast its first purple light on the breaking surf.

Out of sympathy for Mitchell's deteriorating nervous system, the gang agreed it was time for a change of venue. Even the unflappable Reid had to admit he was starting to feel the heat in San Diego. There had been too many mistakes, too many suspicions raised. Sooner or later, the FBI would get lucky. He and JoAnne were also tiring of Mitchell's late-night renditions of beach blanket bimbo—a home without house guests might be nice.

Malibu's strip of opulent mansions and reclusive movie stars is everything eclectic that is America—a welcoming sign that boasts "27 miles of scenic beauty" followed by another posted by the Navy: "Danger! Live Firing!" No matter, a town full of rich hermits seemed a reasonable spot for California's most hunted crooks to hide out for a while.

The house overlooking Seal Point was no mansion at $6,000 a month, but the neighborhood seemed right. The Italian landlord told them Bob Dylan lived next door in the place with the high walls and turrets, and Goldie Hawn's palace was just below them on the point.

Reid told the landlord he was a writer looking for a quiet place to compose his next novel or screenplay—he wasn't quite sure which it would be. The landlord told Reid anything would be better than the crowd of Hollywood types who had just trashed the place during a marathon party. Reid pretended to be aghast at the torn wiring, broken plumbing fixtures, and other post-party debris. He didn't tell the landlord about Paddy Mitchell.

The landlord told Reid they could pay when the place was again livable. Reid handed him $12,000 in cash for rent in advance and said they would be back in ten days.

It was the last time the landlord saw any of them.

The precious-metals dealership was located on the second floor of a commercial strip north of Hollywood. Six years earlier a similar California establishment had taken possession of some gold bricks stolen from a certain Canadian airport. At 1980 prices, they would be worth just over $2 million. Given that the police had eventually found about half of it still stacked in the gold broker's vault, waiting to be made into brooches and wedding bands, Paddy Mitchell figured there must be more where that came from. Besides, he reckoned the industry sort of owed them.

The assault on a bullion dealer had required more complicated planning than all their bank robberies combined. JoAnne was unwittingly enlisted to help Reid case the joint—a grateful husband wanting to buy enough gold for his wife's birthday present: an eighteen-carat statuette of their beloved puppy, Chicago.

Access to the premises was electronically controlled. Video surveillance was heavy. Security was tight. But there was no obstacle too large for Mitchell's criminal creativity—including the fake bomb (compliments of the inventive Denver bandit) that would supposedly be detonated by anyone opening the only door to the place after their departure. The score was timed to be a five-minute operation.

The first minute has gone according to plan. Mitchell pulled the green Camaro to a stop in a loading zone along the curb. His two co-conspirators piled out and disappeared into an inside stairwell. By now, the receptionist should be buzzing them through the steel door into the second-floor offices of the precious-metals dealer.

Mitchell has assigned himself only one task. At the four-minute mark, he has to walk behind the car, check that no one is watching, and fasten a stolen license plate over the real one with two-sided tape and a pair of alligator clips.

He checks the stopwatch lying on the center console beside him. He glances in the rearview mirror, then at the customers entering and leaving the street-level bank beneath the robbery-in-progress.

The seconds pass like minutes, a minute seems like an hour. His fingers drum the steering wheel.

"Oh Mother Mary," Mitchell suddenly sputters aloud. "Not here. Not now. Not today."

The armored truck traveling in the opposite direction has crossed two lanes of traffic and pulled into the curb. It is stopping nose to nose with the Camaro.

The guard behind the wheel is sipping coffee from a styrofoam cup and staring straight at Mitchell. Another one is loading bags of cash for delivery to the bank directly beneath the second-floor bullion heist-in-progress.

The armored transport company has obviously taken seriously the FBI warnings about the Stopwatch Gang. A third guard with a shotgun climbs out of the truck and is walking straight towards the Camaro.

He stops and leans on the right front fender of the truck, the barrel of the shotgun resting across the crook of his free arm, ten feet and a thin windshield away from Mitchell. The guard turns and studies the man with the sunglasses and tweed cap, frozen behind the wheel of the Camaro.

Mitchell forces a smile and raises his hand: Hi there, we're the Stopwatch Gang. But don't sweat it. We're holding up someone else at the moment.

Mitchell glances at the stairwell door. Any second his two partners are going to come bursting onto the sidewalk and straight into a shootout with at least one armed guard, possibly three. The sweat is pouring off his chin.

The guard with the shotgun looks away, then back at Mitchell. The one behind the wheel puts down his coffee cup and lifts the microphone for the two-way radio.

Mitchell reaches for the gearshift. But where can he go? Backward into a parked car. Forward into a parked truck. He can hardly pull away and go for a ride, leaving the others in the midst of a holdup.

He glances at the stairwell door, then at the stopwatch. Four minutes gone. Sixty seconds to a shootout.

The other guard emerges from the bank with an empty trolley. Mitchell prays there is only one load. Now the one with the shotgun is pulling a pack of cigarettes from his shirt pocket and apparently asking for a light.

Mitchell wants to leap out, give him a damn light, and tell them to get the hell out of there. Keep the matches.

The two guards are laughing. The one with the trolley finally disappears into the truck. The one with the shotgun turns and gives Mitchell another long, hard look.

Mitchell's eyes again dart to the stairwell door, then down at the stopwatch. Five minutes. Time's up. The yellow turn signal of the armored truck is flashing as the stairwell door bursts open.

The truck is starting back into traffic as the two bandits scramble into the Camaro. Mitchell looks at the stolen license plate on his lap, throws open the door, and races to the rear.

The chunks of two-sided tape now soaked in sweat are as useless as squares of Teflon. Mitchell fumbles with the alligator clips. One of them falls to the pavement.

"Let's go!" Reid shrieks. "Go! For chrissakes! Now!..."

Mitchell was shaking so badly that it took him most of the two-hour drive back to San Diego to retell his five-minute nightmare. Safely back at the beach house, he didn't stop to admire their glittering cache. He was off to the beach again. He had to get away.

Mitchell returned to the house after a few minutes, and began throwing clothes and bundles of cash into a duffelbag. Without comment, he headed for his car. Reid and Wright followed him out the door.

Paddy tossed the bag into the trunk and slammed the lid.

"That's it. I've had it," Mitchell said firmly, his hands still shaking as he tried to light a cigar.

"Where you going?" Reid asked.

"I can't take this anymore," Mitchell replied. "I don't know where I'm going and I really don't give a damn."

Reid started to chuckle: "So exactly what is it you're planning to do?"

"I don't give a good goddam what I do," Mitchell said forcefully. "I'll grab a pick and shovel before I ever rob another fucking bank. That's it. Never again."

A week after Mitchell's parting "God bless" to the Stopwatch Gang, a Los Angeles radio station interrupted its regular programming for a dramatic news bulletin:

> FBI sources report heavily armed police SWAT teams have surrounded the notorious Stopwatch bank-robbery gang after a dramatic hold-up and shoot-out in the town of Norco earlier today. One deputy sheriff and a gang member were killed...

CHAPTER THIRTEEN

Norco, California

Paddy Mitchell had been right about one thing. The FBI's hunt for the rampaging bandits had become intense. No stone was being left unturned, no street snitch left unsqueezed. Agents unleashed on the case from San Diego to the Canadian border had pieced together every robbery in the string of heists in meticulous detail. Every bank employee had been interviewed, every frame of bank film had run and rerun (the cameras didn't work at all in two of the San Diego jobs). They knew the exact build of each bandit. They knew they were male, probably Caucasian. Unusually polite for gangsters. They knew the gang changed disguises from motorcycle helmets to balaclavas to Star Trek masks. And they knew one of them (Wright) carried his gun in his left hand, his forefinger wrapped around the guard, away from the trigger. They checked the getaway cars against lists of reported stolen vehicles and found only one that came close—the GTO swiped by the gang, abandoned, and boosted by someone else. The license plates were definitely stolen—the real owners hadn't even noticed them missing. The FBI knew one gang member always wore a stopwatch around his neck, though not always the same person. They knew the heists were all carefully planned and well executed—they suspected the commandos were probably Vietnam vets. And they were convinced the rash of robberies was all the handiwork of one gang.

Most of all, the FBI knew everything the agents had gathered in four months amounted to nothing more than a lot of paper in a thick file. The trail was abysmally cold.

Norman A. Zigrossi, special agent in charge of the San Diego bureau of the FBI, spared no effort turning the hunt for the Stopwatch Gang into a media event. Press conferences were called, interviews granted, photographs distributed. Danger, drama, fear—Norman A. Zigrossi knew how to grab headlines when he needed them. He also knew that somewhere, sometime, the gang had to make a mistake.

Friday, May 9, 1980. It is mid-morning and two FBI agents assigned to the Stopwatch case are tailing a late-model American sedan. The suspects have been under round-the-clock surveillance for more than a week. The convoy heads north out of San Diego towards Los Angeles, then east towards San Bernardino. The suspect vehicle turns off the freeway into the town of Riverside, about forty-five minutes east of Los Angeles. The hounds follow. Not too close. Not close enough: the suspects disappear in traffic.

It is shortly after noon. The next call to the FBI comes from the nearby town of Norco.

3:36 p.m. Four men wearing ski masks and carrying automatic rifles enter the Norco branch of the Security Pacific Bank at 4th Street and Hamner Avenue. There are ten customers in the bank. One of the gunmen holds his weapon in the air and orders everyone to "hit the floor." The other three vault the counter and begin scooping cash from the tills.

One of them yells: "Go!"

The bandits rush for the doors. The whole operation has lasted about ninety seconds. One of the tellers has tripped a silent alarm. This time, the police are waiting.

The events that follow are splashed across the front pages of newspapers from San Diego to New York. The Los Angeles Times reported:

> One law enforcement officer and a robbery suspect were killed and nine other officers were wounded during a running gun battle that began Friday afternoon with a bank hold-up here and continued about 50 miles away on the rugged slopes of Mt. Baldy...One suspect was left dead at the scene, while his five companions, including a woman, escaped...
>
> The robbers were met by deputies as they tried to make their way to a waiting getaway vehicle, a green Dodge van...The driver of the van...had been shot and killed by arriving officers...The robbers then exchanged shots with officers as they commandeered a 4-wheel-drive pickup truck in the bank parking lot and escaped... Deputy Sheriff Jim Evans was killed in the ensuing gun-fight. Seven other law enforcement officers and a woman bystander were wounded...

The robbers fled north on Hamner, tossing explosives from the truck at pursuing police. (One of them reported over his radio: "They're throwing all sorts of stuff at us.")...A 40-mile running gun-battle into the wooded foothills of the San Bernardino mountains ensued.

During their escape into the hills, the robbers shot down a police helicopter, but there were no injuries...

Heavily armed SWAT team members pursued the suspects as they climbed up the rocky mountain slopes, but the officers were called back after darkness fell. The bandits eventually holed up in Lytle Creek Canyon during the night...Temperatures in the area, at an elevation of 5,000 to 6,000 feet, were expected to drop near freezing overnight...

Witnesses described the command post scene in the San Gabriel Mountains as reminiscent of an old-time gangster movie—with scores of police officers milling around as plans were being formulated to capture a gang that apparently has no intention of giving up without a fight...The Air Force reportedly was bringing heat-seeking devices to the command post to be used to detect the suspects' location...

At 6:00 p.m., the FBI issue an all-points-bulletin for the suspects in the Norco robbery. A local sheriff's office mistakenly releases the names to the media. Someone in the Los Angeles bureau of the FBI confirms they are all members of the notorious Stopwatch Gang. One is dead. The others are surrounded. Reporters camp out at the police command post overnight with the promise that special commando teams will be moving in on the suspects at first light Saturday morning.

At sunrise, the search resumed in raw, drizzly weather with strong winds and temperatures in the low 30s...A posse of 80 SWAT team members from Riverside and San Bernardino counties, working with three helicopters and a team of police dogs, searched the foothills at dawn.

Three of the men were captured shortly after 8 a.m., so cold they could hardly talk...One was shot in the hip and hospitalized...

The fourth man was in the rugged canyons of the foothill country, with an automatic rifle and about 100 rounds of ammunition...He was sighted from a helicopter and an officer was lowered to the site. The gunman, lightly clothed in the freezing temperatures during the night, was dead...

CHAPTER FOURTEEN

Sedona, Arizona

The last shimmers of the Arizona sun ignite the soaring red rock pinnacles and jagged buttes that seem to teeter precariously above the juniper forest like the overgrown ruins of some antediluvian temple, its giant sandstone spires rough-chiseled by the rains and left to rust in the desert wind. Even as dusk begins to smother the crimson cliffs in shadow, a blaze of auburn and ocher spreads across the skies in a final crescendo. Red mountains. Red skies. Fire in the earth. Fire in the heavens. No wonder the Apache treated the place with reverence. No wonder the cowboys of the Wild West called it Hell's Hollow.

In more modern times the likes of John Wayne, Jimmy Stewart, and Henry Fonda rode off into the same sunsets as the credits rolled on one cowboy epic after another, filmed against the dramatic red stone backdrops of Cathedral Rock, Wild Horse Mesa, and the other eroded geological oddities that dominate the natural beauty of Sedona's landscapes. None is more alluring than Oak Creek Canyon.

A yawning split in the earth's crust, the canyon zigzags fourteen miles from Sedona north to a sheer headwall. There, a cascade of spring water spews from a crack in the sandstone face and plummets into the abyss, then churns and froths over the smooth pebbles of Oak Creek. It is said that Zane Grey wrote his famous 1920s novel *Call of the Canyon* there, describing the area as "a wild, lonely, terrible place...perhaps for outlawed men—not for a civilized person..."

Local legend has it that Oak Creek Canyon was indeed a favorite hideaway for outlawed men of the Wild West. For decades, it is said, runaway rustlers, stagecoach bandits, and other miscellaneous desperadoes shared the canyon forests with Yavapai Apache farmers, a few hardy homesteaders, a fellow named Howard who had gunned down a sheepherder in California, and a prolific counterfeiter named Sterling.

146

A century later, a two-lane highway winds through Oak Creek Canyon, alternately hugging the red rock walls and slithering along the canyon floor through arches of giant oaks and sprawling red maples. About three miles south of Zane Grey's old cabin, an unmarked dirt track drops away from the pavement and into the thick forest, across the creek and past a handpainted sign that reads: "Forest Houses. Quiet Please."

Tucked among the soaring stands of ponderosa pine are ten country retreats, each one meticulously crafted in local wood and stone. The one called Sycamore House is the most magnificent of them all, with its handhewn timbers, high vaulted ceilings, rustic oak furniture, and four giant fieldstone fireplaces, one at the foot of every bed, another forming an entire wall of the spacious downstairs living room. A wall of glass faces south towards the red rock mountains. A cedar balcony overhangs the creek Zane Grey described as "gleaming, boulder-strewn and ridged by white rapids."

It is May 13, 1980. A man is sitting on the deck, smoking a cigarette, and reading the newspaper. The day's editions of the *Los Angeles Times* are headlining the latest titilating installment on the Norco shootout and capture of the Stopwatch Gang the previous weekend. What could have been the public relations coup of the decade for Special Agent Norman A. Zigrossi and the FBI has definitely taken a turn for the worse.

> Law enforcement officials inadvertently made public the names of some suspected members of San Diego's notorious "Stopwatch Gang" because they were mistakenly believed to have been involved in last weekend's Norco bank robbery and shoot-out, authorities admitted Monday.
>
> An all-points-bulletin issued Friday night, when lawmen were cornering the Norco bank robbery suspects in the San Gabriel Mountains, listed the names of five suspects in the robbery.
>
> One of the names may not be a person at all...The other four are San Diego residents who, it turned out, had no involvement in the Norco shoot-out that left three men, including one police officer, dead. They were, however, under surveillance by the FBI as suspected "Stopwatch Gang" members, Norman Zigrossi, special agent in charge of the FBI's San Diego office, said Monday.
>
> "We've had several suspects," Zigrossi said of the San Diego gang, which is suspected of robbing four banks with military-like precision...He acknowledged that the FBI's surveillance of the

San Diego residents has been all but blown...He said it is unclear how the names of the suspects were publicly disclosed, but stressed ...that his office in San Diego was not responsible...An FBI spokesman in Riverside referred all calls to the Los Angeles office where spokesman Lou Bertram offered only "no comment."

The four [suspects] were identified as Jerry Dean Ivens and his wife, Lucille Marie, of Pacific Beach; Michael J. Sullivan of Leucadia; and Rene Ruiz Valdez of Oceanside...

Valdez, 28, a cement contractor, was angry: "My sister called me from Decatur, Georgia, because she thought I was dead. And then my dad and brother and mom called me. So I called the FBI in Riverside and the San Bernardino sheriffs and they said they had no idea [how my name was involved]. Nobody seems to know nothing...I just wish people would be a little more careful when they use my name..."

Ivens, a mobile home contractor, said: "People think we're involved in the Stopwatch Gang...I don't know any bank robbers. I only know Little League people, because I'm a coach..." Ivens, 34, said his wife feels "she may lose her job as a nurse because she's still on [employee] probation at the hospital...She hasn't had so much as a traffic ticket."

Jerry Ivens...was originally identified as the Stopwatch Gang member who was shot and killed at the scene of the Norco robbery. "It's discouraging to work as hard as I have, to have some fool cop throw my name out on the street as a dead man...I'm involved in the Little League, my kid plays ball, and I like apple pie..."

Sullivan, 25, a self-employed commercial artist who works with wood and resin, said Monday he was initially concerned that his name was implicated in the Norco robbery. "At first, when a friend told me he heard my name on the news, I couldn't understand how they'd ever imagine I would be involved in something like that...But the whole thing has gotten kind of funny. When I called my mom up for Mother's Day, I told her I'm robbing banks. She and my dad got a kick out of it..."

The fifth name on the all-points-bulletin was Pascal Ludwig McCoys [who] may not be a person at all...The pick-up truck commandeered at the scene of the Norco robbery and subsequently used by the gunmen was owned by Pascal & Ludwig, a construction firm...

As dusk snuffs the last flicker of fire from the red rock peaks of Oak Creek Canyon, laughter stirs the tranquillity of Sycamore House where another handpainted sign entreats all who enter: "This place is for people who enjoy peace and quiet in this crowded world. Please help us keep it that way. No firearms."

Ten feet away in the living room, a man is chuckling at the arsenal of handguns, shotguns, and machine guns he has spread down the middle of the floor, like the day's catch on a fisherman's wharf. Another man crumples the *Los Angeles Times* into the fieldstone fireplace and touches a match to it. There is more laughter as they mock the voice of Special Agent Norman A. Zigrossi trying to explain to an unforgiving media how the FBI's much-touted "intensive, four-month investigation" of the notorious Stopwatch Gang has wrongly connected the wrong people to the wrong gang wrongly connected to the wrong bank robbery.

As the maple logs crackle in the hearth of Sycamore House, Lionel Wright and Stephen Reid raise a toast: To paradise found. To the FBI lost. To the good health of Patrick Michael Mitchell, wherever the hell he might be.

Reid and Wright had been lounging on the patio of the Pacific Beach condo when they first heard the rather startling news bulletin that the FBI had them surrounded. At first, the two fugitives had just stared at the portable radio in stunned disbelief. Details that followed made it clear that police had cornered some other gang of bandits responsible for the Norco shootout. No matter, the already intense heat was bound to get worse when the FBI—and the media—discovered the real Stopwatch Gang was still on the loose. Wright and Reid agreed it was definitely time to get the hell out of town. Preferably yesterday.

The day after Mitchell's hasty departure from San Diego the week before, a real estate agent had called Reid from Arizona to tell him about a magnificent house for rent in Oak Creek Canyon near Sedona.

Reid and Wright had first stumbled on the area a month earlier, after taking a wrong turn in the mountains en route back to California from a three-day binge in Las Vegas. Like everyone else who discovers Red Rock Country for the first time, they were awed by its beauty and by Sedona's aura of protected seclusion. Nice place to live. Great place to hide. They had left a California phone number at the local real estate office.

Three days before the Norco robbery and shootout, Reid and Wright had driven across the desert to check out the place they called Sycamore House in Oak Creek. It was everything the agent had described, all right.

Discussion ensued. Maybe it was time to split up for a while. Wright could take the house in Sedona; Reid and JoAnne would move to the one in Malibu.

For no other reason than a change of scenery, Reid and Wright decided to drive back to San Diego via Los Angeles. Had they been only a few hours later, two-thirds of the real Stopwatch Gang would have passed the Norco bandits fleeing down the same highway in the opposite direction, shooting down helicopters and tossing dynamite at the pursuing motorcade of screaming police cruisers.

That evening JoAnne was packing for the move to Malibu when Reid heard the stunning news broadcast on the patio and rushed inside to tell her there had been a slight change of plan. He concocted some story about the IRS being after him, the Malibu house not being ready, and his sinuses needing some drier air. He was sure she would like this place they had found in Arizona. And, oh, by the way, they would all be leaving within the hour. JoAnne was not pleased.

At nightfall a blue Buick with a trunk full of guns pulled out of Pacific Beach. A few minutes later a red Camaro followed—a man and a woman crammed in it with piles of belongings, a dog named Chicago, one neon beer sign, and a large duffelbag stuffed with stolen loot. Two rattan chairs from Pier One Imports were roped to the roof; JoAnne won that argument.

As the cars accelerated onto the interstate to head for Arizona, Stephen Reid flipped on the radio to catch the latest news on the hunt for the Stopwatch Gang in the mountains three hours north.

Sedona was every convict's dream—just one quiet, quaint, and beautiful place in which to vanish from the law. Until the early 1970s, cattlemen still drove their herds down the main street. But by 1980 the area had become Trendy Haven, its population swollen to eight thousand by a steady influx of artists and artisans, writers and poets, millionaire urban escapees, yuppie jetsetters, and a small army of real estate agents hawking paradise in hundred-foot lots. The young people worried about the ravages of development. The adults worried about the ravages of recession. The old folks thought it was still a pretty place to die.

As is the custom of small towns, the friendly folk of Sedona subjected all newcomers to plenty of well-intentioned questions. But no one was ever particularly surprised by a dearth of answers in a place that had elevated privacy to a local tourist attraction, where eccentrics didn't have to account for their eccentricities, the rich didn't have to account for their money, and the urban runaways didn't have to account for anything.

Bob and Mary Kitteredge didn't quite know what to make of their newest tenants in Sycamore House. Timmy Pfeiffer and his wife JoAnne seemed like a charming couple, though their friend Stephen Kirkland was a bit odd. Never said a word.

Timmy and the Kitteredges had talked a lot at their first meeting. Mostly about the rules that went along with living in the Forest Houses. More damn rules than a Monopoly game, Timmy thought.

Bob Kitteredge told Timmy the story of abandoning his life as a New York sculptor during the Depression, climbing on a Harley-Davidson with his brother, and heading for the West. Worked for a circus along the way, but there was no money to pay them. So, they settled for one of the animals. Bob laughed a lot when he was telling the part about arriving in Sedona—two men and a chimpanzee on a motorcycle. Other than telling his own stories, Bob Kitteredge didn't seem to laugh much. Life was pretty serious stuff. A lot of rules.

For his part, Reid handed the Kitteredges a business card that read: "Timothy Pfeiffer, President, Spectre Entertainment Marketing, P.O. Box 99391, San Diego, CA." He said his company provided technical equipment for the motion picture industry. Good business. Lots of money. Plenty of free time to spend with his wife and dog...Chicago's a good pup...Oh, no, he won't be running around bothering anyone...Understood...Rules are rules...Stephen Kirkland?...A business associate...Takes care of all the millions of details, eh...Actually, he's a boyhood friend...Just trying to help him out...He's a good guy, a bit shy, but that's just the way he is, eh...Naw, naw, there won't be anyone else living there, just JoAnne and Chicago and me downstairs, Steve upstairs...Understood...Rules are rules...

Timmy paid them the entire six months' rent of six thousand dollars in advance. In cash. The Kitteredges appreciated that a lot. Stephen Reid liked it when people liked him.

"So, what do you think?" Mary Kitteredge asked her husband after their first encounter with the Stopwatch Gang.

Bob shrugged. "I think they're Canadians."

***

For the most part, the newcomers to Oak Creek Canyon didn't do much of anything for the first month except keep their heads down. The FBI's embarrassing bout of mistaken identities in the Norco fiasco was bound to harden Zigrossi's resolve to find the real Stopwatch Gang. Aside from long walks in the surrounding woods and the necessary trips to town for groceries, the three stayed close to home and discouraged new friendships. They junked their telltale California cars and bought Arizona replacements—Wright got a full-sized Ford, Reid another Camaro.

The collection of guns, disguises, and other paraphernalia of crimes past were loaded into a large steamer trunk and stashed at a nearby U-Store shed. The two rattan chairs from Pier One Imports got U-Stored as well. JoAnne lost that argument.

Most of the money was deposited in bank accounts and safety-deposit boxes from Flagstaff to Phoenix. The small bills were stuffed in a large glass jar beside Reid's bed. The stopwatch was deposited in an empty earthen mug on the living room mantel. Just another souvenir.

Reid and JoAnne chose the downstairs apartment in Sycamore House, the one with the large living room, but only one bedroom—Paddy-proof, just in case. There was no television, and only a pay phone on the outside wall of the building. The couple cherished the peace and privacy after the frat-house atmosphere of Ocean Front Walk.

Wright moved into the two-bedroom flat upstairs, stocked it with raisin bread and his eclectic assortment of history books, and passed his days sitting alone on a rock by the creek, tossing sticks to Chicago. Whatever happened seemed just fine with him. If nothing ever happened, that was okay, too. *Que sera sera.*

The newcomers didn't bother the Kitteredges and the Kitteredges didn't bother the newcomers. Those were the rules. Mary did wonder, though, why people with such a perfect lifestyle never seemed to smile.

Dentist George Moore had a sensible approach to his Sedona practice. Assess the mouth, assess the means, and only recommend treatment that fits the two. No point creating a pretty smile, he would say, if the bill leaves a permanent frown.

Timmy Pfeiffer hadn't been in Moore's reclining chair more than a minute before the dentist concluded his new patient's mouth and means were probably similar—that is to say, rough. The only sign of reconstruction was a removable plastic bridge, the cheapest piece of oral hardware available (compliments of Millhaven prison). The rest of the package wasn't exactly a picture of wealth, either—the tatty Levis, the plain white T-shirt, the scruffy running shoes.

"So, where do you live?" Moore asked casually, partly to make small talk, partly to elicit some clues to his patient's financial status.

"Oh, just up the canyon," Reid replied.

"Beautiful up there. Whereabouts exactly?" the dentist prodded congenially.

"Part-way up, in the woods," Reid said vaguely.

Moore thought so much evasiveness a bit odd. But this was Sedona and some people were like that. He came straight to the point. For about two hundred dollars he could replace the flimsy contraption in Reid's mouth with much sturdier and more comfortable bridgework. It would still be removable and therefore a bit of a nuisance, the dentist said apologetically, but anything permanent like porcelain crowns would cost a lot more money. Probably two thousand bucks by the time they were finished.

Reid shrugged in the chair. "Let's do the whole works. I hate waking up every morning with half my mouth on the bedside table."

"If you're sure this is what you want," Moore said, almost pleading for reconsideration, "you can certainly pay us in bits and pieces over a period of time. We don't mind. Lots of people do that."

"Oh, don't worry about the money," Reid said, his voice warming for the first time.

The following day, Timmy Pfeiffer was back in Moore's office with an envelope for receptionist Marilyn Donkersley.

"This is for that million-dollar smile the doctor promised me," Reid said with a chuckle, handing her the blank air-mail envelope.

Reid was barely out the door when Marilyn hauled George Moore aside to show him the extraordinary packet just delivered by that fellow named Pfeiffer—the entire two thousand dollars paid in advance. In cash. In twenties.

Moore's jaw came unhinged. Some of his patients facing big bills paid a little down, the rest later. Most paid it all later. Everyone paid by check. But in his fifteen years of dentistry, no one had ever paid everything in advance, much less in cash.

"Take this down to the bank right now," the dentist sputtered in an excited whisper. "Make sure that money's real..."

The Cessna-172 banked steeply to the left, then to the right, then into a roller-coaster dive and swooping arc back up towards the horizon, the towering red rock mesas spinning and tipping in a dizzying dance. Stephen Reid let out the gleeful hoot of a kid on a Disney ride. Lionel Wright swallowed hard to hold onto his lunch. The toothpick-munching cowboy in the pilot's seat grinned—Jack Seeley's absolutely free, no-obligation, introductory training flights were forever scaring the shit out of prospective students. He could never understand why half of them never set foot in the Sedona Flying School again.

Reid had always liked flying in small planes. Part of it was the sense of excitement, the sense of danger. Part of it was the sense of freedom, soaring along an unfettered freeway above the clutter, calamity, and constraints on the ground below. It was also clear that a small plane and a license to fly it would bring to modern banditry a quantum leap equivalent to the transition from horseback to getaway cars.

It all seemed so simple. Radio ahead for a rental car, land, hit a bank, return the car, and hop back on the plane already refueled in the meantime. No passenger terminals. No baggage scanners. No security checkpoints. No police roadblocks.

Seeley saw nothing at all unusual about Timothy Pfeiffer and Stephen Kirkland when they first walked into the offices of Air Sedona and enquired about flying lessons. They had the required few hundred hours to kill—so did a lot of the rich leisure seekers in Sedona. The fifteen-hundred-dollar deposit in cash didn't faze anyone, either—some of Seeley's clients could drop that kind of dough before breakfast. And there was certainly nothing fishy about the San Diego address on Mr. Pfeiffer's business card, nor the Florida driver's license and social security card produced (quite literally) by Mr. Kirkland—hell, half the town was from somewhere else.

In fact, about the only raised eyebrows that day were on the faces of Stephen Reid and Lionel Wright as they sat on the outdoor terrace of Stretch's Cantina, chewing the fat with Jack Seeley, sipping lemonade, and recovering from their absolutely free, no-obligation, introductory flight with the Sedona Flying School.

"Hey, Gary, pull up a chair," Seeley said to the fellow in the cowboy hat who had approached their table with an outstretched hand and a neighborly smile. "Like ya to meet my two latest flying-aces-in-training...Timmy Pfeiffer, Steve Kirkland, meet my pal Gary. Deputy Gary, we call him..."

Paddy Mitchell's espoused pick-and-shovel salvation tour to Canada got only as far north as Washington State. There he encountered a preacher's homely daughter named Carol-Sue, a young widowed mother trying to eke out an existence with her two small children on a dilapidated farm in the foothills of the Cascade Mountains. Paddy and Carol-Sue met outside a pretty country church where Mitchell had stopped, presumably to ask for God's help getting across the Canadian border.

Life in the country with Carol-Sue and the kids was a pleasant respite from the hectic pace of robbing banks and running from the law. Their days were spent working the farm, their evenings reading to one another from the Bible. Before long Mitchell was convinced the Good Lord had led him to Carol-Sue to give him a chance—quite probably his final one before eternal damnation—to denounce his evil ways, repent, and seek forgiveness.

When the lid blew off nearby Mount Saint Helens, blackening the skies with volcanic fire and ash, Mitchell was sure it was a message from God. Obviously, the Almighty was some almighty pissed with sinners like him.

Unfortunately, Mitchell's dedication to godliness, clean living, and a preacher's girl didn't last long. Overall, repentance turned out to be almost as boring as Carol-Sue. So it came to pass that six weeks after his arrival in the promised land, Paddy Mitchell bade Carol-Sue a final "God bless" and took the southbound freeway back to a bank in Sacramento, California.

The message in the safety-deposit box was not from the Good Lord—twenty thousand in cash, and a ten-digit phone number scribbled on a scrap of paper.

Mitchell locked the door of the bank cubicle, pulled a pen from his pocket and began reworking the phone number, hoping he still remembered the code: add one to the first digit, two to the second, three to the third. Subtract four from each of the next three numbers. Add five to each of the remaining two. Any sum greater than nine or less than zero, use the last digit...Area code six-zero-two. Phone number two-eight-two, nine-nine-zero-six.

The pay phone hanging on the outside of Sycamore House rang three times, stopped, and rang again a minute later. Every Sunday evening at 6 p.m. Lionel Wright had been there waiting. He picked up the receiver on the second ring of the second call.

"Ronnie here," Wright said.

"H-e-e-y, your ol' buddy Mikey here," said the voice on the other end of the line.

"About time," Wright said. "You got my message okay?"

"No, Weirdo, I was sitting here randomly dialing every pay phone in America. Quick, give me directions before I run out of quarters. See you in a couple of days. God bless."

It is the third week of June in Red Rock Country. Another dazzling sunset. Another day in paradise. And the Stopwatch Gang is back in business.

CHAPTER FIFTEEN

Sedona, Arizona

*Seven-three-eight-Uniform-Charlie...You're all clear for take-off...
Have fun...Good flying...*

The afternoon sun danced on the whirling propeller as Stephen Reid pushed the Cessna's nose downwards into a gentle, sweeping arc across the high plains of brittle grass and rolling dust. The wings flattened to the horizon as they streaked over the narrow fringe of tall pine forest. Suddenly, the altimeter spun from seven hundred feet to thousands. Reid gasped as the plane shot over the rim of the Grand Canyon. Ten miles wide. Six thousand feet deep. Jack Seeley laughed. It wasn't easy to scare the shit out of Timmy Pfeiffer.

Stephen Reid took to his new high-flying hobby with the same obsessive passion that had made addictions of so many other pastimes—swimming, hockey, weight lifting, robbing banks.

A lot of students had shared the cockpit with Seeley over the years, but none had been such a quick study. Reid bought every flight book he could find, and read them all with intensity and remarkable retention. In the air, his flying time was limited only by Jack's availability. On the ground, his questions dominated the weekly classes held in Seeley's living room. Tim Pfeiffer didn't just want to know what each gauge in the cockpit did, he wanted to know how it did it. "I hope you never ask me the time," Seeley once said half jokingly to Reid. "I haven't a clue how my watch works."

It was during the ground-school classes that Judy Seeley met Timmy Pfeiffer. The pilot's wife thought the newcomer one of the most congenial, gentle, and considerate fellows she had ever met. The first time they all went out to dinner, Timmy insisted on picking up the tab—in cash, of course. Nothing flashy. Nothing boastful. Timmy just wouldn't have it any other way. If he were going to be even a few minutes late for an appointment, he would always call. Very apologetic. Timmy Pfeiffer was always late for everything. Sedona time, he called it.

Reid told the Seeleys that Spectre Entertainment Marketing was in the business of providing light shows for rock concerts. While he could spin enough jargon to sound convincing, the conversations never lasted long. Jack Seeley assumed Timmy just didn't like talking business on leisure time. Sedona was like that.

The local folk of Sedona seemed fully unsuspecting, if not uninterested in the newcomers. Reid and Wright had even managed to pull off their chance encounter with Deputy Sheriff Gary without getting arrested, so obviously they were in no immediate danger. That first meeting on the patio of Stretch's Cantina had lasted almost an hour. They had talked about flying, about the entertainment biz, about policing in Sedona. Mostly handing out traffic tickets and directions to tourists, Gary said. The odd break-in. Maybe a bar brawl on a good night.

Overall, the Stopwatch Gang thought Gary a pretty good guy, for a deputy sheriff. Gary thought the Stopwatch Gang pretty regular kinda guys, too. He even invited them to a party the following weekend.

"Oh, too bad, Gary," Reid had said with all the disappointment he could muster without laughing. "Thanks for the invite. Love to come, but we'll have to take a rain check. We're all out of town next week. Got some business to do. Out of state…"

The Texas bank has just opened for the day. A man with a dark wig, matching fake beard, glasses, and a briefcase is ushered into the vault. After initialing the signature card, he retrieves a safety-deposit box and retires to a nearby privacy cubicle a few feet away. One minute later another man with a similar blond wig and beard steps up to the counter and asks if the teller would mind changing two thousand dollars in twenties into hundred-dollar bills. Since no teller has that kind of cash on hand—too dangerous—she locks her drawer and heads for the vault. She is still counting out the hundreds when she feels a gentle poke in her back.

"Don't scream and don't turn around," a voice behind her says in a firm whisper. "Just do exactly as you are told and you won't be hurt…You okay?"

The teller, never less okay in her life, nods nervously and unloads the sizeable stash from the vault's cash cabinet into a briefcase the Voice has placed beside her on a pull-out shelf.

"Now listen to me very carefully and no one will get killed," the Voice says, almost soothingly, as he snaps the latches on the briefcase. "Grip the side of that shelf with both hands as tightly as you can, and don't even twitch. I am placing a bomb behind you that will go off if you try to call for help or move a muscle or even turn your head for the next five minutes. Understood?"

By the time the bomb squad arrives, no one is quite certain how long the terrified teller has been frozen in the vault with an empty shoe box on the floor behind her. No alarm was sounded during the robbery, no bank films taken. The FBI is looking for a lone gunman, perhaps two, who made off with an undisclosed amount of cash.

Paddy Mitchell had spent the whole day preparing for the seduction of Miss Beckie. The two had met at the Poco Diablo Bar, one of Sedona's favorite watering holes. She was waitressing. He was drinking. She noticed his friendly eyes and generous tips. He noticed her friendly smile and generous curves. From that moment on no effort was too great, no expense too lavish for the successful courtship of the young and voluptuous Miss Rebecca.

As the Sycamore House residents prepared to abandon their abode to Don Juan and prey for the evening, Reid surveyed the trap. The two place settings at one end of the oak dining table had been purchased by Paddy that morning, just for the occasion. New china and crystal, new silver flatware, and a new white linen tablecloth with matching napkins rolled neatly in new heavy silver rings that matched the new heavy silver candlesticks. The menu for the event was equally *cuisine passé*—shrimp cocktail, vichyssoise, filet mignon in a Burgundy sauce, mushrooms in a sherry sauce, broccoli in a cheese sauce, baked potatoes and sour cream. A few bottles of Mumm's Cordon Rouge before dinner, Beaujolais during, Remy Martin after.

The lighting in the room had been dimmed to near-darkness. A fire was blazing in the huge stone hearth. The pillows on the sofa had been carefully fluffed and strategically placed. The tape on the stereo was a grocery store collection of Nat King Cole love songs.

"Ah, give it some slack, Paddy," Reid admonished. "This isn't *Gone with the Wind*. Like this is the eighties, man, and this broad is twenty-two years old. She probably hasn't seen shit like this since her great-granny croaked."

Mitchell was visibly embarrassed. Aging had always worried him. Lately, it was a toss-up whether he would rather confess his crimes to the FBI or admit to a young woman he was pushing forty.

"Listen, pal," Reid said sympathetically as he turned for the door, "if all this shit doesn't get you laid, you might try something a little more her era. There are a few lines of coke in the top drawer of my dresser. In case of emergency, help yourself."

The next morning, Beckie was still there, along with most of the dinner, half the wine, an unopened bottle of Remy Martin, and a disco tape on the stereo. Nat King Cole was gone. So was the cocaine.

Paddy Mitchell had arrived in Sedona with hugs and handshakes and a friendly plea to live somewhere else. Not for long, Reid had promised. Just until JoAnne could be treated for her latest attack of compulsive nesting. It just seemed easier blaming JoAnne than trying to tell his old friend that the previous two months of living in peace and relative normalcy with a nice home, a girlfriend, and a dog named Chicago had been, well, rather enjoyable. Reid also worried a lot about the Kitteredges—he had a pretty good idea how they would react to the conversion of Sycamore House into Paddy's Party Palace. They'd probably call the cops. Disturbing the peace was not how Stephen Reid wanted to go down.

This time Mitchell took the hint. He rented his own place about three miles up Oak Creek Canyon. It wasn't much of a house: long on drywall and linoleum; definitely short on charm. But the price was right, and that's pretty much all that mattered. It seemed of no consequence to Mitchell that he routinely dropped enough money in Las Vegas in one hour to rent the grandest home in Sedona for six months. Nor did it seem relevant that he could steal ten times that amount in ninety seconds—and routinely did. He just couldn't see parting with an extra nickel for a place to sleep, which was virtually all that home had become to the one-time family man from the suburbs.

Mitchell didn't really mind a house on his own. If there were going to be a raid someday—he was certain there was going to be a raid *every* day—he figured living apart from the others improved his getaway chances. Besides, he could always hang out at Sycamore House when they weren't all out of town. On business.

***

The bank in New Mexico is no different from any other—two doors, a vault, a counter, some tellers, some cash. The heist should be equally straightforward, another typical Stopwatch robbery—one person drives, another takes control of the bank, the third hops the counter and grabs the cash. Out the door and back to the car. Ninety seconds tops. Some employee will have tripped the silent alarm, but police will arrive too late. No one gets caught. No one gets hurt.

Wright is driving. Mitchell takes control of the bank with a long-barreled .45 that certainly could have made Dirty Harry's day. Reid hops the counter and grabs the cash from the teller drawers. He is out the door and running for the car. No more than ninety seconds. Some employee will have tripped the silent alarm, but —

"Okay, ya muthafucka, freeze yo ass, aw youz a deadman."

Mitchell hadn't seen the tattooed hulk flattened against the pillar. Nor could his reflexes match the hand that shot out and grabbed the gun like a lizard's tongue snatching a fly from mid-air.

Mitchell turns his head and is staring straight into the muzzle of his own .45. It is aimed squarely at the alarm-clock scar between his eyes. The gun is vibrating wildly in the hands of the Hulk. The hammer is cocked.

"Git down on dat flo, aw I's goin' to blow yuz muthafuckin' head off," the Hulk sputters.

"Listen, buddy, this is no time to fuck around," Mitchell hisses through clenched teeth. "Just give me the gun and no one will get hurt."

Mitchell starts to move his left hand up towards the gun when the Hulk panics. A finger yanks hard on the trigger.

The hammer slams into the chamber. Click. Nothing.

The Hulk is still struggling to recock the gun when Mitchell's left hand grabs the barrel, and the hard right of a retired teenage boxing champ simultaneously crashes into the Hulk's nose.

"Sorry 'bout that," Mitchell mutters, shaking the pain from his fist as the Hulk sags to the floor.

Always leave the first two bullet chambers empty, Reid had said. You just never know what's going to happen in a bank.

The three sightseers and their dog had been driving almost two hours desperately searching for a bite of lunch that wasn't likely to bite back. The Arizona deserts can be like that—miles of nothing, then a handpainted sign "Food Ahead," then a ramshackle pile of kindling with luncheon fare enjoyed largely by the local fly population. Reid, Wright, and JoAnne were getting grumpy with hunger pangs when they finally pulled into the roadside burger stand. It was no Maxim's, but at least there was a screen over the takeout window. Always a promising sign.

Reid and JoAnne ordered Diet Cokes, fries, and two cheeseburgers, the works, and devoured it all on the spot.

Wright ordered a regular Coke and a plain burger, threw it all into the garbage, and got back in the car.

"Hey, Weirdo, you not hungry anymore?" Reid asked through the car window.

Wright didn't look up from his book. "I ordered a regular Coke and a plain burger. I got a Diet Coke and a burger with mustard on it."

Reid just shook his head—one of the most feared bank robbers in the West would rather go hungry than ask the man at the burger stand to exchange a soft drink and scrape mustard off a burger.

Wright had dropped out of flying school after the second lesson. No excuses. No explanations. He just never showed up again. Instead, he retired to his favorite rock beside Oak Creek, the hobbit comfortably ensconced in Hermit Haven. He never spoke to the Kitteredges nor any of the other inhabitants of the Forest Houses who might pass by. If they happened to say hello, he would just nod. Nice day; another nod. He never smiled. Sometimes he would toss a stick to Chicago who had become his full-time companion, more friend than dog. Mostly, he would pass long hours just watching the water slide over the smooth stones. Alone with his thoughts. Whatever they were.

It was the same on his trips to the Painted Desert, a hauntingly desolate remnant of geological time, rimmed by red rock canyons to the east, the black silhouettes of the snowcapped San Francisco peaks to the west. Here the sediment of ancient rivers and oceans had dried into a vast seabed of solitude, ironed flat and splashed with onyx of pink, mauve, peach, and charcoal. Sometimes Wright would take Chicago there to wander in the bleak wilderness like the Navajo had done for centuries. It was easy to feel at peace, alone with the low growl of the wind churning the red dust in its path like some ghostly stampede charging across the desert floor. Sometimes he would sit there for hours into the night. He used to say the desert only looks empty, so dry and so dead. But listen in the stillness and there is life everywhere. Sort of like Lionel, Mitchell had noted.

Wright rarely joined the others for their nights on the town—he couldn't see the point of spending perfectly good stolen money to eat and drink and stand alone in the corner of some bar, when he could eat and drink and sit alone in Sycamore House for nothing and in considerably more comfort. Besides, he had books to read. Mountains of them. At one point, he had ordered an entire Time-Life series on all his favorite subjects—war and Alexander the Great; Pericles on democracy; the great goddess Athena, protectress of civilized life and defender of righteous causes.

One day Wright abruptly packed up the entire series of books and sent them back to Time-Life. He was muttering something about a single passage in one of the books. The authors, it seems, had tried to inject a little color into one of the battle scenes.

Wright and JoAnne had become close friends. He was forever running her errands, taking her to the airport to meet Reid after his flying lessons, making her tea. JoAnne appreciated the attention and treated her housemate with kindness and encouragement.

Wright showed no apparent interest in finding a mate of his own. Sometimes when the gang was on one of its hedonistic rampages through Las Vegas, Wright would call an escort service, vanish for a few hours, and return without comment. But that was it. Lionel was a loner.

Much as the others tried, nothing seemed to penetrate Wright's introversion. Reid and Mitchell got him drunk on screwdrivers once. He only got quieter, his usual one-word answers reduced to no answers at all. Eventually, he had passed out at the table, spent the next two days in bed, and never drank again.

Another time Mitchell put a substantial mound of cocaine in front of Wright. Lionel dutifully sucked one line of the powder into his left nostril, another line into the right one. Then another line into each again, just for good measure. Then he just sat there. Looking at the wall.

For the next ten minutes the others stared at Lionel staring at nothing, hoping he would show at least some flicker of a high. He didn't move. He didn't speak. He didn't smile. Then slowly, almost mechanically, his hand swept across the tabletop and sent a cloud of white dust settling into the deep pile of the shag carpet.

"Lionel!" Mitchell exploded. "That's six hundred bucks you just blew away."

Wright shrugged. "Didn't do nothin' for me."

Aside from being the hermit robber with a bland palate, Wright was the Felix Unger of the Stopwatch Gang, a compulsive neatnik and habitual organizer with an addiction to watches and calendars. His memory was crammed with more dates, facts, and figures than a bookie's betting log. Every month, Reid and Mitchell would find all of their respective bills-payable stacked neatly on the dining room table, stamps already on the envelopes, the checks filled out and waiting for signatures. Wright not only remembered the electricity bill was due on the thirteenth, he also knew the fifteen-digit account number by heart. The gang had accumulated enough aliases for the cast of a Broadway play, but Wright could recite every birth date and every number on every driver's license, vehicle registration, credit card, and phony baptismal certificate ever used by the trio.

Lionel's filing-cabinet mind was also indispensable to the gang's business interests. Mitchell was chief strategist. Reid was in charge of logistics. Wright's job was detail. Lionel spent a lot of time collecting details.

Wright has spent almost ten days casing Diamond's Department Store in Phoenix. The armored-truck company usually needs a trolley to haul away the deposits. Always a good sign. Lionel can recite the average times for every delivery on the armored-truck route; the number of steps from the parking lot to the second-floor vault in the accounting office; the duration of every stoplight from the plaza to the freeway; the turnover frequency of cars parking in the handicap spaces; the maximum driving time from the underground parking garage to the apartment hideout rented just for the occasion.

Only two details are overlooked: namely, the weather and Paddy Mitchell's insistence they wear bulletproof vests—in case of another ambush by another Hulk with better luck than the first one.

The pavement is smoldering in the July heat wave that has pushed the mercury past one hundred degrees. The temperature inside the car is the same as it is outside. Damn air conditioning is broken. Opening the windows doesn't help. The three men in heavy bulletproof vests are soaking in their own sweat. Mitchell is agitating for them to abandon the whole scheme for another, more temperate day. The armored truck is late.

Reid begins the final review of the gameplan, if only to silence Mitchell and distract them all from the stifling heat in the car.

"Okay, so we are running up the back stairs to the second floor—"

"Twenty-seven steps," Wright interjects as though the statistic were somehow vital.

Reid continues: "And we go through the door and turn left to the accounting department—"

"Five paces," Wright interjects again.

"And I head for the far end of the customer counter —"

"Twenty-two feet," Wright adds.

"Okay, Paddy," Reid continues again, "you pick it up from here. What comes next?"

There is no response from the back seat.

"Paddy?"

Mitchell is slumped over in his seat, motionless under the heavy bulletproof vest. He has fainted in the heat.

Diamond's Department Store is abandoned by the Stopwatch Gang for another, more temperate day.

The queue obediently followed the painted lines on the floor of the Flagstaff bureau of the Arizona Department of Transportation, Motor Vehicle Division. Timothy Pfeiffer was passing the time by reading the license application he had just completed, in duplicate, carbon provided: "Is your license currently revoked or under suspension? Are you addicted to narcotic drugs? Are you presently declared incompetent by reason of a mental disability or disease?" Reid checked all the no boxes and wondered what kind of nitwit would ever walk into a license bureau and confess to being a drug-crazed wacko with a suspended license. "Have you had any kind of seizure within the last three years?" Yes, a few seizures of gold, but mostly money, Reid mused. Applicant also seized by police. Several times. "Persons giving false information or fictitious names will be punished under the law A.R.S. 28-472." Reid wondered whether the judge would make the sentence concurrent or consecutive to the other few hundred years he would get for armed robberies too numerous to mention.

"Next."

Reid handed the application—in duplicate, carbon provided—to the clerk with the sequined spectacles and raspy voice. She read over the form several times, all the while tapping the butt-end of her government-issue pen on the countertop. Something was obviously puzzling her. She turned to her computer and entered "Pfeiffer, Timothy

Douglas, DOB 08-08-51." A question mark flashed back at her from the screen.

"When and where did you last have a driver's license?" the woman asked without looking up.

"Never, nowhere," Reid said in a choked whisper.

"Pardon?"

"I said, I have never had a driver's license anywhere," Reid said politely.

The fat lady's eyes rolled behind the sequined glasses. "Mis-ter Piffeef-fer," she said, "it says here that you are twenty-nine years old, and you are trying to tell me that you have never had a driver's license before?"

Reid took a deep breath and tried to look embarrassed: "That's right, ma'am. I've been in prison most of my life, and I just got out."

Now it was the clerk who was embarrassed.

"I hope you didn't escape," she said with a chuckle as she continued her paperwork.

"Oh yeah, just said goodbye to the guard and ran away," the fugitive said with a big smile. "Didn't even pay for lunch."

She laughed.

Reid had managed to calm everyone in George Moore's dental clinic after his stunning cash prepayment of the two thousand dollars. He explained that he liked to set aside money for specific projects and fixing his teeth was one of them. He always tried to pay everything in cash, if possible. "Frankly, I'd rather pay cash than give a bank thirty cents in check charges."

The dentist and his wife and their receptionist, Marilyn Donkersley, had talked a lot about Timmy Pfeiffer since his first visit. The last time the Moores had seen that much cash was when they had sold a Porsche to three fellows in California. Handed over eight thou in a paper bag. Didn't even test-drive the car. Definitely drug dealers. Timmy Pfeiffer was different. He was polite, well mannered, and didn't even have long hair. The three scars on his right cheek were a little ominous. And he was obviously making a pile of money at his business—as the dental work progressed, so did Timmy's wardrobe. The tatty jeans, plain T-shirt, and blown-out running shoes had been replaced with Calvin Klein, Ralph Lauren, and a pair of four-hundred-dollar handmade cowboy boots. And the jewelry—a new heavy gold chain and matching bracelet, gold rings. Lots of new rings.

But Timmy and his wife JoAnne were just such a darn nice couple, it was hard to even imagine them in any other terms. And for every question, Reid always had plausible answers. The money? Well, the entertainment biz was booming...The natty designer clothes? Well, that kind of thing never meant much to him. Actually, happier in the old jeans and running shoes. But business is business and sometimes you just have to dress the part. That's what the entertainment crowd is like...Goldie Hawn? Sure, he had met Goldie Hawn. Did some work on her last film. Lives in a big house in Malibu, just down the street from Bobby Dylan...

Over the course of the summer, the Moores had come to enjoy Timmy Pfeiffer's regular visits. The dentist was himself an avid flying buff, and the two talked so much it was sometimes hard to immobilize the patient's mouth for treatment. Timmy always had colorful tales of his latest jet-set adventures with JoAnne. One week it would be a whirlwind gambling tour of Las Vegas, the next an outrageous shopping spree in the designer money sinks of Scottsdale, the next a romantic long weekend at the El Tovar Hotel, a magnificent log chateau overlooking the south rim of the Grand Canyon.

It was a wonderful lifestyle, all right, the envy of even well-to-do folk like the Moores. Plenty of money. Plenty of time. Plenty of freedom. But it wasn't all just fun and games, the dentist and his wife had agreed. Timmy did seem to have to spend a lot of time on the road. Out of town. On business.

The bank in Seattle, Washington, is nothing special. Hardly worth the four-day drive from Sedona after Mitchell refused to fly. But there is fifty thousand dollars of the gang's money stuffed in a bank deposit box, put there for safekeeping a few months earlier during Paddy's redemption tour with Carol-Sue. Mitchell had insisted his partners be there when he retrieved the loot, just in case something went wrong. His partners figured that while they were all in town, they might as well knock over the bank up the street.

The score is nothing special, either. Reid takes control of the bank. Wright goes over the counter. Mitchell is driving—he is in no mood to risk another confrontation with another Hulk.

Suddenly, a female customer in the corner of the bank bursts into loud sobbing. Reid moves towards her.

"Oh God, please don't hurt my baby," she shrieks as he approaches. Reid notices something protruding from under the prone body of the terrified mother. He looks closer—two tiny black shoes and a little girl's pink leggings.

"Hey, hey, just relax, lady," Reid says, his own voice choking. "No one is going to get hurt. This will all be over in a minute. Try to take it easy. No one is going to hurt your baby."

Reid glances over at the counter. Wright has barely cleaned out one till and is about to put a crowbar to the second. Three more to go after that.

"Time!" Reid hollers. "Time! Let's go."

It doesn't matter that the aborted take will barely cover the gas for the trip. Reid doesn't care. He just wants to be out of there. Away from the sobbing mother. Away from the two tiny black shoes and a little girl's pink leggings.

The approach of autumn did nothing to cool Paddy Mitchell's heated infatuation with Miss Rebecca. She was his Princess. He was her Sweetie. Together they spent afternoons hiking in the canyon, picnicking in the tall grass of the upper plateaux high above the Verde Valley sprawling to the horizon. Evenings were routinely spent at the Poco Diablo Bar. She worked. He watched. People noticed they touched a lot.

On days when Princess wasn't slinging beer and Sweetie wasn't robbing banks, they would often head out of town in his flashy new van. Fully loaded. AM-FM quad stereo. Leather seats. Tinted glass. A beer fridge in the back. The word "Streaker" was emblazoned in huge letters on both sides. Lionel called it the Paddywagon.

Beckie thought her Sweetie a bit square, especially for someone who was only supposed to be eight years her senior. The night the whole gang and girlfriends went to *The Rocky Horror Picture Show* in nearby Flagstaff, Mitchell refused even to stand in line with the film's cult following dressed to resemble the transvestite star. Inside, the audience participation in the Grade-B musical was more entertaining than the flick, but Mitchell walked out after ten minutes. Said he couldn't hear a damn thing.

Sweetie and his Princess also suffered a considerable generation gap on the issue of the New Age Movement, a curious mix of granola spiritual causes linked by the belief that Sedona is one of the earth's primary vortices of psychic energy. In 1980 the marketing gurus had turned it all into a healthy cottage industry—books, brochures, even authentic vortex tours complete with "frequent sightings of alien spacecraft." Beckie thought this all pretty fascinating stuff. Paddy allowed that the flying saucers seemed to have left behind a lot of space cadets, all right.

Overall, Beckie figured she had stumbled upon nothing more complicated than Mr. Nice Guy. Maybe even Mr. Right. He was gentle and fun to be around. Obviously, he had lots of money; the family chateau sounded pretty nice. Some of his stories didn't quite jibe—like the big inheritance from his dead parents who were still running a winery in the south of France. And if he were such an avid skier, how come he thought the Matterhorn was in Colorado? But none of that seemed to matter much. He was her Sweetie and she was his Princess. Beckie had never met anyone quite like Paddy Mitchell before.

After Beckie, Mitchell's greatest love seemed to be Las Vegas. Glitter Gulch embodied everything that Paddy's imagination could concoct for the Mike Garrison who had spun life's wheel of fortune and won: wealth, power, success, and excitement. It was all there in a kingdom of tuxedos, chandeliers, and scantily clad waitresses—his idea of a classy place full of classy people who showed him respect and kowtowed to his every nod as though they really cared.

Mitchell would settle for nothing less than Caesar's Palace, glitziest of the glitzy, the penthouse of Fantasy Island. A thousand-dollar suite with jacuzzi and more television sets than there were channels. Dinner in the Bacchanal—a gluttonous seven-course meal, half-naked "slave-girls" pouring wine from goatskins held shoulder-high. Then it would be off to a show—Paddy would pay anything to see Wayne Newton.

Usually Mitchell would head for Caesar's famed baccarat pit, where security guards hover over more than seven hundred thousand dollars in chips at each table, where minimum wagers are a grand, and routine bets are fifty times that much. Sometimes he would wager, but mostly he would watch the others at play in the pit. If that kind of money couldn't buy happiness, he and his Princess could at least have a lot of fun shopping for it.

Paddy Mitchell didn't just want money; he wanted *that* kind of money. All he needed was one big score. The Dream Score...

While Mitchell was busy trying to replay adolescence, Reid and JoAnne had become the perfect yuppies of Sedona. Timmy Pfeiffer, entrepreneur of the entertainment biz, was eating homemade muffins and skinless chicken, and could usually be found jogging before bed. No more drugs. Booze in moderation. He was even thinking of joining a money-back-guaranteed program to quit smoking—maybe next week. His flying lessons were going so well after only two months that Jack Seeley was already talking about booking the final licensing exam.

At the same time, JoAnne had enrolled in photography and sewing classes at the nearby Yavapai College. Her instructors were certainly impressed, if not slightly overwhelmed, with her beginner's camera kit. Every week she would show up with a motordrive or telephoto lens. Always the most expensive. JoAnne said she had a generous husband.

"Funny thing about him, though," JoAnne once told a classmate. "Wow, is he camera shy. Just for fun, I'll hide and try to ambush him. Boom! He gets furious if I even point a lens in his direction. Weird, eh?"

In their earlier days in Sedona, Reid and JoAnne hung out a lot at the rough-and-tumble Oak Creek Tavern, birthplace of the famed Cowboy Artists of America, all of whom had long since moved along to the trendier hangouts. Similarly, as time rolled on and the money rolled in, Timmy and JoAnne preferred the sedentary sophistication of Rene's Restaurant at the chic end of town.

Jan Bauda and her husband Rene thought their two regular patrons were perfectly delightful. JoAnne always ordered a sherry; he drank Heineken. DeeDee Nigh usually served them and thought Timmy seemed a bit bored, or maybe nervous. It was hard to tell in the dim lighting. But he also left behind generous tips. Twenty bucks for a couple of drinks. She sure appreciated that a lot. Even mentioned it to her husband a couple of times—nice folks, big tippers. He was a deputy with the local Coconino County Sheriff's Department.

Over the summer Reid and JoAnne had also become pals with a Texas couple who played butler and maid and general housesitters to a California tycoon with a mansion on the edge of Sedona. John and Cathy had pretty nice jobs for a couple of young vagabonds. Eight hundred a month each, use of a Cadillac Seville, and a pile of gold cards to keep the place stocked when the tycoon was in town. Conveniently, that was only about six weeks a year, which left the palace open for unauthorized parties the rest of the time. With Reid's money and his pals' access to the mansion, the two couples entertained in grand style. Reid thought it all just good mischief at the expense of the absentee tycoon, who happened to be absent running one of the largest armored-truck companies in the West.

But no one was closer to Timothy Pfeiffer than Jack and Judy Seeley—quite likely, he had never had better straight friends. They in turn considered him more family than friend—Judy didn't just refer to him as Timmy, he was her Timmy.

One day Jack suggested that it would be a wonderful idea for Timmy to join the Sedona chapter of the Jaycees. Reid ranked that idea right up there with Judy's invitation to dinner with the sheriff and his wife, but allowed that he would attend a breakfast meeting as Jack's guest. Surely there could be no harm in that.

The next morning Reid sat in the parking lot across from the restaurant where the local Jaycees were gathering. He waited for just the right moment, not early enough to have to mingle, not late enough to be noticed winding his way through the tables to join Jack. There were two others at the table, an insurance salesman and a real estate agent. Reid feigned interest in acquiring large amounts of both commodities to steer the conversation away from his own business interests.

"Fellow Jaycees and guests," a man said into the microphone. "We are truly honored today to have with us as our guest speaker one of Arizona's most prominent and respected judges who is going to tell us what we can all do to help get criminals off our streets and behind bars where they belong..."

As the room burst into applause, Jack Seeley noticed his guest was gagging on a mouthful of scrambled eggs.

Reid had bumped into Deputy Gary a lot since the gang had moved to Sedona. Usually, they met at the airport. The lawman was a flyer himself and, like just about every other buff in the place, when he wasn't in the air, he was on the tarmac kicking tires and talking aviation. Their chats were friendly if trite—a comment about the weather, a jealous sneer at the line of private Learjets parked beside the runway. One of America's most-wanted bandits wasn't about to invite a pair of handcuffs to dinner at Sycamore House, but he had no fear of their encounters, either. In fact, Stephen Reid quite reveled in the charade.

One afternoon in mid-September, Deputy Gary walked into the airport coffee shop, slapping the red dust from his Stetson.

"So, what are Sedona's two worst excuses for working folk up to today?" the deputy sheriff chuckled as he joined his pals Timmy and Jack for coffee.

"Just about to take the Cessna for a run up to Jerome for a look at a piece of real estate," Reid said casually. "Supposed to be a nice place—two acres, four bedrooms, three fireplaces, a pool. You know, all the toys."

Deputy Gary let out a long, low whistle. "I just don't know where people get that kind of money," he said, shaking his head. "I mean, the real estate prices these days."

Reid took a deep breath and stretched: "Yeah, you pretty well gotta be robbing banks, all right."

"A *whole lot* of banks," the lawman retorted, laughing at his own apparent wittiness.

Deputy Gary was still chortling to himself as he left the coffee shop. So was Stephen Reid.

A few days later, on Wednesday, September 17, 1980, Lionel Wright placed a long-distance call from San Diego to the pay phone at Sycamore House.

Friday morning, Patrick Mitchell kissed his Princess good-bye, climbed into his car, and drove south out of Sedona.

Sunday evening, Stephen Reid was reading the newspaper in the Seeleys' living room. Judy was in the kitchen making dinner. The two had just finished exchanging barbs about his new short haircut, and how different his face looked without his mustache.

"Well, Jude, guess Jack told you he's flying me to Phoenix in the morning," Reid half shouted to the kitchen.

"What's up, Timmy?" she hollered back.

"Ah, just running a little low on cash. Gotta go back to work."

CHAPTER SIXTEEN

San Diego, California, September 23, 1980

The widening spots of sweat on Reid's blue dress shirt are cold to his skin. He glances at the gold chronometer strapped to his right wrist, just above his gun hand. 10:35. Dammit. Where the hell is that Loomis truck? They have been sitting in the middle of the bank for a full quarter of an hour. Still no sign of the money. Someone is bound to get suspicious. Banks are boring places; no one but an employee spends a lot of time there. Someone is bound to start asking questions. Or call the cops.

He shuffles the loan application papers on the round table in front of him and scans the bank. Three customers are at the long counter, doing their banking with three tellers. Another half-dozen people are hunched over desks piled high with canceled checks and computerized statements. He recognizes one of them. Held her up in April before the branch moved down the street. She doesn't recognize him without a Klingon mask. In fact, no one seems to be paying him any heed. But who knows what calls have been made from a rear office? Who knows if someone has hit the silent alarm?

He glances up at the security cameras. Big Brother is watching. Big Brother tells all to Norman A. Zigrossi and his fellow agents of the San Diego bureau of the FBI. Where the hell is that Loomis truck?

The pounding in his ears is getting louder and faster. He glances across the bank at Lionel Wright fidgeting with the knot in his yellow tie. Maybe Paddy was right when he said the whole idea was insane: two of the most hunted fugitives on the continent sitting in a Bank of America branch, thinly disguised as bearded businessmen in full view of the staff and security cameras, waiting to ambush an armored transport company guard with a .38 Smith & Wesson on his hip and a pump-action shotgun in the truck. If the truck ever arrives...

Paddy Mitchell hadn't liked the plan from the beginning. It was one thing to storm into a bank, steal some money, and run away in less than ninety seconds. But sauntering in and just hanging around waiting for an armored truck to arrive with the money, well, that was a whole different ballgame.

First, there was the danger of going gun-to-gun with armed guards. The whole reason for meticulous planning, Mitchell noted, was precisely to avoid going gun-to-gun with anyone. As the Norco bandits had discovered the hard way, shootouts heavily favor the Good Guys winning in the end. Besides, Paddy Mitchell had no inclination to kill anyone, much less be killed.

But what had bothered him most were all the variables involved in robbing a bank from the inside out. Clearly, a hit on an armored-car delivery in broad daylight was going to take months of painstaking preparation, and more ingenuity than any other twenty Stopwatch robberies combined. It was also going to cost a bundle to pull off, probably more than most others in their profession would steal in a year.

In short, about all the mastermind liked about the plan was the money. Paddy Mitchell just wanted one big score. Then they could all retire.

The Stopwatch Gang hadn't exactly picked the Pacific Beach branch of the Bank of America at random. The same outlet with the same staff had originally been located further up Garnet Avenue. The gang had knocked that one off in April, back in the days when Mitchell was still wearing the stopwatch around his neck. Apparently, that heist had been the last straw—after five holdups in one year, the battle-weary branch was relocated in late spring to a spiffy brick building down the street. New location; same old problem. More precisely, the B of A had unwittingly moved next door to the gang it was trying to shake. At that time, Lionel Wright's Emerald Avenue apartment was a block away. Stephen Reid and Paddy Mitchell were still five blocks in the other direction, shortly before they abandoned their hideout condo on Ocean Front Walk.

Since all three robbers had opened accounts at the old branch so they could case the joint before knocking it off in April, the bank was kind enough to mail them invitations to continue their patronage at the new location. The Stopwatch Gang was only too happy to oblige.

At first they had planned nothing more than the usual—in the door, over the counter, grab the money, leave. All they had to do was rerun their April score at a new address. But their early surveillance of the new bank revealed a remarkable coincidence: the Loomis Armored Transport Company made cash pickups and deliveries at the bank each Tuesday morning between 10:20 and 10:30. Never later, never earlier. Remarkably punctual. It was also the only pickup of the week. Remarkably large.

Wright was dispatched to gather necessary data for a preliminary assessment. His first stop was the public library where he pored over the city directory, a treasure chest of information that matches each municipal address with the names, professions, and phone numbers of the occupants. By the time he was finished, Wright had a detailed profile of the neighborhood within twelve blocks of the bank.

The police department was a safe distance away, and there were no hidden substations. A lot of the residents were listed as "retired," and none was listed as a police officer. A mid-robbery encounter with local pensioners was manageable. A mid-robbery encounter with local off-duty lawmen was not. American cops always carried a gun somewhere.

The next stop was the local office of the AAA—Wright was a member—for the latest and most detailed street maps of the area. What was their best getaway route (the bank was almost close enough for them to run home with the money)? Where were there medians that could hem them in? What was the most likely route the police would take to get to the scene?

Just as the plan was taking shape, it was suddenly abandoned with the hasty exodus of the gang from California in early May—Mitchell north towards salvation, the others to Sedona. But Wright kept the Emerald Avenue apartment as a future command post—just in case they changed their minds.

Their minds changed the day after Mitchell arrived in Sedona, fresh from his salvation tour and still pushing that one big score. Just one.

In the ensuing months, the gang had kept bankers' hours in and around the target bank. Even from Sedona, they frequented San Diego "on business" specifically to continue their surveillance. Each of them had a jogger's stopwatch on his wrist to time every move of the Loomis guards making their weekly deliveries, every move the gang would have to make to relieve said guards of their burden.

Every dimension of the bank was paced and repaced—Lionel eventually had enough measurements to rebuild the place on a vacant lot. Every inch of the short getaway route was driven and redriven, always on Tuesday mornings between ten-thirty and eleven o'clock. Three alternative routes were chosen and driven, just in case the fleeing bandits encountered road construction, an accident, or a stray police cruiser in the neighborhood.

There were the usual arguments about the most suitable location to switch getaway cars and the best place to hide out while they changed clothes, cut the cash, destroyed the evidence, and waited for the police roadblocks to be removed. Reid always wanted to get as far away from the scene of the crime as possible, preferably four exits down the freeway—a relatively short drive to a whole different part of town. Paddy Mitchell would have preferred to hole up in the bank's basement, if possible—he could never get into hiding fast enough.

Someone has entered the bank and is approaching Reid's back. The footsteps are getting closer. They stop only a few feet from his right shoulder. There are movements and noises he cannot decipher. He strains to hear. Sounds like keys rattling. He closes his eyes in relief. A female customer is rummaging through her purse in search of something evidently vital to her banking. He watches her pass en route to the customer counter. Where the hell is that Loomis truck?

Reid mops the perspiration from his forehead and grimaces at the thick, brown residue on his white handkerchief. Smeared make-up. Someone is bound to get suspicious now. He touches his fingers to the corners of his fake heavy black beard and mustache. The black wig feels like it is starting to ride back on his forehead. Maybe it's just his imagination.

He checks his watch again and shoots an anxious glance across the floor to the short counter where Lionel Wright is pretending to fill out a withdrawal slip. The blond Vandyke beard, styled wig, heavy horn-rimmed spectacles, and tan suit with brown stitching have transformed the homely hermit into a homely beatnik...Shit...Eighteen minutes and still no Loomis truck... Someone has to be suspicious by now...No one really takes that long to fill out a withdrawal slip...No one really looks like Lionel.

By the time the gang gathered around the oak dining table at Sycamore House one evening in late summer, they figured they knew as much about the Pacific Beach neighborhood as the city planners; as much about the Bank of America branch as the branch manager; as much about the Pacific Beach pickups and deliveries of the Loomis Armored Transport Company as the guards themselves. But there remained one rather significant question—how to steal the money.

Mitchell spent the entire evening at Sycamore House studying Wright's meticulous bank blueprints spread out on the oak table.

"Okay, we know the truck is going to arrive between 10:20 and 10:30, and back in here," Mitchell began, pointing to the handicapped parking spaces in front of the side entrance to the bank.

"What if a couple of real cripples get there first?" Wright asked.

"I dunno, Lionel," Mitchell sighed. "Maybe the Loomis guys will have the cars towed. It's not important. I'm sure they'll find a place to park. Anyway, we know there are always two guards. The driver stays in the truck. The poor sucker in the back gets to do all the legwork."

"What if there are three of them?" Wright asked.

"What if the whole U.S. Army shows up?" Mitchell snapped. "We'll get to that. Anyway, the first loads are going to be boxes of Federal Reserve coin going into the bank, bags of unrolled coin coming back out to the truck."

"Forty-seven pounds apiece," Lionel interjected. "I called the feds."

"Jesus, Weirdo," Mitchell said with obvious frustration. "Unless you've got a lot of laundry to do, we don't care about the goddam boxes of quarters."

Mitchell lit a fresh cigar and took a long drag. "Anyway," he continued, "the last load in and the last load out are always the bags of bills. But grabbing the delivery is out of the question. The clerk in the vault locks herself up with the cash until she's got it all put away. One of those plexiglass doors over the entrance, just like the one that shut us out over on Balboa. My bet is it's all on timers—she couldn't let us in if her life depended on it."

Mitchell punched his cigar into the ashtray: "Somehow we've got to get at those bags between the time they leave the vault and the time they get loaded into the wagon."

"So we take down the guard," Reid said casually.

"Yeah, right," Mitchell scoffed. "You seem to forget those guys are both packing .38s, and God-knows-what kind of artillery in that truck. I'm not doing all this just for something to leave in my will."

"Ah, relax," Reid sighed. "We're the ones with a plan. We've got surprise on our side. And we've already got our guns drawn. These guys ain't no Wyatt Earp."

"Yeah, well, we ain't no John Wayne, either," Mitchell said. "No shootouts, period."

Discussion went on into the night. They all agreed that attempting anything outside the bank was out of the question. It would be certain to engage both guards, and that would be almost as certain to get someone killed.

They talked about rushing through the front door of the bank to intercept the one guard entering and leaving with his loads through the side entrance. But that plan was discarded, too: there would be no way of telling from the outside whether a particular trolley load leaving the vault would be carrying bags of loose coin or the target haul of paper currency.

"The only way to pull this off would be sitting in the bank, watching for the paper load," Mitchell said with a shrug. "And that would be totally insane."

There was silence around the table. Mitchell's mind was groping for another plan—maybe a sudden diversion outside the bank would get the guard to leave his loaded trolley long enough for them to grab the cash and bolt out the other door.

Wright was jotting numbers on a scrap of paper. For weeks, he had been trying to calculate the number of bills in a bank bag.

Reid was pondering the imponderable.

"Well, I'm ready to plead insanity," Reid finally said with a broad smile.

"Sit in the bank?" Mitchell laughed. "You can't be serious."

"How 'bout you, Lionel?" Reid continued. "You up for joining me in the loony bin?"

The snaps on the briefcase open with two thwacks that sound like rifle shots to the bandit-in-waiting. Reid scans the bank. The noise doesn't seem to have attracted attention. But who knows? He lifts the corner of the newspaper folded in the case and rearranges the snubnosed revolver. A siren wails in the distance. He reaches under the newspaper again and clicks open the safety latch on the Uzi submachine gun. God have mercy on him if he has to use it. God have mercy on everyone in the place.

A suspicious teller is staring at Reid's bowed head. He can feel it. Maybe just his imagination again. He is afraid to look up, afraid to meet her eyes. Dammit, where the hell is that Loomis truck?

The siren fades, then nothing. He closes the lid of the briefcase and goes back to filling in the loan application...Paddy was right: this is insane...But what does Paddy care? He's sitting pretty in the car while we're sitting ducks in the bank.

Paddy Mitchell had finally given in to the plan he still thought insane. If the other two wanted to sit in a bank playing Mr. Dress-Up for the security cameras, that was their choice. But no one was getting him any closer to the action than the driver's seat of the getaway car. In return, Reid and Wright would be able to leave town clean—no guns, no money—after the robbery. Mitchell would drive himself and the evidence back to Arizona.

In the subsequent months, Mitchell's reluctance had turned to enthusiasm as they watched the weekly Loomis ritual. He estimated at least a million dollars left the bank on that last trolley trip every Tuesday. A third of that would put him into retirement quite nicely for a long time. Wright's mathematical calculations came to a fraction of that amount, but Paddy would never listen—he wanted every job to be their last. Just one big score.

September had been a busy month for the gang's one-man-detail detail. Wright's crime shopper's list of necessities was unusually long and complicated. He began ticking the items off one by one.

Disguises: Check. Wright found everything he needed to know about disguises at the San Diego Public Library. The book was called *Theatrical Make-Up*, a handy guide to temporary plastic surgery. Fake beards and wigs were bought at various costume shops in Los Angeles—the masquerade store just up the street from the target bank was certain to be the first stop for the FBI. The phony eye glasses were a little more difficult—no one walks into the neighborhood optometrist's asking for two pairs of plain lenses. But Mitchell had the lie for that one—he just wanted a light tint to cut the glare from his computer screen.

Guns: Check. There were already enough guns in the steamer trunk at the Sedona U-Store for a small coup d'état. Reid had recently added two stolen Uzi submachine guns to the collection. Bought them from a gun thief driving a Mercedes 450-SL. Stolen, of course.

Bearcat Scanner: Check. The perfect gift for audio voyeurs and other busybodies, the compact radio receiver scans police frequencies to eavesdrop on their communications. Plugged into the cigarette lighter of the getaway car, the device would instantly alert Mitchell to any dispatcher calling all cars to a robbery-in-progress. Three long blasts on the car horn would mean bad news on the airwaves. Abandon the bank and run like hell.

Bank Parking: Check. Reid and Wright would be coming out the door facing Garnet Avenue. Fifteen steps to the getaway car. Mitchell could even keep an eye on the Loomis truck from there. Perfect. Except it was a no-stopping zone. The alternative was to wait around the corner on Bayard Avenue at the opposite end of the bank from the armored truck. It would be further for the fleeing fugitives to run, and Mitchell couldn't see a damn thing from there. But it was better than Reid and Wright, bank bags in hand, running head-on into a traffic cop writing a parking ticket.

Getaway Car: Check. The vehicle suitable for such a dangerous mission sparked much heated debate among the trio. No one wanted to risk stealing a car—the stakes of getting caught at such a relatively petty criminal act had become just too high. Buying one would require registration. Renting one would also leave a paper trail, but a much harder one for the FBI to find among all the hundreds of leasing agencies in California. Finally, all three agreed: renting was probably safe. Besides, it was easy.

Underground Parking: Check. An apartment building close to the Emerald Avenue hideout conveniently had two indoor parking spaces for lease, complete with a remote door opener. In less than two minutes, the gang could switch the money, guns, and disguises from the getaway car to Wright's Buick, change their clothes, and walk to the Emerald Avenue flat only half a block away.

Waste Disposal: Check. When he hadn't been busy following the Loomis Armored Car Company on its rounds, Wright had been dogging the local garbage truck. Aside from the stolen money, nothing would pin them to the robbery faster than a bag of make-up, wigs, and fake beards. Wright was taking no chances—the telltale refuse had to go straight from the trunk of his car into the garbage truck compactor. The rendezvous would take place at Hospitality Point in nearby Mission Bay Park where the city emptied the trash bins every Wednesday afternoon between one o'clock and one-thirty. The timing was perfect. He could drop off the evidence on his way out of San Diego en route to the Los Angeles airport.

Miscellaneous: Check. One attaché case and two bank loan applications for Reid. One two-inch belt holster for Wright. Three rolls of fluorescent red tape to create diversionary pinstripes on the car. One freshly stolen license plate to be attached with four pieces of double-sided, picture-hanging tape. One large plastic trash bag for Wright's garbage rendezvous in the park. One box of Band-Aids to keep the bandits' fingerprints off bank property—gloves with business suits in September were obviously out of the question.

At 3:04 p.m. on September 22, 1980, one Ronald P. Scott, Arizona driver's license FF26391, rented a navy blue Ford LTD, four-door model, at Lindbergh Field, San Diego, from Hertz. Approximately thirty minutes later, Scott met one Timothy D. Pfeiffer of Spectre Entertainment Marketing, who had just arrived on air commuter service from Phoenix. The two left the airport together and drove off in a navy blue Ford.

Paddy Mitchell might as well be waiting for a bomb to drop on the hood of the Hertz getaway car. For over twenty minutes he has been squirming in the driver's seat of the Ford LTD, his eyes searching wildly in every direction—towards the front doors of the bank, out the rearview mirror, then at his watch, out the front, out one side window, then the other, then at his watch again. Hands wringing the wheel. A cup of early-morning instant coffee has turned to bile in his throat. Where is that truck? Why are they still in the bank?...Told them this whole thing was insanity...

Mitchell has already done his duty. The stolen California license plate is securely fastened over the rear rental tag with four pieces of picture-hanging tape. Now all he can do is wait for his partners in the bank. Or for a SWAT team.

The Bearcat scanner on the front seat is flipping automatically from one emergency channel to another. He hears a dispatcher's voice with a coded call to action, then static, then another voice on another channel, then more static..."We have a ten-thirty-two house fire..." Static. "...we show no outstanding warrants on the registered owner of vehicle number..." More static. "Car five-nine, are you responding to that ten-sixteen multiple vehicle on..." More static. "...we are confirming that alarm..."

Alarm! What fucking alarm? Mitchell lunges for the hold button on the scanner to lock on the channel, but it is too late. The machine has gone on to another channel…"dispatch, this is three-six…I'll be ten-thirteen for lunch in about five minutes…"

Mitchell grabs onto the key in the ignition and twists hard enough to bend the metal. The V-8 roars. The heel of his left hand slams into the padded steering-wheel center. The scanner is silent. So is the horn.

The gang's Emerald Avenue command post had been shrouded in an early-morning mist as Paddy Mitchell stood in front of the picture window, running and rerunning every second of the plan, the cup of tepid instant coffee in his hand. He was trying to think it all through again. Too many damn angles; that's what was wrong with this whole insane scheme. Too many things that could go wrong.

Stephen Reid has been in front of the mirror, transforming his complexion to Arabian with smears of dark make-up, the three telltale scars on his right cheek smothered under paste and powder. He secured the heavy black wig with bobby pins, and glued down the matching beard and mustache. He tightened his blue silk tie and buttoned the vest on his natty, dark blue business suit. Finally, he wrapped Band-Aids over the thumb and first two fingers of each hand to cover his fingerprints.

Lionel Wright had been over at the underground garage, taping red racing stripes on the dark blue Hertz rent-a-car. He walked back into the Emerald Avenue apartment, and let out a rare burst of laughter, noting that Reid looked more the part of a terrorist planning to blow up a bank.

"Well now, no one would ever suspect you're going to rob a bank, that's for sure," Wright snickered. "They'll think you're going to blow the fucking place up. Ladies and gentlemen, please welcome Carlos the Terrorist. Cute."

An hour later it was Reid's turn to laugh as Lionel emerged from the bathroom in full goatee and blond wig. The tan suit with dark brown stitching looked like something from the boys' department, circa 1960. Reid wondered why his odd friend would want to make himself look nerdier than usual. He wondered how that was possible. The .38 hanging from Wright's belt looked as incongruous as the Gerber baby with a bazooka.

Mitchell spread the blueprint of the bank on the kitchen table and began the final rehearsal.

The model prisoners—
Paddy Mitchell and
Stephen Reid at Mill-
haven Penitentiary.
Being good boys meant
doing less time—in
their case, a whole lot
less time.

Lionel ''the Ghost''
Wright (left) poses in
the jail-yard for a
going-away shot with
Stephen Reid (right)
and an unidentified
friend. Not long after
this, the Ghost
vanished.

Paddy Mitchell's first mug-shot (right) before his infamous heart attack. In this and subsequent shots, he would close his eyes or screw up his face to make it harder for police to recognize him. (Below) Paddy's last mugshot, taken thirteen years and two prison escapes later. By then, he was enlisting plastic surgeons to really change his face.

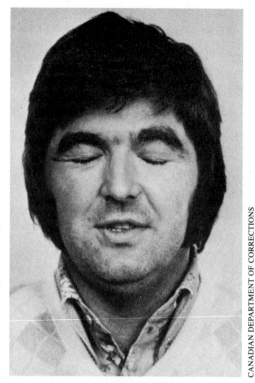

CANADIAN DEPARTMENT OF CORRECTIONS

OTTAWA CITIZEN

MINISTRY OF THE SOLICITOR GENERAL

Stephen Reid's first mugshot, taken before the former flower child had perfected the technique of dine-and-dash: two identical escapes, only the menu changed.

SUSAN MUSGRAVE

Stephen Reid eventually returned to Canada, married well-known poet Susan Musgrave, and began raising a family in a pretty seaside cottage on Vancouver Island.

Lionel Wright's first mugshot (below). The shy former clerk took care of all those annoying details of the bank robbery biz.

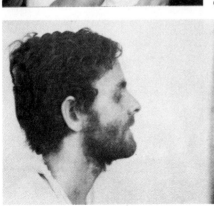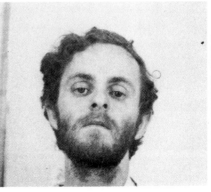

MINISTRY OF THE SOLICITOR GENERAL

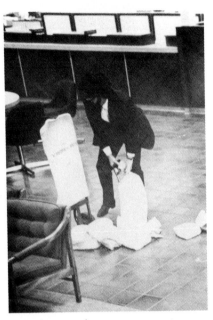

"Okay, folks, this is a holdup," yells a heavily disguised Stephen Reid. "Let's not have any heroes today, please."

Reid struggles with the money bags. Darn, just too many to carry.

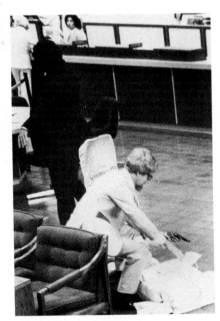

Lionel Wright, disguised more as a beatnik than a bandit, gives it a try.

Now they have the bags, but there goes the briefcase . . .

Moneybags and briefcase finally under control, Wright and Reid head for the getaway car, where Paddy Mitchell waits—if he hasn't panicked and left.

Photos of the Stopwatch Gang's final bank heist in 1980, the largest in San Diego's history.

Every fugitive's dream (left)—the gang's magnificent cedar-and-glass hideout in Oak Creek Canyon near Sedona, Arizona. They befriended the local townsfolk, including the deputy sheriff, who thought they were all just nice fellas with too much money and plenty of time on their hands.

"Ah, the Good Life," Paddy (below) used to say. He figured it couldn't get much better: a pretty girlfriend, a beautiful home, and lots of money.

The many faces of Patrick Michael Mitchell.

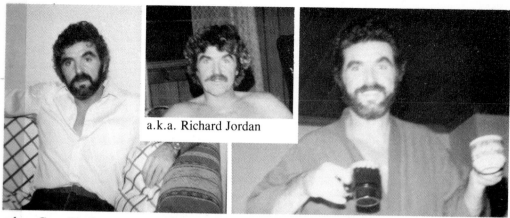

a.k.a. Richard Jordan

a.k.a. Gary Blackstone

a.k.a. Michael Lawrence Garrison

a.k.a. Richard
Joseph Landry

a.k.a. The Galloping Gourmet

a.k.a. Richard Jordan Baird

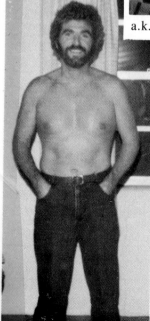

a.k.a. Michael Brewer

a.k.a. Gary Weber

a.k.a. Roger L. Lanthorn

Paddy Mitchell graduates to the FBI's notorious "Ten Most Wanted" list with this poster showing "the most widely traveled fingerprints in America."

LA PRESSE, MONTREAL

The Dream Score: in 1990, $16.5 million in cash, securities, and gold bars were stolen from this Brinks chartered aircraft at Montreal's Dorval Airport en route from New York. Paddy Mitchell had talked about it for years before, "just one big score and we can all retire."

"Okay, we make a pass by the bank at 10:15 and check for the truck, just in case it's early," Mitchell began. "If it's not there, we continue up Garnet, swing around here, and head back to the bank again—"

"Two minutes, thirty seconds," Wright interjected.

"Right," Mitchell continued. "So I pull us up here, at the end of the bank and you guys head for the score. That should put you inside at 10:20."

"What if the truck's late?" Wright asked.

"Then we complain to the company," Mitchell snapped. "You're the ones who wanted to go in there ahead of the truck to give you time to read the place. I think it's insane, but—"

"Okay, okay," Reid grumbled. "Let's keep going. They've never been late yet."

Detail by detail, they plodded through the plan. Wright would take up his position at the withdrawal-slip counter just inside the front doors. Reid would be seated with his back to the side entrance used by the guard, facing the vault and the oncoming loads heading back to the truck. The positions would give them control of both doors—a customer chancing on the scene could be discouraged from running back onto the street and screaming for help.

"If they are late, how long do we wait?" Wright persisted.

"Until it's time to go to lunch," Reid said sarcastically, not wanting to even contemplate such an event. "We'll know when we've overstayed our welcome. We'll know."

"What if there are three guards," Wright asked, "and one of them happens to be wandering around outside with a shotgun?

Mitchell lit his first cigar of the morning, the smoke pouring onto the blueprint like the morning mist still rolling over Pacific Beach.

"You pray he's a lousy shot."

Reid twists his head and glances at the glass doors behind him as though the missing Loomis guard might somehow be frozen back there somewhere. He checks his watch. 10:43. They have been in the bank for twenty-three minutes. It's time to call the whole thing off. A teller stares at him for a moment, then turns to talk to another employee.

Reid's face looks more burn victim than Arab under the blotched make-up. He glances over at Wright, now dancing nervously from one foot to the other, crumpling another withdrawal slip. It's definitely quitting time.

Reid opens his briefcase and begins stuffing it with the half-completed loan application forms. He just wants to get back to Sedona and the easy life of Timmy Pfeiffer, back to JoAnne, back to his dog, back to his friends. Most of all, he just wants to get the hell away from the Bank of America...Lionel was right—what if the truck is late?...It is late...Too late...Paddy was also right...The whole thing was nuts...Should have listened to Paddy...

Reid's back suddenly stiffens. Paddy. He had almost forgotten about Paddy...

What if Paddy had panicked and left?

CHAPTER SEVENTEEN

San Diego, California

Stephen Reid would never forget the sound.

It was 10:48, almost a full half hour since he and Wright had entered the Bank of America. Reid had been twitching his head towards the front doors. Wright seemed in a trance, frozen at the stand-up counter, another crumpled withdrawal slip clutched in his fist. The eyes behind the horn-rimmed glasses were locked onto something else, something at the other end of the bank, something behind Reid's back.

Then the sound. Faint at first. Then louder.

Just a low hiss, the sound of rubber tires on the freshly waxed tile floor.

There are two thwacks of snap locks on a briefcase. A thin smile splits a fake black beard from a fake black mustache. Then the rustling of loan papers being spread on the small round customer table.

Harlen Lee Hudson of the Loomis Armored Car Company passes with a .38 on his hip and a trolleyload of coin bound for the Bank of America vault. Twenty-five boxes. Forty-seven pounds apiece.

The man who looks like a terrorist with a badly peeling tan nods at the beatnik in the beige suit with dark brown stitching. Somehow, the long-awaited arrival of the Loomis truck has suddenly erased the anxiety of sitting in the bank so long. No point quitting now. Stephen Reid is already tingling at the thought of cutting the cash. One big score and they can all...

The euphoria evaporates. Reid's eyes are riveted on the far end of the bank, on the smoked-plexiglass security door over the entrance to the vault. The guard has been in there too long...Unload the boxes coming in, pick up the bags going out, get the bank clerk to sign a receipt ...How long can that take?...Something is going on in there...Maybe it's all a set-up…Maybe he has been sent in with instructions from the SWAT team outside…Something is wrong. Reid pokes his bandaged thumb and forefinger under the dark-rimmed glasses. Sweat is stinging his eyes.

Reid glances over at Wright, then back at the vault. Loomis guard Harlen Lee Hudson has finally left the vault and is coming straight towards him, pushing a load of white canvas bags. The bandit sizes up his prey—the mirrored sunglasses, the long sideburns, the pencil mustache, the black hair slicked back and receding at the temples, a paunch straining the blue uniform. Cool dude in the 1950s maybe, Reid concludes.

The trolley is only fifteen feet away and closing in. Reid reaches for the briefcase and glances up at the guard again. He bows his head and goes back to the loan application…Shit…Just outbound bags of coin…

Reid scans the bank. Five customers at the counter. How is it possible? Twenty-nine minutes sitting in a bank and no one has become even suspicious enough to advance a may-I-help-you?…If anyone does, it's all over—the blotched make-up is too obvious.

10:50. The hiss of rubber on tile. Harlen Lee Hudson passes again. Another twenty-five boxes of rolled coin. Forty-seven pounds apiece. A teller looks up and catches the mirrored sunglasses looking her way.

"Nice day," he says, and vanishes back into the vault.

Reid reaches into his briefcase and wraps his right hand around the butt of the .38 under the rolled newspaper…This is it…This must be the load of bags stuffed with currency…Nice day, my ass…Showtime…He glances at Wright to exchange a final round of here-we-go signals. But all Reid sees is the top of a styled blond wig. Lionel is struggling with another withdrawal slip.

Reid's grip tightens around the gun handle as Harlen Lee Hudson rounds the end of the customer counter with another load of canvas bags…Another load of coin?…What the fuck is this, national piggy bank week?

The two perspiring bandits exchange shrugs. Reid can hear the hiss again…This has to be the last load…Maybe it doesn't matter…The whole goddam U.S. Marine Corps could be waiting outside for them by now.

Harlen Lee Hudson passes for the fifth time. Only fifteen boxes this time. It is the last load…Please, God, don't let him stop to chat… Please don't let the wheels fall off the fucking trolley…Please—

The sudden blare of a car horn might have been a shotgun blast. Reid's eyes are darting around the bank, first to one corner, then another, to the vault, to the customer counter. He twists in his chair and stares at the doors behind him. Then back towards the vault, the customer counter, then at Wright. Lionel has obviously heard the horn, too. His body stiffens, his left hand reaching beneath the suit jacket for the snubnosed revolver on his belt...Only one honk, not three...But who the hell knows? Someone must have hit the alarm by now...Maybe Paddy forgot his signals in a panic...Maybe it wasn't Paddy at all ...Maybe Paddy left long ago.

Reid already has the briefcase open and his hand on the revolver when Harlen Lee Hudson rounds the customer counter with another trolleyload bound for the armored truck. It is 10:53. Thirty-three minutes late. Bingo. There is no mistaking the cargo: three canvas bags with "Bank of America" stenciled on the outside, each about thirty inches high with corners made almost square around the neatly piled bundles of currency.

The guard is moving at a near run towards the parking-lot doors, towards the small round table, towards the man with a black beard and a loaded .38 in his lap. The chair wheels move silently over the loans department carpet. Reid stands, the gun in his right hand covered by the loan application forms in his left.

He steps into the aisle.

Within seconds, one of them will be richer. Or one of them will be dead.

A woman passes Reid en route to the customer counter, her red dress pasted to her thighs.

Reid's eyes are locked on the mirrored sunglasses locked on the red dress. The gun barrel collides with the flesh below the guard's ribcage.

"Hold it, or I'll kill you."

The handcart swerves as though to avoid nothing more menacing than an unforeseen trash can. Reid staggers backwards against the guard's momentum. He jabs again with the gun. This time Harlen Lee Hudson freezes.

"Don't try to be a hero or I'll make you a dead one," Reid says.

The loan application forms are still in Reid's left hand as he reaches to the guard's right hip, flips the snap on the thin holster strap, and removes the Smith & Wesson.

Another jab to the guard's ribs. Harlen Lee Hudson lifts his hands from the cart, shuffles backwards, and raises his hands. Reid scans the bank, searching for a gun being drawn from a purse or a pantleg. But there is nothing, save the odd puzzled face. Most don't know anything has happened. The guard is staring down a gun barrel aimed squarely between his mirrored lenses. He isn't going anywhere.

"Okay, folks, this is a holdup," Reid yells in a calm, may-I-have-your-attention-please voice.

"Everyone get down on the floor and let's not have any heroes today."

They watch as the bank employees disappear behind the long customer counter. Reid knows at least one of them is hitting a silent alarm.

A man is standing at a counter against the wall, a pen in one hand, a deposit slip in the other, his body as paralyzed as a wax dummy...Just like that other jerk who didn't want to get his suit dirty...Not again.

"You, too, pal!" Reid barks. The man slumps to the floor.

Harlen Lee Hudson is sprawled face first on the carpet at the edge of the loans department when Wright runs to the scene and takes the guard's gun from Reid.

"Let's go!" Reid says in a near whisper. "Let's get out of here."

Wright tucks the gun into the waistband of his pants and picks up a sack of cash in each hand. Reid grabs the other bag and slings it Santa-style over his left shoulder, his right hand sweeping the bank with the guard's Smith & Wesson.

They are halfway to the doors, halfway out of the bank. Reid sweeps the revolver back to where Loomis guard Harlen Hudson is lying on the floor. The briefcase containing one Uzi submachine gun is still lying on the round table in the loans department.

"The briefcase," Reid whispers to Wright. "Get the briefcase."

Wright drops the two sacks of cash and heads back to the table, one hand on the gun in his waistband, a wary eye on the prone armored-truck guard. His fingers fumble with the latches. He can't get them closed. Something is holding the lid open. Reid is rocking from one foot to the other...Hurry up, Lionel...Let's go...Reid suddenly glances at the parking lot door. The other guard. The Loomis driver. He must know something is wrong. His partner has been gone too long. There'll be a shotgun coming through those doors any second...Let's go, Lionel...For fuck's sake, what's wrong?

One of the latches on the briefcase finally catches. Wright grabs the attaché by the handle and runs back to the two sacks of cash lying on the floor. He tries to grab one of the bags and the troublesome briefcase in his right hand, but his fingers aren't long enough for both tasks.

Cover all the angles, Mitchell had said. Cover all the angles. Running out of hands hadn't been one of them.

"Come on. Come on," Reid whispers through clenched teeth. "Let's go. Let's go."

Reid spins towards the parking lot doors. He is certain he heard something from that direction. The other guard. The driver...There is no one...The guy is either grabbing his shotgun or on his radio to the cops. He must know something is wrong...Someone must have hit the alarm by now...It seems like an hour since they heard the blast of the car horn...The cops are probably waiting outside...With any luck, so is Paddy...

Wright has finally managed to grab both money bags with his left hand. The briefcase dangles from his right. They are heading for the front doors.

Suddenly, there is the clatter of metal bouncing on tile. The briefcase has fallen open, spilling a submachine gun and the rolled newspaper onto the floor.

Wright drops the bags and frantically scoops the rubble back into the bothersome briefcase. He is struggling with the lid. Can't get it closed. Reid is sweeping his gun around the bank at nothing. A siren wails in the distance...Dammit...Let's go...Let's go...

Wright has given up on the latches. He has two ten-pound bags of money in one hand, the half-open briefcase tucked under his other arm.

They wheel past the stand-up counter littered with Wright's spent withdrawal slips and shuffle backwards towards the exit doors. Reid swings the revolver towards the guard still sprawled on the floor.

"Okay," Reid shouts. "Everyone stay on the floor and no one will get hurt. No heroes today, please."

Reid turns for the door, then back again with a final thought borrowed from Wacko.

"There's someone outside with a shotgun," Reid yells into the still bank, his voice calm and flat. "And anyone who sticks a head out there is going to get it blown off."

There is a moment of silence, as though the two terrorists are expecting questions from the floor.

A phone is ringing. Probably the FBI confirming the alarm. Checking to be sure the bandits are gone. No one wants a hostage taking.

Suddenly, the door behind Wright and Reid opens. Now it is their turn to freeze. The look on the woman's face is more confusion than fright. She is still standing in the door, holding it open with the palm of her left hand.

"Just go ahead and do your banking," Wright says softly. "And make sure nobody comes out the door or they'll be killed."

There are no cars passing on Garnet Avenue. Maybe the cops have it roadblocked. Maybe they are just waiting until their targets are clear of the bank, then they'll start shooting. Another siren screams. Maybe the Loomis driver is out there waiting in ambush. Maybe...

"Okay, let's go!"

The doors at both ends of the bank seem to crash simultaneously. Harlen Lee Hudson is running for the shotgun in the back of his armored-truck.

Lionel Wright and Stephen Reid are running for their lives. Out the door. Down the cement sidewalk. Turn right...Don't run...Faster... Faster...Where the hell is the blue Ford?...What if Paddy has left? ...Okay, you pricks, if you're going to shoot, do it now...

Harlen Lee Hudson yanks the pump-action shotgun from the rack in the back of the Loomis truck. Reid can hear him screaming, "We've been fucking hit...I said, we've been..."

The tires on the blue LTD squeal in reverse as the car roars backwards to meet the galloping terrorist and the beatnik loaded down with guns and cash and a half-open briefcase.

The two bandits have never been happier to see Hertz. Paddy Mitchell has never been happier to see them.

Harlen Lee Hudson is making his way, leg over leg, along the front wall of the bank. He reaches the corner and flattens himself against the wall.

The Loomis armored-truck roars in low gear as driver Henry Koppen wheels onto Garnet Avenue and makes a half-U-turn to block traffic away from the shootout.

Harlen Hudson pumps a shell into the chamber of the shotgun. Chuck-chuck. He begins counting to three.

One...

Reid yanks open the rear door of the blue Ford and tumbles headlong onto the seat. Wright lands in the front seat with flying bags of cash and the troublesome briefcase.

Two...

"Hit it!" Reid shrieks from the back seat of the Hertz getaway car. "Go! Go!"

Three...

Mitchell stomps on the gas pedal. The Hertz getaway car is still in reverse and rockets backwards. The car screeches to a stop. Mitchell finds the right gear and the car lurches forward.

Harlen Lee Hudson wheels around the corner of the building and aims the shotgun at the dark blue LTD.

An elderly woman screams and throws herself backwards to miss the fender of the wildly swerving car, her bag of groceries spilling onto the pavement.

Harlen Hudson's shotgun can find only parked cars and the rooftop of a speeding, swerving Hertz rent-a-car.

Mitchell's thumb is frantically pumping the button on the electric garage opener as though somehow that will make the door lift faster. "Come on," he shouts. "Come on."

The Bearcat scanner sounds like the Kennedy Airport control tower on Christmas Eve. The sirens screaming from every direction sound like World War III.

"Come on. Come on."

The antenna thwacks the half-open garage door as the car roars into the underground and slams to a halt alongside Wright's blue Buick.

Mitchell is already stripping the red racing stripes off the Hertz getaway car by the time the other two untangle themselves from the back seat. There is a flurry of flying wigs, business suits, and sweatpants as the three gentlemen bandits transform themselves into late-morning joggers.

Reid mops the remnants of smeared make-up from his face. Wright rips the stolen license plate off the rent-a-car and tosses it into a green garbage bag with the discarded disguises. The three canvas sacks of cash are stuffed into two nylon sports bags along with the revolvers and the Uzi. Everything is dumped in the trunk of the Buick. Wright flings the briefcase on the front seat, climbs in, and pulls out of the garage.

Reid and Mitchell follow on foot, just two joggers loping their way to good health.

Mitchell is glued to the window of the Emerald Avenue apartment to watch for the arrival of the SWAT team. The money is overwhelming, but so are the odds of getting caught or killed before they can spend it.

The excitement in the room is electric—the breathless relief of finishing a marathon mixed with the overpowering euphoria of winning the lottery. But underlying it all is the renewed anxiety of being hunted with relentless ferocity by Norman A. Zigrossi and his agents of the FBI.

Reid is peeling the bandages off his fingers, wondering what happened to the one on his left thumb.

Wright is scribbling numbers from the tags on the three bank bags—two hundred thousand, plus seventy-five thousand, plus eight thousand, makes two hundred and eighty-three thousand, divided by three...

Mitchell's pacing comes to a halt back at the table. He strips the plastic wrapper off a bundle of twenties and slowly fans them with his fingers. The Irish eyes are smiling.

"Ladies and gentlemen." Mitchell says, holding the bundle of bills high like a trophy. "It is with great pleasure that I announce my official retirement from the Stopwatch Gang."

September 24, 1:45 p.m. Lionel Wright is drumming his fingers on the steering wheel of the dark blue Hertz getaway car in the middle of Mission Bay Park, four blocks from their Emerald Avenue hideout and the scene of the previous day's crime. None of them slept the night before. Too many trips to the apartment window to watch for the arrival of the SWAT team.

Shortly after noon Wright had been dispatched to drive his Buick through the back streets of Pacific Beach as far as the Interstate and back to Emerald Avenue. All clear. The police roadblocks were gone.

Minutes later Reid took a cab to San Diego Airport with a first-class ticket to Phoenix. Mitchell loaded the guns and the cash into the wheelwell of the Buick, bid a final "God bless," and headed for Arizona.

Wright's only remaining job was to rendezvous with the garbage truck at its routine stop in Mission Bay Park, return the Ford to Hertz at the Los Angeles Airport, and hop a jet to Phoenix.

Wright knew he would be clean once he had rid himself of the telltale trash bag stuffed with wigs, beards, bank bags, a stolen California license plate, a wig box, and the dozens of paper and plastic money wrappers. Once he had tossed the bag into the hopper of the garbage truck, he would just be Ronald Scott, businessman, driving a Hertz rent-a-car. No money, no guns, no bank bags, no disguises, no red racing stripes.

In the meantime, he is a sitting duck. The cops are certain to be checking every dark blue sedan in the area that even remotely resembles the getaway car. And if they find the LTD, they are certain to find the green garbage bag. And if they find the green garbage bag, he might as well plead guilty on the spot.

Wright gets out of the car and scans Mission Bay Park. Yachts are moving in and out of Ventura Cove. Traffic is moving along Mission Boulevard. But nothing is happening at the dumpster beside the sign that says "Hospitality Point."

Dammit. First the Loomis truck, now the garbage truck. For months he had watched the dumpster being emptied every Wednesday. Neverearlier than one o'clock. Never later than one-thirty. It is already fifteen minutes late...Damn, the whole city must be operating in a different time zone this week.

Wright gets back in the car, checks his gold Rolex, and stares at the green garbage bag on the floor of the Ford...Where the hell is that truck?

Shortly before two o'clock Wright finally grabs the neck of the green garbage bag, checks the surroundings for witnesses, and opens the car door.

He has one foot on the pavement. He stops cold.

A San Diego police cruiser has appeared out of nowhere and stopped on the far side of the laneway, no more than twenty feet away. The lone patrolman is speaking into his two-way radio, staring straight at the man in the dark blue Ford LTD with a bag of garbage on his lap.

For a moment, Wright simply stares back, paralyzed with panic. Wanted for the biggest bank robbery in San Diego history. Nabbed with a lousy bag of garbage.

The door of the patrol car opens.

Now what?...Get rid of the garbage and drive away...Forget the garbage, just drive...Ram the cop...Run across the park...Shit, don't even have a gun...

Wright gets out of the car and walks toward the dumpster. He can hear the squawking on the police radio. He is afraid to look back. His ears will tell him everything—the chuck-chuck of a shotgun, a voice yelling: Police! Maybe even that final blast before his life is splattered on the park lawn.

The bag lands in the dumpster. Wright pauses, as though waiting for the trash bin to give change. Slowly, he turns.

The door of the patrol car is still open. The lawman is back on the radio.

Take it easy...Don't run...Wright looks as though he is walking on hot coals by the time he reaches the Ford and flings himself into the driver's seat. He is still closing the door when he passes the parked police cruiser.

Lionel Wright's eyes are locked on Doomsday in the rearview mirror. The door of the cruiser slams shut.

Wright eases down on the gas pedal...Not too fast...He swings onto Mission Boulevard.

The cruiser is still sitting in the park.

CHAPTER EIGHTEEN

San Diego, California

Within minutes of the robbery, Garnet Avenue outside the Bank of America was a curb-to-curb traffic jam of San Diego PD cruisers overrun by a surging crowd of Pacific Beach oddballs, the sirens having attracted every skateboard and spike of green hair within a ten-block radius. The Bearcat scanners in newsrooms across the county also brought a horde of reporters, photographers, and camera crews to swarm the scene of the crime. Three hundred thousand dollars, the police dispatcher had said over the air. The cops *never* broadcast the amount of any robbery. Then again, there had never been a robbery quite like this before.

As the deadlines for the lunch-hour news shows approached, all hell broke loose on the police lines: cameras were pressed to the bank windows, pens scribbled quotes from eyewitnesses who weren't, and microphones were jammed in just about any face with an open mouth.

Around the corner on Bayard Avenue police were trying to comfort an elderly woman sobbing and shaking, her scattered groceries now being pulverized into the pavement by the stampede around her.

The FBI didn't usually make it to Page One much anymore. Not since the formation of the U.S. Drug Enforcement Agency (DEA). The FBI still had the odd kidnapping, maybe an extortion case, but mainly a lot of bank robberies and those were mostly penny ante, back-page stuff. The DEA got all the high-profile narcotics busts and media attention, along with lots of money from Congress. It was hard to tell which agency resented the other more. Despite the best efforts of the brass in Washington to engender cooperation in the interests of law and order, the competition between the two agencies remained fierce. The DEA usually won in the headline department.

But the Stopwatch Gang changed all that, if only temporarily; the FBI weren't competing with anyone on this baby. And special agent Norman A. Zigrossi knew how to run with a hot story. Press conferences were called. "Exclusive interviews" were granted to any reporter who asked for one. Even the dramatic bank photographs of two bearded men with guns and sacks of money were distributed to news outlets coast to coast. Most of all, Norman A. Zigrossi made sure the public understood the gravity of the crime being investigated by his agents of the Federal Bureau of Investigation—someone, somewhere had to know something about the bandits.

"It is the largest armed robbery in the history of the City of San Diego," he told reporters the same day as the heist. "There is nothing that even comes close to this amount—two hundred and eighty-three thousand dollars."

That was good enough for the headline writers.

"Bank here hit for $283,000," screamed the front page of the San Diego *Evening Tribune*.

"Biggest S.D. Holdup?" bannered *The Union*, evidently not entirely convinced of Zigrossi's claim.

Even the giant international *Los Angeles Times* cleared a full two columns on its front pages for a story under the headline: "Gunmen Get $300,000 in Bank Holdup—Armored-Car Guard Waylaid as He Totes Cash in Pacific Beach."

The next day, Norman A. Zigrossi tossed some fresh meat to the media hounds. The *Tribune* quoted the FBI boss as saying: "Agents are looking into the possibility that the men involved in yesterday's heist may have been behind the robberies dating back to April...We are looking very closely at those robberies where the crooks used disguises."

Zigrossi refused to say specifically whether he was suggesting the record-setting Bank of America heist had been the work of the notorious Stopwatch Gang that had terrorized the neighborhood back in the spring. After the Norco fiasco of connecting the wrong people to the wrong gang at the wrong robberies, no one in the FBI was going out on a limb this time—at least not publicly.

Privately, Zigrossi and his agents were convinced. There were too many similarities in the bank films. The statures of the two robbers in the big heist were identical to those of the culprits in at least four of the earlier scores. Their modus operandi was also the same. No one hurt. Unusually polite for gangsters.

Then there was the way the shorter fellow held his gun. Always in his left hand. Always with his forefinger wrapped around the outside of the trigger guard. No killer that one. Had to be the same guy in all the pictures. There was no stopwatch in the latest haul, but that made sense—they could have timed this one with an hour glass.

The Stopwatch Gang was back in business, all right. All the FBI had to do was find them...

Paddy Mitchell pulled the bottle of Dom Perignon from the silver ice bucket, wrapped the neck in white linen, and gently poured another glass of champagne for Beckie. Nothing was too good—nor, apparently, too expensive—for his Princess. His hand swept around the room, like some game show host about to reveal the winning contestant's grand prize behind Door Number Two. Princess had to admit she'd never seen anything quite like it—one of the most opulent suites in the Phoenix Biltmore. Two king-sized bedrooms. Three bathrooms with sunken jacuzzi tubs—all-gold fixtures, no less. A balcony for twenty guests overlooking Camelback Mountain and the shimmering Catalina-tile swimming pool. The parlor was only slightly larger than the living room at Sycamore House, complete with an imposing oak and brass wetbar, two fireplaces, a built-in stereo with quadraphonic sound, a remote large-screen television, and a baby grand piano—a vital touch of class.

The brochure said the place was suitable for a party of thirty-five. Not bad for nine hundred bucks a night. Certainly comfy enough for a thief and a barmaid. Precisely what Paddy Mitchell had in mind for the official victory party and retirement celebration of the Stopwatch Gang.

FBI special agent James M. Bird and his partner had been sitting in a north San Diego parking lot, staking out the latest wrong suspects in the earlier Stopwatch robberies, when they heard the police call on their radio: "nine-one-two...Garnet...approximately three hundred thousand dollars...armed guard in pursuit."

Bird jammed the car in gear and sped off towards the scene of the crime. Three hundred grand? And they're broadcasting it? To hell with the stake-out—in the realm of the FBI holdup squad, this was the once-in-a-career Great Train Robbery, and FBI special agent James M. Bird and his partner couldn't wait to be part of it.

The agents added their car to the chaos outside the Bank of America and pushed their way through the crowd of city police and oddball gawkers.

In the midst of the pandemonium stood FBI special agent William M. Ayers, an urban cowboy with western boots, tan corduroy suit, dark shades, and a thick Texas drawl. Other agents wondered where he came up with all those weird things he was always saying. Stuff like: "Well, ain't that just the skin off a rattler's nose." Other agents called him Cowboy. On a bad day, they called him Magnum Force. Never to his face.

San Diego bureau chief Norman A. Zigrossi had promoted the lanky Texan to the job of Supervisor, Bank Robberies. As such, agent Ayers had sole responsibility for coordinating investigations of incidents involving financial institutions with deposits insured by the government of the United States of America (the only bureaucratic quirk that allowed the FBI anywhere near bank heists). As Ayers's daily duties included the assignment of individual agents to each case, he had developed a rotation system to keep everyone's workload just as fair and square as a cockfight in heaven. Had it all written down, too, on the clipboard he always carried under his arm.

Cowboy was saying something about the bank robbery and turkey stuffin' when special agents James Bird and partner found him in the crowd outside the Bank of America.

"So, Bill, who's up for rotation here?" Bird asked, nodding towards the neatly typed duty rosters on the clipboard.

Special agent Ayers didn't even bother to look at the dang thing. "Don't rightly know," Cowboy replied with a deep sigh, jamming his thumbs under his belt.

"Reckon I best take this baby myself."

In another Biltmore penthouse down the hall from Mitchell, Stephen Reid finished admiring his digs and turned his attention to something of even greater exotic appeal—namely, JoAnne. The two had celebrated his "collecting on a couple of light shows" by dropping a small bank bag of stolen cash in the expensive boutiques of the Borgata and Phoenix Fifth Avenue. Now JoAnne was modeling her retail rampage—a vision in black silk and diamonds. Reid was taken aback—he had always thought of JoAnne as a bit of a country girl, not rough, just rather plain. He had certainly never thought of her as the stylishly elegant woman now gracefully twirling in front of him.

"What do you think?" JoAnne bubbled gleefully.

"I think I'm the luckiest man on earth."

Special agent William M. Ayers knew he was probably looking at a trail 'bout as cold as a coyote's howl. His boss had told the dang media pretty near everything the FBI knew about the case and, hell, that wasn't enough to fill a jackrabbit's eye.

Ayers's first important move had been to send special agent Bird into the victim bank to get a special number from the manager, thereby confirming it was a federally insured financial institution over which the FBI had jurisdiction in the conduct of the investigation. Discussions ensued as to whether the theft of funds from an armored-truck guard inside a bank was really a robbery of funds from a federally insured bank, or from an armored-truck insured by the armored-truck company over which the FBI might not have jurisdiction. Since no one from the city PD was raising the issue, the FBI agents decided they would proceed as though the thought had never occurred to them, either.

Over the next forty-eight hours, FBI agents interviewed every employee in the bank and every customer who had walked through the place since it had opened the morning of the robbery. Every thirty-five-millimeter snapshot taken by the bank cameras was studied under a magnifying glass. The city PD stopped a dozen dark blue four-door sedans in the area, but none of them seemed to be carrying the Stopwatch Gang. The Highway Patrol were put on alert for a Ford sedan, but they weren't about to roadblock the Interstate. Local detachments were also stationed at the airport, train station, and bus depot, but they turned up nothing but a few troublesome vagrants. Finally, the FBI combed every line of the reports on the earlier Stopwatch robberies, hoping to match any two pieces of the puzzle.

By the second day of the investigation, special agent William M. Ayers would have happily settled for even one puzzle piece that meant something. He knew the gang had made its getaway in a dark blue, four-door Ford with red pinstripes and California plates. The model could be wrong—witnesses were always getting that kind of detail screwed up. No one got the license number; they were too busy remembering the red pinstripes. If they came with the car, they would probably be painted over by now. The whole car could be painted over by now. Anyway, none of it mattered much. The gang had made no attempt to conceal the vehicle—in FBI-speak, they had "fronted" it— which usually meant it was stolen, or the plates were stolen, or both. A check of the California police computers didn't come up with a missing Ford Fairmont of any description. But that didn't mean much, either— the car could have been swiped in New Jersey.

The car could have been rented, but where and when and by whom? Rental agencies took up five pages in the San Diego directory. And what if it was rented in Los Angeles or San Francisco or New York City, for that matter? These guys could certainly afford the drop-off charges.

It would take every agent in the San Diego bureau of the FBI weeks just to phone all the car-rental agencies in California alone. It would take them months to check out everyone who had rented a blue Ford four-door in the month of September. And even then, it wasn't likely the culprit had used his real name and address and was conveniently listed in the phone book.

The bank didn't cough up a lot of leads, either. The ID boys had been over the place with a microscope and came up with nothing of value. Zip. Zilch. Special agent Ayers was there when they dusted the small round table where the tall one had been sitting, and the counter where the smaller one had been standing. There were plenty of different prints, all right, and none of 'em worth a rat's tooth in a rain storm.

The stack of carefully typed witness statements didn't help much, either. The employees gave pretty good descriptions of the robbers. Hell, they'd had enough time to count the dang hairs on the thieves' wigs. Strange nobody noticed a couple of guys sitting in a bank for a half hour. A little asterisk went beside that observation.

Unfortunately, the witness accounts didn't tell special agent Ayers anything he didn't already know from the bank films. The tall one was wearing make-up. Smeared all to hell. Probably trying to hide a scar or something. Maybe he was just trying to look Arab or Mexican. The same guy had bandages on his thumb and on the first two fingers of each hand. Clever. No gloves, no prints. Except in those last frames, one bandage on the left thumb was missing. The agents had gone back to the bank to scour for the Band-Aid. Didn't find it.

There was also no question from the photographs that both bandits were wearing disguises. The black beard on the tall guy had fallen loose on the left sideburn, and his hairline had receded somewhat in the course of the robbery. And the little guy with the puffed hair and the Vandyke— heck, that was a fake for sure. Nobody really looked like that.

As for the clothes, they could have come from anywhere. Same with the handguns. Even the Uzi could have been bought in the back of a corner store—hell, the Israelis had been dumping them on America by the boatload.

The FBI and city PD officers had already combed the neighborhood, questioning the shopkeepers, knocking on doors, stopping pedestrians. Have you seen a dark blue, four-door Ford sedan? Do you recognize either of the two men in these photos, with or without the beards? Have you noticed anything the least bit unusual lately?

Unusual? That one always got a lot of laughs—by Pacific Beach standards, the President of the United States in drag would barely rate a second glance.

These Stopwatch fellas were pros, all right. Slick as beetle juice on buttered toast. Heck, they hadn't left behind enough leads to feed an ant in a drain hole.

In fact, it all seemed just a little too slick. Two guys looking like that, sitting in a bank for over a half hour, and no one in the gall-dang place thought that was strange? And how did the thieves know that was going to be one of the biggest armored-truck pickups in the county?

The whole thing smelled like an inside job, all right.

"Is there any possible way that we might offer our assistance to help you today, monsieur et madame?" the maître d' of the Biltmore's famed Gold Room asked in the longest rendition of what-d'ya-want Paddy Mitchell had ever heard.

"My name is Michael J. Garrison the Third," Mitchell said in an abysmal British accent. "And this is my wife, Lady Rebecca. We are residing in the Persian Suite. I believe my private secretary made reservations for dinner in your establishment."

The maître d' leaned towards Sir Michael and away from Lady Rebecca.

"I am terribly sorry, sir, I truly am. It must have been our dreadful mistake in not informing your private secretary, or perhaps she might have inadvertently neglected to mention it to you, but—"

"Is there a problem?" Sir Michael interrupted.

"I am afraid there is, sir," the maître d' sighed. "You see, we do insist that our guests in the Gold Room be in black tie."

Mitchell looked down at his brand new two-thousand-dollar suit, then at Beckie's equally pricey evening gown, and tried not to laugh.

The best-dressed couple in Phoenix, staying at the most expensive suite in the place, with a quarter of a million dollars in tips sitting upstairs, and they can't get into a restaurant?

Sir Michael smiled and flashed two hundred-dollar bills at the maître d'.

The maître d' looked at the bills and smiled back at Sir Michael.

"Oh, yes sir, I am sure you will find that will be more than sufficient to rent a very fine dinner jacket, indeed..."

In the hours that followed the San Diego heist, a visibly shaken Harlen Lee Hudson had tried to reconcile all that had just happened to him. At first, he had been angry that some two-bit hoods had stuck a gun in his face, scaring the piss out of him like that, making him smell the dirty carpet, holding a gun to the back of his head—his own fucking gun, for chrissake—and then just waltzing out of there with all that money he was supposed to be protecting. It was all pretty humiliating. All he had wanted to do was grab that shotgun and kill the bastards.

But by the time Ray Hudson had finished a beer after work with one of his buddies, it finally hit him—he had just come within a hammer's click of spending the rest of the week at his own funeral. As he walked through the door of his suburban home that evening, he was pale and shaking. His wife was paler and shaking harder, which didn't help matters. She had cursed his job every morning he put on a uniform. Back in the spring, her nagging had turned to pleading with him to find a new job somewhere.

The morning after the robbery, Hudson had come out of the shower to find a business suit, tie, and freshly pressed dress shirt lying on the bed.

"You're going for a job interview today," his wife said. "I don't care what it is or where it is or with whom, but you're going to call that damn suicide company of yours and tell them you've decided to look for another job. Period."

Hudson had managed to calm his wife long enough to get out of the house with his Loomis uniform intact. Don't worry, he told her, the worst is over. Life can only get better.

Wrong.

The last nice thing anyone would do for the man who had risked his life in the line of duty was hand Ray Hudson the mirrored sunglasses he had left lying on the bank floor when he ran for his shotgun.

First, there was less than a hero's welcome from the Loomis Armored Car Service, whose insurers had just coughed up $283,000 to the Bank of America within two days of the heist. The guard was promptly marched into the office of the company's security chief.

"It seems obvious those robbers must have been casing that bank and our company's operations for months," the security chief wisely surmised. "How is it possible that you didn't notice them?"

"Well, sir, maybe I should ask you who the hell can spot someone sitting somewhere else with a pair of binoculars?" Hudson replied curtly.

"And you say that you noticed the two suspects sitting in the bank?" the security chief continued, checking his notes. "And you say they were there during the course of your, ah, I believe it was three separate trips in and out of the bank immediately before the incident?"

"Yes, sir, that's correct," Hudson said calmly. "I was able to describe them to a tee."

"And may I ask why you didn't do anything?"

"Do anything?" Hudson exploded. "Sir, with all due respect, sir, instead of asking me about them guys, why don't you ask the Bank of America? They must have been sitting in that bank for fifteen goddam minutes before I arrived. I ask you, sir: did anyone call the cops? No. Did anyone turn on the cameras? No. They just sat there and waited for me."

The security chief made some notes and concluded the interview with one final question: "You said that you got up and ran out of the bank, retrieved the shotgun from the truck, and gave pursuit to the suspects."

"Yes, sir, that is correct."

"I am sure you now realize that your actions may have endangered the lives of innocent civilians in the bank—"

"Well, sir, now just a—"

"May I ask you why you took this action?"

"Because, sir, that bastard had a gun and I didn't and I wanted one. It's that simple. Sir."

For all the anxiety that Ray Hudson suffered from his near-fatal brush with the Stopwatch Gang, the Loomis Armored Car Service awarded him with an official reprimand for running out of the bank to get his shotgun and thereby possibly endangering the lives of others.

The *Evening Tribune* quoted Armando Cisneros, San Diego branch manager for Loomis, as saying that no added security precautions were planned in the wake of the B of A heist, and adding, "But I'm sure our guards and drivers will be more aware of the people around them now."

Just when Harlen Lee Hudson figured life couldn't get any worse without dying, he saw a huge headline splashed across the *Tribune*: "Armored-car firm workers quizzed in huge bank heist."

> Federal investigators were questioning present and former employees of the Loomis Armored Car Service after two armed men yesterday took about $300,000 which was being loaded into a Loomis truck at a Pacific Beach bank. Norman A. Zigrossi, FBI agent in charge here, said the men who robbed a Loomis guard of the three bags of cash at the Bank of America, 912 Garnet Ave., at 10:55 a.m. "were obviously familiar with the Loomis routine as to bank pick-ups.
>
> "The FBI plans to talk to former and present employees of the company and the bank," Zigrossi said.

But the FBI had more than a few perfunctory questions to ask Hudson. After days of "intensive investigation by dozens of agents"—Norman A. Zigrossi's words—the posse landed at the guard's kitchen table.

As it happened, Hudson had been thinking about buying a 1931 Model-A from a neighbor who restored antique cars. Hudson's mother had offered to lend him the thirteen thousand dollars he needed for his dream buggy, but he had balked at taking the money. After the Stopwatch Gang had given him an unsolicited preview of the Afterlife, however, Hudson promptly bought the car while he was still alive to drive it.

The agents of the FBI were on Hudson's doorstep faster than a chicken hawk in a hurricane.

"So, Mr. Hudson, may we ask where you got the money to buy that nice Model-A out there?" the FBI man asked, all but rattling his handcuffs.

"From my mother," Hudson growled. "Why?"

"Uh-huh. Your mother," the FBI man said. "And just how much did your mother give you?"

"Thirteen thousand dollars," Hudson said stiffly.

"Uh-huh. Thirteen thousand dollars," the FBI man repeated. "How old are you, Mr. Hudson?"

"I am forty-two years old, sir."

"Uh-huh," the FBI man said with a doubting smirk. "Forty-two years old and your mother is giving you thirteen thousand dollars to buy an old car. Is that what you are telling us, Mr. Hudson?"

"Yes, sir. That is exactly what I'm telling you. And if you don't believe me, sir, then (a) you can ask my mother, and (b) I don't really give a shit whether you believe me or not."

Lionel Wright had finally managed to rid himself of the Hertz getaway car at the Los Angeles airport after his parkside brush with the law and the longest two-hour drive of his life to Los Angeles. His chosen suite in the Biltmore was sumptuous enough, but lacked some of the finer appointments, like the baby grand. Mitchell had made quite a scene at the front desk, insisting that his pal treat himself to no less grandeur than the others. But Lionel only became agitated: "I don't play the fucking piano."

Wright spent his first two days at the Biltmore pouring drinks for the others, making their dinner reservations—including the one for the Gold Room—and generally keeping himself busy. He did call an escort service and vanish for a few hours. And he had managed to drop a bundle on a new Rolex. Otherwise, he didn't venture far from the hotel.

Just before dinner on their second evening, Wright dialed Reid's suite. He came straight to the point.

"We've got a problem."

Reid's grip tightened around the receiver.

"What is it?"

"Tell you when you get here," Wright muttered and hung up.

It had been less than three days since the San Diego heist, well before the FBI would declare the gang's trail was even cool, well before the most wanted trio in the West could even start to relax. Reid slowly turned the brass door handle, opened the door a crack and checked for waiting police rifles. The hallway was empty.

The scene in Wright's suite hardly resembled the preparations for a police raid. The entire San Diego haul—including 10,000 twenty-dollar bills—had been placed in neat little piles in perfectly straight lines exactly eight rows deep and running the entire length of the sunken living room. Lionel was pacing, scratching his head.

"What the hell's wrong?" Reid sputtered in amazement.

"We each took ten grand, right?" Wright said.

"Yeah, so what?"

"Well, then, that should leave $253,000, right?"

"Shit, Lionel. What the hell is the trouble you called me about?"

"Just can't figure it out," Wright said, shaking his head. "I keep coming up a $140 short."

Cowboy and his posse had finally scratched Loomis guard Harlen Lee Hudson from their list of suspects after his story about Mom's loan for the Model-A checked out. That left the FBI with eight prime candidates for stalking and stake-outs. A few of them had done time for armed robbery. Several others were on bail awaiting trial for armed robbery. The rest fell into that oft-quoted category of unsavory characters "known to the police"—they were certainly capable of getting time for armed robbery.

Otherwise, the pursuit of the Stopwatch Gang hadn't hit a dead end so much as an endless series of forks. There were a few thousand registered owners of blue Fords and almost as many rental agencies to be checked. There were hundreds of restaurants where these guys could have blown a bundle and left behind a credit card number. There were thousands of people in the Pacific Beach area who could be interviewed—somebody must have seen these guys somewhere.

And there were eight suspects.

As Cowboy sat looking at a file three inches thick, he knew his best chance to catch the Stopwatch Gang was probably for the Stopwatch Gang to catch themselves. Sooner or later, they had to make a mistake. Just one good clue, that's all Cowboy reckoned he would need. Just one suspicious neighbor, one angry girlfriend, one underworld crony with a big mouth. Just one broken alias, one piece of phony ID flashing negative on a computer screen. Sooner or later those crooks had to spend a pile of dough. Someone, somewhere, had to notice.

Friday, September 26. On the third day of the Biltmore binge, Paddy Mitchell's hangover was verging on a medical emergency. Reid placed a call to Jack Seeley at the offices of the Sedona Flying School to say they would be coming home soon with a surprise for the flying instructor and wife Judy—a pair of $800 tickets to the Ali-Holmes prizefight in Vegas. The friendly response suggested there were no big surprises awaiting the Stopwatch Gang back in Sedona. Reid hung up and announced the coast was clear.

Shortly before noon the fugitive trio checked out of the Arizona Biltmore with girlfriends, shopping bags, hangovers, and a sizeable flourish of hundred-dollar bills at the front desk. By the time the desert sunset lit Red Rock Country in its daily blaze, the three desperados were safely holed up again in Oak Creek Canyon.

Paddy Mitchell promptly announced that he was moving into Sycamore House "just for a few days" until he could find a new honeymoon hideaway for himself and his Princess. Seemed one of the richest bank bandits in America had neglected to pay his rent.

And that's pretty much when the trouble started.

The same morning that Patrick Mitchell, Stephen Reid, and Lionel Wright checked out of the Arizona Biltmore, the phone rang on the desk of FBI special agent William M. Ayers.

"Y'all found *what?*" Cowboy drawled at the excited babbler on the other end of the line.

"Well I'll be a..."

CHAPTER NINETEEN

The Arizona Desert

The wind wraps the barren clutch of cinder-block houses in gusts of howling melancholy, rattling rusted sign posts, churning the dust of empty streets. A thousand feet below, the tinted checkers of the Painted Desert lie flat to the horizon like a faded quilt on a lifeless slab. Perched atop the soaring rock faces of an Arizona mesa, the nest of human habitation has been ignored by centuries of civilization below the rugged cliffs. The Hopi inhabitants call their few acres of desolation Shungopavi, and think it is the center of the universe. Most would think it the end of the earth. The reclusive Hopi would find no contradiction between the two.

Stephen Reid turned his collar to the bluster and sucked in the solitude like the fresh scent of wet pine. What a wonderfully forlorn and lonely place, he thought. It was hard to believe that somewhere across that desert were all those meaningless milestones along the road to the American Dream. The Biltmore. Vegas. Hollywood. Monuments to another world. His world.

But the Hopi had it all figured out centuries ago, living alone to enjoy what little the gods had given them, settling out of harm's reach atop nature's geological fortresses like Shungopavi. The other tribes reverently called them the Ancient Ones and thought them a direct link to the gods, a belief no doubt enhanced by the Hopi's choice of real estate. Theirs was a peaceful existence—a thousand years ago, the Hopi had no words to describe violence. A thousand years later, they still don't.

Timmy Pfeiffer loved his day trips north of Winslow to Shungopavi, alone with Chicago and an aging Hopi friend named Victor.

"Hey, Timmy, Timmy!" Victor shouted. "Look at this one. Wow! Isn't that a beauty? Timmy, come look!"

Victor was among the most celebrated of Hopi artisans, his jewelry routinely fetching five-figure sums in the trendiest of trendy showcases from Los Angeles to Manhattan. Reid liked Victor for his sheer simplicity of spirit—this old man with a rotting twill hat, living in the back of beyond, routinely taking calls from the starlets of Hollywood wanting a fifty-grand necklace and some fast spiritual advice. Victor didn't know what Timmy did for a living and didn't much care. Victor liked Timmy because Timmy was his friend.

Victor's spartan cement-block house in Shungopavi is littered with the tools of his trade, a half-finished masterpiece lying on the kitchen counter like yesterday's newspaper. But all Victor cares about this day is his latest harvest of squash in the tiny garden.

"Look, Timmy! Isn't this one a beauty? Oh, here, look over here..."

It was after dark when Timmy Pfeiffer bade farewell to Victor and turned the Camaro down the steep switchbacks out of Shungopavi. It had been another glorious day at the center of the universe, but Reid was troubled.

Somehow, Victor's creative talents, his penetrating wisdom, his simple life—it all made Reid's self-indulgent existence of guns, lies, and running from the law seem vacuous and spiritually obscene. The kindly old Hopi had entrusted to Timmy Pfeiffer something as sacred as the setting sun—his friendship. In return, Stephen Reid could offer only the passing acquaintance of a fugitive's alias.

The problem wasn't Timmy Pfeiffer. He was everything that Victor could have wanted in a friend—bright, engaging, sincere, and loyal. The problem was Stephen Douglas Reid who had time to serve, a face to hide, some stolen cash, and half the FBI hunting for him. It had been almost three weeks since the San Diego heist and still no sign of the posse. But that didn't mean they would stop looking. Once a fugitive, always a fugitive. The best he could do was make himself harder to find.

While Wright had been busily manufacturing new sets of ID for all three gang members, Reid had been designing a new appearance to match. Getting the colored contact lenses to make his brown eyes blue had been no problem. He had also consulted a plastic surgeon in Phoenix about removing the three telltale scars on his face—leftovers from a traffic accident, he told the doctor. And while the scalpel was out, he wanted a new nose. The physician understood—lots of people hate their noses. Surgery was scheduled for Thursday, November 6.

Mitchell agreed it would probably be a good idea to rid himself of the "Fat and Heller" tattoo on his arm, and the alarm-clock scar between his eyes. But most of all, Paddy wanted a facelift—age was worrying him more than the FBI.

The others ragged Lionel about his potential for a physical make-over, but Wright seemed content in his homeliness. *Que sera sera.*

But putting new names to new faces does not a new identity make. There were all those little things—Mitchell's conflicting stories; Wright's oddly suspicious solitude, and his invisible means of support; even the small quirks in Reid's speech patterns.

Bob Kitteredge had openly teased his favorite tenant about staying in Sycamore "Hoose" and coming from "Canada, eh." Reid had spent hours in front of his bedroom mirror, giving his reflection a self-administered Dale Carnegie course in the art of not using notoriously Canadian pronunciations and expressions. He was getting better.

"Eh" wasn't a problem for Mitchell. And nothing was a problem for Wright—a nod is the same in every language.

After the surgery and speech therapy, all that would distinguish the Stopwatch Gang from their aliases would be their fingerprints. No law-abiding physician would touch one of those without first phoning the local police detachment—the only people with hangups about their fingerprints are criminals.

But the underworld breeds crooks of all persuasions, and a friend of the gang in Los Angeles was a walking Yellow Pages of all such unsavory types. Sure, he knew a guy who could do new fingerprints. A doc fresh out of the slammer. Did three years for prescribing drugs to patients whose only afflictions were prescription drugs. All he needed was a clear set of prints and he'd make these little plastic molds with lasers and stuff. Then he'd take the skin off the fingers, wrap 'em in these molds for a month and, bingo, new prints.

As the Camaro's headlights groped through the desert blackness, Reid imagined the new life that lay ahead of him. He had JoAnne and their puppy—not exactly a stable family with a white picket fence, but it was a start. He had Jack and Judy Seeley—they had become his best friends. And he had his airplane—that was the main reason he wanted to run the big San Diego score. He'd already picked the aircraft he wanted—a sleek little Moonie 201. Four-seater. Fast. Seventy grand. Saw a black one on the cover of last month's flying magazine. He wanted that one. A black one. Maybe start a charter service. Go into business with Jack.

Life was certainly going to be different without his partners in crime, he mused. Lionel would probably go back to being a clerk at a motel somewhere. Maybe buy his own motel so he could be his own clerk.

Paddy would do okay. Shit, Sweetie and the Princess would be happy rolling around under some palm tree for the rest of their lives. Or until she turns twenty-five and he dumps her for someone younger.

Or until he has to dump her to run.

Or until he gets caught.

Reid's mind was racing the Camaro down Oak Creek Canyon. There was a flash of police cars and sirens and shotguns. A flash of a prison cell and Wacko's ugly face. A flash of two tiny black shoes and a little girl's pink leggings.

The Camaro turned into the laneway to the Forest Houses. It was all a nice dream. But Stephen Reid knew fugitives don't build lives for themselves. At best, they just rent them between aliases.

Reid pulled up beside Sycamore House. It was after midnight. He could hear the laughter and blaring music with his car windows up.

"Damn you, Paddy."

For Paddy Mitchell, the Biltmore binge and victory celebration had not ended at checkout time. It had simply moved to Sycamore House. Every evening there was champagne. Every morning there was more champagne mixed with orange juice as Paddy went for his daily stroll around the Forest Houses estate in his silk bathrobe and floppy slippers, a drink in one hand, cigar in the other. Ah, this is the life, Mitchell was always saying when a simple hello would have sufficed. Ah, this is the life.

Paddy Mitchell figured life at Sycamore House was about as close to paradise as he was going to get without that final message from God. He felt safe there. The rest of the world was still full of prying eyes. Every passing police cruiser, every glance his way, every haircut above the ears, everything was a prelude to arrest, prison, maybe even death. Paddy Mitchell was paranoid just getting out of bed in the morning— except in Oak Creek Canyon. Somehow, the place just seemed out of bounds to the law.

By the third week after the San Diego robbery it had become clear to Reid and JoAnne that their house guest had become a permanent resident of the upstairs apartment. Beckie had her own place just up the Canyon Road, but Paddy spent most of his waking hours at Sycamore House. In return, he volunteered to be chief chef. One day he arrived with a carload of cookbooks on everything from wok vegetables to stewed reindeer. Three days later he drove all the way to Phoenix to buy three thousand dollars worth of copper cookware and kitchen gadgets. The following week, he enrolled in cooking classes two nights a week at Yavapai College, where JoAnne was taking photography.

Reid and Wright didn't mind. They were no hell in the kitchen, and JoAnne could barely butter toast. Besides, anything that kept Paddy busy was okay with them. A chef running from the law—Lionel thought that was pretty funny. Called him the Galloping Gourmet.

The Kitteredges had other names for Mitchell, none of which was remotely flattering. The other tenants in Sycamore House all seemed very nice, courteous folks. But that friend of theirs, that Garrison guy, well, he just ignored all the rules of living in the Forest Houses.

"Ah, Mr. Garrison, may I remind you that our rules prohibit the consumption of alcoholic beverages outside of your home," Bob Kitteredge said to Mitchell, who was out on a morning stroll with stogie and champagne.

"Well now, Bob, I don't really see that I'm bothering anyone, am I?" Mitchell said pleasantly enough.

"You're bothering me, Mr. Garrison," Kitteredge scowled, "and I happen to own this place. I don't like to wake up every morning to find you wandering around out here in a bathrobe."

"Well then, Mr. Bob," Mitchell chided sarcastically, "I suggest you sleep in a little later. Other than that, take a hike."

Bob Kitteredge headed back to his house to call the sheriff, but was intercepted by his wife. She persuaded him the police weren't likely to arrest someone for wearing bedroom slippers in public.

At the end of the second week of October, Mitchell and Bob Kitteredge had their final run-in. The landlord came straight to the point.

"Okay, Mr. Garrison, I've had it up to here with you," Kitteredge said. "You wander around here like you own the place and you don't even pay rent. Either you leave, or everyone in your place leaves."

"Who pays your exorbitant rent on that place is none of your goddamn business, Bob," Mitchell retorted, spitting out the name.

"Well, I'm making it my business, mister," Kitteredge said in welling anger. "You're nothing but a freeloader and a slob, and either you leave or I'll throw you out."

The words *freeloader* and *slob* hit a nerve with the thief who thought himself every bit the aristocratic gentleman.

"Listen, Mister Bob," Mitchell said, waving a finger in the landlord's face, "I'm staying here at the invitation of my friends, and if you try anything, I'll have five of the hottest lawyers in America crawling all over your ass. Got it?"

Two days later a man with a brushcut was standing on the landlord's doorstep, talking to Mary Kitteredge. For the rest of the day he wandered back and forth along the banks of Oak Creek, fishing for trout, right under the balcony of Sycamore House.

With no banks to stake out and no hauls to count, Lionel Wright busied himself with the Stopwatch family chores. There were always bills to pay, shopping to do, errands to run. Sharing the upstairs apartment with Mitchell also meant enough housework for an industrial cleaning staff. The rest of Wright's days were spent down by the stream, reading a book, tossing sticks to Chicago, or just staring into the frothing waters of Oak Creek.

By and large, money didn't seem to change Lionel's life much. More of it just meant more accounting—and more laundering of all those small bills. The San Diego heist alone had produced 11,000 of them, certainly far too many for the glass jar beside Reid's bed. For days at a time, Wright would go from store to store, unloading the mountain of nuisance bills a dozen at a time. But there were only so many jugs of milk, tanks of gas, and packs of cigarettes he could buy in any given week. It was a long, boring process, all right. But Lionel didn't mind. Lionel liked to keep busy.

Retirement from the holdup business had also created an unlikely prankster. Every day Wright had some new joke to play on his two unsuspecting gangster friends. One day it was a rubber tarantula in Mitchell's underwear drawer. Reid's attempt to stick to the Scarsdale diet was thwarted by chocolate donuts everywhere he turned—in his bed, in the shower, in his car, even on the seat of his training aircraft.

Wright never pulled any nasty pranks on JoAnne. He would never do anything to upset her, even in jest.

Mitchell's retaliation was swift and severe. He kept hiding Lionel's raisin bread and cans of Coke.

But underneath Wright's playfulness, something was bothering him more than the missing hundred and forty bucks from the huge San Diego heist: the dumpster.

Why had he tossed that bag of criminal trash in the damn park dumpster? Why hadn't he just taken it with him? He would have found a garbage truck somewhere. Any garbage truck would have been fine.

On the second Sunday of October, Reid, Wright, and JoAnne had lunch at the airport restaurant with Jack and Judy Seeley. Lionel was visibly anxious. The place was packed, but it was the two men at a nearby table who were attracting Wright's attention. Reid had spotted them, too. Maybe it was their cleancut military appearance. No, it was the way they were talking and laughing, two people who seemed to be trying much too hard not to look at someone they wanted to watch.

Reid's regular dental appointments with George Moore had become something of an event for the dentist and his staff. JoAnne would usually sit in the waiting room chatting with receptionist Marilyn Donkersley, while Reid was having his mouth rebuilt in the next room with Moore. Every visit brought new tales of jet-setting adventure by the gallivanting couple. The latest was their fabulous long weekend in Vermont, a transcontinental flight so JoAnne could shoot the autumn colors for her photography class. The dentist had already heard about that one through the local grapevine—Reid had walked into the travel agency down the street and peeled off fourteen hundred bucks, all in twenties, for the first-class airfares.

By mid-October, Reid's new set of teeth was almost ready for installation. As usual, he and Moore talked a lot about flying and airplanes, especially the new Moonie 201 that Reid was getting ready to buy from Superstition Air Service outside Phoenix. Seventy thousand bucks.

"I suppose you're going to pay for that in cash, too," the dentist said with a laugh.

"Oh, yeah, for sure," Reid said around the dentist's finger. "You know me. Ain't giving those banks a nickel I don't have to."

Moore didn't bother to ask whether his patient planned to plunk down the seventy grand in twenties. But even by certified check, the cash purchase didn't make any sense. Then again, a whole lot of things about Moore's high-rolling acquaintance didn't quite make sense. Like all those stories being told in the waiting room by JoAnne that didn't quite jibe with the stories being told in the dentist's chair by Timmy Pfeiffer.

The folks in Moore's office couldn't wait for the next appointment to hear the next installment—or to compare contradictions. On one occasion, JoAnne had been telling receptionist Donkersley all about her dream of getting married in a nice little New England church. Donkersley later mentioned it in passing to Moore.

"That's odd," said the dentist. "Timmy has been telling me all along that they are already married. I think he even told me where they were married. Big ceremony. Lots of movie stars."

After a while it all became something of an office game to get together after an appointment and compare notes. One day JoAnne would say they had been shopping in Mexico at the same time Reid put them in New York on business. Another day Reid was going on about their being high-school sweethearts in Maine, while JoAnne was in the next office talking about the day she and Timmy met in Florida. (Reid had insisted that she never mention Canada, nor use her real name on any official documents. Said he didn't want the IRS to trace him through her.)

For the most part, nobody treated the couple's inconsistencies with any concern. Moore and his staff agreed Timmy and JoAnne were probably up to something. But it couldn't be too terribly bad. They were both just such darn nice folks.

Towards the end of the second week of October, receptionist Donkersley cornered George Moore and told him about a strange encounter with JoAnne the previous night at Yavapai College. JoAnne was talking to her photography instructor when Marilyn came by and said hi.

"She just stood there and looked at me as though she had never seen me before," Donkersley said. "I introduced myself a couple of times, but she kept saying I must be mistaken. Then I found out that everyone else around there knew her as Marci somebody. There's something definitely wrong here. Something's going on."

That same week San Diego FBI boss Norman A. Zigrossi called a three o'clock press conference to announce that the Loomis ArmoredCar Service was doubling its initial ten-thousand-dollar reward for information leading to the arrests and convictions of the Stopwatch Gang.

Shortly after noon, the press conference was canceled without explanation.

Paddy Mitchell had reluctantly moved out of Sycamore House and into Beckie's the day after his final blow-up with Bob Kitteredge. Wright finally convinced his housemate that sooner or later the sheriff was going to get a call from Mr. Bob. Risking life in prison over a landlord-tenant dispute didn't make a lot of sense.

It was the third week of October when the entire Stopwatch Gang got together for brunch with their housesitter friends John and Cathy at the absentee tycoon's mansion. Cathy was none too comfortable with Beckie's latest, Sweetie, and had already asked Reid point-blank if Mitchell had ever been in prison. It was the way he played Scrabble, she said. Ex-cons are supposed to be some of the best players around.

Princess and Sweetie arrived considerably overdressed for the occasion. She was noticeably excited. Mitchell was grinning.

"So where have you two been?" Reid asked Mitchell when they were alone in the kitchen.

"We went to church," Mitchell said proudly, "and on the way home, I told her I thought we should get married."

"You went *where* and were talking about *what*?" Reid exploded. "Jesus, man, you better stop bouncing that poor girl; it's shaking all your bolts loose."

"Well, I didn't actually—"

"Listen, my poor oversexed friend," Reid interrupted. "This is a small town. You start going to church and you're going to attract a lot of attention to all of us. And for chrissakes, don't go around promising to marry—"

"Well, we didn't set a date or anything," Mitchell said sheepishly.

"Oh, that's a different story then," Reid said sarcastically. "For a minute I thought maybe you had forgotten you are still married to your first wife. Gawd, Pat, I've never seen anyone who can reel them in like you do. And that's fine, that's your business. But dammit, man, don't go around promising to marry them."

Mitchell was indignant. "This one is different. I love this woman. And, frankly, I'm tired of running. I don't want to do it anymore."

"We're all tired of running," Reid said. "Unfortunately, we can't just call the cops and tell them we've decided to drop out of the race to become respectable citizens."

Mitchell looked so woebegone that Reid put a consoling hand on his shoulder.

"Do what you want with Beckie, but don't go around promising to marry her. Sooner or later, you're going to have to run."

The following week, the Kitteredges' dog barked on and off every night. No one seemed to have an explanation. It was almost as though there was somebody in the woods.

***

It was almost dusk when Reid and Mitchell drove north out of Phoenix. They had stuffed close to three hundred thousand dollars in a safety-deposit box, and spent the rest of the day just driving around talking. Both agreed it was time to take a long vacation from the bank-robbery business, and that the welcome mat in Sedona was getting a bit threadbare.

Reid admitted he was perturbed by the blow-up with the Kitteredges, the barking dog, the cleancut fisherman under their veranda, and those other two chaps at the next table during Sunday brunch.

Mitchell admitted he was perturbed by just about everyone around him. Sweetie and his Princess had already decided to spend a few weeks holidaying at her family's condo back in St. Petersburg, Florida. Paddy was then planning to surprise Beckie with a three-week luxury Caribbean cruise as, well, sort of an engagement present. Mitchell had wanted to leave Sedona the day he got the boot from Sycamore House. But Beckie had insisted on giving the proper two-weeks' notice to her employer at the Poco Diablo bar.

Reid also planned to leave. All he needed was his pilot's license and a brand new Moonie 201. A black one. The airplane was on order, and the flying test was booked for the first week of November. Then he and JoAnne would be airborne for a winter in the Cayman Islands. Probably take Lionel with them. The whole gang would keep in touch through Jack and Judy Seeley—everyone agreed that the couple wasn't the least bit suspicious—and reconvene at the Biltmore in the spring. Then they could cut the three hundred thou from the safety-deposit box and decide where everyone wanted to go from there.

As the car rounded the last bend of the highway from Phoenix to Sedona, Reid was dozing in the passenger seat, Mitchell was driving with a half-empty can of Bud between his legs. Suddenly, his eyes locked on the rearview mirror.

"Shit," he sputtered. "We've got company."

Reid snapped awake to the reflections of red flashing lights...Damn ...This is it...

"Do exactly as I tell you," Mitchell whispered. "Without turning in your seat, reach across with your left hand and grab the beer from my lap."

Reid did as he was told, amazed at his partner's preoccupation with an illegal can of beer at a time like this.

"You're twenty miles an hour over the limit," the officer said, shining his flashlight at the two faces in the front seat. "Oh, Tim, it's you," said Deputy Gary. "Been flying a lot lately?"

After a short chat two of the most hunted fugitives in America were sent on their way with a half-empty can of beer and a warning to ease up on the gas.

A few days later Reid was driving up the Oak Creek Canyon Road when Deputy Gary nabbed him again, but this time the conversation was a little less cordial and the warning a little more stern. Reid suspected the lawman might have been just a little pissed at him for taking off from a bar one night with a local cowgirl named Louella. She had professed no interest in the deputy, but Reid suspected the deputy didn't feel quite the same way about her. Or about him after that, either.

"The next time, I'm going to have to slap a ticket on ya," the deputy sheriff warned Reid.

The next afternoon Reid arrived at Sycamore House to find a telephone company truck parked beside the Kitteredges' house, and a repairman strapped to the pole. For a long minute, Reid watched the repairman watching him. When the van was still there at nightfall, Reid went upstairs to Wright's apartment.

"I don't like it," Reid said. "I just don't like it..."

On Wednesday, October 29, Timmy Pfeiffer and JoAnne had lunch with the Seeleys at Stretch's Cantina near the airport. The official reason for the gathering was to give Jack and Judy a couple of presents the globetrotters had brought back from their weekend in Vermont—a can of fresh maple syrup and a T-shirt for Jack that read: "Smilin' Jack's School of Ero-Naught-Icks—Flying instructors do it with class." The Seeleys thought that was pretty hilarious.

Unofficially, the luncheon was to celebrate Timmy's gift to himself. He and Jack had just flown back from Phoenix where Reid had plunked down a ten-thousand-dollar deposit with Superstition Air Service for a brand new Moonie 201. The aircraft would be ready for delivery the following week—the company just needed a few days to paint the plane black. There was only one hitch.

"How would you like the aircraft registered, Mr. Pfeiffer?" the selling agent had asked. "In your name or under Spectre Marketing Enterprises?"

"Ah, well, I'm not exactly certain," Reid stammered. "I'd better check with my accountant in San Diego. I'll get back to you."

The name Timmy Pfeiffer and the phony company were about to be buried in the alias graveyard, along with his car, credit cards, and everything else about him. Reid had overlooked the plane registration.

It was a painful glitch that certainly canceled the gang's plan to stay in touch through the pilot and his wife. Reid loathed the idea of pulling a sudden vanishing act on the Seeleys. But the awkward encounter over the aircraft registration had made his disappearance inevitable—he couldn't simply tell Jack and Judy that he had decided to register the plane under Bob Smith. He couldn't tell anyone anything about his new alias. In fact, he could never again see anyone he knew, other than his criminal friends.

Lunch with the Seeleys ended shortly after two o'clock so Reid could get to his dental appointment for the long-awaited installation of the permanent crowns.

George Moore had done a truly fine job on the new collection of teeth, and his patient was delighted to be rid of the plastic temporaries. But there was an air of awkwardness—receptionist Marilyn Donkersley had barely looked up when Reid entered the office.

The receptionist booked another appointment so the dentist could check his handiwork in a month or so. Reid had no intention of keeping the date. He would be long gone by then.

That evening Reid walked up to the Kitteredges' home and signed a new one-year lease on Sycamore House. For almost two hours he sat in their living room telling them all about the laundry service he had bought in Tucson. Only had four trucks. He wanted to expand it to twelve, run the business for a couple of years, and sell it. He'd got himself a real nice condo down there as well, but he thought he would keep Sycamore as a ski place for the winter. Said a couple of lawyer friends might be up to use the place as well.

For the first time, Reid paid nothing in advance. Wright didn't even sign the new lease.

The following day Reid took his final flying lesson with Jack Seeley and spent several hours reviewing everything he would need to know for his licensing examination the following week.

There was one other final bit of business—Reid was color blind and would have to pass a special "light-gun" test or be barred from night flying.

"It's no real problem," Jack explained. "They flash white, green and red lights at you. Even you'll be able to distinguish them. Just don't tell them something looks amber, 'cause there ain't one. You'll be fine."

Seeley offered to book the test for the following week after the main flying exam. But Reid insisted they try for something earlier; he had already decided the signing of his pilot's license would be the last time he would ever see Jack Seeley.

Later that afternoon, Reid picked up the pay phone outside Sycamore House and called the Seeleys. Jack had some good news and some bad news.

"The good news is they can fit you in for a light-gun test in Phoenix tomorrow morning," Jack said. "The bad news is they can only take you at eight-forty-five, which means flying out of here at seven-thirty, latest."

Jack gave a throaty laugh. "So why don't you pretend we have to leave by five in the morning, and maybe you'll get here on time for a change."

"Is that seven-thirty your time or Sedona time?" Reid quipped with a chuckle. "Just kidding, Jack. See you tomorrow morning at the airport. Seven-thirty. Promise."

As Reid hung up the phone, he thought he heard snapping twigs. He wheeled around. A man with a fishing rod was trudging away from Oak Creek and up through the woods not twenty feet away. It was the same guy again, the fisherman with the short haircut.

CHAPTER TWENTY

Sedona, Arizona, Halloween 1980

Stephen Reid put the go-cup of hot coffee on the dash, started the Camaro, and checked his watch. Friday, October 31, 7:30 a.m. Dammit. He was already due at the airport, at least twenty minutes away. He had promised Jack Seeley he wouldn't be late for the FAA test, but he was. As always. Just snoozed through the alarm. Other than that, didn't get much sleep at all. Couldn't get that fisherman out of his mind, the one with the short haircut just like the telephone repairman, just like the two fellows at the airport restaurant. Any one of them could have been FBI. Or all of them. But it didn't make sense—no lawman was going to wait to take down the Stopwatch Gang.

The first rays of daylight were igniting the red rock peaks as the Camaro pulled out of the Forest Houses laneway and sped off down the empty two-lane highway toward Sedona. A wispy-cotton mist hung over the canyon, the sheer walls echoing the whirring symphony of locust-like cicadas. Reid rolled down the window to let in the crisp autumn air. He pushed the speedometer up to fifty-five.

Reid sipped on the go-cup and turned his mind from the suspicious strangers of days past to the sleek Moonie 201 that would be waiting for him on the airport tarmac Monday morning. JoAnne would be leaving the house within the hour to get a bank check certified for the sixty thousand dollars outstanding on the plane—even he wasn't about to try to pass off that much in twenties. Then, with his pilot's test on Tuesday and his plastic surgery on Thursday, they could be airborne for the Cayman Islands by Friday. One week to go and life would start anew.

About a mile before Slide Rock the Camaro roared around a bend in the road and past a tourist pull-over marked, "Scenic View." Reid hit the brakes, but it was too late.

The car shot past the parked police cruiser of the Coconino County Sheriff's Department. Reid glanced at the speedometer, then at the familiar face of the deputy sheriff in the patrol car.

"Ah, shit, Gary," Reid muttered angrily. "Not again. Not today. I'm already late."

On the morning of Thursday, October 30, FBI special agent Stephen Chenoweth was a half hour north of Oak Creek in Flagstaff, teaching a course on SWAT-team tactical assaults. After twenty-one years of chasing bank bandits, prison escapees, and other dangerous fugitives across Arizona, there wasn't much he didn't know about bringing criminals to justice—dead or alive.

Just before noon Chenoweth was called out of the classroom to take an urgent phone call. He returned a few minutes later to say the afternoon session had to be cancelled.

"I'm afraid we'll have to take a rain check," Chenoweth announced. "Unfortunately, I've been asked to put all this classroom theory into practice rather urgently. By the sounds of it, we had better not plan to reconvene until sometime next week."

Special agent Chenoweth reckoned the case wasn't going to involve a lot of hunting for suspects—he had been given three names, three photographs, three sets of fingerprints, two automobile license numbers, and one address for all of them: SR 3 Forest Houses, Oak Creek, Sedona, Arizona. Arresting them, however, might be a different matter. Suspects have propensity for violence, a subsequent telex had warned. Known to possess automatic weapons. Make: Uzi.

Chenoweth would have liked to invade Sedona with every SWAT team in America, but he couldn't risk it. In his words: "Oak Creek and Sedona were nothing. So trying to put the number of people we needed to put in strategic positions to observe everything we needed to observe was not easy, and of course to stay unobserved."

The telex had said the suspects were extremely evasive. That meant they were smart enough to notice a cavalcade of chromeless Chevys in a small town like Sedona. It also meant: don't let them get away.

At approximately 2 p.m. two FBI agents walked into the Sedona sheriff's office and flashed their badges at the local lawman sitting with his cowboy boots on the desk, his long-barreled six-guns draped over the hat stand.

"Now, sheriff," one of them began, laying out three black and white photographs on the desk. "Have you ever seen any of these men before?"

"Mind tellin' me what this is all about?" the sheriff asked.

The FBI man didn't answer. The sheriff studied the pictures.

"Nope. Can't say I have," he said. "So, what's—"

"Now, sheriff," the FBI continued, "do the names Timothy Pfeiffer, Ronald Scott, or Michael Garrison mean anything to you?"

The sheriff thought for a moment. "Yeah, Timmy Pfeiffer. Now I do know that name. Yeah, for sure. Nice fella. Lives up the canyon. From Hollywood or something. Good friends with one of our deputies. Yeah, nice fella."

The sheriff leaned forward on his desk. "Now, you mind telling me—"

The FBI man smiled: "Well, sheriff, your deputy ought to be more careful about the company he keeps."

Mary Kitteredge thought it only happened in the movies—two FBI badges in black cases, dangling from outstretched arms poking in her face on the front doorstep of her home.

"Oh, dear, is someone hurt?" she sputtered in sudden panic. "Is it my son?"

The FBI managed to calm Mrs. Kitteredge long enough for her to call her husband up from the garden.

"I guess you're here about the bad check," Bob Kitteredge said, assuming the FBI had spent the past year hunting down the former tenant whose rent check had bounced.

"Do you recognize any of these three men?" Chenoweth asked, handing the Kitteredges the three black and white police photos.

"Oh sure, that's Timmy Pfeiffer," Mary Kitteredge said. "Looks pretty scruffy in the picture, but that's him all right. He and his girlfriend live just down below us in Sycamore House. And that's Steve Kirkland. Lives in the upstairs apartment. And, oh, there's that Garrison fellow," she said sourly, studying the photo of Mitchell. "Look at that smirk on his face."

Special agent Chenoweth proceeded to relay the necessary information to the Kitteredges—namely, their tenants were wanted across America as suspects in dozens of armed robberies, including the biggest bank holdup in San Diego history.

"No, no, I'm sure you've made some mistake," she interjected. "Timmy and JoAnne are two of the nicest people we've had stay with us here. And Mr. Kirkland, well, he's so quiet, you'd never know he even lived here. Spends his whole day down by the creek with their puppy. The guy wouldn't hurt a flea. Now, that Garrison character. I could believe anything about him. He was a slob—"

"Was a slob?" Chenoweth interrupted.

"He lived with the others for a while until I threw him out," Bob Kitteredge said with some bravado. "I told him to get out of here or I was going to call the, well, ah, anyway, I threw him out."

There was a knock at the door. Mary Kitteredge opened it slowly until she recognized the face of the man outside. It was the fisherman with the short haircut, the same one who had dropped by two weeks before to ask permission to toss a line in the creek. This time he had his rod in one hand, his FBI badge in the other.

Fishing under the veranda of Sycamore House two weeks before had certainly put FBI special agent Blain McIlwain closer to the Stopwatch Gang—and for longer—than any other lawman in America. The only problem was, he didn't know it. Just took a day off work to cast for trout and he wasn't getting any nibbles further upstream.

Now that everyone knew there was more to be caught around Sycamore House than rainbow trout, special agent McIlwain, cleverly disguised as a fisherman, was dispatched back to the creek to conduct surveillance of the suspects.

McIlwain didn't have much to report from his fishing-hole lookout so far: only a few good bites, and just one close encounter with the Stopwatch Gang—his brush with Reid after the call to Jack Seeley on the outdoor pay phone. Suspect said something about being at the airport by seven-thirty the next morning. Other than that, all suspects were at home and accounted for—except Mitchell.

No one seemed to know where Paddy was.

It would have been easy enough to uncover the whereabouts of the suspect described in the FBI telex as the suspected leader of the suspected Stopwatch Gang. Hell, Deputy Gary probably knew about Paddy. But special agent Chenoweth wasn't taking any chances, even with the local lawman. No one but the sheriff and the Kitteredges were to know the FBI agents were even in the area. One misplaced question in a town like Sedona, one tip that the FBI were around, and the culprits would be running for the hills.

Special agent Chenoweth also knew the Stopwatch Gang was big time. National news material. He didn't just want two of the suspects. Special agent Chenoweth wanted all of them.

That left him with some tough decisions. They could take down Reid and Wright and risk losing Mitchell. Or they could wait for Mitchell and risk losing all of them. One way or another, they couldn't wait long for anyone—the Kitteredges had mentioned Reid had signed a new lease, but paid nothing in advance. Wright hadn't even signed, and the following day was the last day of the month. Then there was that call from the pay phone, something about being at the airport by seven-thirty. Chenoweth concluded the suspects were getting ready to move.

As night fell on Oak Creek Canyon, special agent Chenoweth pored over blueprints of Sycamore House and topographical maps of the surrounding roads and countryside. A dozen agents with heavy artillery had been called in from Phoenix, but were sent to Flagstaff— nowhere to hide that many of them in Sedona.

Finally, special agent Chenoweth made his critical decision: they would do nothing before daybreak. All existing evidence suggested the suspects did not yet guess they were under police surveillance. And if there were going to be a stand-off or a gun battle, Chenoweth would rather be standing off or shooting it out in daylight. Besides, he had a plan that was a lot safer than trying to storm Sycamore House. And maybe, just maybe, Paddy Mitchell would show up in the meantime.

That night agent Chenoweth was so certain of his plan, so confident the FBI's cover had not been blown, that no one was even left behind to keep watch over Sycamore House.

Mary Kitteredge went to bed early with an allergic reaction to a flu shot, while her husband Bob sat by their front window, peering through the darkness at Sycamore House, wondering how he could have liked people that bad that much. He was also more than a little peeved the FBI weren't giving him and his wife police protection. That fellow Chenoweth had said just to act normally, to stay indoors for the evening and there was probably nothing to worry about. Easy for him to say. Bob Kitteredge didn't sleep at all that night. Just like Stephen Reid.

As the Camaro shot down the Oak Creek Canyon Road beyond the parked police cruiser, Reid's eyes barely left the rearview mirror. But there was only empty pavement disappearing around the curves. He took a long slug of coffee from the go-cup and heaved a whistling sigh of relief. "That a boy, Gary," Reid said aloud. "Owe ya one, pal...Anything you want...Promise I'll never drive Louella home again."

Then he heard it. A distant whine at first, then louder. A siren. Then the flashing lights in his rearview mirror.

"Ah, shit, Gary," Reid growled. "Why today?"

Reid brought the Camaro to a stop in the tourist pull-over at Slide Rock. Through the open window, the crescendo of whirring insects mixed with the splashing of Oak Creek, tumbling and frothing over the smooth stones in the canyon beside the road. He grabbed his coffee, opened the car door and stepped into the brisk morning air.

Suddenly, his brain froze.

It was Deputy Gary, all right. Crouched behind the open cruiser door, staring at Stephen Reid down the barrel of a shotgun.

Reid's eyes flicked to the other side of the cruiser. Another deputy. Another shotgun.

"What the fuck's going on here, Gary?" Reid sputtered.

Now there was movement to his left, more to his right, the screeching of rubber on pavement behind him. Car doors opening. The chuck-chuck of rifles and shotguns being cocked. He twisted without moving his feet. More guns. A bloody invasion of M-16 assault rifles.

"FBI!" a voice behind him said.

"No shit," Reid muttered.

"Okay, just put your hands over your head and don't move or you're dead," the voice behind him continued.

Reid raised his arms, the half-full go-cup still in his right hand.

"Just drop the cup and lie flat on the pavement."

The go-cup bounced on the asphalt, splattering the black coffee on Reid's pant leg. His nose had barely touched the ground before he felt the pinch of FBI handcuffs on his wrists, frisking hands patting the length of his body.

Two agents helped him to his feet, and for a moment Reid's eyes caught the glare of the deputy sheriff.

"What's going to happen now, Gary?" Reid asked.

"Sorry pal, I'm the wrong guy to ask," the deputy sheriff said with the smirk of someone getting the last laugh.

"So you know this guy?" one of the FBI agents asked the deputy sheriff.

The deputy sheriff didn't answer. The smirk vanished.

As Reid was led away to one of the waiting cars, police radios were crackling in five different locations. Team alpha to leader. Over...

Ten-four, alpha. This is leader. Go ahead. Over...Ah, team leader, suspect apprehended without incident. Over...Ten-four, alpha, this is leader. Good work. Move to your next assignment. I want all firepower here. Over...

"Holy shit, you guys!" Reid exploded at the two FBI agents gripping his arms. "You don't have to blast your way into the fucking house. There are no guns in there. There's a goddam woman and a dog in the place, for chrissakes."

"Uh-huh," said one of the lawmen as he pushed Reid into the back seat and slammed the door.

One down. Two to go. Chenoweth was pleased with the success of Plan A. The previous night he had called the sheriff to ask that two of his deputies be deployed to Slide Rock in the early morning to assist in effecting the apprehension of the three suspects. That was normal procedure—the plainclothes FBI like to have a uniform at the scene, just so citizens don't think they are being ambushed by a bunch of short-haired crazies in blue business suits.

But Chenoweth didn't want just any two deputies. He wanted Deputy Gary. If Reid already knew the lawman personally, he would be less likely to go for a gun. The deputy was to be told nothing other than the location of his early-morning rendezvous with the FBI on Oak Creek Canyon Road. And if all went well, the suspect would think he was merely being stopped by a familiar, friendly officer for a routine traffic violation. Special agent Chenoweth had it all planned.

At 8:20 a.m. JoAnne came out of the house, bundled Chicago into her Volkswagen, and headed for the bank to get a certified check for her sweetheart's new airplane. She was barely a mile from Sycamore House when the highway was suddenly littered with police cruisers and chromeless Chevys. The VW skidded one way, then the other, and finally crashed into the ditch. When she looked up, she was surrounded by an army of men shoulder-to-shoulder with rifles and shotguns aimed through every window in the car.

A local deputy finally opened the driver's door and found only a pretty young woman shuddering in terror, tears dripping from her cheeks, her arms wrapped around a puppy named Chicago.

The FBI were courteous and consoling, but there was still a job to be done. Through JoAnne's tears, they did manage to ascertain that suspect Wright was alone in bed in the upstairs apartment, the room at the back away from the creek.

"Oh, please dear God, don't shoot him," JoAnne pleaded. "He's just a harmless little guy."

"Harmless," the FBI agent repeated. "Uh-huh."

"I just spoke to him a few minutes ago," JoAnne said, as though that somehow reinforced her character reference. She broke into tears again. "All he wanted was for me to pick him up a loaf of raisin bread. Oh, please—"

"So he is expecting you back then?" the FBI agent continued.

"Yes he is. Sure he is. In about an hour," JoAnne sputtered. "Oh, my God. Oh, please, don't kill him."

The police radios crackled again...Ah, leader, this is team beta, do you copy?...Ten-four, beta. This is leader. Go ahead. Over...Team beta reporting female suspect apprehended without incident. Female suspect indicates a single male suspect, apparently suspect Wright, is situated in bed at the north end of the residence. Female suspect indicates male suspect is not in the company of other persons. Over...Ten-four, beta, this is leader. Good work. Ah, does female suspect give any indication male suspect is expected to depart the residence? Over...Negative, leader. Female suspect indicates male suspect is expecting her to return to the residence by the bottom of oh-nine-hundred hours to deliver single loaf of raisin bread at male suspect's request. Over...

Special agent Chenoweth lowered his walkie-talkie and stared down at Sycamore House from his perch beside the Kitteredges' home. The broadcast was not particularly good news. If suspect Wright had asked for a delivery of raisin bread, it could thereby be inferred the suspect was not intending to depart the target residence within the one-hour time period alleged by the suspect female to be her ETA back on the premises with the male suspect's raisin bread. If, on the other hand, the suspect female did not deliver the requested raisin bread within the prescribed time period, suspect Wright could become suspicious and resort to evasive action, possibly arming himself in the process.

Leader was left with no choice: they were going in after suspect Wright. As always, FBI special agent Chenoweth had a plan.

The first part of the plan was to pack the woods around Sycamore House with a small army of sharpshooters. The second part would either make special agent Stephen Chenoweth a brave hero or a dead cop. He was going in himself.

Leader studied the diagram of Sycamore House. Ten steps down from the driveway to the side entrance of Wright's apartment. All stone, no creaking boards. No windows. A screen door and a solid wood main door. The entrance opened onto a hallway landing. The suspect's bedroom was up four stairs, to the right, down the corridor, at the end on the left. His bed was parallel to the hall. The suspect would be facing anyone entering the room —if the suspect was still in bed. If the suspect didn't greet Chenoweth in the hallway with a spray of bullets from an Uzi submachine gun.

Bob Kitteredge handed the FBI a door key and hid behind a large tree. Special agent Chenoweth headed down the hill to Sycamore House.

At 9:25 a.m., precisely when suspect Wright would be expecting delivery of his raisin bread, Chenoweth turned the brass doorknob, pushed open the door, and stepped onto the landing in the hallway. Four other agents with high-powered rifles followed and flattened themselves against the wall. Chenoweth looked at the stairs, the empty corridor, and the open bedroom door at the far end on the left. If the Uzi came around that corner, they'd be sitting ducks. Dead ones.

Chenoweth silently counted down from three with his raised fingers and began trudging up the stairs as though he were JoAnne returning with a loaf of raisin bread. His brain was screaming: Where is he? Where is he?

Chenoweth moved down the hall, paused, jumped past the open bedroom door, and jammed his back into the pine wallboards. He motioned to the others.

"FBI!" Chenoweth shouted. "Don't move a muscle or we'll kill you!"

Lionel Wright's body jumped a foot off the bed as though a thousand volts had just shot through his electric blanket. By the time his eyes had blinked in the daylight, he was staring at a bedroom packed with bulletproof vests, assault rifles, and pump-action shotguns. One of the agents reached over and yanked the bedding onto the floor. Lionel was now lying in a roomful of guns and strangers. Daring not to move a muscle. Not even a hand to cover his shyness. He was totally naked.

"Okay, who's going to frisk him?"

The lawmen laughed.

CHAPTER TWENTY-ONE

Sedona, Arizona

With two-thirds of the Stopwatch Gang safely under lock and key in the Flagstaff jail, and every route in and out of the valley roadblocked, the agents of the FBI descended upon Sedona in search of the elusive Patrick Michael Mitchell, alias Michael Garrison, alias just-call-me-Mikey.

Stephen Reid certainly wasn't helping—he was still insisting his own name was Timothy Pfeiffer, a respectable businessman with a hankering to sue for false arrest. Lionel Wright wasn't much help, either—reading the Ghost his right to remain silent gave new meaning to the word redundant. The police tried to question JoAnne, but she rapidly became a basket case and a doctor had to be called to administer sedation.

Coconino County Deputy Sheriff Bill Nigh, husband of the gang's favorite waitress, DeeDee, of Rene's Restaurant and Bar, had been in the cruiser that morning with Deputy Gary when they arrested Reid on the canyon road. It had been among the more thrilling moments of Nigh's career—certainly a lot more exciting than his next assignment.

For the next twenty-four hours, Deputy Nigh was given the job of chauffeuring two FBI agents around town to gather evidence and conduct interviews with individuals who might be in possession of information necessary to locate and apprehend one Paddy Mitchell. His passengers were a couple of Leadfoots, all right. Not a lot basically wrong with them, mind you, nothing a steamroller over their egos couldn't fix.

It was late afternoon when Bill Nigh and the two FBI agents pulled up in front of the mansion belonging to the absentee armored-truck tycoon. Someone had said the two housesitters, one John and one Cathy, had been friends of the entire gang.

Cathy was home alone when the deputy and two FBI agents arrived on the doorstep. Like everyone else in town, she had already heard sketchy details of the arrests that morning. Leadfoot One did all the talking. Leadfoot Two took notes.

"So you know these individuals?" Leadfoot One said, spreading the three well-worn police photographs on the kitchen table.

"Oh yeah, sure," Cathy said helpfully. "That's Timmy Pfeiffer. He and JoAnne are a super couple. And—"

"*Were* a super couple," Leadfoot One amended.

"Yeah, I guess," Cathy sputtered. "And that's Steve Kirkland. Funny sort of guy. Really shy type. We didn't see a lot of him. I'm not sure anyone did much. Pretty well did his own thing—"

"Like robbing banks, maybe?" Leadfoot One asked with an accusing edge, as though Cathy had been driving the getaway car.

Cathy was starting to shake. "And, ah, that's Mike Garrison. Naturally, we saw a lot of Mikey 'cause he and Beckie are, ah, sort of an item, and Beckie's my best friend, but I'm sure she didn't know—"

"And I suppose you're going to tell us," Leadfoot One began sarcastically, "that you didn't know your best friend was hooked up with a group of individuals wanted for armed robberies from one end of this country to the other? Is that what you want us to believe?"

"Well, no. I mean, yes. I didn't know any of that stuff. I mean, I had my suspicions—"

"Suspicions?" Leadfoot One asked.

"Well, yeah. Like I remember once asking Timmy if Mike had ever been in prison, 'cause I sort of suspected he might have been, 'cause, well, it was the way he played Scrabble."

The agents roared with laughter.

"Scrabble?" Leadfoot One said. "Did you say Scrabble? What, did he use the word escape a lot? Come on now, Cathy."

"No, no. Someone once told me ex-cons are really good at the game, and Mikey was really good at the game, so—"

The Leadfoots rolled their eyes at one another in obvious disbelief. Cathy was starting to buckle. She wiped the first tears from her cheeks. The deputy sheriff wondered if the FBI carried their own bare, swinging light bulb.

"And when was the last time you saw your best friend Beckie and this nice fellow Mikey?" Leadfoot One continued.

"The last time I saw them was the last time everyone else around here saw them, and if you have any more questions—"

"And when might that have been, Cathy?"

"Five days ago," she snapped.

"Where?"

"At the Poco Diablo Bar," Cathy said flatly. "We had a huge going-away party for Mike and Beckie. Half the goddam town was there, including, I might add, a few folks from the sheriff's department."

The Leadfoots shot the deputy an oh-really sneer, as though the local lawmen should have known the departing guest of honor was on the FBI's Most Wanted list.

"And have you talked to the happy couple since they left town, Cathy?" Leadfoot One continued.

"Listen, if you think I had something to do with all this stuff, then I want to call a lawyer," Cathy said angrily.

"Oh no, no, heavens no, Cathy," he said smoothly. "We don't think anything of the kind. We just need some information. Your friend Beckie might be in a lot of danger."

"All right," she said reluctantly, "I spoke to them last night. They're at a condo somewhere in Florida. Don't ask me where. We are supposed to get in touch with each other at six o'clock every Thursday evening. But there's no phone in the condo. Just a pay phone somewhere around their place."

She dissolved in tears. The agents nodded at each other, and snapped their gold-embossed FBI business cards on the kitchen table.

"If you should happen to hear from your good friends, you will be sure to give us a call, won't you Cathy?" Leadfoot One said, as they turned for the door.

Cathy barely nodded her bowed head. Bill Nigh turned to the two agents standing at the door.

"I'll catch up with you in a minute."

As the two men from the FBI headed back to the police cruiser, the deputy sheriff put his hand on Cathy's shoulder and tried to console her.

"Sorry about all this," the deputy said soothingly, "but I guess they're just trying to do their job."

The shaken woman mopped her face.

"Cathy," the deputy continued, "you wouldn't by any chance have the number of that pay phone in Florida so we can find out where your Beckie's at?"

"Sure. It's on the pad beside the phone. Eight-one-three-something, I think."

Deputy Sheriff Bill Nigh climbed back into the cruiser.

"Here, you might need this," he said, holding a slip of paper over his shoulder without turning.

"And what might this be, deputy?" one of the Leadfoots asked.

The deputy sheriff was trying hard to keep a straight face.

"That's where you'll find Patrick Mitchell."

"There must be some terrible mistake," JoAnne kept repeating to the FBI between sobs, the sedatives doing little to diminish her grief. "This can't be happening. It can't be true. There must be a mistake..."

But as she watched the FBI turn Sycamore House upside-down, it became painfully clear there had been no mistake. Every day she had pulled her clothes from the bedroom dresser. Now the police were pulling ten thousand dollars from Reid's socks. For over a month she had been making love on another twenty-eight thousand dollars stuffed between the mattresses. Another eight thousand was taped to the bottom of the laundry hamper. Then there was the two grand in small bills the FBI found in a glass bowl beside the bed.

For hours FBI agents took turns trying to interrogate the weeping woman who had shared her bed with one of America's most hunted bandits and, apparently, one of America's most persuasive liars. Most of what little JoAnne was able (or willing) to tell the lawmen between sobbing fits was either contradictory or evasive or simply beyond credibility. But there were no indictments naming her as a suspect, no warrants for her arrest. Whatever her involvement had been with the gang, the FBI concluded she wouldn't know an Uzi submachine gun if she fell on it.

"You're free to go," special agent Chenoweth finally told JoAnne, her arms clutching Chicago like a stuffed toy.

Free to go. But where? How? For what? The FBI treasure hunt in Sycamore House and seizure of Reid's bank account had left her with clothes, a beat-up Volkswagen, fifteen dollars, and a confused puppy.

JoAnne drove to the Sedona airport to see Jack Seeley, hoping that Reid's habit of paying everything in advance had left some cash on credit at various establishments around town, including the flying school.

When Reid had not appeared at the airport by nine o'clock that morning, Jack Seeley had called the sheriff's department to ask if there had been an accident of some kind involving a Camaro and/or one Timothy Pfeiffer. On instructions from the FBI, the dispatcher said she had no record of anything of that kind. Seeley then called home, but Judy said Timmy had left no messages there, either. Strange, they thought. Tim was always late for everything, but he always called.

JoAnne walked into Jack's flying school office with the unlikely news that Timmy had been arrested in New Mexico. The Internal Revenue Service had nabbed him, she said. Something to do with overdue taxes. He had called to ask her to collect whatever money was left on credit for his flying lessons. JoAnne couldn't lie her way out of an empty phone booth, but it didn't much matter—the balance on Reid's account was only sixty-eight dollars.

After JoAnne left, Jack Seeley was back on the phone to the sheriff's department dispatcher.

"I am afraid I cannot give out any details on the whereabouts of Mr. Pfeiffer," the woman told Seeley. "But just a friendly word of advice, Jack—I wouldn't be getting myself involved with those characters if I were you."

An hour later, Jack finally reached Deputy Gary who gave him all the sordid details about the arrest of the man the Seeleys had come to regard as family.

"Oh god! Not my Timmy," Judy Seeley exclaimed. "Arrested? Armed robbery? It can't be. Not my Timmy. And that meek little Steve Kirkland? And Mikey? Sticking up banks with guns, for heavens sakes? No. There must be some mistake."

Judy suddenly remembered Reid telling her two days before the big San Diego heist that he was running out of cash and had to get back to work. Jack wondered how many times he had unwittingly driven the getaway plane on all those training flights to places where Reid said he had "business."

Jack and Judy Seeley stared at each other, not knowing quite whether to laugh or cry.

"Well, I for one don't care," Judy finally said with some indignation. "Timmy would still be welcome in my house anytime—or whatever his name is..."

As the afternoon progressed, word of the arrests spread through Sedona like brushfire. Deputy Sheriff Bill Nigh dropped by Rene's Restaurant to tell his wife the stunning news about her favorite patrons. The great tippers. Too bad it wasn't their money.

The deputy's wife rushed to the phone to call the restaurant owner's wife, Jan Bauda, who wasted no time calling the landlord's wife, Mary Kitteredge, at Forest Houses.

Mary Kitteredge was a fountain of exciting information about their barking dog, the fisherman's strange visits—geez, the FBI must have been staking out the place for two weeks at least, she said. And then that fellow Timmy sitting in their living room not a day before, saying how he had bought this laundry service in Tucson.

"Some laundry service," Mary Kitteredge said with a hearty laugh. "At least now we know what they were going to launder."

When JoAnne walked into George Moore's dental office in search of more leftover credit, she was greeted by awkward stares and a visibly nervous Marilyn Donkersley behind the reception desk. JoAnne sputtered something about their having to leave the state for a long time on business, but it was all to no avail. The amount of money left on account from the two thousand in twenties was an even zero.

George Moore had been telling everyone his office must have been under FBI surveillance the previous day when his high-flying patient came in for his new mouthful of molars in permanent plastic.

The dentist's first reaction to the news about his favorite patient was an excited comment to his wife: "Boy, just think. If we hadn't got all those crowns submitted yesterday and he goes to jail, those temporaries would have been shot within a year and they'd have to pull every tooth in Timmy's mouth—or whatever his name is."

JoAnne returned to Sycamore House to find Mary Kitteredge tidying up after the FBI scavenger hunt. Local treasure seekers had already swarmed the surrounding woods, checking every tree trunk around the place for a stash of stolen booty. So far, they had come up with seventy-seven cents in loose change.

"What will you do now, JoAnne?" Mary Kitteredge asked the forlorn figure wiping tears with one hand and patting her pup with the other.

"I just want to go home to my family for a while," JoAnne said through the sniffles.

"My husband and I would be happy to take care of Chicago for you, if that would help," Mrs. Kitteredge said kindly.

"Oh my God," JoAnne sputtered, bursting into tears again. "Thank you, but, but, oh God. He's all I have left."

Mary Kitteredge finally said goodbye with a hug and a final wish of good luck, as JoAnne finished packing her dog and her few belongings into the Volkswagen.

JoAnne counted the eighty-three dollars in her purse and took one last nostalgic wander through the beautiful house. She already knew she wouldn't find a penny in the place—the FBI had it all. Almost as an afterthought, she walked over to the huge stone fireplace and turned over the pottery jar on the mantel.

Something fell into the palm of her hand. Strange, she thought. Never seen it before. The FBI must have missed it somehow. Must have belonged to a previous tenant.

As dusk darkened the red rocks of Sedona, JoAnne dropped the stopwatch into her pocket, flicked off the lights, and closed the door behind her for the last time.

CHAPTER TWENTY-TWO

San Diego, California

Norman A. Zigrossi wasted no time summoning the media for his victory speech and press conference. Heck, Lionel Wright wasn't even behind bars before the FBI's public relations department was cranking out its first communiqué on the dramatic arrest of the Stopwatch Gang. Well, most of the Stopwatch Gang. Well, the arrest of two individuals suspected of being in the Stopwatch Gang. Well, no, the FBI couldn't say with absolute certainty they had connected the right suspects with the right gang this time. And, no, the FBI had not charged anyone with all those earlier robberies executed with a stopwatch and military-like precision. But the FBI had "information."

Not mentioned in the FBI's ensuing San Diego media hoopla was Arizona agent Stephen Chenoweth, who had just risked his life to capture two of the notorious bandits. Also conspicuously absent was the name of special agent William M. Ayers, alias Cowboy, who had tracked down the gang in the first place. The PR boys in San Diego apparently knew on what side their bread was buttered.

NEWS RELEASE
10/31/80

Norman A. Zigrossi, Special Agent in Charge, Federal Bureau of Investigation, San Diego, California, advised that as a result of a joint investigation conducted by the Federal Bureau of Investigation and the San Diego Police Department, Stephen Douglas Reid, 30, and Lionel James Wright, 35, were arrested today by FBI Agents in Sedona, Arizona, on a Federal warrant issued October 30, 1980, at San Diego, California, charging them with Conspiracy and Armed Bank Robbery. The arrest resulted from

237

the robbery of a Loomis Guard in the Bank of America, 912
Garnet Avenue, San Diego, California, on September 23, 1980,
in which $283,000 was taken. A third subject, Patrick Michael
Mitchell, is still being sought on the same charges.

If convicted of the charges, they each face a maximum prison
sentence of thirty years or a twenty-thousand-dollar fine or both.

In addition to the Bank Robbery charges in the United States,
all three subjects are wanted by the Royal Canadian Mounted
Police for Unlawful Escape from prison in Canada...

The official release and the press conference that followed were
guaranteed to generate the kind of Page One coverage that appeared in
the Saturday editions of the *LA Times*.

> Two members of a notorious gang of thieves were arrested Friday by
> FBI agents in Arizona in connection with the $283,000 Sept. 23
> holdup of a Pacific Beach bank...The gang members...also are
> suspects in the so-called Stopwatch Gang bank robberies in San
> Diego earlier this year...Zigrossi said there are enough similarities
> in the styles of the two gangs to suspect Reid and Wright...

It was apparent from the *Times* article that Zigrossi could also tell a
good yarn.

The story had romance: "Shortly before their arrest, Wright and
Reid 'were spending money, having a good time and running around
with women,' Zigrossi said. He said the suspects were with women at
the time of their arrests..."

The story had violence: "Canadian law-enforcement authorities
confirmed...the trio is wanted in connection with the December, 1979,
holdup of a Brinks armored car in Hull, Quebec, in which a guard was
killed and $350,000 taken..."

The story had plenty of action and intrigue: "According to news
reports, on April 17, 1974, a gunman wearing an Air Canada uniform
bound and blindfolded a night watchman guarding gold bars awaiting
transport to the Canadian Mint from a cargo shed at Ottawa International Airport...During investigation of the gold robbery, the largest in
Canada's history, authorities also uncovered a major narcotics smuggling ring..."

And finally, the story of the Stopwatch Gang had plenty of ongoing
drama and suspense. Three days after the arrests of Reid and Wright,
Norman A. Zigrossi finally conceded the obvious: Paddy Mitchell had
given the FBI the slip.

Zigrossi told reporters: "If we could have waited one day, we would have had them all. But we were afraid we wouldn't get any of them if we didn't move."

It would have been a long day of waiting. The two Leadfoots had taken a few hours too long to alert their FBI colleagues in Florida to check for the fugitive Mitchell in the vicinity of a certain St. Petersburg pay phone.

The Florida hideout was easy enough to find: the phone company coughed up the location of the pay phone conveniently bolted to the outside wall of Mitchell's condominium unit. But by the time the local FBI barged into the place, all that remained were two empty coffee cups in the sink.

At that moment Sweetie and his Princess were uncorking a bottle of champagne on the deck of a luxury ocean liner, toasting life and love and the launch of their romantic three-week Caribbean cruise. First class, of course.

FBI official spokesman Norman A. Zigrossi subsequently reported with some severity: "Mitchell will definitely go on our Ten-Most-Wanted List...He has let it be known in no uncertain terms that he intends to go down blazing."

Stephen Reid sat on the hard steel cot in his San Diego jail cell, laughing as he read. He had expected the FBI to play up to the media, but Paddy go down blazing? Trapped in a house fire, maybe.

Reid also anticipated the usual police hype to make the Stopwatch Gang appear just slightly more dangerous than Jack the Ripper with a chainsaw. But killing that Quebec Brinks guard...Shit...All three of their suspects were thousands of miles away in Florida at the time. What will the folks back home think?

But neither Reid nor his partners in crime ever expected the four-paragraph story tucked in among some earlier clippings provided by a legal-aid lawyer.

The story was dated Friday, September 26, three days after the San Diego heist, and the same day the gang had checked out of the Biltmore, too hung over to bother buying a newspaper.

FBI reports break in big bank heist

The FBI today reported a "significant" breakthrough in its hunt for the robbers who took a record $283,000 from a Pacific Beach

Bank of America branch Tuesday, said Norman Zigrossi, special agent in charge of the bureau here.

He refused to elaborate on the development which he said came early today and could result in arrests today or over the weekend.

"We feel this is very positive," he said. "With some luck, we'll identify them very soon…"

Zigrossi said the robbers are believed to have been from outside San Diego and are thought to still be somewhere in California…

Had they seen the story, the Stopwatch Gang would have been on the first flight to Timbuktu, instead of lounging around Sedona for the next month, thinking they had nothing but time and money to burn.

As it happened, the "significant break" for the FBI three days into their investigation had been a phone call from the San Diego Police Department to special agent William "Cowboy" Ayers. Seems that Wright's planned post-robbery rendezvous with the garbage truck in Mission Bay Park would have been a long wait had he not been scared off by the arriving police cruiser. The following afternoon an old man rummaging in the dumpster for empty pop cans came across one of the Bank of America money bags and turned it over to the nearest cop. Closer inspection by the FBI produced the entire trash bag of goodies—including a couple of fingerprints.

The rest of the story was spelled out in the indictments sworn by agent Cowboy two days before the arrests of Reid and Wright:

On September 25, 1980, evidence from the bank robbery which included the three Bank of America cloth bags with shipping tags still attached, paper money wrappers and plastic money containers, was recovered from a trash container located in the vicinity of Hospitality Point, Mission Bay, San Diego. Included in the same trash bag which had been secured shut at the top, were theatrical make-up, two wigs similar to those worn by the robbers, license plates apparently used on the getaway car, false facial hair, one pair of broken glasses, styrofoam food containers, and a wig box.

On October 21, 1980, the Latent Fingerprint Section of the Federal Bureau of Investigation (FBI) Identification Division advised that some latent prints on the recovered money-bag tags matched those fingerprints of Stephen Douglas Reid, FBI Number 778-025-J7, currently an extraditable escapee from Canada.

On October 27, 1980, the Latent Fingerprint Section of the FBI Identification Division advised that some latent prints on a recovered plastic money container matched those fingerprints of Patrick Michael Mitchell, currently an extraditable escapee from Canada.

Information received from Canadian authorities shows that Patrick Michael Mitchell, Lionel James Wright and Stephen Douglas Reid are known criminal associates...Each of the three is currently an escapee from Canadian prison and is sought by Canadian authorities.

A review of the bank robbery surveillance camera photographs from the Bank of America...reflects that Lionel James Wright, also known as Ronald Peter Scott, fits the description and appearance of the smaller robber in the light suit and blond wig, and Stephen Douglas Reid fits the description and appearance of the robber in the dark suit and dark wig.

On October 27, 1980, it was determined that one Ronald P. Scott, Arizona driver's license FF26391, rented a Hertz navy blue Ford LTD, four-door vehicle, at Lindbergh Field, San Diego, on September 22, 1980, at 3:04 p.m. This car was turned in at Los Angeles International Airport on September 24, 1980, at 4:41 p.m. This vehicle fits the description of the getaway car.

On October 27, 1980, inquiry of the California Law Enforcement Telecommunications System (CLETS) disclosed a California driver's license CO144435, for a Ronald Peter Scott, white male, date of birth May 25, 1951, with an address of 1623A Emerald Avenue, San Diego, California, 92109. Also reflected was a second address of 3509 Ocean Front Walk, San Diego. The first address is in very close proximity to the victim bank. The second is in the general area of the bank.

On October 27, 1980, inquiry of the Arizona Department of Motor Vehicles (DMV) disclosed that Ronald Peter Scott, date of birth May 25, 1951, was issued Arizona driver's license FF26391, on June 16, 1980. The address reflected on the printout is POB 1564, SR 3 Oak Creek F.H., Sedona, Arizona. Records of Arizona DMV show that an automobile was registered in that state to an individual using the name Timothy Douglas Pfeiffer and an address of POB 1564, SR 3 Forest Houses, Oak Creek, Sedona, Arizona, the same address used by Scott. Timothy Douglas Pfeiffer was found to have a previous California driver's license reflecting the same date of birth. A comparison of the

California DMV photographs of Ronald Peter Scott and photographs of Lionel James Wright supplied by Canadian authorities shows that they are the same person. A comparison of the Arizona DMV photograph of Timothy Douglas Pfeiffer and a photograph of Stephen Douglas Reid supplied by Canadian authorities shows that they are the same person.

Reid reread the affidavits and the thick file of news clippings. Just their luck: hunted by half the cops in North America, pinched by some vagrant pop can collector. As he pieced it all together, the story of their capture seemed to boil down to a bit of bad housekeeping, and a lot of slick detective work by special agent William M. Ayers. Very slick, indeed.

But Reid had a gnawing feeling there was something wrong with this picture. Some things just didn't add up. He began leafing through the file again.

September 23: Bank of America robbery.

September 24: The garbage truck arrives ahead of schedule. Gone by the time Wright arrives. Lionel panics when the city cop car arrives. Pitches trash and drives to Los Angeles. Returns Hertz rent-a-car to Los Angeles Airport.

September 25: The pop can collector finds garbage and collects the biggest refund of his life in cut of ten-thousand-dollar reward.

September 26: FBI pull Reid's print from tag of money bag; Mitchell's are on one of the money wrappers. That afternoon Zigrossi announces his big break in the case to media. Says he expects arrests "today or over the weekend." Says robbers are believed to have been "from outside San Diego and are thought to still be somewhere in California."

October 10: Zigrossi schedules a press conference to announce the previous ten thousand dollars in reward money is being doubled, but he cancels at the last minute. No explanation.

October 21: The FBI identification section in Washington comes up with a fingerprint match on Reid, almost four weeks after the recovery of the telltale trash bag.

October 27: The FBI ID-boys make a match with Mitchell's prints. That same day special agent Ayers identifies the Hertz getaway car that had been rented by Wright under the name of Ronald Peter Scott.

Reid stopped reading. How did they find the car? Maybe Cowboy just took a flyer because the address on the Hertz form was in the vicinity of the bank. Talk about a needle in a haystack. Maybe someone in Pacific Beach had recognized Ronnie Scott from a Canadian police photo of Wright, supplied on the hunch he would be running with Reid.

However Cowboy had solved the riddle of the aliases, the rest of the puzzle would have been a breeze. A check with the California license bureau not only would have led police to the Emerald Avenue apartment, but also to the previous address listed in the computer—namely, the condo on Ocean Front Walk. The landlord at Emerald Avenue would have been able to identify his ex-tenant Ronald Scott from the Canadian photos of Wright.

A telex to the Arizona authorities would have connected Ronald Peter Scott to the address on his license—Forest Houses, Oak Creek, Sedona. A computer check of the same address would have coughed up Timothy Douglas Pfeiffer and a license picture matching the Canadian police photo of Stephen Douglas Reid.

It all seemed like a pretty slick piece of detective work by Ayers. Or maybe he just got lucky on a tip. Norman A. Zigrossi did tell the media that the reward money "might be shared by a number of acquaintances [of the gang] along the beach." That pretty well ruled out the gang's friends along the beach—the FBI never say anything accurate about their tipsters.

There were plenty of other candidates for honorary snitch of the year, of course. The Stopwatch Gang had left a small army of doubting acquaintances in their wake.

In San Diego there was ol' Rob-O and that whole crowd of straight friends. Then there was the insurance lady in the restaurant who had caught Lionel with his alias in a knot. She even had the Emerald Street address. But how were the fugitives tracked to Arizona?

In Sedona there were any number of prime candidates—the Kitteredges fuming about Paddy; the dental office receptionist who had caught JoAnne pretending to be someone else at night school; the Seeleys—no, never Jack and Judy. Then there was Deputy Gary. Maybe he had finally figured out that people with the gang's kind of money really do rob banks.

The list was endless. But what difference would a tip have made anyway? Reid wondered. None of those people had any way to connect the known aliases of the trio to their real identities. And those fingerprints—it would be a banner day at the FBI labs in Washington if they could actually take a smudge and put a name to it.

Suddenly, something occurred to Reid. He dug through the file and began rereading a San Diego *Tribune* news clipping on Norman A.

Zigrossi's triumphant post-arrest press conference: "Zigrossi said the men were arrested without incident after being under surveillance for at least two weeks."

That would certainly account for the two FBI look-alikes that day at the Sedona airport restaurant, Reid thought, and the mysterious fisherman, and the Kitteredges' barking dog, and the telephone repairman, and all the other danger signals the gang should have heeded.

But how was that possible? Phoenix FBI boss Steve Chenoweth swore his bureau didn't know anything about the Stopwatch Gang until the day before he arrested two of them in Sedona. And according to agent Ayers's affidavits, the FBI didn't even connect the Stopwatch Gang to Arizona until the motor vehicle computer check four days before their arrest—until October 27, to be precise.

The day after Paddy Mitchell left town.

CHAPTER TWENTY-THREE

Federal Court, San Diego

"Stephen Douglas Reid, also known as Timothy Douglas Pfeiffer, is charged that on or about September Twenty-Third, Nineteen Hundred and Eighty, in the County of San Diego in the Southern District of California, he did by force and violence and intimidation, take from the person and presence of another, about $283,000 belonging to and in the care, custody, control, management and possession of the Bank of America...

"How does the defendant plead?"

Defendant Reid: "Not guilty, Your Honor."

Whereupon the same charges were read to the co-accused, Lionel James Wright, a.k.a. Ronald Peter Scott.

"How does the defendant plead?"

Defendant Wright: "Not guilty, Your Honor."

Whereupon the two accused were remanded into the care and custody of the state pending trial or until such time as they could fulfill the conditions and obligations of bail set by the court at $1.5 million—each.

Whereupon began one of the more bizarre episodes in the saga of the notorious Stopwatch Gang...

"How do you feel?" the reporter asked Reid.

The prisoner glanced at the handcuffs, at the leg irons, then at the peeling paint on the jail walls.

"Fucked."

After apologizing for the profanity and for looking so sloppy for his first-ever press interview, Reid talked for hours about the life and times of the Stopwatch Gang—albeit disavowing any connection to same. The journalist later wrote: "Reid talks painfully about his predicament, but his past stirs animation and lively reflection, as though reminiscing to a grandchild on his knee."

Reid began the interview philosophically: "The hardest part isn't landing in a hellhole like this with nothing but a bad cold. It's having everything you ever wanted and then losing it.

"You know, when I was younger, all I wanted to do was party. Drugs, booze, women—anything I could get my hands on any way I could. Fun, yeah. But it was all meaningless. So when I got put away the first couple of times, the only real difference was having to make my own prison moonshine. It was just more of a meaningless existence."

Reid paused to gather his thoughts and blow his nose, red and raw with influenza.

"But this time was different. For the first time in my life, I was starting to feel straight on the inside. I know it is hard for anyone to swallow, but you're looking at a guy who had become the picture of the perfect square. And I was never happier—a real stand-up girl, my dog, my house, my new plane—I had everything I ever wanted. One more week and I was headed for a lot of straight time.

"From nothing to everything and back to nothing again," Reid said, holding out his handcuffs like some ignominious trophy. "*C'est la vie*, I guess..."

Despite his neatly combed blond hair, Lionel Wright looked pathetically forlorn in his grossly oversized jail uniform, every cuff rolled up a good foot for his encounter with the reporter. The twenty-minute interview was a series of shy shrugs and nods and a few whispered responses that filled less than a page in the journalist's notebook.

Reporter: How do you feel?

Wright: No complaints, no regrets.

Reporter: How did you feel when you woke up with all those guns in your face?

Wright: I would have to say it came as something of a shock to everyone.

Reporter: Have you any idea how you got caught in Sedona?

Wright: Evidently, we overstayed our welcome.

Reporter: If you get time in the U.S., you then have probably another twenty years left to serve in Canada. How do you cope with that prospect?

Wright: I'm in no hurry.

Reporter: As you probably know, Paddy Mitchell has been placed on the FBI's Ten Most Wanted list. Do you think they will ever catch him?

Wright: Paddy can take care of himself.

Reporter: They seem to have a pretty air-tight case against you and Reid. How do you plan to fight the charges?

Wright: Pray a lot...

The act of pleading "Not guilty" when obviously guilty as hell is known in underworld parlance as the "Disneyland denial"—in short, a complete lie proffered in the hope the legal system will gag on some obscure technicality, thereby disgorging back onto the streets one more crook with a clever lawyer.

In the case of Stephen Reid and Lionel Wright, even Disneyland was less fanciful than pleading innocence in the face of such overwhelming evidence to the contrary. The fingerprints, the disguises, the bank bag, the money wrappers—it was all there in one big green trash bag.

The only bits of evidence the FBI hadn't found were the infamous stopwatch and the steamer trunk crammed with guns, disguises, and other paraphernalia—enough evidence to connect them to dozens of other Stopwatch robberies across the U.S. The whole collection was still sitting in the U-Store in Sedona. Reid had chanced across the storage receipt in a drawer at Sycamore House the night before his arrest. It was the last thing he had burned in the big stone fireplace. But it didn't much matter—FBI special agent Cowboy had those two hombres roped tighter than a hog-tied bronc in heat.

Bail was out of the question. Even if the two captives knew someone dumb enough to forfeit three million bucks for the pleasure of watching the pair disappear, the FBI had publicly warned that "anyone showing up with that kind of money is going to be asked a lot of questions."

If life is lonely at the top, it was perfectly desolate at the bottom of the Municipal Correctional Center in San Diego where Wright and Reid would be held in virtual solitary confinement over the ensuing months, pending trial. Aptly called the Hole, their "basement suite" was a damp, cold dungeon of windowless cement bunkers, each equipped with one steel cot, one frayed blanket, and a fifteen-watt light bulb. The place was designed for segregated punishment, not residence. But the authorities apparently thought it perfectly suited for a couple of well-known escape artists.

Time was up for the Stopwatch Gang, it seemed, and nothing much was likely to change that. Nothing much, that is, except Big Sam Stone.

Stone was the walking phone book of underworld connections to whom the gang had turned for new faces and fingerprints shortly before their arrest by the FBI. At six-foot-four and three hundred pounds, the former pro-football fullback commanded certain respect.

Stone had been a long-time friend of Paddy Mitchell and had provided the invaluable California links that ultimately disposed of the five gold bricks. Paddy claimed the guy owned half the judges, prosecutors, and cops on the west coast—or at least his known associates did, the shady ones with the Italian-sounding names. The guy got into a heap of trouble in the 1970s, but barely did enough time to get the number stitched on his prison shirt. Big Sammy had connections, all right. Paddy claimed there was nothing this guy couldn't arrange.

Stephen Reid had first met Big Sam Stone back in the winter when the gang was starting to run roughshod over bank counters in southern California. The gang was planning a big score that would require the services of an efficient jewelry fence, and Paddy was sure that Big Sammy would be able to arrange someone like that. Big Sammy could arrange anything.

Stone had instructed Reid to meet him at a Denny's Family Restaurant just off the Ventura Highway north of Los Angeles. He was to park in the side lot and go for a walk along the Topanga Canyon Road. Reid arrived two hours early and parked at the rear to watch for a possible set-up. Stone arrived early in his Rolls-Royce for the same reason. After two hours of Reid unknowingly watching Stone unknowingly watching Reid, the two met and got along just fine.

The last time the two had met was at Solley's Deli on Ventura Boulevard. Stone always seemed to eat a lot when he was nervous, and on this day, he was downing a double order of coconut cream pie. Seems he and some druggie friends had just been busted at a homestyle amphetamine factory up in Borrego Springs east of Los Angeles. Big Sammy had walked away from that rap after diving through a plate glass window during the raid. Said the boys from the Drug Enforcement Agency had nothing on him—he just happened to be in the wrong place at the wrong time.

Reid concluded Big Sammy's friends must own half the DEA agents, as well. Paddy was right—there was apparently nothing this guy couldn't arrange.

Unfortunately, some of Stone's druggie friends hadn't been so lucky and now Big Sam needed some quick cash to bail them out. Get them back in business and they'd be able to repay it all in a couple of weeks with interest of say, double the loan. Big Sam didn't dare use his own money. He wasn't even admitting he knew any of the fellas who got pinched, and the DEA were watching him like a hawk.

Reid liked the idea of investing his money at a hundred percent interest every two weeks—the profits would have almost covered the price of his new Moonie aircraft. Wright, too, thought it all a good investment—if only to keep someone like Big Sam Stone happy.

Curiously enough, Paddy Mitchell had said thanks, but no thanks, to the deal. Wright and Reid hadn't given their partner's decision much thought at the time.

Three days after the meeting at Solley's Deli, Wright flew from Sedona to Los Angeles with enough cash to bail out the Borrego Springs bunch. He and Stone retired to the Aku Aku Motel across the street from the deli where they discussed arrangements for plastic surgery to the faces and fingertips of Reid, Wright, and Mitchell. No problem, said Big Sammy. He would arrange everything.

The day after the two captured members of the Stopwatch Gang were transferred from Arizona and tossed in the basement of the San Diego lockup, a call was placed to Sam Stone at his house in a suburb north of Los Angeles.

If anyone needed some serious arranging, it was Lionel Wright and Stephen Reid. Big Sam said he would be only too happy to oblige. He would arrange everything.

Los Angeles defense attorney Ralph Larsen wasn't thrilled to get Stone's call asking him to represent a member of the Stopwatch Gang. The last time Larsen had been involved with one of Big Sammy's fugitive friends, the attorney had been arrested by the FBI. The threatened charge of obstructing justice was never laid, but the experience didn't leave Larsen begging for more of Stone's business. After some prodding by Stone, Larsen reluctantly agreed to at least talk to Reid. One did not say no to a guy like Big Sam Stone.

Larsen was surprised by his first encounter with the man portrayed by the FBI as a lethal felon. Allowed to shave only once a week, Reid certainly looked the part of hardened criminal. But the bandit was friendly, engaging, intelligent, and full of good humor, all of which were hardly expected under the circumstances. The attorney had met a lot of crooks in his day, but no one quite like Stephen Reid. No one that bad had ever been that pleasant. Ralph Larsen agreed to take the case.

"How are we going to handle the fees, Ralph?" Reid asked.

"Our mutual friend has already said he would take care of all that," the attorney replied with a shrug.

Stone was certainly living up to his reputation. Big Sammy was arranging everything.

Michael J. Aguirre had never met anyone quite like Lionel Wright before, either. Their first meeting consisted of questions from the attorney and a lot of blank stares from his new client. Under different circumstances the lawyer might have thought he was just dealing with a shy, rather simple-minded fellow. But those sad eyes had been out there doing all those daring and dangerous things like robbing banks. The case at hand was for the biggest bank robbery in San Diego history, for heavens sake. The lawyer concluded his client was probably one of those dangerous, silent types. Aguirre had never represented one of those before.

In fact, the young attorney hadn't represented a lot of crooks of any persuasion. Most of his still-budding law career had been spent trying to put criminals like Lionel Wright behind bars. Eighteen months as an assistant U.S. attorney in the office of the federal prosecutor. Another eighteen months in Washington working for the high-profile, crime-busting congressional subcommittee on investigations. Then a couple of years in Los Angeles in private practice. Then back to San Diego to set up the law offices of Aguirre & Meyer with the dream of someday running for Congress. No doubt about it, Michael J. Aguirre was ambitious, particularly on the political side. He just didn't have much experience defending bank robbers.

Aguirre had been appointed by the court after one of the three most successful bank robbers in North America pleaded abject poverty worthy of a public defender (whose bills would be picked up by the American taxpayer). No way the penny-pinching clerk of the Stopwatch Gang was spending a nickel of his hard-earned stolen money on a damn lawyer.

January 1981: Stephen Reid angrily paced the floor of the jailhouse consultation room. He was moody and agitated. Federal prosecutor John J. Robinson wanted to throw the book at the bandits. He was going for the maximum sentence. Twenty-five years, not a day less. Called the case "open and shut." No deals.

For two months, Reid had been playing jailhouse lawyer to no avail, other than driving both Larsen and Aguirre crazy.

Finally, Reid and Wright were persuaded to cut their losses and go for a deal: plead guilty in return for a shorter sentence. But they hadn't counted on a hard-nosed prosecutor named Jack Robinson, who was rarely in a dealing mood, and certainly not with the Stopwatch Gang.

"What the hell do you mean, no deals?" Reid exploded.

"That's what Robinson said," Aguirre said, shrugging. "No deals. He's not interested."

Reid glared at Larsen and Aguirre. "You mean to tell me, if we agree to plead guilty and throw ourselves on the mercy of the court and save the taxpayers all that time and expense for a damn trial, you mean to tell me, we still get to spend the next two-and-a-half decades in the joint? Where's the justice in that?"

"Listen, Steve," Aguirre said patiently. "You have to understand that Jack Robinson isn't some evil prosecutor. He has to work with the FBI, and all the FBI care about is bank robberies, and this is the biggest one they've had. They'd have Robinson's head if he let you guys skate. Let's face it: they have a good case against you. And the damn media are watching like a bunch of vultures for someone to screw up. So don't be too hard on Robinson. He's under a lot of pressure. I know, I've worked in that office with him."

Aguirre's close ties to Jack Robinson and the prosecutor's office from his days of working there had already inflamed the paranoia of both Wright and Reid—all of it unfounded—and neither crook wanted to discuss anything but the weather in front of the attorney.

For his part, Robinson didn't need any pressure from anyone on this case—he would have been perfectly content to see both felons behind bars forever.

The next day Reid was on the phone again to Ralph Larsen. "I'm worried, Ralph. I've got fourteen years to go in Canada, and Lionel's got seventeen and probably twenty by the time they finish with him. If Robinson goes for twenty-five down here, both of us are going to be collecting old-age security in the joint. There's got to be a way. Maybe Big Sammy can arrange something..."

Michael J. Aguirre was already stinging from some bitter encounters with the prosecutor over the Stopwatch Gang. He decided to give Robinson one last shot.

"These guys aren't your average gangland crazies," Aguirre said pleadingly. "Actually, other than their criminal side, they are both rather pleasant. I mean, they didn't kill anyone. I really do think—"

"If they're so full of good intentions," Robinson snapped, "then why haven't they returned all that money they stole?"

Aguirre thought for a moment: "Supposing they did, would you deal on a plea?"

"If they don't, I won't even talk about it."

Wright and Reid conceded there was plenty of cash that could be returned to the state, but neither was anxious to hand over a penny of it. Somehow, their accumulated wealth was all either of them had to show for their lives. On the other hand, buying their way to shorter sentences definitely had more appeal than spending their loot on a lifetime supply of prison cigarettes. Aguirre was probably right—the stolen money was the only bargaining chip they had left.

"The problem as I see it," said Reid, "is that Robinson says he won't deal until the money is returned. But what if we return the money and he says, 'Ha, ha, still no deal; see ya all around in twenty-five years'?"

Wright added: "It may be difficult to admit we have stolen money to return without admitting we stole it."

Michael J. Aguirre listened and pondered the problem. If the prosecutor's office wasn't in a dealing mood, there was one other possibility.

The courtroom of the Honorable Leland C. Nielsen had become something of an institution in San Diego legal circles. Rarely did a beseeching lawyer approach the bench without a wince, or leave without ringing ears. Prosecutor or defense attorney, it didn't much matter—the wrath of His Honor Leland C. did not discriminate. But more than anything else, the purveyor of so much reproach was also known as one of the fairest judges in the land, especially when it came to creative cures for docket congestion. As it happened, no one seemed to dislike long trials before Leland C. Nielsen more than Leland C. Nielsen. The judge had something of a reputation for impatience with those choosing to fight lengthy, losing legal battles. On the other hand, His Honor was also known to have been something of a Santa Claus to those crying *mea culpa* early in the game.

Of course, Nielsen would never get involved in plea bargaining. Instead, it became a well-known game around the courthouse for defense attorneys to chance upon the judge's clerk, a fellow named

Bob, in the courthouse corridor. The ensuing conversations might go something like this:

"So, what are you planning to do with the accused Smith?" Bob might ask.

"Oh, dunno, Bob," the attorney might lie. "If we thought he was going to get something like three years, he'd probably plead, but you just can't be sure what the judge will do, eh, Bob?"

Sometime later Bob might just happen to bump into the attorney again and say something like: "You know that Smith case of yours? Well, I took a look at the file and I don't think the judge would give him more than three on that."

And more times than not, that's exactly what Smith would get upon entering a guilty plea. Nielsen's clerk was affectionately known around the courthouse as "Judge Bob."

In the second week of January, Aguirre convened a meeting at the jail with Larsen, Wright, and Reid to announce that a deal was on the table—return the stolen money and they would get fifteen years.

"What do you think, Lionel?" Aguirre asked. "This is obviously an extremely important decision that only you can make."

Wright's lips barely moved: "Whatever Steve says."

Reid summoned Larsen back from Los Angeles again the next afternoon and told him to go for the deal. Fearing the room might be bugged, Reid communicated with his attorney through a series of scribbled notes.

The first note said the person returning the stolen loot would be referred to as "Mr. X" and his identity would never be revealed to the FBI, the federal prosecutor, or even Aguirre—"No one. *Ever!*" Reid underlined.

Secondly, Aguirre was not to be told details of the planned money drop. Thirdly, the cash would be delivered in a way that would ensure the FBI couldn't nab Mr. X in the act.

Finally, Reid scratched his last note and passed it to Larsen: "Contact Sam. He will arrange everything."

At the same time that Stephen Reid and Lionel Wright were trying to plea bargain their way from virtual life in prison to most-of-life in prison, Paddy Mitchell was having a fine time partying his brain cells to a pulp in New Orleans.

Parting with his beloved Princess had been painful. The day before their loveboat docked back in Florida after a three-week luxury cruise, Beckie had called her pals in Sedona from the ship-to-shore phone. The news from the other end of the line left her paralyzed, more in disbelief than fright.

Mitchell had tried in vain to calm her. Yeah, it was true his two friends had been in some trouble with the law. But, gosh, he never imagined they could be in that much trouble. And certainly he had nothing to do with any of it. No, no, a thousand times no, Princess. Who me?

When the boat docked the next morning, Sweetie bid his Princess a teary "God bless" and vanished.

Sometime later Mitchell made a rather daring return visit to Phoenix and retrieved the $300,000 he and Reid had stuffed in the bank safety-deposit box for their planned reunion the following spring.

The day after Reid and Wright agreed to their plea bargain, Ralph Larsen met secretly with Mr. X.

Ordinarily, Jack Robinson's skin would have crawled at the thought that Patrick Mitchell, member of the FBI's exclusive Ten Most Wanted Club, would be invited to return the gang's stolen loot as part of an officially sanctioned plea bargain in the interests of justice. But the federal prosecutor seemed convinced that the money would never be returned anyway, and the wrath of His Honor Leland C. Nielsen would then descend upon the heads of Stephen Reid and Lionel Wright. Twenty-five years of hard time, for sure. Nothing would make Jack Robinson happier.

By the last week of January, even defense attorneys Aguirre and Larsen were beginning to wonder if the money would ever be returned. Reid and Mr. X had alternately torpedoed every scheme the two lawyers had concocted for recovering the stolen booty. Of primary concern was Mr. X—he had to be protected at all cost. The FBI weren't just going to sit there and watch him dump a bundle of stolen bills on Cowboy's desk.

Reid and Larsen had discussed leaving the loot in a bus-station locker and then telling the FBI where to find it. But Wright didn't trust anyone: "What if the cops claim they found the locker empty?"

The money could have been safely handed over to either Larsen or Aguirre and delivered to Robinson's office—except neither Larsen nor Aguirre wanted anything to do with possession of stolen funds.

Finally, Reid had a plan: Mr. X would place the loot in the overnight depository of a certain branch of the First California Bank in suburban Los Angeles. The money drop would take place on a Sunday when Mr. X would run the least chance of being observed. Monday morning the bank would be instructed to place the funds in an account Reid had opened at the branch back in the spring just before the gang robbed the place. The funds would then be transferred from the account to the court.

Everyone liked the scheme—except Mr. X. He sent word back to Reid that the whole plan could still turn into an FBI trap. Aguirre extracted a promise from Norman A. Zigrossi of the FBI that there would be no surveillance, no arrests, no interference of any kind. But the nervous Mr. X was still not satisfied; he wanted one of the lawyers to accompany him on the mission.

Wright's attorney was out of the question. Getting pinched in criminal company in possession of stolen funds was definitely not the fastest route to Congress. Besides, Aguirre hadn't been entrusted with even the sketchiest details of the plan.

Larsen didn't want to do it, but one did not refuse a request from Big Sam Stone.

Stone had arranged everything.

The evening of Sunday, February 1, 1980, Los Angeles attorney Ralph Larsen drove north up the Ventura Highway and west through the Sumi Hills. Satisfied he was not being followed, he circled back towards suburban Panorama City.

As the attorney pulled into the parking lot of the Pink Pig Restaurant, he spotted a blue TransAm parked under a street lamp in the far corner. Larsen flashed his headlights twice. The TransAm's highbeams winked back.

The attorney parked and began walking towards the other car. Under the glow of the street lamp, Larsen watched the driver's door of the TransAm open. Mr. X moved to the rear of the car and lifted the trunk. The attorney slowed his pace. Mr. X was hunched over, his head and torso leaning into the trunk of the TransAm. He was wearing surgical gloves.

"Okay, let's get this over with quickly," Larsen said with obvious agitation.

The two rubber-coated thumbs snapped the latches on a brown attaché case lying in the trunk. Ralph Larsen stared at the bundles of American currency arranged like paper bricks in the briefcase.

"It's all there," Mr. X said. "Fifty-three thousand, seven hundred. Go ahead. Count it."

Larsen had been expecting a considerably larger sum, but he wasn't about to quibble. "I believe you," he said impatiently, scanning the parking lot.

"No, I insist."

"I'm sure the money is there. Let's get this over with, and the sooner the better."

"Okay, if you insist. The bank is just down the street. Hop in."

Larsen opened the passenger door and climbed into the TransAm. Mr. X slammed the trunk lid and slid into the driver's seat. The attorney looked at the briefcase perched on the console between them and listened in the darkness. No sirens. No screeching tires. No guns. The FBI had apparently kept their word.

Larsen began to relax. In a few minutes it would all be over.

Ralph Larsen called Mike Aguirre the morning after the encounter with Mr. X.

"The money is at the First California Branch in Panorama City," he said with no introductory pleasantries. "Fifty-three thousand and change in eight brown envelopes. It went into the night depository."

Larsen related the story of meeting Mr. X at the Pink Pig, the briefcase full of cash in the trunk, the surgical gloves, and how X wanted him to count it all.

"There was no way I was touching that goddam money so I can't say for sure how much was there. He told me there was $53,700 and that was good enough for me. All I wanted to do was get the hell out of there."

"Can't say I blame you, Ralph," Aguirre chuckled. "Did you deposit the money?"

"I didn't; he did. We drove to the bank and it has one of those drive-thru night depositories, you know, the ones with the carousel you turn and it drops your deposit into the locked compartment underneath. Anyway, the guy says he is going to pull up on the left side of it so I can deposit all this money. And I told him I didn't want to be any part of it, and he could bloody well pull up on his side and put the cash in there himself. So that's what happened. He pulled up to the depository and we've got the briefcase between us and he's making this big production about showing me the money going into these envelopes and into the night depository. He's saying things like, 'Okay, here it goes. Now listen to it.' And I'd hear the thing dropping into the locked compartment. I mean, the guy was in no hurry. He really wanted me to know that money was being deposited. As I said, I just wanted out of there.''

"I think I can understand that. So what now, Ralph?''

"I suggest you call the bank or Jack Robinson or the FBI or whoever the hell you want, and tell them there are eight brown envelopes stuffed with cash that require pickup and delivery to the court. Either that, or Stephen can write a check. Frankly, Mike, I don't give a damn.''

The phone never left Mike Aguirre's ear—one button to hang up on Larsen, another for a line to the First California Bank in Panorama City.

"An unmarked night deposit was made at your bank last evening and I wanted to give instructions on its transfer,'' he began. "I believe it was approximately $53,700. The deposit was made in eight brown envelopes.''

"One minute, please,'' a female voice said. "I'll put you through to the manager.''

The manager came on the line and Aguirre repeated the information—$53,700 in eight brown envelopes.

"This is all very odd,'' the manager said.

"What's very odd?'' Aguirre snapped, his hand suddenly clammy around the phone receiver.

"Well, Mr. Aguirre, we had no such deposit made at this branch over the weekend—''

"Excuse me?''

"Well, we did find eight envelopes in our night depository, but they were empty.''

"Empty?'' Aguirre repeated in a near-whisper.

"There were eight other identical envelopes stuffed with shredded newspaper. And, oh, we did find a single hundred-dollar bill.''

CHAPTER TWENTY-FOUR

San Diego, California

The news that the Stopwatch Gang had just been robbed did not go over well at the San Diego lockup.

"How the hell could this happen, Ralph?" Reid shrieked, slamming his fist on the jailroom table inches from Larsen's wincing face.

"I wish I had the answer, Steve," Larsen said, shaking his head in dismay. "I could swear—"

"Well, fuck, Ralph," Reid seethed, "you were sitting there in the car with him, for chrissakes. Fifty-three grand just doesn't turn to shredded newspaper overnight."

Larsen swore he had seen the attaché case full of cash in the boot of the TransAm. Reid figured there could have been a briefcase switch between the trunk and the front seat. Or the money could have been swapped for the look-alike bundles of shredded newspaper. But Larsen said he was sure money went into the envelopes on the car console, and he was equally certain the envelopes went into the night depository.

Wright's face was emotionless: "If all eight bundles were just newspaper covered in a couple of real notes, why did the bank find only a single hundred-dollar bill?"

Larsen said an investigator he knew had suggested it was possible the night depository had been rigged with a catchall bag on a string, making it possible for a third party to have retrieved the loot sometime after the drop.

"Doesn't make sense," Wright droned. "If someone pulled the money back out, why would anyone then bother to deposit all the shredded newspaper and empty envelopes?"

A bank employee could have pocketed the loot in the morning, one of them suggested. But the shredded newspaper made even less sense in that scenario.

Another possibility was that Larsen himself had taken the money, or he and Mr. X were in cahoots. But Reid was the first to dismiss that notion—no attorney would be that stupid.

Larsen said Mr. X had a suspect of his own, the one he had suggested to the attorney earlier that morning, just seconds before the attorney slammed the phone in Mr. X's ear: the FBI had enlisted the bank manager and taken the money as part of an elaborate sting operation. The story about the sixteen worthless envelopes was invented to make Wright and Reid think there had been a switch and they had been ripped off by their friend. If revenge then compelled the two condemned crooks to finger Mr. X, the FBI would have a clean sweep of all three.

Reid and the two attorneys dismissed the FBI sting theory as unlikely—no lawman was going to risk his badge for that kind of stunt. Wright commented: "The FBI aren't that smart."

Reid slumped in a chair. Whoever had ripped off their money had also just stolen their last chance of seeing the outside of a prison wall before the next century.

"What do you think, Ralph?" Reid said gravely.

"I think we're all in a lot of trouble."

Federal prosecutor Jack Robinson had his own theories about the funny thing that happened on the way to the bank—namely, nothing had happened on the way to the bank because no one ever went to the bank. He was convinced the stolen money had never been re-stolen by anyone and that it was still out there with Mr. X for safekeeping. Reid and Wright would claim they had tried to keep to their end of the deal, but were the victims of someone else's larceny. Nice play if it worked—they would get their plea bargain and keep the loot at the same time. But it wasn't going to work as long as Jack Robinson had any say in the matter. "The whole story," he told Aguirre, "is a lot of bullshit."

Robinson did agree it was possible that Paddy Mitchell had ripped off his friends—crooks are known to do those kinds of things, he pointed out.

But Robinson wasn't about to lose any sleep worrying about who stole what from whom. As far as he was concerned, no money, no plea bargain. And no deal meant twenty-five-year sentences for Lionel Wright and Stephen Reid. The federal prosecutor could already hear the gavel falling.

Judge Leland C. Nielsen, on the other hand, looked as though he might at any moment bring his gavel down on the heads of the three shouting attorneys turning his otherwise orderly court into a raging circus of accusations and counter-accusations. A defense attorney in the midst of a swindle of his swindling client? Money switches? Shredded newspapers? FBI plots? Crooks cheating crooks? Order! Order!

Larsen returned to the San Diego jail to see Stephen Reid for the last time.

"I hate to do this to you of all people, Steve," Larsen began slowly. "But I've talked to Judge Nielsen, and I don't see how I can go on representing you."

Reid shrugged. "That's your choice, Ralph. I'm certainly not firing you."

Larsen drew a long breath: "Judge Nielsen is going to put me in front of a grand jury, and I am going to be asked to identify our Mr. X."

"No way," Reid said firmly. "I just can't authorize you to do that. There are a lot of things I'd like to do to the sonofabitch, but I've never snitched on anybody and I'm not about to start now. Case closed."

"If I refuse to identify him," Larsen continued, "I think Nielsen is in the mood to cite me for contempt and toss me in here with you."

"Bring lots of good books," Reid quipped, not knowing quite what to say next. He threw his head back and stared at the ceiling. No money. No plea bargain. And now, no lawyer.

"Do what ya gotta do, Ralph."

The grand jury remained spellbound for almost forty-five minutes as Ralph Larsen related the tale of his clandestine meeting with Mr. X and the mysterious disappearance of $53,700.

Federal prosecutor Jack Robinson had been remarkably pleasant throughout the proceedings, neither accusatory nor particularly aggressive toward Larsen. If anyone in the courtroom really cared who stole the stolen loot, Larsen apparently was not high on the list of suspects.

"One final question," Robinson began politely. "Mr. Larsen, were you positively able to identify this person you are calling Mr. X?"

"Yes, ah, absolutely."

"Would you kindly tell the court the name of this individual?" Robinson asked.

Larsen complied. Robinson was stunned.

"I'm sorry?" the prosecutor stammered, his eyes wide at Larsen. "Would you please repeat that?"

An hour later, Jack Robinson was on the phone, railing at FBI chief Norman A. Zigrossi.

Suddenly, the Stopwatch Gang had given the federal prosecutor a few problems of his own.

His Honor Leland C. Nielsen was not pleased. His determination to get to the bottom of the matter had so far unearthed only new layers of swamp. Larsen was barely out of the grand-jury room when the judge called San Diego defense attorney Michael McCabe.

"I've got a real mess on my hands," the judge said gruffly. "I want you to represent this fellow Reid and see if we can't make some sense of this case. His counsel is a guy named Larsen from Los Angeles—at least he was his counsel. Got mixed up in a money switch or some damn thing, and the whole plea has gone sour. Aguirre is counsel for a co-accused, but I'm not sure he knows what's going on, either. Anyway, call Larsen."

The judge didn't wait for a response and hung up.

Mike McCabe was known as one of the hottest defense attorneys in San Diego. The cons in the jail certainly gave him high marks, and that was always a pretty good reference.

McCabe quickly made the rounds to Reid, Larsen, Aguirre, Robinson and back to Reid, who scratched a few words on a scrap of paper and pushed it across the table to McCabe.

"It's just a hunch, Mike," Reid said cautiously.

"I'll check it out," McCabe said, and left.

Three days later McCabe was back at the jail to meet with Wright, Reid, and Aguirre.

"I had an interesting phone conversation with some fellows I know in the Drug Enforcement Agency," McCabe began. "Seems they're not very happy with their brothers in the FBI over the handling of your case."

Even Lionel was paying attention. McCabe continued.

"It would appear from court documents and from my discussions with the DEA, gentlemen, that the FBI's brilliant detective work was a lot of bullshit, most of it gathered after the fact to protect their real source of information—an informant."

"Damn!" Reid shouted, his fist making the table jump. "I knew it!"

"If my information is correct," McCabe continued, "your good friend Mr. X didn't just steal your money and your plea bargain. He first traded your skins to save his own neck."

Michael J. McCabe could spot a legal loophole from the courthouse parking lot. And this one certainly seemed big enough even for two members of the Stopwatch Gang to climb through. It was one thing for a plea bargain to have been soured by another crook's larceny. But it was a whole different matter when the intended restitution to the state was swiped by an agent of the state, working as a police informant.

Federal prosecutor Jack Robinson listened to McCabe's theory, and came straight to the point: "I have absolutely no idea what you are talking about."

"Ah, come off it, Jack," McCabe snapped. "You know damn well he fingered my client, you let him off, and then he walked off with the restitution."

But Robinson was sticking to the FBI's version of events—Wright and Reid had been captured through clever and diligent investigation. As far as the alleged informant was concerned, the prosecutor said, he had been let off other charges only because there wasn't enough evidence to convict him. There had been no deal for information.

"Frankly, Jack, I think that's all a load of crap," McCabe said angrily. "And if you won't come across with all the reports on this case and give me the true version of what happened, I'm damn well going to see the judge about it."

Jack Robinson was not easily cowed. "Well, Mike, you do whatever you want to do," the prosecutor said finally. "But I am not going to participate in any such conference with the judge."

"All right, Jack," McCabe said tersely, "if you won't participate, I'll go see the judge myself."

Most judges wouldn't let a defense attorney within ten feet of their chambers door without the prosecution present. But the Honorable Leland C. Nielsen was different—if the prosecutor didn't want to participate, too bad.

McCabe met with Judge Nielsen in chambers—Aguirre said he was unable to attend—and ran through the whole scenario.

"Unfortunately, Judge, I don't know whether this amounts to a hill of beans in terms of my client's position," McCabe finally concluded.

"There doesn't seem to be any motion that could be made that would drive a stake through the heart of Dracula here."

McCabe paused, hoping Nielsen might at least offer some encouragement. Or maybe blink. But there was nothing.

The attorney gave it one last try: "I mean, well, frankly, Judge, I think the whole thing still stinks and the government should not be permitted to go around doing this kind of thing."

The judge looked at McCabe with a stone face. His lips barely moving, he said, "I agree."

In the days that followed McCabe's visit to the judge's chambers, Jack Robinson had been burning up the phone lines to the FBI. The federal prosecutor seemed more than a bit apprehensive that the whole mess could blow up any minute.

Michael J. McCabe tactfully suggested to Robinson that, surely, it would not be in the best interests of the Office of the United States Attorney to have the entire sordid tale splashed across the front pages of every newspaper in California. In other words: deal on a plea bargain, or deal with the press.

By the third week of February, Robinson was starting to talk about a deal.

But inside the Drug Enforcement Agency, someone was evidently still fuming at the FBI and the federal prosecutor's office for their collective handling of the case. Just as McCabe was finalizing a plea bargain with Robinson, the bizarre tale of Mr. X and the mysterious theft of the stolen loot was bannered across the front page of the *San Diego Union*.

Negotiations came to an abrupt halt: if Reid and Wright pleaded guilty, the prosecutor would recommend twenty years in federal prison—take it or leave it.

Meanwhile, Nielsen's trusty clerk, "Judge Bob," seemed to be running into McCabe and Aguirre every time they rounded a courthouse corner. And every time, the subject of the Stopwatch Gang just happened to pop up in conversation. Judge Bob said he might just take a look at the file, if he could find the time. Sometime later he would be happy to offer his opinion on what His Honor just might do under the circumstances. Just an opinion, though.

On Monday, March 2, Stephen Douglas Reid and Lionel James Wright were back on the front pages after pleading guilty to the largest bank robbery in San Diego history.

The San Diego *Evening Tribune* reported:

They each could receive up to twenty-five years in prison when they return to court for sentencing.

At the recommendation of Assistant U.S. Attorney John J. Robinson, [Judge] Nielsen advised the defendants that local sentences might have to be served [first] in addition to the substantial time remaining on their Canadian sentences at the time of their escapes...

Wright and Reid told Nielsen that no promises—other than the recommended dismissal of a remaining bank-robbery charge—had been made by the prosecution in exchange for their guilty pleas. And neither Reid's counsel, Michael McCabe, nor Wright's attorney, Michael Aguirre, mentioned the defendants' earlier offer to return $53,700 in loot as part of a plea-bargaining attempt.

The same day, Norman A. Zigrossi, special agent in charge of the San Diego bureau of the FBI, told reporters "there is a strong possibility Mr. X was the fugitives' partner-in-crime, Patrick Mitchell, who is also wanted for the San Diego robbery..."

April 20, 1981. Reporters packed the courtroom of the Honorable Leland C. Nielsen to witness the sentencing of two of America's most highly publicized bandits.

Federal prosecutor Jack Robinson played to the audience with all the apparent fury he could muster, denouncing Reid and Wright as "extremely competent, dangerous bank robbers [who] will continue to be so." The protection of the public from vicious criminals, he railed, demanded nothing less than the maximum twenty-five-year sentences.

McCabe and Aguirre rose one after the other to plead that their clients were oh-so-remorseful for their misdeeds, and had showed nothing but the best intentions in trying to return their cuts of the stolen loot.

Aguirre got particularly nasty at one point, suggesting that the prosecutor needed to look no further than his own files to know exactly what had happened to the stolen money.

Robinson got nasty right back: "I don't know what office you're running for today, Mr. Aguirre."

The Honorable Leland C. Nielsen looked profoundly bored as he watched the courtroom theatrics. Finally, he ordered the two defendants to rise for sentencing. He noted that all their best intentions still came up about fifty-three-thousand dollars short, not to mention the two-hundred-odd thou also still missing from the Bank of America heist.

"The defendant is hereby committed to the custody of the Attorney General or his authorized representative for imprisonment for a period of twenty years..."

The media was happy and said as much in banner headlines the following day. Federal prosecutor Jack Robinson seemed happy enough—twenty years, twenty-five years, what's the difference? The FBI were certainly happy. And curiously enough, even Stephen Reid and Lionel Wright seemed rather happy, too.

Four days before Reid and Wright were sentenced, at precisely ten-thirty in the morning, defense counsel Michael J. McCabe and federal prosecutor John J. Robinson met in the chambers of the Honorable Leland C. Nielsen. Again, Wright's lawyer was unable to attend. The exchange went as follows:

Robinson: An informant in the case involving Mr. Reid and Mr. Wright was a man named Sam Stone. Part of the agreement with Sam Stone was that his identity and the fact that he'd provided information would not be disclosed. Subsequently...I was informed that Reid contacted Stone about obtaining an attorney for him. Mr. Stone sent Mr. Larsen to contact Mr. Reid to represent him.

Judge Nielsen: Mr. Stone is the gentleman who went out by the window at Borrego Springs in another matter.

Robinson: That's correct, Your Honor.

Judge Nielsen: Was he not prosecuted in that case as a result of his information provided in this case?

Robinson: That's correct, Your Honor...As a result of this, I wasn't quite sure what the situation was, once I learned about it, and then when Mike McCabe came into the case, replacing Mr.Larsen, I assumed there would be no further problem.

And then, in the course of discussing it with Mike, he suggested to me as we were discussing it hypothetically, that there could very well be a Sixth Amendment problem with the fact that Mr. Stone had, to any extent, been involved in obtaining an attorney for Mr. Reid at the time that Mr. Stone was providing information to the government. And after thinking about it, I think Mike is absolutely right...I think it is important that we put it on the record for the Court to know, for Mike to know, so that any appropriate action could be taken...

Mr. Stone told the FBI that the reason he had agreed to recommend an attorney to Mr. Reid was so that he could, in his words, maintain his cover so that Reid would not know that he was the one who had provided information. Apparently, shortly after he had done this, in other conversations with the FBI, he did inform the FBI agent that he was responsible for Mr. Larsen's being the attorney. The agent I talked to believed that he had relayed that information to me. I don't recall hearing any such thing until the affair with Mr. Larsen came up, when—

Judge Nielsen: The money.

Robinson:—it came to my attention that the loss of the money—

Judge Nielsen: While we're on the money, was it Mr. Stone who was with Mr. Larsen [at the bank depository]?

Robinson: Yes, it was. Yes, sir.

On October 13, 1981, almost six months after Reid and Wright had been sentenced to twenty years in federal prison, Mike McCabe filed a legal motion for the consideration of the Honorable Leland C. Nielsen:

> The defendants, Stephen Douglas Reid and Lionel James Wright, by and through their counsel Michael J. McCabe, and pursuant to the provisions of Rule 35, Federal Rules of Criminal Procedure, hereby move this court for an order modifying the twenty-year sentences imposed upon them in the above-entitled case on April 20, 1981, to any period of time less than the original commitments which the court may deem appropriate.

Two months later, with no attorneys or news reporters in attendance, Judge Leland C. Nielsen signed identical orders with respect to Stephen Reid and Lionel Wright:

> On this 15th day of December, 1981, it appearing in the interest of justice to modify the sentence heretofore imposed, it is adjudged that the defendant is hereby committed to the custody of the Attorney General or his authorized representative for a period of Ten Years.

Judge Bob had guessed right all along.

CHAPTER TWENTY-FIVE

San Diego, California

The whole truth about the arrests, prosecution, and convictions of Stephen Reid and Lionel Wright—and the funny thing that happened on the way to the night depository—will likely always remain a matter of some mystery. Federal prosecutor Jack Robinson has never publicly identified Mr. X, saying: "As far as I know, the deal I made in 1980 still stands today."

Reid's attorney Ralph Larsen is sticking to his story that the money was deposited, and to his supposition that someone must have rigged the depository and pulled the loot back out.

Stone's attorney in Los Angeles subsequently denied reports linking his client to the theft of the stolen loot. In a letter of protest the lawyer claimed: "Mr. Larsen took the money to the bank, not Mr. Stone. He was questioned by the grand jury about its disappearance, not Mr. Stone. He was owed money for legal fees by Reid and Wright, not Mr. Stone.

"Your depiction of Reid being turned in by a friend is also inaccurate. These individuals were caught by their own mistakes..."

Stone denies he ever informed on anyone, and says it was a court-ordered handwriting analysis—not information given to the FBI—that exonerated him in the Borrego Springs drug affair.

The FBI remains equally mute on the identity of Mr. X and its pursuit of the Stopwatch Gang. Former special agent and San Diego bureau chief Norman A. Zigrossi does confirm that not everything reported in the media at the time was exactly the whole truth. In his words: "I was never loath to use the media to advance an investigation...And in a case like this where no one was getting killed [by the Stopwatch Gang], I guess we didn't mind having a laugh or two."

The laughs started with the pop-can collector's recovery of the garbage bag stuffed with Bank of America money sacks, the gang's discarded disguises, and the fingerprints of Mitchell and Reid three days after the record-breaking heist. Zigrossi's announcement that day that the FBI had a "major breakthrough...and expected arrests today or over the weekend," was a deliberate ploy to panic the culprits into trying to make a run for it. At that point the FBI had eight prime suspects under continuous surveillance. Unfortunately, none of their fingerprints matched either of the two in the trash bag.

The announcement, of course, didn't panic anyone into trying to run anywhere—the FBI were again watching the wrong eight people, and the real culprits were too hung over at the Biltmore to read a newspaper.

The two recovered fingerprints were immediately sent to the latent fingerprint section of the FBI's Identification Division in Washington, D.C. In 1980, however, the national and international fingerprint files were still not fully computerized. As a result, their batting average in connecting even a known suspect with a set of prints was, at best, mediocre. But without a name, the chance of identifying the owner of a recovered print was poor to nil.

The Identification Division subsequently telexed the San Diego bureau of the FBI: "Searches were conducted in the single fingerprint file, but no identification was effected."

In other words, FBI special agent Cowboy had nothing but a couple of fingerprints from a couple of unknown individuals, and the entire Stopwatch Gang might well have gone merrily into their planned retirement.

But something happened on October 10, almost three weeks into the investigation. That was the day FBI chief Norman A. Zigrossi called a press conference to announce a doubling of the bounty on the heads of the Stopwatch Gang, and then canceled the announcement at the last minute without explanation. "That was the day we got the real breakthrough," he later said. "We had them."

Well, not quite.

October 10 was the day arrest warrants were issued for Sam Stone and four others, charging them with conspiracy and manufacturing amphetamines at the Borrego Springs speed factory—a rather odd story in itself.

Two days before, in broad daylight, a blond woman driving a yellow Volkswagen had dumped a man's naked body on the front lawn of the

Borrego Springs fire department and driven off. The corpse was later identified as one Robert C. Scott II, an employee of the local illegal amphetamine laboratory. Seems he had either got too much of his own medicine, or the chief chemist couldn't quite get the formula straight. Either way, it killed him.

That evening Deputy Sheriff J.K. McKenna got a tip that the yellow Volkswagen was parked outside a cottage at the La Casa Del Zorro resort on the outskirts of Borrego Springs. It turned out to be the speed factory. The deputy pounded on the door.

"Who is it?" a woman's voice asked.

"Sheriff's department."

According to court documents, the deputy then heard the loud crash of breaking glass from the far end of the bungalow. When he arrived on the scene, the ground was littered with one shattered plate glass window, and one prone and slightly stunned Sam Stone, now face-down under a lawman's shotgun.

Two days later, the FBI went to federal prosecutor Jack Robinson and told him they might be able to get Stone to deal. (Robinson was also prosecuting the Borrego Springs drug bunch.) Unfortunately, they didn't tell Robinson that their would-be informant had a criminal and prison record in Los Angeles, nor did they mention he had suspected ties to the mob, nor that he was of considerable interest to a half-dozen other law-enforcement agencies, nor that he was wanted on an out-standing warrant in Canada, nor that the Drug Enforcement Agency had spent the better part of two years trying to crack the Borrego Springs speed operations. Jack Robinson thought he was dealing with a first-time offender of no particular consequence.

The DEA knew better—they had been busting their butts on the Borrego Springs case and were furious that one of their drug suspects was being traded for a couple of FBI bank suspects. But local FBI boss Norman A. Zigrossi was prepared to go right to the top of the DEA on this one, and that's where the grumbling stopped.

Meanwhile, it was roughly a week after the Borrego Springs bust that Stone met with Reid at Solley's Deli and arranged to borrow $65,000 of the gang's stolen Bank of America loot, supposedly to post bail for the four other drug co-conspirators. (Lawyers for the foursome later said no such funds were ever received from Stone.)

Immediately following the FBI's "real breakthrough" in the case, a flurry of telexes was sent between the San Diego bureau of the FBI and their labs in Washington, asking the Identification Division to have another go at their fingerprint files. But this time, the two prints in the trash bag were accompanied by the names of three possible owners: Stephen Douglas Reid, Lionel James Wright, and Patrick Michael Mitchell.

The Identification Division reported that Stephen Reid and Paddy Mitchell were not listed in any FBI files. Either Canadian authorities had forgotten to report that two of their own Most Wanted were wanted, or the fugitives' names were simply lost somewhere in the system. Lionel Wright's dossier was there—suspect still presumed dead—but his prints did not match either of the two pulled from the contents of the trash bag.

All of which was naturally causing considerable hair-pulling around the San Diego headquarters of the FBI. Norman A. Zigrossi had turned up the heat on his agents, but there was nothing anyone could do. Without fingerprints or some other more conclusive evidence than just Stone's secret and suspect information, the FBI had no chance of getting an indictment and arrest warrant for Reid, Wright, or Mitchell.

In the third week of October, there was another blizzard of frantic telexes, this time to the Royal Canadian Mounted Police. The FBI were urgently requesting photo files on the trio to match with the bank films, and fingerprint files to match with those on the bank bag and money wrapper.

There was no response.

Other notations in the official Stopwatch investigation file suggest the FBI were led directly to the Emerald Avenue hideout in San Diego, or to the rental papers of the Hertz getaway car—or to both. Either would have provided police with Lionel Wright's alias, Ronald Peter Scott. Another tip to look in Sedona led the FBI to Mr. Scott's driver's license, on which was written the address of the gang's hideout in Oak Creek Canyon.

At this point, Zigrossi was going crazy. He dispatched four of his San Diego agents to Arizona so they could at least keep the Stopwatch Gang under surveillance in Sedona until he could cut through enough red tape to get the fingerprints and mugshots of three of the most-hunted fugitives in America.

Reid and Wright should have trusted their instincts. The two brushcuts at Sunday brunch; the Kitteredges' dog barking at something in the woods; the telephone repair truck parked near Sycamore House—they were all part of Zigrossi's FBI stake-out. So was Arizona FBI agent Blain McIlwain, who happened to go fishing in the creek in front of the fugitives' hideout. Zigrossi's boys had him under surveillance for almost two days before they figured out he was one of them.

While the FBI were busy watching themselves, Operation Stopwatch seemed to miss one rather important bash at the Poco Diablo bar in Sedona, namely, the going-away party for Paddy and his beloved Beckie. No one mentioned anything about the whole operation to the FBI bureau in nearby Flagstaff or Phoenix, under whose jurisdiction it should have been conducted. This was Norman A. Zigrossi's case, and he wasn't about to entrust it to anyone else, and that was that.

Meanwhile, back in San Diego, Zigrossi and his agents were climbing the walls. More telexes were dispatched to Canada, each expressing increasing exasperation: "RCMP URGENT! HELLO CANADA! ANYBODY HOME?"

Finally, someone in the FBI decided to hell with proper channels and placed a call directly to the Gloucester Police Department in Ottawa, the local lawmen who had first arrested the trio for the gold robbery and other related misdeeds back in the 1970s.

Gloucester PD immediately dispatched photographs and fingerprints of the wanted threesome to Washington. By October 27 the FBI's Identification Division was finally able to match both Mitchell and Reid with the two sets of trash-bag prints—seventeen days after the three members of the Stopwatch Gang had been identified by name, located in Sedona, and put under surveillance by a lot of harried FBI agents.

It took another two days for special agent Cowboy Ayers to process the indictments. While the information in the documents—the photograph and fingerprint matches—was accurate, all of it was carefully drafted to obscure the existence of an informant by making the whole operation look like so much clever police work.

Finally, the FBI were ready to move in.

But Norman Zigrossi didn't want just Reid and Wright—he wanted all three members of the Stopwatch Gang. He decided to leave his men in the bushes for a few days in the hope that Mitchell would come back to Sedona.

Then Reid paid nothing in advance on his new lease for Sycamore House. Then Wright failed to sign it. Then Reid got a phone call from Jack Seeley to say they would be flying to Phoenix the next morning for the final color-blindness test required for Reid's pilot's license.

Zigrossi panicked. Two out of three was infinitely better than losing them all. It was at that point, according to protocol, that the San Diego

272 THE STOPWATCH GANG

chief called upon his FBI counterpart Stephen Chenoweth in Phoenix to effect the arrests of the two suspects—preferably all three of them, if Chenoweth could manage it.

On November 24, about three weeks after the arrests of Reid and Wright, the following letter was sent to Edward J. Harris, United States Magistrate:

> Please dismiss Complaint filed on October 10, 1980, against Samuel Stone. Charge: Conspiracy to possess a controlled substance with intent to distribute. Reason: In the interest of justice...

The letter was signed by federal prosecutor Jack Robinson.

The truth about the subsequent money-switch and theft of the gang's stolen loot also seems destined to remain in the files of unsolved mysteries.

The two men who supposedly went to the night depository—Big Sam Stone and Reid's lawyer Ralph Larsen—continue to point accusing fingers at each other. Federal prosecutor Jack Robinson says he had no idea that his informant—and not Paddy Mitchell or some other friend of the gang—was the mystery courier until a week after the money supposedly disappeared. He didn't really care, either—he was convinced all along that the money wouldn't be returned. And when it wasn't, he became equally convinced that it was all just a ruse by Reid and Wright to get lighter sentences.

When Reid's attorney Ralph Larsen subsequently told the grand jury that Stone was the man behind the money drop, Robinson was furious. For some time, he had been increasingly concerned that he had cut a bad deal with the wrong kind of individual. Now he was all but certain. Most of all, he was peeved at the FBI.

Exactly how much the FBI knew and when is not entirely clear. Zigrossi says he would have approved the deal not to bust Mr. X or otherwise interfere in the planned money drop, and "we probably thought it was Mitchell or one of the gang's other friends." The FBI didn't have much choice—without such a deal, the money wasn't going to be returned and they still wouldn't have nabbed Mr. X.

The former FBI boss also emphatically denies that officialdom had made the money disappear as part of an attempted sting operation to compel Reid and Wright to testify against Stone by making them believe that they had been ripped off by their friend.

When defense attorney Mike McCabe took over the case from Ralph Larsen after the alleged money switch, Reid suggested his new counsel might want to do some checking into one Samuel Stone.

McCabe hired a private investigator who had to dig no further than the public court files on the Borrego Springs drug factory. Anyone caught jumping out the window of a speed lab into the arms of an arresting deputy was not simply in the wrong place at the wrong time, as Stone claimed. But no indictment was ever filed against Stone in that case.

Meanwhile, a few agents of the Drug Enforcement Agency were fuming. It is widely suspected they had a hand in the embarrassing news leaks about the officially sanctioned freeing of Stone, including the fact that the FBI and Robinson had made a sweetheart deal with a man alleged to have serious Mafia connections.

For his part, Judge Leland C. Nielsen seemed to agree with Reid's attorney Mike McCabe that the whole mess reeked of impropriety, especially having an informant for the state retaining counsel for a couple of accused upon whom he had just snitched.

It was at that point that Judge Bob and the two defense attorneys began bumping into each other in the courthouse corridor with unusual regularity.

Two days before Reid and Wright pleaded guilty, they were told that twenty-year sentences would be imposed in open court for media consumption, while a quiet application for a reduction of the jail terms to ten years just might be given a favorable hearing sometime later. At least that's what had been conveyed in the courthouse corridor. Just an opinion, of course.

Prosecutor Jack Robinson was never part of those discussions, and had no idea that the two bandits were going to get a day less than the twenty-five-year maximum he was demanding.

Reid and Wright steadfastly refused to testify against Sam Stone, in spite of all that had happened to them.

Three days after sentencing, Reid was ordered before a grand jury. Mike McCabe warned his client that refusing to testify could kill the whole plea bargain and any arrangement to reduce the twenty-year sentence. No matter. Reid refused to testify and was given an additional sentence of one year for contempt of court—or as long as it took him to change his mind about testifying. He never did.

Nor did Lionel Wright, who told Mike Aguirre, "Sorry, but I'm just not a testifying kinda guy," and fired the attorney.

At first Judge Nielsen refused to consider any sentence reductions so long as Wright and Reid continued to thwart his efforts to solve the great stolen-loot caper. Eventually, however, the judge relented.

Ordinarily, a hearing would have been held to allow both defense and prosecution a chance to argue for and against sentence reduction. But it never happened. While the court was in Christmas recess, a memo was delivered to Jack Robinson informing him that Judge Leland C. Nielsen had cut the sentences of Stephen Reid and Lionel Wright to ten years from twenty. Robinson hit the roof. But there was nothing he could do.

Ironically, Big Sam Stone had in the end lived up to his reputation—albeit inadvertently—for being able to arrange anything. The original twenty-year sentences were to run concurrently with the fourteen years Reid had left to serve in Canada, and with the seventeen years remaining on Wright's prison record. When the whole fiasco involving Stone compelled Judge Nielsen to reduce the sentences to ten years, however, they nonetheless remained concurrent—that is to say, they would be served at the same time as the longer sentences still outstanding in Canada.

In other words, Stephen Reid and Lionel Wright ended their careers with the Stopwatch Gang with no more time to serve than when they started.

Then there's Paddy Mitchell. Unless he was getting a blizzard of messages from God, Mitchell was simply blessed with the luck of the Irish. It was pure coincidence he got out of Sedona with Beckie just as the FBI were watching and waiting for the elusive fingerprint files. And it was only a rare stroke of good sense that he didn't buy into Stone's windfall investment plan as Reid and Wright had done.

At the same time as his two partners-in-crime were being set up and robbed, Mitchell took more than a quarter of a million dollars to New Orleans and threw his own private three-month Mardi Gras. When the king of party animals wasn't seducing the young ladies with checkbook charisma, a small fortune in cocaine was going up his nose.

Alas, it all got him nowhere but right back where he started—flat broke and hiding from the law in Arizona.

The day before Judge Nielsen signed the final order reducing the sentences of Stephen Reid and Lionel Wright to the effectively redundant ten years, Patrick Michael Mitchell was back in the news.

Only this time, he was alone. And this time, he walked straight into the sights of a loaded police revolver.

CHAPTER TWENTY-SIX

Phoenix, Arizona

December 14, 1981. The forecast is for light breezes and a comfortable high of seventy-two, certainly a nicer day to hold up Diamond's Department Store than when the Stopwatch Gang last tried it. That was eighteen months ago, the time Paddy Mitchell fainted in the back seat under the swelter of a bulletproof vest in the midst of a July heat wave in a getaway car with faulty air conditioning.

This time, there is no heat wave, no bulletproof vest, no backseat ride in the getaway car. More importantly, there is no Stopwatch Gang.

Paddy Mitchell is alone.

Launching a solo career in armed robbery was the last thing on Mitchell's mind when he bid a final "God bless" to his two partners-in-crime fourteen months earlier and headed off to Florida for his honeymoon cruise with Beckie.

First he lost Beckie. Then he lost his money.

Even Mitchell couldn't remember exactly how he managed to blow a quarter of a million dollars without buying anything more expensive or durable than a $3,000 used Chevrolet. But it is a safe bet the last big bundle was eaten by the ponies at a track in Hot Springs, Arkansas.

On November 25, 1981, a man named Richard Joseph Landry had pulled out of Hot Springs and headed south to Shreveport, Louisiana, where he purchased a silver, snubnosed .32-caliber revolver at a gun shop. He registered the weapon in his own name and gave an address in New Orleans.

On December 4, Landry arrived in Phoenix and checked into a furnished room in the Royal Suites apartment motel, a drab, yellow, two-story walkup in the north end of the city. More precisely, it was exactly four-fifths of a mile of back streets from Diamond's Department Store in the giant Metro Center shopping plaza.

The Stopwatch Gang had estimated their haul from Diamond's at the time of the aborted mid-summer heist would have been a few hundred thousand at least. Richard Joseph Landry had figured the haul from the large department store eleven days before Christmas should be at least five times that amount.

A million was all Paddy Mitchell wanted. Then he could retire.

After casing Diamond's and chasing armored trucks for a week, Mitchell had picked Monday, December 14, as the day to collect his million—with no armored pickups over the weekend, the vault room should be piled high with the receipts from two of the busiest shopping days of the year.

Picking the time and the place had been the easy part. Then there were all those little details. Paddy Mitchell had never had much time for details. That had always been Lionel's job.

On the morning of December 14 no one is missing Stephen Reid and Lionel Wright more than the mastermind without a gang. Lionel would have known the precise layout of the department store, the running times in and out of the place, the frequency and duration of every stoplight along the getaway route, the exact schedule of the armored truck pickups on any given day of the week. He would also have provided disguises, guns, a getaway car, a stolen license plate, and even the tape to stick it over the real one.

Stephen Reid would have provided the logistics of the actual stickup. One of them would have taken control of the store's second-floor customer-service area, securing the getaway route, and watching for any would-be hero with a gun. The second bandit would have retrieved the loot from the vault room to the rear of the customer counter. The third would have been waiting with the getaway car.

Paddy's preparations for the heist wouldn't impress a candystore shoplifter. He hasn't bothered to try stealing a car, or even to rent one. He plans to use his own Chevrolet Caprice with an Ohio license plate stolen from the parking lot next door to his apartment. The only other attempt to disguise the Chev is a piece of gray tape over the name of the Louisiana dealership where he bought the car. Mitchell has sloppily felt-penned the word "FORD" on it.

He hasn't given much thought to disguising himself, either. True, Richard Joseph Landry doesn't look much like the old Paddy Mitchell—plastic surgery and a black beard have knocked ten years off his face; jogging and cocaine have knocked thirty pounds off his frame. But it doesn't much matter whether witnesses identify Richard Landry or Paddy Mitchell—the police will be looking for the same person.

Mitchell checks his watch. It's almost 12:30, time to drive to the scene of the crime. Instead, he is frantically using a kitchen knife to carve eyeholes in the cut-off pant leg of his beige corduroys.

He pulls it over his head. It looks ridiculous.

He snaps open the cylinder of the silver pistol and inserts four .32-caliber shells. The chamber behind the hammer and the next one up are left empty.

He folds a pillowcase tightly and stuffs it into the front pouch of his jogging suit, along with the silver pistol, the pant-leg balaclava, and a pair of green rubber dishwashing gloves. He pulls on a blue Wrangler shirt, extra-large and untucked at the waist to hide the belly-bulge of burglary tools underneath. He tugs to get his Levis over the sweatpants.

If all goes well, the corduroy pant leg, jeans, shirt, and rubber gloves will come off after the robbery, and he will just be another jogger in sweats. Just like the big San Diego job. If all goes well.

Finally, he reaches into the bottom of his suitcase for his last ten one-hundred-dollar bills and stuffs them in his jeans pocket.

It is 12:45 when Paddy Mitchell laces his blue running shoes, crosses himself, and heads for Diamond's Department Store.

Next stop: second floor, men's washroom.

Julie was at the cashier's wicket of Diamond's when Paddy Mitchell came storming out of the men's washroom at a full run towards the customer counter, a blur of green dishwashing gloves, silver revolver, and a pant leg over his head. She froze.

"This is a holdup," came the muffled voice from under the pant leg with no mouth hole. "Just get me the money bags."

Julie just stared at him in disbelief.

"This not a joke," the pant leg sputtered.

Mary, the supervisor, had just finished serving a customer at the other end of the counter and was busily stuffing paperwork into a drawer. When she looked up, she was three feet from Corduroy Head and his silver revolver.

"Oh my God!" she yelled.

The gun swung towards her.

"Just get the money bags from the back room," the pant leg barked. "And don't scream."

She opened her mouth to scream. Mitchell panicked. In a single movement he vaulted the counter and landed with his left hand over Mary's mouth.

"Dammit, stop screaming," the pant leg growled in her ear. "I just want the money bags."

Mitchell and his terrified victim shuffled backwards ten feet to the door of the vault room.

"Open it, and don't scream," Mitchell whispered as he released his hold.

As Mary turned the door handle, Mitchell fanned his gun at the crowd of stunned Christmas shoppers at the customer counter.

No one moved, not even the man in the blue cardigan with the .38-caliber revolver under his left pant cuff.

Detective George Edward Harden had never shot anyone in his thirteen years with the Phoenix Police Department. He had never been shot, either, although a shotgun blast had blown in one rear side window of his cruiser and out the other during a race riot.

In fact, Harden's worst injury was inflicted by a sixty-nine-year-old woman arrested for refusing to sign a traffic citation. By the time the feisty grandmother reached the police station, four burly officers were struggling to subdue her. As Harden grabbed her feet, Granny kicked out and sent him crashing backwards into the edge of a wooden table. The sharp corner drove into his spine like a wood splitter, and he was never quite the same again.

At first he had loved being a cop—the excitement, intrigue, and sense of purpose, all missing in his previous job as a greeting-card salesman. But by the time he reached thirty-five, Detective George Edward Harden had a wife, two children, three stab wounds, chronic back pain, and a transfer from downtown homicide to suburban shop-lifting duty at the Metro Center shopping plaza.

The voluntary duty demotion was okay with him. No nightshifts or weekend duty. No one trying to kill him. The ten-minute drive to his home meant never having to use a public washroom. And generally he could run his own show without all the bureaucratic hassles at the station.

George Edward Harden liked to run his own show. He had five official reprimands to prove it. Nothing serious; he just wasn't always inclined to follow the rules. They were forever on his back about handcuffs, for instance. He hadn't carried a pair in years. Just kept losing them and having to pay the department twenty-two bucks for new ones. To hell with that. And sunglasses—hadn't owned a pair of those in years, either. Always sitting on them. It was the same with his portable police radio. He usually left it in the car. Damn thing was bulky and always squawking and blowing his cover.

The Metro Center beat, therefore, suited Detective George Harden just fine. Most of his days were spent wandering around the giant plaza in a sweater and casual slacks, looking like Joe Shopper, nailing shoplifters and flashers. Didn't need handcuffs or a radio to arrest someone wearing two pairs of pants, or none at all.

He never left home without his gun, though—a handy little .38 in an ankle holster strapped to the inside of his left leg under his trousers so no one would notice. Didn't bother with the regulation supply of spare ammunition. He figured if the day ever came when six bullets couldn't solve a problem, he'd fucking well throw down his gun and run.

Shortly after one o'clock on the afternoon of December 14, 1981, Detective George Edward Harden was summoned to Diamond's Department Store to discuss a minor theft case with the company's security chief. Metro Center was jammed with Christmas shoppers and shoplifters, and Harden was in no mood to be kept waiting.

When his appointment didn't show by 1:15, Harden went to the second-floor customer-service counter. The area was crowded with people paying off their bills so they could run up bigger ones for Christmas. But there was no sign of the security chief there, either.

Harden stomped into the administrative offices a few feet to the right of the counter and asked the switchboard operator to page the absentee security official as quickly as possible. He would wait two more minutes, and then to hell with the appointment.

Suddenly, he heard a commotion out by the customer counter. There was a loud noise, more like a woman's yell than a scream. The detective rushed around the corner.

In his thirteen years with the Phoenix Police Department, George Edward Harden had never seen anything quite like it—an armed robber wearing bright green dishwashing gloves and a beige pant leg over his head. Paddy Mitchell and his female hostage were already at the vault-room door.

A thought flashed across Harden's mind: "Shit, I'm going to spend Christmas in hospital with bullet wounds."

Elissa and Raye-Jean were in the vault room counting the weekend's receipts for the scheduled armored-truck pickup when they heard Mary yell. A few seconds later, the door opened.

The first thing they saw coming through the doorway was a green dishwashing glove gripping a silver revolver. Then Mary entered, thoroughly traumatized. Then the bandit with the pantleg over his head. He closed the door.

"Where's the money?" he shouted at the two accounting clerks.

Mary started to walk towards the safe in the far corner of the room.

"Hold it!" Mitchell shouted. "Don't touch the safe or any drawers with alarms on them or I'll start shooting."

Elissa pointed to two metal containers about the size of shoeboxes on the table.

"Get the money, and get it fast," Mitchell said, his voice quivering. He pulled the white pillowcase from the front pouch of the sweatsuit. His hands were shaking. His fingers were jammed only halfway into the rubber gloves, the tips hanging like deflated balloons. He fumbled with the tightly folded pillowcase, but couldn't get a grip on it.

Mary picked up the bundles of cash from the two boxes on the table. Her whole body was quivering.

Mitchell finally got the pillowcase open with a snap in the air.

Mary let go of the money—$42,000 in bills fluttered in every direction.

Mitchell waved the gun in the air, first at Mary's head, then at the other two women, then at nothing in particular. "Hurry up!" he shouted. "Let's go. Hurry up. I haven't got all day."

Elissa helped Mary gather the money on the floor and put it in the pillowcase.

Mitchell stared into the bag. Sure didn't look like a million. "Is this all there is?" he boomed. "If I don't get it all, and get it fast, I'll start shooting."

"Well, there's all this," Elissa said, picking up a pile of rolled quarters from the table.

"I just want the paper, no coins," Mitchell said, nervously rocking from one blue sneaker to the other.

Raye-Jean, who had been frozen with her hands up, slowly lowered one arm and pointed to three plastic money bags on the floor—another $43,000 in cash and a lot of non-negotiable checks and credit card receipts.

"Give them to me and hurry up," Mitchell shouted at her. "If I don't get all the money now, I'll start shooting."

Raye-Jean picked up the three bags from the floor, straightened up, stepped forward, and dropped them on the floor again.

The silver revolver swung towards her head.

"I'm sorry," she pleaded. "I'm sorry. I didn't mean—"

"That's okay, that's okay," Mitchell consoled her through clenched teeth. "Just take it easy. Don't anyone panic."

Raye-Jean finally got the three plastic money bags into the pillow-case.

Mitchell looked as nervous as his victims, his body twitching, the gun wildly vibrating in the palm of the rubber glove with droopy fingertips.

The silver revolver made a last jerky sweep of the three frightened faces.

"Is there any more?" Mitchell demanded. "I told you, if I don't get everything I want, I'm going to start shooting."

The big money was in the safe he wouldn't let them open, but no one mentioned that. No one said anything.

Suddenly, Mitchell wheeled around and left, the pillowcase in his left hand, the silver revolver in his right. The door slammed behind him.

A few seconds later, the three women heard the crack of a gunshot. Then a piercing shriek. Another gun blast. A loud crash.

Then there was silence.

The instant Mitchell disappeared into the vault room and slammed the door, Detective George Edward Harden stopped worrying about Christmas in hospital and flew into action. Going in after the gunman was out of the question. Three of the clerks were missing; they had to be in the room with him. Barging in could get them all killed. Harden made his decision: kill the bandit on his way out.

The detective looked around the area. Everywhere there were milling shoppers, gawkers, and panicked witnesses to Mitchell's. dramatic arrival. Everywhere there was potential slaughter if the gunman decided to shoot back.

Harden glanced at Julie, alone behind the customer counter, still rigid with fright.

"Get the hell out of there. Now!" he said in a loud whisper.

Julie looked at the man in the blue sweater and grey wool slacks and seemed even more confused.

"I'm a police officer," Harden said in the loudest whisper he could muster. "Get out of there! Now!"

Julie vaulted the chest-high counter and scrambled for cover in the adjacent administration offices.

Harden turned to the crowd. It was no time for manners.

"There's a holdup!" he whispered as he unceremoniously shoved women into the men's washroom.

"I'm a police officer," he growled at several men who resisted a shove into the ladies' room.

"Get in there and shut up," he sputtered as he herded a gaggle of gawkers into an adjacent photography studio.

"Beat it!" he shouted at others wandering into the battle zone. "There's a robbery in progress...Get out of here...Call the police... Yeah, I'm the police...Goddammit, just call the police!"

In a matter of seconds Harden had the area cleared of would-be targets and rushed back into the administration office.

"Call the police," he whispered hoarsely to the switchboard operator. "Tell them there's an armed robbery in progress. Say there's an officer on the scene and he needs backup. Now! Got it?"

Unfortunately, the detective's cry for help had already reached so many well-meaning bystanders that no one could pass along the message to police headquarters. Throughout Diamond's Department Store everyone was dialing at the same time. The entire phone system jammed.

Detective George Edward Harden reached under his left pant cuff, drew his .38-caliber revolver, and stared at the closed door to the vault room.

Now he was all alone against the gunman. Or was that gunmen? The vault-room door had been open when he arrived on the scene. Two or three others could have barged in ahead of the one with the pant leg over his head.

Any second that door would fly open. Then what? Harden's mind was spinning. How do I take him?...Standing up, point-shoulder, both hands on the gun—best chance of hitting him...Also best chance of his hitting me...If there's more than one, I'm dead...Lie on the floor—they'll shoot high...should be able to take out a couple before they get their aim down...Where do I hit him, or is it them? Can't do it in the doorway...could be a hostage in the way. Might hit one of the girls behind him by mistake. That's the goddam problem: cops have to worry where they shoot; crooks just shoot.

Suddenly, the door flew open.

For an instant Detective George Edward Harden was staring point-blank at Patrick Michael Mitchell, hunted member of the FBI's most-wanted, a stuffed pillowcase in one hand, silver revolver in the other, corduroy pant leg over his head.

For the same instant Paddy Mitchell was staring point-blank at an ordinary-looking man in a blue sweater, casually leaning on the corner of the customer counter, his right hand tucked under his left armpit.

Mitchell slammed the door behind him. Harden now knew he was facing a lone gunman. His grip tightened around the revolver.

The bandit took a few steps towards Harden, then wheeled to the right, and disappeared behind a short partition wall. He re-emerged about ten feet from a steel fire door that led to an emergency stairwell.

Harden straightened, spread his legs, and raised his gun.

Mitchell reached for the bar on the fire door, his back to Harden.

"Freeze! Police!" Harden boomed.

Mitchell started to turn around. Harden fired.

Mitchell had turned sideways when the bullet passed within an inch of his chest and blew a hole through the plaster wall. He let out a shrill scream and smashed into the steel door.

Harden re-aimed and fired again through the plaster wall, this time where he thought the fleeing bandit would be in the stairwell. Paddy Mitchell felt the bullet whiz under his nose.

Harden rushed to the top of the stairwell. Three flights down to the first floor. Three landings. Harden listened. Nothing. The gunman must be waiting for him. Christmas in hospital. Or a graveyard.

Harden turned and began racing back through Diamond's. He knew Mitchell would be running a parallel route, one floor down. The detective would exit on the second floor, the bandit on the first. The two men would then be separated only by a set of outside stairs down a landscaped embankment.

The sight of a man in a blue pullover racing through the children's-wear department waving a revolver over his head sent Christmas shoppers screaming and diving into the clothing racks.

The scene one floor down was no less dramatic. Paddy Mitchell crashed through the men's department with a white pillowcase in one hand, a silver revolver in the other, a pant leg over his head. In this case, he was doing the screaming.

"He's trying to kill me!" the pant leg shrieked as Mitchell lunged down the aisles, leaving a litter of upended shoppers and strewn Christmas gifts in his wake. "That crazy bastard is shooting at me!...He's got a gun...He's trying to kill me!"

One level up Harden skidded on the freshly waxed parquet floor. His feet went out from under him. With both hands still over his head clutching his gun, there was nothing but his tailbone and already-damaged spine to cushion the fall. The pain shooting up his back felt as though he'd landed on a three-foot spike.

Now Harden was mad. The detective crashed into the exit doors with a force that left them rattling on their hinges. Now he was on the cement walkway to the upper lower parking lot.

As though on cue, thirty feet below Harden, Paddy Mitchell came scrambling out the first-floor exit doors and began running across the lower parking lot.

Harden reached the top of the cement stairs joining the two levels. He stopped and lowered his gun. The bandit was in his sights. But so were shoppers and parked cars. He raised the revolver over his head again and glanced at the stairs. About forty of them, twisting and turning, with five-foot cement walls on both sides that would obscure his view of the fleeing bandit. No way he was letting that bastard out of his sight for a second. He ran towards the embankment, a landscaped series of rock gardens terraced with railway ties. The pain in his back was agonizing.

Harden took three steps down the embankment and tripped. He ricocheted like a pinball from a jagged pumice stone that ripped open his arm, to a tree trunk that smacked his back, to a thorny cactus that gouged his face, to another hunk of volcanic rock that tore a strip of flesh from his leg. Now he was in a rage.

Bleeding and in pain, he stumbled forward, his eyes still locked on the fleeing fugitive still shrieking and weaving among the parked cars below. Harden jumped down a three-foot wall of railway ties separating two terraces of the perilous garden. His left foot landed first, twisted at the ankle, and sent him sprawling chest first into a bush with dried branches that felt like barbed wire. Now he wanted to cripple that little prick with the pant leg over his head.

By the time Harden finally reached the lower parking lot, it occurred to him that, having watched a robbery in progress, been nose-to-nose with the bandit, then shot at him twice and missed—well, he'd look pretty damn stupid letting the bastard get away. He spotted Mitchell and started after him again at a hobbling run.

An elderly Christmas shopper in the parking lot watched in amazement as the man with a pant leg over his head raced past, still shrieking: "He's shooting at me! The sonofabitch is trying to kill me!"

Mitchell had that right.

At that moment, Harden yelled, "Halt! Police!" and promptly caught his toe on a parking curb. He skidded face-first along the asphalt, ripping still more flesh from his chin, arm, and leg. Now he really did want to kill the bastard.

Mitchell reached the green Chevy, flung himself into the driver's seat, ripped off the mask, put the gun in his lap, turned the key, and threw the car into reverse. He glanced out the side window.

He was looking straight down the barrel of a loaded and cocked .38, not three feet from his face.

The man on the other end of the gun looked like he had just done fifteen rounds with a street gang and lost. His sweater and trousers were in shreds, blood poured from his face, chest, and every limb.

"If you move that car, I'm going to kill you," Harden yelled.

Paddy Mitchell froze, his mouth hanging open.

Harden pulled out his billfold with the police badge in it and snapped it open. Credit cards and papers flew in every direction. Even the metal badge parted company with the leather and hit the pavement with a tinkling bounce. The flustered detective threw the wallet on the ground.

Mitchell put his hands up and started screaming hysterically through the closed window. "Don't shoot! Don't shoot! I've got a gun on my lap! For God's sake, don't shoot! The gun's on my lap! Don't shoot!"

The car was rolling backwards.

"Keep your hands up and put your foot on the brake," Harden yelled. "A wrong move and I'll kill you."

Mitchell did as he was told. Then he started screaming again. "Don't shoot! Don't shoot!"

Harden reached over and pulled open the car door. The sawed-off pant leg was lying on Mitchell's left thigh. The silver revolver was in his lap. The white pillowcase stuffed with loot was on the seat beside him.

"Now, do as you're told or you're a dead man," Harden growled. "Reach over with your left hand and put the car in park. Now, spread your legs and let the gun drop onto the seat. Now, slowly roll out onto the pavement on your face. Do it, or I'll kill you."

Mitchell rolled face-down onto the pavement. Harden landed on the suspect's shoulder blades with both knees and poked his gun into the crook of the bandit's neck.

"How the fuck did you get here so fast?" Mitchell asked.

Harden didn't answer.

"Bad luck," Mitchell muttered from the pavement. "Bad luck. What a lot of bad fucking luck."

"You're under arrest," Harden snarled.

Mitchell didn't answer.

Suddenly, Harden started to panic. He had no handcuffs and no way to call for help. His police radio was on the front seat of his cruiser where he always left it.

Worse, a crowd was starting to gather at the arrest scene. Harden's eyes darted around frantically, searching the faces for danger signals. Big-time armed robbers like this guy never work alone...One robs, another drives...No one ever tries a heist like this solo...His buddies must be out there somewhere...One of them is going to step out of that crowd any minute and blow my head off...

The elderly gent who had watched the bandit scream past him in the parking lot now stepped out of the crowd.

"Anything I can do to help, officer?" he asked.

"Just get these people back," Harden shouted. "Everyone get the hell out of here! Get them back. Get these people away from here!"

A siren wailed in the distance. Someone had finally managed to get a phone line out of Diamond's. Harden scanned the crammed parking lot. A backup cruiser could take a week to find him in that mess. No way to radio his location, either. Damn.

"Somebody go to the entrance of the parking lot and flag down the first police cruiser you see and tell where I am. Somebody go! *Now! Hurry!*

The police cruiser screeched to a halt and the officer stepped out. He stared at the battered and bleeding fellow in the shredded cardigan, kneeling on another man's back with a gun at his head. For a moment, the policeman stood there, trying to decide which was the bad guy.

"Put the cuffs on him and get him into the cruiser," Harden barked.

Paddy Mitchell was still wearing the green rubber gloves with the droopy fingertips when he was handcuffed and tossed into the back of the police car.

Within minutes the scene looked as if there had been a mass murder. When someone finally got the message to police headquarters, the call went out to all cars as a Code 999. Loosely translated: police officer involved in shooting; needs help—yesterday. Now the place was swarming with enough members of the Phoenix PD to subdue every armed robber west of the Mississippi.

Suddenly, there was a shriek from the back seat of the police cruiser.

"I've been shot!" Mitchell screamed at the sight of blood on the front of his shirt. "Oh my God, I've been shot. Somebody call an ambulance. I've been shot!"

An ambulance was already on its way, having responded to the original Code 999. The attendants took one look at Detective Harden and rushed towards him with their medical kits.

"No, no, not me," Harden grumbled. "The guy in the back seat of the cruiser. Says he's been shot."

But Mitchell wasn't even scratched. He had simply rolled in a pool of Harden's blood.

As the boys from internal affairs questioned Harden about the shooting, the identification team dusted the getaway vehicle and everything in it for prints. Detective Carley Anderson picked the silver revolver off the front seat and cracked open the cylinder.

"Hey, look at this," Anderson said to another detective, showing him the cylinder.

If Mitchell had, in fact, been waiting in the emergency stairwell for Harden, it certainly wasn't to shoot him. Beneath the hammer of the silver pistol, the chamber and the next one up were still empty.

Detective Anderson climbed into the police cruiser and read Mitchell his rights.

"Please state your name," Anderson said.

"Richard Joseph Landry," the suspect replied.

Anderson asked all the other usual questions and got all the usual answers—which is to say, only that Mr. Landry wanted a lawyer.

"Do you have anything else you wish to add at this time, Mr. Landry?" the detective asked.

"Yeah," Mitchell said in a half-whisper. "I wish one of those bullets would have hit me."

CHAPTER TWENTY-SEVEN

Phoenix, Arizona

Detective Jim Thomas had questioned a horde of suspects in his two decades with the Phoenix PD, but he had never run across anyone like the man sitting in interrogation room Number Five.

The suspect sure didn't look like the average scruffy armed robber, with his neatly trimmed black hair and beard, the clear complexion on a tanned face, the slim athletic build of someone who obviously kept himself in good physical shape. The designer sweatsuit, the Wrangler shirt, and new Levis weren't exactly Salvation Army issue, either.

He didn't sound like a run-of-the-mill deadbeat. The crisp and articulate speech, the politeness tinged with self-assured arrogance. Most of those hauled in for interrogation turn the air blue. But not this guy, not a single obscenity.

Thomas and another detective tried for about fifteen minutes to squeeze information from the man, but had little success. The driver's license said he was Richard Joseph Landry, aged thirty-five, and the photograph on it matched the face.

"When was the last time you were arrested?" Thomas asked, assuming that such a major holdup was not a first-time offense.

"Never," Mitchell said softly.

"Uh-huh, and other than armed robbery, what do you do for a living, Mr. Landry?" the detective continued.

"I'm a salesman," Mitchell said rather proudly.

"What kind of salesman, Mr. Landry?"

Mitchell stared blankly at the detective as though the question had evaporated somewhere in mid-air.

"Who is your next of kin?" the detective continued.

"No one—my whole family is dead," said Richard Joseph Landry, who had himself been dead for thirty-three years.

Mitchell allowed that he had not lived at the New Orleans address on his driver's license for more than a year, that he had been in Arkansas before arriving in Phoenix about three weeks earlier, and that he had been staying at a motel he wouldn't name with a girl he wouldn't identify, partly because she didn't exist.

All other questions got roughly the same response: "I know my rights. I don't have to tell you anything about myself. Just get me an attorney."

The two detectives left the interrogation room. Outside in the corridor, they agreed the $90,000 heist at Diamond's Department Store wasn't Mr. Landry's first brush with the law—the guy obviously knew the ropes. Thomas decided to have another go at the suspect, alone.

Mitchell was still wearing the two layers of clothes, his sleeve soaked in the sweat he had been mopping from his face. He hadn't stopped quivering since he arrived at the station. Thomas suggested he might feel more comfortable if he took off some excess clothing.

Suddenly, the suspect was animated. "I'm not sweating from the clothes," Mitchell sputtered. "That guy darn-near killed me. Do you know how close those bullets came? Like he was shooting at me. Somebody ought to do something about that guy before he kills someone."

"Well, Mr. Landry, surely that's an occupational hazard for someone committing a rather large robbery with a loaded weapon," Thomas said, stifling a laugh. "If you hadn't tried to run, the officer probably wouldn't have tried to shoot you."

"That's no reason to try to kill me," Mitchell retorted. "I mean, I've never hurt anybody in my life and here's this maniac shooting at me. There was no reason for it. Someone ought to do something about him. He's dangerous."

Thomas asked Mitchell if he would like a cup of coffee.

"No, thank you very much for offering, but I don't drink coffee. It's bad for your heart. A glass of water would be nice, though, if it wouldn't be too much trouble."

Thomas returned with a glass of water, lit a cigarette, and offered one to Mitchell.

"No, thank you—I jog every day," Mitchell said forcefully, as though he were offended by the mere offer.

"Yeah, you look like you're in pretty good shape, all right," the detective said.

"I run about ten miles a day, and you can't do that if you smoke," Mitchell said piously. "And frankly, it's none of my business, but you should really give some thought to quitting. I mean, if cancer doesn't get you, you'll end up with heart disease or emphysema. Have you ever seen anyone with emphysema? Hacking and coughing up blood all the time. It's awful. Do you have a family?"

Thomas was starting to wonder if Interrogation Room Number Five had slipped into the Twilight Zone.

"Speaking of running, Mr. Landry," the puzzled detective said, trying to regain control of the conversation, "what made you take off when the officer told you to freeze?"

"You would, too, if some crazy was shooting at you," Mitchell said.

Thomas tried again: "At the time of your arrest, Mr. Landry, you were in possession of a .32-caliber handgun. Where did you get it?"

Mitchell leaned across the table and began shaking a lecturing finger at Thomas. "Instead of asking me all these questions, you should be talking to that guy who tried to kill me. He's the one who was doing the shooting. He's the one who shouldn't have a gun. He tried to kill me. Someone like that should be reprimanded and thrown off the force. I'm telling ya, he's going to kill someone."

"Can I get you anything else, Mr. Landry?" the detective said finally.

"Yeah, a lawyer."

Later that afternoon, Richard Joseph Landry was arraigned in county court on charges of armed robbery, aggravated assault, and kidnapping.

Despite the gravity of the alleged crimes, the prosecutor had to admit that, as far as anyone knew, this was Mr. Landry's first offense. And, no, your honor, the defendant had no apparent assets other than the impounded Chevy and a thousand bucks in his pocket.

Mitchell started to suggest the court "ought to do something about that guy Harden before he kills someone." The judge rolled his eyes and cut him off. Bail was set at $16,000.

As the man on the FBI's Ten Most Wanted list was shuffled out of the courtroom and taken to the Maricopa County Jail, he was still shaking and sweating profusely.

The night after his encounter with the unlikely bandit, Detective Jim Thomas barely slept. He was back in his office early the next morning.

The pieces just didn't fit. The massive computer files of the National Crime Information Center, tied into every law-enforcement agency in America, had drawn a blank with the name Richard Joseph Landry, born September 2, 1946.

Paddy Mitchell's fingerprints were on ten thousand FBI Most Wanted posters across America, but they weren't in the police files of either the City of Phoenix or the State of Arizona.

Thomas would eventually send a set of prints directly to the FBI identification division in Washington. But there was no rush. Since Diamond's was not a federally insured institution like a bank, the robbery was not an FBI case and it would probably take weeks to get a response.

The detective was puzzled. It was almost as though Richard Joseph Landry had indeed walked out of a law-abiding life in suburbia to stage a daring daylight holdup. But that didn't make sense. All the first-time bandits Thomas ever encountered had been clumsy, tripping over their own feet, passing holdup notes that didn't make any sense, running away at the first scream or other sign of trouble.

The Diamond's job, on the other hand, was obviously planned. It was evident Landry had studied the armored-truck routines. He knew exactly where to find the money in that back room and when it would be out of the vault for counting. The stolen license plate, the tape over the dealer's sticker on the trunk of the car—those weren't the marks of a total greenhorn. In fact, had Detective Harden not been standing at the scene of the robbery, the thief probably would have got away with it.

Thomas's first big clue that the affable thief might not really be Richard Joseph Landry was all the identification saying he was Richard Joseph Landry. There was just too much of it—almost twenty pieces. In addition to a driver's license, social security card, and other usual ID, there were credit cards, a Playboy Club membership, even a birth certificate. That made Thomas more suspicious: how many people carry a birth certificate?

Then there was the checking account at a bank in New Orleans. The bankbook showed a thousand dollars had been deposited almost a year before, but had never been touched. The first check, No. 001, was still in Landry's checkbook. How many people put money in a checking account and never write a single check?

Late on the afternoon of December 15, the day after the robbery, Detective Jim Thomas took another close look at the mountain of identification for Richard Joseph Landry. That's when he noticed it.

All the credit cards had been issued in New Orleans in December of the previous year. So had his driver's license, car insurance, the birth certificate—every piece of ID had been issued in the same month.

Now Thomas knew something was amiss.

The next morning the detective walked over to the courthouse on West Jefferson to see the assistant county attorney. Thomas started to show him the mountain of ID, piece by piece, all of it issued in the same month.

"Yup, yup…For sure…Yeah…No, that doesn't look right," the assistant prosecutor kept interjecting, checking his watch every time Thomas reached for another piece of the suspect ID.

"I suggest you make a motion asking the court to increase his bond to, say, a hundred grand or something," Thomas said. "That will give me a bit of time to check this guy out some more."

"Yeah, good idea," the assistant prosecutor said briskly, checking his watch again. "Leave it with me. I'll take care of it."

As Thomas walked back to his office in the police station, he was certain he was on to something.

That afternoon Thomas placed a call to a fellow detective at the New Orleans Police Department and asked him to check out the address on Landry's ID—1205 St. Charles Avenue, Apartment 1023. The lawman at the other end of the line said there was nothing unusual about a stack of phony identification papers from Louisiana. For the right price counterfeiters in that part of the country would crank out enough of the stuff to wallpaper the county jail.

The Louisiana officer promised to get back to Thomas in a few days.

Shortly after noon on Thursday, December 17, Detective Thomas re-interviewed the clerks at Diamond's to complete his report on the robbery three days before. On returning to his office, he noticed that the officers who had booked the suspect had neglected to seize the robber's clothes for evidence.

The clothes would still be among Richard Landry's possessions held at the jail, but it was a nuisance nonetheless: Thomas had to draw up a search warrant, take it over to the courthouse to get a judge to sign it in triplicate, then go to the jail to serve it and retrieve the missing clothing.

Thomas arrived at the police entrance, hit the buzzer, and showed his badge. The door locks clicked open.

"I've got a warrant for the personal clothing of Richard Joseph Landry, booking number 81-137756," Thomas said to the man behind the wicket of the prisoners' effects department, handing him the necessary paperwork.

The man behind the wicket ran his finger down a page of the booking log, looked up, and shrugged at the detective.

"Afraid you can't have 'em," the man said.

"What do you mean, I can't have them? You've got the warrant right there."

"Sorry, detective," the man said casually, "can't give ya somethin' we ain't got."

"You don't have the clothes?" Thomas said impatiently. "Well, where the hell are they?"

"I suspect they're probably on Mr. Landry's back," the man said impassively. "Got bonded out of here about three hours ago."

For a moment, Thomas just stared at the man behind the wicket, hoping for a smile and a laugh and a confession that it was just a bad joke.

"You're kidding."

"Nope. He left at twelve fourteen, to be exact."

The detective slammed his fist against the wall in a rage. "Are you absolutely sure?" he shouted. "Check again. It must have been someone else."

The man behind the wicket shoved the forms at Thomas. It was all there: the Arizona Bail Bond Company had posted the necessary amount for the release of one Richard Joseph Landry: $16,000.

The detective rushed to the offices of the Arizona Bail Bond Company. The manager there said that a man by the name of Gil Minski had posted bail in the amount of $16,000, plus another $800 in fees. Paid it all in hundred-dollar bills.

"I don't suppose this Mr. Minski showed you any identification," Thomas growled.

"No, sir, he didn't," the bondsman said. "Nothing in the law says he has to and we didn't ask for it. As long as the money was good—"

"What about Landry?"

"Well, he gave us power of attorney over his '77 Chevy, signed all the papers, and left. Seemed a nice enough fella—"

"When did he leave?"

"Oh, 'bout two hours ago. This is the address he gave us. Some place called Royal Suites apartment motel. Is there a problem?"

Thomas jumped in his car and raced north to the Royal Suites.

The manager didn't have to check his files. "Mr. Landry checked out, oh, I'd say about an hour ago."

***

The encounter between Detective Jim Thomas and the assistant county attorney that followed contained an abundance of language not suitable for the six o'clock news. The prosecutor explained he had planned to ask the court for an increase in Landry's bail at the same time Landry applied for a reduction of it.

"Had he applied for a bond reduction?" Thomas asked.

"No, he hadn't," the prosecutor said flatly.

"Well, what made you think he was going to apply for anything?" Thomas shouted.

"They usually do."

"Well, thanks to you, he's gone, and you can be damn sure we aren't going to see Mr. Landry in court next week."

"Now, now, detective," the prosecutor said, "I suggest you take care of your job chasing the bad guys, and leave my job to me. If you are so convinced this Mr. Landry has disappeared, you're certainly not going to find him while you're standing here yelling."

Fortunately, the prosecutor's door had strong hinges.

A week later, to no one's surprise, Richard Landry did not show up for his scheduled court appearance. That afternoon a grand jury indicted him in absentia, and a warrant was issued for his arrest. This time the assistant county attorney was right on top of the case. He requested that bail for the missing Mr. Landry be increased to $56,000.

In the ensuing months Detective Jim Thomas would engage in the most dogged fugitive hunt of his police career. It wasn't a job so much as an obsession. Nights, weekends, any spare time would be spent on the phone or hunched over a police computer trying to track the elusive bandit.

His first stop was a friend's office in the Phoenix bureau of the FBI. Agent Tony Olaham had previously worked at the bureau's ID section in Washington. He promised to expedite a fingerprint check.

With each fingerprint reproduced on special three-by-five cards as required by FBI regulations, Paddy Mitchell's unique collection of lines and whorls must have passed dozens of identical sets plastered on the FBI's own bulletin boards from Phoenix to Washington and back again.

A week later, agent Olaham called Jim Thomas and read him the telex from Washington: "SEARCHES CONDUCTED IN LATENT

FINGERPRINT FILES, BUT NO IDENTIFICATION WAS EFFECTED."

Thomas was dumbfounded. No record anywhere in the United States? He went through the same process with the U.S. military files—perhaps the mysterious bandit was a former vet gone berserk. Negative. Nothing there, either.

Further enquiries of the manager of the Royal Suites apartments in Phoenix produced nothing useful. No, Mr. Landry had not made any long-distance phone calls while he was staying there—the rooms had no phones. Yes, he had left a forwarding address for the return of his seventy-five-dollar damage deposit: 1205 St. Charles Ave, Apt. 1023, New Orleans.

On January 6, 1982, almost three weeks after Mitchell's disappearance, Thomas got a call from the New Orleans police detective who had promised to check out the Charles Street address. At least he had some information.

The apartment had been rented from November 1980 to February 1981 by a man giving the name Michael Baxter. He had told the landlord he was self-employed, and had provided a former address of Box 635, Dundee, Florida. As a reference, he had given his mother's name, Jean Baxter, along with an address and phone number in Iowa City, Iowa. Mr. Baxter had also advised the landlords that he would be receiving mail for Richard Joseph Landry.

And there was something else. While the mail was always picked up, no one ever saw Michael Baxter after the day he rented the apartment.

Other than his alias, Michael Baxter, Paddy Mitchell had not been overly inventive. The box number in Dundee, Florida, was the one used by Lionel Wright when he had been a motel clerk there. As for the maternal reference, Jean Baxter, Mitchell's mother's name is Jean, and the Iowa City address and phone number were each a few digits off the parental home of his beloved and abandoned Beckie.

Of course, Detective Jim Thomas knew none of that at the time, and all the information supplied by the New Orleans detective seemed as worthless as everything else in the already-thick file of dead ends. First the guy opens a checking account and never uses it. Then he rents an apartment and is never seen there again. A phantom in Louisiana disappears in Phoenix. Geez.

Thomas called the Iowa City PD to learn that Jean Baxter and her supposed address and phone number were all non-existent.

The detective then checked out the Ohio plate found taped over the New Orleans tag on Landry's getaway car. Stolen. Next he contacted the sheriff's office in Dundee, Florida. They had no record of either a Michael Baxter or a Richard Joseph Landry.

A month later Thomas again telephoned the New Orleans detective and asked him to check out Landry's birth certificate. In a matter of days the Louisiana lawman called back.

"I've got good news and bad news," the New Orleans detective began. "The good news is I managed to track down the records on your boy Richard Joseph Landry, d.o.b. September 2, 1946. The bad news is he died in a traffic accident before he was two years old—April 30, 1948, to be exact."

The phone call confirmed what Thomas had suspected all along. But if the fugitive bandit was not Richard Joseph Landry, who the hell was he?

Thomas didn't know it at the time, but the other significant lead in his file had come from two girls in Clintwood, Virginia, whose telephone numbers were found in Landry's wallet at the time of his arrest. Vicki and Sally told the detective they had partied a lot—one of them romantically—with Rick Landry in Florida in September of the previous year, three months before the Diamond's heist. He had told the girls he was a Los Angeles businessman, originally from New Orleans, who had just bought a home in Winterhaven, Florida.

Thomas did contact the Winterhaven PD, who told him what had become a familiar story—they had no record of a Richard Joseph Landry in that town nor in any of the surrounding communities. He tucked the Winterhaven connection in his file with all the other clues that had similarly amounted to nothing.

Finally, he sent off photographs, fingerprints, and full descriptions of Richard Joseph Landry to the police departments in New Orleans, Los Angeles, and Winterhaven. No one replied.

Every lead that Thomas had followed for Landry was rerun in the search for an equally elusive Gil Minski, the mystery man who had bailed Mitchell out of jail with fourteen dozen hundred-dollar bills.

But, like Richard Landry, the man named Gil Minski seemed to have evaporated.

Almost three months into his investigation, Detective Jim Thomas had run out of leads. The trail of Patrick Michael Mitchell had led straight to the middle of nowhere.

***

The sleepy town of Hot Springs, Arkansas, isn't exactly the baccarat pits of Las Vegas. But life on the lam was taking its toll on Paddy Mitchell's nerves, and a southern dullsville seemed the perfect respite from it all.

Richard Landry had first landed in town the previous fall after a seven-month fugitive's odyssey from New Orleans to New Mexico, Florida, Texas, Kentucky, Oregon, back to Florida, and finally back to Arkansas. Hot Springs was no playpen for the rich and famous, but it did provide most of Mitchell's other favorite amusements—horse racing, fishing, and a cute young nurse named Suzi.

Suzi had fallen in love with the man who first came to her public-health clinic for treatment of a dose. He introduced himself as Richard Joseph Landry.

Mitchell had kissed Suzi goodbye the previous November, saying he was going to visit his mother in New England for Christmas. That was two days before he bought the silver revolver and headed to Phoenix for his ill-fated shopping spree at Diamond's Department Store.

Immediately after the benevolent Gil Minski had bailed him out of that jam, Mitchell had run for cover back to central Florida. Down on his luck and cash flow, he managed to get through the winter with a little help from his old friend Chuck Hogan, the motel-owner who had once employed the fugitive Lionel Wright.

The following March, about the same time Detective Jim Thomas was giving up his hunt for Richard Landry, Paddy Mitchell arrived back in Hot Springs, desperately seeking Suzi. He was driving a Lincoln Continental with tinted windows and Florida license plates.

The luxury car looked incongruous alongside Mitchell's new abode, a small motel cabin on the shores of Lake Hamilton. It had probably been a real nice spot, right after World War II. No matter, the place was comfortable, the fishing was good, and Suzi was glad to have her lover back after his extended Christmas visit with Mom.

Mitchell had rented the place under the name C. "Rick" Hogan. He had nothing to identify him as Richard Joseph Landry—the Phoenix PD had all that ID—and he hadn't bothered to buy or manufacture a new alias. Instead, he had simply "borrowed" pieces of identification from his old pal Chuck Hogan in Florida.

Rick Landry explained to Suzi and her friends that he had lost his license in San Diego for drunk driving, and was using the name Hogan so no one would know he had obtained another one illegally in Florida.

Suzi introduced Rick Landry to her ex-boyfriend and his new lover, and the foursome got along famously. Paddy had actually become quite accomplished in the kitchen, and his friends were routinely treated to gourmet extravaganzas of Cajun and Mexican cuisine. Cocaine for dessert.

Most of the other folk around the resort area got to know Rick Landry—or Rick Hogan, depending on the day—as the compulsive jogger who would clock at least ten miles every morning, always with a friendly wave and a g'mornin' as he passed.

Mitchell had become obsessed with aging. Vitamins, skincreams, herbal medicines, even supposed wonder drugs like Retin-A—every doubtful age-retardant espoused by any supermarket tabloid got sucked up in twice the recommended daily dosage.

Paddy Mitchell was about to turn forty.

April 5, 1982. It is opening day of the horse racing season at the Oaklawn Track on the outskirts of Hot Springs. The otherwise peaceful town is a curb-to-curb traffic jam, its normal population of 30,000 swelled to almost double that number. Most of the local constabulary are busy coping with the congestion. On this day, only the ponies are going anywhere in a hurry.

The perfect day for a bank robbery.

Paddy Mitchell is only marginally better prepared than he was for the fiasco in Phoenix. He has a gun, an armored-truck schedule, skin-tight surgical gloves, and a knitted balaclava instead of a sawed-off corduroy pant leg.

He has a plan: park the getaway car some distance from the bank—running will be faster than driving in all the congestion. Let the cops get caught in traffic. But he is stumped again by the problem of a suitable getaway vehicle. He can't be bothered stealing one, and wouldn't know how to, anyway. He can't rent a car—he has only one set of identification papers, and those would lead police straight to his pal Chuck Hogan in Florida.

He is reluctant to use his own car—trying to sneak away in a Lincoln Continental semi-limo with tinted windows might be a bit obvious. Besides he wants to keep it. So he does the next dumbest thing—he borrows a car from Suzi's ex-boyfriend and slaps a Florida plate on it.

It is shortly after one o'clock when Paddy Mitchell parks his friend's gold-colored Firebird in the lot of the Bonanza Restaurant, and walks to the First National Bank of Hot Springs.

At 1:29 p.m. the armored-truck finishes its delivery to the bank and noses into the bumper-to-bumper traffic.

Less than a minute later Paddy Mitchell pulls the balaclava over his face, roars into the bank, waves his revolver, demands the two money bags just dropped off by the armored-truck, and races back out again.

A man in the parking lot spots Mitchell tearing off the balaclava at a full run, and begins yelling: "Thief! Thief!"Another civic-minded fellow, ignoring all the warnings about chasing people with guns, pursues the fleeing bandit.

Mitchell weaves in and out of the congested traffic, then darts down an alley, turns right down a side street, across a parking lot, down another alley—all the detours just can't seem to shake the dogged citizen still in hot pursuit.

Finally, Mitchell ducks into a Wendy's restaurant, pushes his way deep into the crowd, and runs out the other door. As the footrace nears the finish line in the parking lot of the Bonanza Restaurant, Mitchell glances over his shoulder. There is no sign of the competition.

Mitchell jumps into the gold-colored Firebird and speeds off down a side street.

That evening back at the lakeside cabin the happy foursome dined on French champagne and Rick Landry's house speciality—Cajun chicken with a ginger stir-fry. Cocaine for appetizers and dessert.

Opening day at the track had certainly been a bonanza for ol' Rick. Had stories to tell about every race and most of the horses. Rickie sure knew how to pick 'em. Claimed he hadn't even bothered to count his winnings, but it was well over ten grand, for sure. Betting on the ponies is all a science, you know—

There was a lull in the lies and the laughter just long enough for the radio announcer to fill the dead air.

"...in a daring daylight holdup at the First National Bank at about one-thirty this afternoon...Police said the witness chased the lone gunman until he sped off in a late-model, gold-colored sports coupe, possibly a Firebird or a Camaro, with Florida license plates."

For a moment, there was silence around the table. All four faces were troubled—three of them wondering the same thing, the fourth suddenly realizing he hadn't shaken his tail after all.

Paddy Mitchell started to cackle around a mouthful of spicy chicken. "Hey, did you hear that?" he said as he chewed. "A gold-colored sports coupe. Geez, that could've been me driving your car this afternoon."

Mitchell looked up at Suzi's ex-boyfriend and started to roar with laughter. "Can't you just see it now? Stick 'em up, pants down, ol' Rickie the robber's back in town. What a picture! Can't you just see it? Ha! Ha!"

Soon they were all laughing.

The holdup alarm at the First National Bank had barely finished ringing when every agent in the Hot Springs bureau of the FBI was unleashed on the case—that is to say, both Floyd Hays and Tom Ross.

The drowsy community had never been considered a hotbed of federal crime, but the two agents were no banished-to-the-boonies amateurs, either. By the night after the robbery the pair of sleuths had found the gold-colored Firebird and its rightful owner, Suzi's ex-boyfriend, who in turn led them to Suzi. As the ensuing interrogation dragged into the early-morning hours, the FBI were finally pointed to a cabin by the lake. There they found a small library of cookbooks, some fishing tackle, and the Florida license plate used on the getaway car. The former occupant of the cabin had obviously left in a hurry.

They also found a photograph of Suzi and her beloved Rickie. Sure didn't look like a bank robber, FBI agent Ross concluded—the combed brown curly hair, a neatly trimmed mustache, laughing blue eyes. Handsome fellow. A gourmet cook and an avid jogger, too.

After that it took the FBI no time at all to discover the cabin had been rented to one C. "Rick" Hogan, also known to his friends as Richard Landry. He had last been seen by his friends after dinner the previous night, just before he drove off in a Lincoln Continental with tinted windows.

Everyone said the car had arrived in town with a Florida license plate, but no one could remember the number. The FBI assumed it was the one they found in the cabin. Tom Ross made a special note of the tinted windows—didn't see many of them in Arkansas. Probably was a Florida car, all right.

Later that week a Hot Springs police officer recovered a bag of garbage in the parking lot of the Royal Vista Inn. It contained ten money wrappers, an adding-machine tape, deposit slips and envelopes from the local K-Mart, $7,049 in personal checks, and some miscellaneous scrap paper. The FBI determined it had all come from the two money bags stolen during the First National robbery.

The FBI sent off the contents of the trash bag and the recovered Florida license plate to the latent fingerprint section of their Identification Division in Washington. As the full set of Richard Landry's prints was already on file from the previous futile enquiry from the Phoenix PD, it took only three weeks and four haranguing phone calls from the Arkansas bureau of the FBI to get the following response from their lab in Washington:

> The specimens were examined and six latent fingerprints and seven latent palm prints of value appeared or were developed— ...The latent fingerprints are not the fingerprints of Richard Joseph Landry, FBI #517427X10. No palm prints are contained in our Identification Division files for Landry...Searches were conducted in the single fingerprint files [of everyone else], but no identification was effected...

Meanwhile, shortly after the robbery, FBI agent Tom Ross had contacted Phoenix Detective Jim Thomas on noticing in the national crime computers that Richard Joseph Landry was wanted in Arizona for armed robbery, kidnapping, and aggravated assault—the legacy of the botched Diamond's Department Store job. The two lawmen compared notes and agreed they were both looking for the same friendly fitness freak.

Detective Thomas had the names of two Florida towns in his file: the girls whose phone numbers had been found in Landry's wallet said he had mentioned buying a house in Winterhaven. The fugitive had also given his New Orleans landlord a post-office box number in Dundee, Florida, as his previous address. Thomas gave Ross a description of mystery bondsman Gil Minski, just in case the FBI happened to stumble across him.

Ross said the Florida connection seemed to fit. Landry was last seen driving a Lincoln Continental with tinted windows, probably from Florida. He had also used a second alias—one C. "Rick" Hogan—to rent the cabin near Hot Springs.

Within a matter of days, FBI agents in the Winterhaven district of Florida arrived on the doorstep of Mitchell's old friend and motel owner, Chuck Hogan.

Seems Mr. Hogan had been on a bit of a losing streak lately. So far he had lost a Lincoln Continental with tinted windows and numerous pieces of identification. He was also missing $16,800 paid to the Arizona Bail Bond Company.

CHAPTER TWENTY-EIGHT

Phoenix, Arizona

Eleven days after the Hot Springs bank robbery Phoenix detective Jim Thomas sounded as though he had just won the lottery. FBI agent Tom Ross was on the other end of the phone from Arkansas saying an informant in Florida had revealed the elusive Richard Joseph Landry was staying at the Bahia Motel in San Diego. The FBI even had the license number and exact description of the fugitive's 1979 Lincoln Continental with tinted windows.

What the FBI did not have was the jurisdiction to do anything about it. Despite all the circumstances pointing to Landry in the Hot Springs heist, the FBI still didn't have sufficient evidence to get an arrest warrant. They had one witness who had picked the suspect out of a photo line-up, but that was it. They had no weapon, no disguises, no fingerprints, no stolen loot, and no idea their suspect was already on their own Ten Most Wanted list. All they had was a bag of garbage, a pile of cookbooks, a Florida license plate, and a missing jogger named Rick Landry.

But Jim Thomas had plenty of evidence and a warrant and a burning obsession to nab Landry. He couldn't wait to hang up on agent Ross and call the San Diego PD.

The duty officer in San Diego dutifully took down all the details from the excited Phoenix detective and promised to have someone check it out. Two hours later Thomas couldn't stand the suspense and called the San Diego PD again. He was assured someone there was investigating. Three hours after that the anxious detective called again. He got the same story. That was the last Jim Thomas heard from the San Diego police department.

Almost two months later the FBI got another tip. This time Landry was in Seattle. Seems Mitchell had driven north for another fling with

302

godliness and the preacher's daughter named Carol-Sue. But this time she announced that forgiveness for his unceremonious disappearing act two years before was something he might want to discuss with God. She slammed the door.

Dejected and lonely, Mitchell drove to Seattle and checked into a suburban motel. He called a friend in Florida, who promptly called his neighborhood FBI agent, who called Tom Ross in Arkansas, who called Jim Thomas in Phoenix, who immediately called the Seattle PD for help.

When police arrived at the motel, the steam was still on the bathroom mirror. Paddy Mitchell was gone.

And so it went throughout the summer and early fall of 1982. Tips led police in a dozen different states to a dozen different abandoned hideouts. Sometimes they would miss Mitchell by hours, sometimes by days. Sometimes there was no trace of his ever having been there in the first place.

But in all that time no one anywhere connected the Richard Joseph Landry with the Stopwatch Gang and Paddy Mitchell's smiling face on the FBI's own Most Wanted posters.

In early October, Jim Thomas called his local FBI friend Tony Olaham and, joking, asked why the mighty feds had not located his boy Richard Joseph Landry. Olaham promised to get back with an update.

During Olaham's subsequent conversation with his FBI colleagues in Arkansas, agent Tom Ross mentioned a rather interesting titbit. Apparently during the Hot Springs bank robbery, Ross said, the bandit had said that "anyone sticking a head out that door is going to get it blown off." One of the bank employees told the FBI she thought maybe the thief was a Canadian. It was the way he had pronounced "oot that door."

Olaham called Detective Thomas back to say he knew some folks in the ID section of the Royal Canadian Mounted Police. Both agreed it was worth checking.

On October 22 Tom Ross called Jim Thomas in Phoenix with some fascinating news. The RCMP had identified the fingerprints of Richard Joseph Landry as belonging to a prison escapee on Canada's Most Wanted list. Ross reported: "Landry's real name is Bobby Mitchell from Ottawa, Canada."

Either the RCMP had mistakenly identified Paddy Mitchell's brother (not wanted for anything), or something had got lost in the translation inside the FBI bureaucracy. One way or another, the FBI still did not make the connection to their own most-wanted Patrick Michael Mitchell and the Stopwatch Gang.

"And there's something else," Ross told Thomas. "We have received information that the suspect is currently living somewhere in Lakeland, Florida."

If Thomas would issue the proper paperwork to give the FBI jurisdiction in the case, Ross said, agents in Florida would be only too happy to apprehend the fugitive.

Paddy Mitchell had arrived in the central Florida community of Lakeland in early September. He rented a small cottage and promptly lapsed into a reclusive funk. He was depressed, paranoid, lonely, and generally sick of running from the law. He was also suffering from a back injury sustained during a holdup. Seems he had underestimated his own level of physical fitness—he'd flown over the counter at a full run, twisted in midair, and landed backwards on a desk halfway to the loans department.

For more than a month he lay in bed in Lakeland, drinking gin, and snorting cocaine. The former good-time bandit rarely ventured outside and chatted with no one. There was no point—even a beer in a bar meant having to fear every glance.

A gangster without a gang, a party animal without friends, a romantic without a lover—Paddy Mitchell had come to loathe his life on the lam. He missed his partners in crime. Stephen Reid was rotting in Illinois's notorious Marion prison, one of the ugliest, most violent dungeons in America. Lionel Wright wasn't faring much better behind bars in Leavenworth, Kansas. Paddy sent them money from time to time, and wished them well. There was nothing more he could do. And while he had no inclination to join them in captivity, he no longer much cared if he got caught, either. If it happened, it happened.

His carelessness showed: not coding the Virginia girls' phone numbers, then leaving them in his wallet; not changing his alias after his arrest in Phoenix; using a car and ID belonging to his traceable friend Chuck Hogan.

With a trail of clues strewn from one end of America to the other, Paddy Mitchell had become akin to the wartime soldier once described as "a fugitive from the law of averages."

As the November storms battered the sleepy town of Lakeland, so too came the agents of the FBI.

***

Jim Thomas would have done just about anything for the pleasure of personally slapping the handcuffs on Richard Joseph Landry. But the FBI's tip on October 22 that Mitchell was living in Lakeland demanded immediate action, not interdepartmental turf wars. If finally nabbing the elusive crook meant handing jurisdiction to the feds, Thomas was happy to oblige.

Specifically, what the FBI required was a warrant alleging that Richard Joseph Landry had engaged in "unlawful flight to avoid prosecution"—in bureau-ese, a UFAP. The process was invented, in part, to keep the already overworked FBI from becoming the national lost-and-found for every municipal, county, and state police force that happened to be missing a suspect.

In order to obtain a UFAP on Mitchell, therefore, Thomas had to prove in writing that the Phoenix PD had done everything within its power and jurisdiction to apprehend the fugitive, and that there were reasonable grounds to believe the suspect was no longer in the state of Arizona.

Eleven months of chasing Richard Joseph Landry across half the states in the union certainly seemed to fit the criteria for a UFAP. The problem was that the UFAP didn't quite fit the criteria for catching someone like Patrick Michael Mitchell.

It took three days for Thomas to complete the UFAP paperwork, and another three days to get the four pages typed on the proper forms. A week for the same four pages to clear the brass in the Phoenix PD and the county prosecutor's office. It took another ten days for the papers to get to the top of the right pile at the Department of the U.S. Attorney General. Finally, it took another five business days for the approved UFAP warrant to reach the FBI who wouldn't have needed the damn thing in the first place had they figured out that Bobby Mitchell was really Paddy Mitchell, one of their own Ten Most Wanted.

No matter; almost a month after the fugitive had been pinpointed in Florida, FBI agents armed with one UFAP warrant and a lot of guns converged on the small community of Lakeland.

Surprise, surprise.

At the same time as the UFAP warrant was crawling from Phoenix to the FBI, Paddy Mitchell was sitting in the Hee Haw Bar on the outskirts of Leesburg, Florida, about two hours north of Lakeland. After almost two months of drowning his sorrows in numbing doses of booze and cocaine, Mitchell had left Lakeland in search of company for his misery.

He found her the evening of November 3 in the Hee Haw, a favorite watering hole for rednecks, deep in the heart of cracker country. Mitchell had dropped by to soak up some cold suds and a bit of achin'-hearts country music. He spotted her as soon as she walked into the place, a cute young brunette with friendly eyes and a shy smile.

She couldn't help noticing him at the bar. Most of the men in the place looked as though they had just overhauled a Mack truck with their teeth. He was different—handsome, tanned, and muscular, with black curly hair and mustache, and those laser-beam blue eyes. She guessed he was in his late twenties. The others were old enough to be her father. Actually, so was he.

She ordered a sloe gin fizz and caught his eye across the bar. Or maybe he caught hers. They danced and talked and drank and danced some more. She was lonely. So was he.

At the end of the evening she drove home with him in his new Thunderbird to a small house he had rented in nearby Astatula. They drank some more and talked all night.

At the age of twenty, Janet Lynn Rush was two years younger than Mitchell's son. No matter. She had managed to pack a lot into her short lifetime. A lot of misery.

Janet Rush had married at sixteen to escape a violent home life in Elyria, Ohio. A year later, she had a hundred dollars and a '73 Olds Cutlass, and an ex-husband, so she drove south in search of a fresh start. She ran out of gas and money in a small central-Florida town called Lake Papasoffka.

The lonely runaway soon fell in love with a fellow named Billy, whose own childhood story made Janet feel like Cinderella by comparison. Billy was no rocket scientist, but he was gentle and generous and generally good company. He was out of town on business a lot, though he never said much about what he did for a living. Janet figured she had found her fresh start.

A year later, at nineteen, Janet Rush arrived home one day to find four men in business suits and Billy in handcuffs. Seems her beloved was a fugitive from New Jersey with a criminal record longer than Janet's face as she watched him being dragged off by the agents of the FBI.

Janet got a job as a delivery girl for a Leesburg autobody shop. Convinced she was born to lose, she studiously avoided getting close to anyone for over a year. Then she met the handsome fellow in the Hee Haw Bar.

Mitchell introduced himself as Richard Jordan, an insurance investigator from Allentown, Pennsylvania. Despite forty-one years of hard living and his latest two-month binge of substance abuse, his jogger's body remained youthfully taut. Another plastic surgeon had also worked another facial miracle—Richard Jordan said he was thirty-one; Janet was amazed he was that old. As dawn began to break over the little house in Astatula, she curled up with her handsome new friend and fell asleep smiling.

By all appearances, the wedding of Florida motel owner Chuck Hogan was fit for the cover of a glossy bridal magazine. The happy couple and guests assembled amid the floral splendor of the Bok Tower botanical gardens. White suits, colorful garden dresses, floppy straw hats, the thick perfume of blossoms everywhere—everything just oh-so-special.

It was special, all right. Not every happy couple has wedding vows witnessed by agents of the FBI. The uninvited guests showed up in droves—brushcuts in the bushes; brushcuts behind the trees; brushcuts wandering conspicuously among the flowerbeds—a small army of them with binoculars and guns and chromeless cars.

The matrimonial stake-out, an exercise normally reserved for updating FBI photo files of Mafia families, was only slightly less peculiar than the tip that prompted it.

Paddy Mitchell was on the guest list. And in honor of the occasion, the funny guy they called "Rickie the Runner" was planning to stage a ceremonial jog-past just as the confetti was flying. Just for laughs.

The I-dos were concluded shortly before three o'clock. Binoculars scanned the jogging path, the gardens, the wedding crowd, the jogging path again. Police radios crackled in earplugs in a dozen different locations.

The fastest jogger alive couldn't have dodged the trap. The agents of the FBI had the place surrounded. All they had to do was wait for their prey to run straight into their handcuffs.

They watched and they waited.

And watched and waited.

Maybe it was Irish luck. Maybe another message from God. Something at the last minute told Paddy Mitchell that the perfect day for a wedding could be a perfectly lousy day for a fugitive on the guest list.

While the FBI watched and waited, the man on their Most Wanted list sent a message of regrets and went fishing.

***

Paddy Mitchell sat silently in the rowboat, peering into the aluminum minnow bucket, watching the tiny mouths groping and gobbling the morsels of cornmeal falling gently from his hand. Their last supper before the hook.

Janet Lynn Rush wanted to cry. Finally, she had found her Perfect Ten, a fisherman who fed his bait because he felt sorry for them, a lover she would later describe as "the kindest, most gentle man I have ever known."

Paddy Mitchell was happy, too. He and Janet had moved into a new house he had rented at Eighteen East Cove in Astatula. It was a pretty place—two stories, two bedrooms, two bathrooms, a big living room with cathedral ceiling, and a view of the canal leading to a nearby lake. Nothing was too good for his Princess.

Typically Mitchell's day would begin with a ten-mile jog along the canal, a healthy breakfast, and a joint with his morning newspaper. When he wasn't out fishing on the lake, one of America's Most Wanted was a semi-reclusive househusband. He never complained, and seemed perfectly content to pass his time cleaning house, running errands, washing the Thunderbird, shopping for groceries, reading cookbooks, and preparing elaborate evening meals.

Janet would arrive home from work to a hug and a kiss and a hot bath already drawn for her. He would bring her a drink in the tub, and set a fire in the hearth. Every dinner was some culinary delight—she would kill for his tostadas—and always set to candlelight, soft music, and no shortage of French wine.

Other than visiting his friend Chuck Hogan in Winterhaven, Mitchell rarely ventured far from home.

All of which was fine with Janet. She would have loved nothing more than to show off her Prince. But in a town of rednecks and retired rednecks, Paddy Mitchell just didn't fit in. She tried to tell him time and time again—in cracker country, you don't try to tip the waiter with a toot of coke. But her Prince would just laugh and tell her she worried too much.

Janet Rush did worry a bit at first. The Richard Jordan she had met at the Hee Haw suddenly became Richard Graham a month later, and Rick Baird a month after that. Finally, she peeked in his wallet and found a social security card for someone named Michael Lawrence Garrison. Everything else in the billfold—credit cards, driver's license, the registration for the Thunderbird, even a birth certificate—was for someone named Richard Jordan Baird.

Mitchell apologized and told his Princess that, yes, his name really was Richard Jordan Baird. He had certainly meant no harm by the rest of the fictitious names—as he had told her before, anonymity was all just a regrettable part of being an insurance investigator.

The street-smart runaway didn't really believe his explanations. She didn't even believe he was an insurance investigator. But she didn't care much, either—Janet Rush had never loved anyone like she loved Richard Baird, and she wasn't about to risk her Prince turning into a frog.

On the three-legged coffee table in their living room, Janet kept a book of poetry she had been writing since her tormented teens. The first part was filled with the violence and fears of her childhood. The second was all the hopes and dreams and the ultimate devastation of her romance with Billy the fugitive. Now she had started a third part for the love and ecstasy she had found in her Prince. Life, she said, just couldn't get any better.

For his part Paddy Mitchell never stopped missing his family, and regretted the choices that put him into exile. But short of turning back the clock twenty years, there wasn't much he could do about any of it now.

For the time being the reclusive Richard Jordan Baird was happy to let his tranquil version of the Good Life roll on forever. He had everything he needed.

Except money.

On December 19, 1982, Richard Baird told Janet Rush the same story Richard Landry had fed to Suzi the year before in Hot Springs— he was heading north, this time to Pennsylvania, to visit his aging mother for Christmas. Two days later in Ocala, Florida, two masked bandits robbed a bank with what police later described as "military-like precision." Three days after the Ocala heist and five days after Mitchell had left for Pennsylvania, Richard Baird was back home in Astatula. It was Christmas Eve.

The next morning Janet found her Christmas present parked in the driveway—a baby blue Cadillac Coupe de Ville.

It was mid-afternoon in late January 1983 when Paddy Mitchell drove to nearby Leesburg to buy a special frying pan for enchiladas. He parked the Thunderbird in a lot along the main drag and walked across the street to the kitchen store. When he returned to his car fifteen minutes later, a man was standing behind the Thunderbird, jotting the license number in a small notebook.

"Hey! What the hell are you doing?" Mitchell shouted from thirty feet away.

The man gave Mitchell a startled glance. "I collect license numbers," he shouted back, then hurried away across the parking lot.

For a moment, Mitchell just stood there, watching the license-plate collector disappear around a corner. His insides knotted. He knew danger when he saw it. And there was no doubt he had just stared it in the face. Mitchell called Janet to say he had to go out of town on an urgent insurance investigation. God bless.

Three days later, he called her from a pay phone in southern Georgia. Had anyone dropped around to see him? Had she noticed anything unusual around the house? Were there any strange cars parked on the street? This was one dangerous insurance investigation, all right.

At any other time in his fugitive's career, he would have kept right on driving. But to where? To what? To another strange town full of more strange faces, any one of them his potential nemesis? And what about the young lover waiting for him at his home in Astatula? Paddy just couldn't bring himself to leave her.

Satisfied the coast was clear, Mitchell returned home. He would rather risk the FBI than run back to the loneliness he had come to fear and loathe. Besides, he rationalized, if the license-plate collector had really been a cop looking for him, why hadn't the arrest been made on the spot?

Three weeks after the incident, Mitchell dropped by the Hee Haw for a pint on his way home from Friday-afternoon grocery shopping in Leesburg. The bartender put the beer on the bar and casually asked Mitchell where he was staying.

"In Astatula," Mitchell said as he dug in his pocket for money. "Got a nice big house on the canal."

"You from these parts?" the bartender asked.

"No, no way," Mitchell said with a laugh. Then, without thinking much of it, he added: "I'm originally from Canada."

"No kidding," the bartender said, picking up the money. "Those two guys at the end of the bar are Canadians, too."

Mitchell turned on his barstool and was staring at a familiar stranger. The license-plate collector.

"Jesus," Mitchell muttered at no one. "This is it."

***

More than two months after Richard Joseph Landry was identified as Bobby Mitchell of Ottawa, Canada, the FBI finally figured out the man they had been chasing all over America was the Patrick Michael Mitchell who had been on their own Most Wanted list for almost two years.

The FBI paid another visit to their Florida tipster. He was already in the bad books of a few frustrated agents tired of bursting into Mitchell's vacated hideouts. He was also heading for a heap of trouble with the DEA if he wasn't more cooperative. The Leadfoots came down hard on their informant.

Look for a Thunderbird, the tipster said, somewhere in the Leesburg area.

Finding a T-Bird among the pickup trucks of Leesburg wasn't hard. Nor was the license check that coughed up the name Richard Jordan Baird. The address was useless—Mitchell's previous hideout in Lakeland.

But the date of birth produced something interesting. Richard Jordan Baird's records in Pennsylvania indicated the owner of the Thunderbird had died approximately twenty-seven years before the car rolled off the Ford assembly line.

Then the T-bird and its owner vanished.

The license-plate collector sitting in the Hee Haw was therefore just as astonished to see Mitchell as Mitchell was to see him.

But Paddy wasn't waiting for introductions. He ordered another beer, left his jacket hanging on his chair, headed for the men's room, and slipped out the back door.

He was a nervous wreck all weekend. Nothing was making any sense. If the FBI knew who he was and where he was, why the hell hadn't they busted him? If they didn't know, why was he worrying? Maybe it was just a lot of paranoia. Too many cocaine desserts.

Mitchell knew he should run. Get out of Florida. Leave Janet. But he couldn't. Not yet.

Thursday was her birthday. He wanted to do something really special for his Princess. After all, she was turning twenty-one.

Then he would leave town and set up somewhere else.

Then he would knock off that planeload of loot in New York or Montreal, his old Dream Score.

Then he could retire.

Then he would send for Janet and marry her.

Then the doorbell rang.

"FBI—"

CHAPTER TWENTY-NINE

Astatula, Florida

The morning of February 22, 1983, had been overcast and cold when the FBI converged on the pretty little house by the canal in Astatula. Special agent Dennis Wicklein stood on the doorstep of 18 East Cove, bracing himself for the long-awaited encounter with the elusive bank robber described in FBI files as: "Armed and Extremely Dangerous!!!"—always with the three exclamation marks.

Three other agents positioned themselves between the house and the canal, hoping they wouldn't have to go swimming. Wicklein rang the front doorbell with the tip of his revolver. The door opened without so much as a who's-there.

For an instant the two men just stared at each other. Mitchell was understandably surprised to find an FBI revolver in his face. Wicklein wasn't exactly expecting to find a gangster in a designer jogging outfit, either. The notorious felon wasn't armed, and he certainly didn't sound particularly dangerous when he offered to make coffee for the lawmen.

"Obviously, there has been some mistake, gentlemen," Mitchell said with a smile and a shrug. He insisted his name was Richard Jordan Baird, an insurance investigator from Allentown, Pennsylvania. And he had a walletful of identification to prove it.

"Patrick Mitchell? Hmmm. Mitchell. Mitchell—sorry, gentlemen, can't say I know anyone by that name. And who did you say that other fellow was? Somebody Landry? Richard Landry? Nope. Sorry, doesn't ring any bells, either."

But Wicklein knew there was no mistake. Plastic surgery may have removed all those years of aging so important to Mitchell, but everything important to the FBI was still there—the alarm-clock scar between his eyes; the Fat-and-Heller tattoo on his arm; the small crucifix stenciled on his chest. And soon they would have matching sets of ten of the most widely traveled fingerprints in America.

The unyielding morning temperatures had sent Janet home for a jacket in the midst of her delivery rounds for the body shop. The scene in her living room required no explanation. She had seen it all before— four men in business suits, her Prince in handcuffs, pleading that it was all just a big mistake.

No introductions were required, either—the men in her living room were the same four FBI agents who had hauled away her beloved Billy eighteen months before.

She started to cry.

The capture of Patrick Michael Mitchell made front-page news across the United States and Canada. But the story didn't end with his arrest. Four days after he had been tossed in the Seminole County slammer, Mitchell was back on Page One of the Ottawa *Citizen* under the headline: "Mitchell insists he's someone else."

> Four days after FBI agents in Florida arrested famed Ottawa fugitive Patrick "Paddy" Mitchell, the colorful crook whose face has adorned international most-wanted posters for over three years insists he's not the man most wanted...
>
> "For some crazy reason, he refuses to admit he is Paddy Mitchell," said Dennis Wicklein, one of the FBI agents who made the arrest. "There is no doubt in our minds who he is. But we've never seen anyone try to hang onto an alias as long as he has.
>
> "We have no idea what he is up to..."

The reporter at the newspaper had barely put down his pen when the phone rang. It was a collect call from a Mr. Mitchell in the Seminole County jail.

"Hi there; it's Paddy Mitchell," announced a friendly voice. "I gather you might want to talk to me."

"Ah, er, you sure this phone call is, ah, er, a good idea?" the reporter stammered. "I mean, I just finished filing a story saying you were saying you aren't who they say you are, and—"

Mitchell was laughing: "Oh, yeah, that. Don't take it too seriously. I'm just having a bit of fun with them. If you want to chat, c'mon down to Florida. I'm not planning to go anywhere for a few days."

***

Janet Rush was devastated. From a used Olds and a hundred bucks to a used Caddy and some cookbooks. Nothin' from nothin' leaves nothin', the song goes. But somehow, her losing everything from everything left a far more devastating nothin'. She would later reflect:

> The hard thing was realizing when it was all over that all the things he had told me, and all the things we had shared, were lies. He was leading a dual life—he was two different people.
>
> When they took him away, Richard Baird died, and in his place was this Patrick Mitchell person who did things that Richard Baird would never do.
>
> The Richard Baird that I was in love with would never pick up a gun and put it to somebody's head and demand their money...The guy was a wimp. He wouldn't hurt a fly...He spoiled me rotten. He ruined me for other men. I have never loved anyone like I loved Richard Baird. [But] that person was dead, and all the wonderful time we had together was a lie...

Rush later told the FBI that a few hours after they had led her latest lover away in handcuffs, Chuck Hogan had arrived at the Astatula house, gone straight to the trunk of Rush's baby-blue Cadillac, and removed a packet containing a considerable amount of money.

The FBI say that they had searched the car thoroughly and found nothing at the time of Mitchell's arrest. Florida FBI agent Tony Salemmy, who was largely responsible for trying to get information out of Hogan, says if Chuck took anything from Mitchell's car, "it would have been shortly *before* [Mitchell's] arrest."

The FBI never publicly identified their Florida informants, other than to say that they included a few women. And, yes, Chuck Hogan was known to the DEA. The FBI had turned up the heat on him somethin' awful in the end.

Hogan admitted he was the mysterious Gil Minski who had posted $16,800 bail to spring Mitchell from jail in Phoenix. But that was not a criminal offense. And, yes, he owned the Lincoln with the tinted windows. He also knew something about Mitchell's enjoyment of recreational drugs. And, yeah, his old motel might have been visited by Mitchell. But he denied that he'd snitched.

"I love the guy. He's my friend..."

Various lawmen across the United States and Canada would subsequently spin a variety of thrilling versions of the capture of Paddy Mitchell. Some included wild tales of Mafia contracts and hitmen. Others had a more familiar ring—the FBI had traded another of the

DEA's suspected drug dealers for the third member of the Stopwatch Gang.

During his first days in captivity in Florida, Paddy Mitchell didn't appear to much care how he had been caught. Running eight miles a day around the jail yard certainly lacked the aesthetic appeal of his morning jogs along the canal in Astatula. Other than that, he didn't seem overly perplexed. In his promised newspaper interview, he sounded more like a hockey coach who had just lost the season opener than a fugitive who had just lost his freedom, possibly forever.

The reporter subsequently wrote: "Mitchell is one of the world's most likeable convicts—he doesn't swear, he grins, he laughs at himself, he tells stories."

The interview was vintage Paddy Mitchell.

How did it all start? the reporter asked.

"Aw, I guess it's easier to steal money than make it. I'm lazy, that's all. I wanted the good life...After four or five years in jail, you just want to relax."

Are you rich?

"I'm empty. Broke. You spend money like water when you're on the run. Hey, I partied a lot in New Orleans."

You started your career looking for one big score, then you could retire, was how you put it. Did you ever find it?

"That was a goddam dreamer talking, pal. There is no big score. You just keep doing it again and again. Once you start, you can't stop. You just keep doing it. Like a politician who takes a bribe...one dollar, then a thousand...I've sat with really big money in front of me and wanted more."

Do you regret your criminal career?

"Oh man, do I ever. There's nothing I would want more than to be back years ago, driving a Pepsi truck and leading a decent life. God, I wish I had an education. I know what it means now. I could have done anything, couldn't I?"

Do you miss your family?

"I really miss my brothers, my wife and my son, and my mother. Tell them I do...And tell people I'm really not the bad guy I'm cut out to be, will you?"

The FBI characterize you as a pro, as one very cunning bandit.

"If I'm so damn smart, what I am doing in jail?"

Are you there for the rest of your life?
Paddy Mitchell just smiled.

Reality shattered Mitchell's good humor about thirty seconds into his first phone conversation with Stephen Reid in over two years. The voice on the other end of the line was monotonous and despairing. Reid strained to sound happy to hear from his old buddy again, but he wished it were under different circumstances, and thanked Mitchell for the money he had been sending his former partners-in-crime.

But Reid's descriptions of life in the maximum security prison at Marion, Illinois, were chilling. Most of the inmates were demented killers, he said, and the guards would have scared the shit out of the Gestapo. Overall, the place made Millhaven seem like the Promised Land.

The good news was Reid and Wright would both be getting transfers under the Canada-U.S. prisoner-exchange treaty and serving the rest of their sentences in Canadian pens. Any inmate from either country could apply to do his time in his native land. Most of the traffic was northbound. Reid suggested Mitchell apply early.

"Whatever it takes, whatever you have to do," Reid told Mitchell, "get your ass back to Canada as soon as you can. Don't get stuck in an American joint. You'll never make it."

Mitchell listened with surging terror. If a hardened jailbird like Reid wasn't coping, there was no way Paddy would fare any better. Probably a lot worse.

"And there's one other thing," Reid added ominously, "if you've got federal charges in San Diego and state charges in Arizona, make sure you get sent to a federal pen. It doesn't matter which one. Take your pick. They're all equally bad. But the word around here is that Arizona State is even worse."

A Florida judge having finally determined that Paddy Mitchell was Paddy Mitchell, proceedings were moved to San Diego for trial on the big Bank of America heist that had already sent the rest of the Stopwatch Gang to prison. He might just as easily have been sent to Arizona to be tried for the Diamond's Department Store robbery. But the FBI had caught him and the California case was an FBI case and the boys in the Phoenix PD could damn well wait their turn.

The basement of the Metropolitan Correctional Center was hardly designed for a fitness freak; jogging ten miles of laps around the range only made Mitchell dizzy. Most of the other inmates thought he must be crazy. And that was fine with him. He was certain they were crazy, and wanted nothing to do with any of them.

On March 5, 1983, Mitchell made his first appearance in San Diego court. Bail was set at $250,000. Mitchell appealed, hoping for an amount his friends could better afford. The judge increased it to $1,500,000. So far, things weren't going well.

The court appointed Barton Sheela III to defend the destitute Patrick Mitchell at the state's expense. Bart the Third was thirty-two and bright and dedicated, but he still had a few things to learn. Mitchell didn't care. He already had the whole thing worked out.

The evidence against him in San Diego amounted to his fingerprint on one of the money wrappers taken from the Loomis guard in the big Bank of America heist. That didn't mean he had stolen the cash. Maybe he was just laundering some loot for a couple of acquaintances. Maybe he'd sold the robbers a set of wheels for a freshly wrapped bundle of hundreds. He hadn't been in the bank. No one had seen him driving the getaway car. And his long-time criminal relationship with the other members of the Stopwatch Gang was circumstantial.

Mitchell figured a plea bargain of five years for being an accessory after the fact sounded good. Sentence to run concurrently with his fourteen years left in Canada. Very important. Court to designate a federal prison. Extremely important.

Phoenix was another matter. He'd been caught red-handed, and certainly not empty-handed, in the parking lot of Diamond's Department Store. But the way Mitchell saw it, they got their money back, he hadn't shot anyone, and he'd damn near been killed by that crazy cop Harden.

Five to ten, max. Sentence to run concurrently with his sentences in San Diego and Canada. Very important. Court to accept previous designation to a federal prison. Extremely important.

If all went according to plan, Mitchell would be shipped back to Canada on the prisoner-exchange program, and could pick up where he left off in 1979. The new concurrent U.S. sentences would add nothing to his old Canadian sentences. And, by Canadian law, that would make him eligible to apply for parole in five years. Make that six, given his escape.

Barton Sheela III got the case transferred to the court of the Honorable Leland C. Nielsen. The feisty judge and Paddy Mitchell had a few things in common—they were both Irish and neither one had any love of lengthy trials.

On March 16, 1983, Patrick Michael Mitchell was marched into court. On cue, he pleaded not guilty to the bank-robbery charges, just to give everyone time to fine-tune the plea bargain on the lesser accessory charges.

Assistant U.S. Attorney Patrick O'Toole took over the case for the state. Mitchell thought so many Irishmen on the case seemed a good omen.

Bart Sheela had run across a lot of crooks in seven years of practice, but never one he would have liked to take home for a family dinner. Paddy Mitchell made quite an impression:

He was just a great, wonderful guy. The first thing I noticed were those sparkling blue eyes. I loved going over to see him [in jail]. I will always remember the good feelings I had about him. Every time I would go over to see him, he would be a delight to talk to. We would laugh. We would talk. He was always a very alive, very bright, an incredible human being...I had never met anyone like him before, and certainly not a bank robber...He said quite openly that it was a regrettable life he had chosen, and those were things he had done, and he knew he was going to have to pay the price for it...

Prosecutor Patrick O'Toole was cooperative enough. The prosecutor said he would accept a guilty plea from Mitchell on the lesser charge of being an accessory after the fact. He also had no objection to the sentence being served in a federal pen or in Canada. But he wasn't buying a five-year sentence. The Stopwatch Gang was too high profile. Ten years was a bargain.

Mitchell thought ten years was rather harsh, but if it was concurrent with his twenty-year Canadian sentence, five or ten didn't make any difference. He just wanted to go back to Canada.

It was early June when Bart Sheela just happened to bump into Judge Bob in the courthouse corridor, and just happened to run the proposed plea bargain by him. A few days later Judge Bob just happened to run into Bart Sheela in the corridor again.

"You know that Mitchell case of yours," Judge Bob said. "Well, I had a look at the file and I think Judge Nielsen might go along with that plea agreement. Just my opinion, of course."

Everything was going exactly to plan. All Mitchell needed to do now was cut the same kind of deal in Arizona and he would be homeward bound for Canada.

The plan, however, did not take into account the FBI. They were furious.

The FBI in San Diego had never fully recovered from the media whippings they took over the Stopwatch Gang back in 1980—naming the wrong people in the wrong gang, letting Mitchell get away, allegations of their involvement in the mysterious money switch, and finally, trading a suspected drug felon with Mafia connections for a couple of bandits. The only consolation prizes had been the stiff twenty-year sentences slapped on Wright and Reid. (The FBI were never told of the quiet deal that cut those terms in half.) They expected nothing less for the purported leader of the gang.

News that the man who had caused them so much grief was about to get ten years and a one-way plane ticket to Canada made more than a few brushcuts bristle.

Four months after Mitchell's arrest in Florida, the FBI in Arkansas filed an indictment charging him with the armed robbery of the bank in Hot Springs in April 1982. The evidence was still as tenuous as it had been a week after the robbery—no fingerprints, no weapons, no recovered funds. Just one witness who had yelled "Thief!" and picked Mitchell's picture from a photo line-up of five people.

"This is absolutely ludicrous," Mitchell stormed at his lawyer. "They haven't got a damn thing on me. One witness who thinks he saw me."

Bart Sheela agreed the evidence was thin, but suggested it might be a good idea to plead guilty anyway.

"Plead *guilty*?" Mitchell couldn't believe his ears. "You must be kidding, Bart. This is just harassment by the damn FBI. It'll get laughed out of court on the first day."

Sheela was almost apologetic. "I'm worried that if we draw some hanging judge up there in small-town Arkansas, and he doesn't like the way you walk, you may never see daylight again."

"Geez, Bart," Mitchell said with exasperation, "we can't just let the FBI kill us with no evidence. I mean—"

"If this were the only charge against you, I would probably say you're right—we should fight it," Sheela continued. "But if I can get it packaged up with everything else, with no extra time for you, why fight it?"

Sheela called prosecutor Patrick O'Toole with a proposition: transfer the Arkansas case to San Diego, and Mitchell would plead guilty for a sentence of five years to run concurrently with the ten he was already getting for the Stopwatch heist in California. No added time.

"Ten," said the prosecutor.

"Six," said the defender.

"Ten," said the prosecutor.

"Fine," said the defender.

Pleasantries were once again exchanged in the courthouse corridor with Judge Bob, who later happened to mention to Sheela that the deal seemed reasonable to him. Just an opinion, of course.

Bart Sheela went back to the jail to deliver the good news to Mitchell—the ten years for the Arkansas job would run concurrently with the ten for San Diego and both would run concurrently with his remaining stint in Canada. Overall, no extra time.

Then he told him the bad news.

"I have spoken to the county attorney's office in Phoenix," Sheela began sheepishly. "Now I don't want you to panic. We'll work something out."

Mitchell looked terrified.

Sheela explained that the hang-'em-high legislators in Arizona had recently decided the courts were being too soft on criminals. Judges were therefore tied to strict sentencing guidelines for each offense. Prison time for repeat offenders rose exponentially.

"They're out for blood," Sheela said.

"So what are we talking here, Bart?" Mitchell asked apprehensively.

"The minimum for armed robbery is seven years," Sheela said cautiously.

"Phew, Bart, you had me worried," Mitchell said with obvious relief.

"Unfortunately," Sheela continued, "the prosecutor over there is talking the maximum. He's talking twenty-one years."

Barton Sheela III had never put so much of his time and soul into a case. He liked Paddy Mitchell and wanted to get the best deal possible for him. The problem wasn't just the harshness of punishment looming in Phoenix. The real threat was that a longer sentence in Arizona than in

San Diego meant Paddy Mitchell was headed for hard time in the dreaded Arizona State Penitentiary.

Sheela finally worked out a plan. Mitchell would plead guilty on the federal bank charges in Arkansas, then be shipped off to Arizona to dispose of the state case there. Then he would be brought back into federal custody for the Bank of America case in San Diego. Whatever sentence he got in Arizona, they would match it with concurrent time on the federal charges.

If the scheme worked, Mitchell would be finally sentenced in federal court in San Diego, sent to a federal prison somewhere, and immediately shipped back to Canada on the international prisoner exchange.

On August 2, 1983, Patrick Michael Mitchell pleaded guilty to the armed robbery of the bank in Hot Springs, Arkansas. He thought the whole thing quite crazy—confessing to a crime for which the FBI hadn't had enough evidence even to get an arrest warrant. But nothing was too crazy if it would keep him away from Arizona State pen.

Mitchell's transfer to Phoenix in early September gave him regular newspaper reports on the horrors of the state pen about fifty miles away in the desert. Stephen Reid's information had been right—the place was a zoo:

> Some inmates at Arizona State Penitentiary have experienced in the past month perhaps the worst punishment the penitentiary dishes out, short of the death penalty: they were served meatloaf for twenty-one consecutive meals…Prison Director James Ricketts said he could find no other means to prevent the damage prisoners were creating by hurling their food against the walls to protest prison conditions. "Meatloaf wouldn't stain the walls like beets…"

> A certified sanitation expert said…filthy floors, dirt-encrusted walls, unclean showers, accumulations of dead insects and soiled areas beneath mattresses present potential health risks for prisoners.

> Inmates refer to the shower area as the "Wild Kingdom" because it is so infested with roaches, spiders and other insects…One inmate who trapped a rat in his cell hung it from the slot in his

door to draw the authorities' attention to the problem. Corrections officials just laughed and left it hanging there to rot.

The dramatic arrest of Paddy Mitchell in the parking lot of Diamond's Department Store had made detective George Edward Harden the most decorated officer in the Phoenix Police Department. Medals, citations, and other bravery awards completely covered what he called the "I-love-me wall" in his suburban home.

Mitchell's accidental release on bail had covered the county prosecutor's office with embarrassment. Two years later Mitchell could be thankful the offending prosecutor had gone into private practice. But his replacement, Deputy County Attorney Marc Budoff, was definitely no pushover. He knew he had Mitchell cold on the case—a confession wouldn't make it any stronger. He also knew a light sentence would bury his office under bad press. Marc Budoff couldn't wait to throw the book at Paddy Mitchell.

Mitchell wasn't overly impressed by his newest court-appointed public defender. The feeling seemed rather mutual. In the ensuing four months Charles McNulty spent most of his time on the case listening to his client giving orders.

"I'll cop a plea for the minimum seven years," Mitchell instructed his lawyer. "Anything I get has to run concurrently with the other federal cases in San Diego and the time I've got left in Canada. That's very important. And I want the judge to direct that any time be served in a federal pen. That's extremely important."

McNulty passed Mitchell's message along to Budoff who promptly passed a message of his own back to Mitchell. "Budoff says he is planning to go for the maximum—thirty-five years."

In the third week of November, Mitchell's lawyer visited his client in jail. "The prosecutor has apparently got tired of my grovelling. He's finally agreed to deal. Eighteen years. Hard time. That would bring you up for parole in twelve."

"Jesus, man!" Mitchell scowled. "Is that the best you can do?"

"It's better than I ever thought we would do," McNulty snapped. "If you want to go to trial, he'll go for the full thirty-five and he'll probably get thirty."

On November 23, 1983, Patrick M. Mitchell signed away his freedom for eighteen years.

Two months later, federal marshals drove Mitchell back to San Diego for sentencing on the outstanding federal cases there. Then he would be on his way back to Canada.

The Paddy Mitchell who returned to San Diego was thin and drawn and broken, the months in the Alhambra crazy-wing having slashed deep furrows of age across the plastic surgeon's portrait of youth.

Mitchell was not only despairing of his future, he was also deeply troubled by his pre-sentencing report in Arizona. Throughout his criminal career, he had never thought he was hurting ordinary people—his victims were all big banks, big insurance companies, big department stores. Big deal. But he had hurt people, lots of them. It was all there in the parole officer's report on the Diamond's robbery in Phoenix:

> The defendant maintains that he is not a violent person and that he never touched any of the "girls" [at Diamond's]. He emphasizes that no one got hurt in the offense and that he had no intentions of injuring anyone. He says that he never shot at the policeman when the policeman fired at him. He also points out that he did not get away with any of the money...
>
> Jo McGovern, who is in charge of Diamond's security, advised that because of the defendant's actions, Julie had quit her job at the store. Julie indicated that...she was scared and jumpy...Melissa reported that she was very frightened after the robbery occurred...Mary said the incident upset her greatly...Ray Jean stated the defendant "scared the crap out of her." She stated that she has become apprehensive and nervous working at the store...
>
> Because the defendant was apprehended at the time of the offense, the store's money was recovered. However, what cannot be recovered is the sense of security that the victims had prior to their contact with the defendant...
>
> Because this officer believes the defendant is a danger to society when he is allowed to live his life as he pleases, it is thought that the defendant needs to be removed from the community for a long period of time...

Shortly after Mitchell's return to San Diego in January 1984 lawyer Bart Sheela just happened to bump into Judge Bob in the courtroom corridor. The judge's clerk had long ago offered a positive opinion on the deals worked out before Mitchell went to Arizona—ten years for the San Diego robbery; ten years concurrent for the Arkansas bank job.

"So, ah, in your opinion," Sheela began, "what do you think the judge might do if we, say, stuck to the ten years for the San Diego case, but doubled the sentence on the Arkansas case to, say, twenty years?"

Judge Bob didn't have to go away and reflect on this one. The judge would probably think everyone was nuts. Just an opinion, of course.

Paddy Mitchell thought someone was crazy: "Let me get this straight, Bart, I pleaded guilty to the Arkansas job they couldn't have proved. In return, we got a deal for ten years concurrent with the ten in the San Diego case. Now you want to increase the Arkansas term to twenty? Some deal, Bart."

"If we don't," Sheela said, "you'll be doing your federal time and then be shipped off to the Arizona State pen for the rest of the time owing over there. It may be a long stint before you get back to Canada, if ever."

Mitchell thought about it and called his lawyer: "Do what you gotta do, Bart. Just get me into a federal pen so I can get back to Canada. Whatever you do, don't let me near that Alcatraz in Arizona."

On February 27, 1984, Patrick Mitchell appeared before the Honorable Leland C. Nielsen and was sentenced to twenty years for the Arkansas bank robbery, and ten years for being an accessory in the San Diego heist. Both terms were to be served concurrently with the eighteen years imposed in Arizona. The judgment concluded: "It is also recommended that a Federal Institution be designated as the place of incarceration."

Sheela had already started the paperwork to have Mitchell shipped back to Canada to serve all his sentences there concurrently—all twenty years of them. Parole in seven if he were lucky.

A week after sentencing, a federal marshal arrived at the San Diego lockup with a clipboard and orders to transport Mitchell out of the place.

"So where are we off to?" Mitchell asked.

The marshal looked at his clipboard.

"Arizona State Penitentiary. Lucky you."

CHAPTER THIRTY

Arizona State Penitentiary

And on the eighth day, the Lord created Arizona State pen. And He looked down and saw that it was bad. Real bad. And so on the ninth day He created another place much better and called it Hell.

Inmate graffiti

The aging prison van rattles and lurches along the final mile of potholed highway they call Hell's Gate Boulevard. Beyond the high barbed-wire fences, dust swirls across the flat desolation carved from the desert and left to bake and crack under the scorching Arizona sun. A rusting water tower looms like a huge toilet tank ready to flush out the human sewer clogged in the sickly yellow buildings below. Beside the roadway inmates bang their hoes hopelessly on the bulletproof earth, their blue prison shirts sweatsoaked in the hundred-degree heat. Guards watch over them from horseback, their navy trousers tucked into high leather boots, steel spurs glinting in the sun, white straw Stetsons pulled down over rawhide faces, one hand always on the shotgun jammed into the front of the saddle. Nowhere for anyone to run. Nowhere to hide. Those who try will be shot.

The last highway sign on the left is a peeling billboard that reads: "Jesus Is Lord." And as the ugly iron gates of Arizona State Penitentiary swung open that day, Paddy Mitchell must have wondered if he hadn't missed an important message from Him.

The Arizona prosecutor had been smarter than all of them. Sure, he would knock the Phoenix sentence down to eighteen years. But what Mitchell's lawyers had missed was the obscure federal regulation that only those first sentenced in federal court go to federal prisons. Since the State of Arizona got him first, so did the state pen.

Mitchell now faced at least twelve years in the dreaded state prison even before he could be shipped back to Canada for perhaps another dozen years behind bars there. Paddy Mitchell would be lucky to be free by his sixty-fifth birthday.

In the meantime he considered himself lucky to see daylight each morning. Life in the maximum-security Central Unit of Arizona State pen would have given Alfred Hitchcock nightmares. The horror stories were a regular feature in the *Arizona Republic*:

A prisoner who complained about having to shower in the so-called "wild kingdom," was smeared with feces and doused with urine by other inmates as guards stood by and watched. He was locked in his cell, unable to wash, for the next twelve hours. Asked why the inmate had not been allowed to shower after the attack, guards said it was the end of their shift and they were ready to go home.

Patrick James Sadivy, 24, suffered third-degree burns over most of his body by setting fire to trash he had piled around him in his cell. He died Wednesday. A Corrections Department spokesman said the inmate had been housed in the prison's maximum-security section because he had been "acting strangely."

An Arizona State prison employee strip-searched three young children in front of their mother in search of contraband. The mother was also strip-searched in front of her children by the guard.

A 23-year-old inmate being treated for depression in the maximum-security Arizona State prison committed suicide Thursday. Officials said the probable cause of death was an overdose of anti-depressants...

Paddy Mitchell quickly became a hermit amid the perpetual madness of both the keepers and the kept of Arizona State pen. Most of his time was spent in voluntary isolation in his cell. He did what he was told and was polite to the guards. Otherwise, he rarely said anything to anyone. While he had enough years ahead of him to learn every trade in the Yellow Pages, he never went near the prison shops. Too many sharp instruments. Instead, he begged for solitary maintenance jobs—at least he would be armed with a broom handle. He jogged a lot to keep in good enough shape to fend off attackers—or at least to outrun them.

But he avoided the weights and other equipment in the exercise yard. Too many blunt instruments.

Mitchell gave little thought to escape. The punishment for trying was a long-term lease in Cell-Block Six, CB-6 for short, a hideous relic of the Dark Ages that made the Shoo at Millhaven seem like the royal daycare center by comparison.

In a letter to Bart Sheela, Mitchell wrote: "Hope my letter finds you in good health and spirits. Is there anything you can do to get me out of here? This place is horrible. I guess it was my destiny. Whoa! This is one rough joint. The whole place is run by three gangs—the Aryan Brotherhood, the Black Brotherhood, and the Mexican Mafia. Everyone is six-three and three hundred pounds. All muscle. I stay home a lot..."

Mitchell was in no hurry to join a fraternity. He was the wrong color for one gang, spoke the wrong language for another, and figured the fanatical white supremacists were as much a danger to themselves as anyone else.

The Aryan Brotherhood was a swell bunch of guys, all right. "No outsider must ever know anything concerning our business," their rules stated. "Any violation of our code of secrecy will mean a MANDATORY death penalty for the violator." Early retirement was definitely out of the question: "On entering this family we pledge our blood—on leaving, it will be shed."

Paddy Mitchell wrote: "The Aryans spend their days plotting to kill the Blacks who spend their days looking for ways to kill the Aryans. The Mexicans don't seem too picky, one way or the other. It's like the whole place is packed in dynamite. The tensions are unbelievable. Any day, it's going to blow..."

October 6, 1984. Shortly before 9 a.m. more than three hundred maximum-security prisoners gather in the walled recreation yard to watch a little Saturday morning football.

White supremacists versus the Black Brotherhood. The Mexican mafia will referee.

Paddy Mitchell's assessment was right—for months, the place has been described by guards and inmates alike as a "pressure cooker." The warden knows about the planned racial scrimmage, but lets it go ahead anyway. Should blow off a little steam.

The angry mountains of meat and muscle on the field are intimidating, to say the least. Most are convicted killers. The Mexican mafia don't bother calling unnecessary roughness—flying fists and bloodied faces are all part of the fun.

About halfway through the second quarter the intended receiver for the Black Brotherhood is out cold on the field. One of the Mexican mafia understandably calls pass interference against the white supremacists. The last thing the referee remembers is the offending player's fist crashing into his face.

The whites and Hispanics in the crowd follow suit. The Blood Bowl is suddenly turning into a full-blown riot.

Some of the two hundred medium-security inmates, who have been watching the game from behind a twelve-foot-high wire fence, break into a prison vocational shop. Minutes later, hammers, screwdrivers, two-by-fours, and pieces of lead pipe are being tossed over the fence into the war zone on the field.

The six guards assigned to watch over five hundred inmates run for cover. No one fires so much as a warning shot.

At the end of the day seven prisoners are in hospital, one is in the morgue.

The final score? White supremacists: one dead; one stabbed abdomen; one perforated chest; one face caved in; dozens injured. Mexican mafia: two stabbed; one broken back; one eye missing; dozens injured. Black Brotherhood: minor injuries. Prison administration: eight to nothing for the good guys.

Paddy Mitchell had abandoned his front-row seat at the Blood Bowl at the first sign of trouble. Desolate and desperate after only four months in Central's maximum-security crazy house, he knew he would be lucky to last more than twelve months, much less twelve years. His only hope was a transfer back to Canada, and getting involved in a riot would definitely not help the process.

Less than a year into his sentence, Mitchell received some wonderful news. And some not-so-wonderful news. Stephen Reid and Lionel Wright had both been transferred out of their respective American prisons and shipped back to separate pens in Canada. What's more, due to some miraculous miscalculations by the Canadian parole authorities, both would be eligible to apply for early release within the year. The bad news was that someone somewhere in the American legal bureaucracy was incensed that the two members of the notorious Stopwatch Gang were getting off so lightly.

Early in 1985 Paddy Mitchell's application to join his two partners-in-crime north of the border was suddenly, mysteriously, and indefinitely lost under a tangle of red tape.

Time for Plan B.

Throughout his first year in the ugly yellow lockup at Central Unit, Paddy Mitchell was the model prisoner. That should have surprised no one who read the assessments in his prison files:

> On examining Patrick Mitchell's background, there does not appear to be any obvious reason why he began his life of crime as an adult in Canada. Nor does there seem to be any good reason why he continued these illegal activities in the United States... He would like to return to Canada [in prison] to be near his family. When he is released from confinement, he says he wants to reside with his wife. He does not desire to commit any more crimes, but rather to devote his life to doing good deeds. He plans to lead the Christian life that he knows he is capable of leading...

The rest of the file was crammed with the usual warrants of committal and other bureaucratic forms. One listed all of his personal particulars, including a rather long list of aliases. All of his latest sentencing papers were there. And there was a separate page for next of kin—just in case the prison needed someone to claim the body.

And finally, there was his criminal record: seventeen years for the cocaine conspiracy; another three for the gold robbery; another eighteen for the Diamond's heist; ten for the San Diego bank robbery; twenty for the one in Arkansas.

Remarkably, no one in the Arizona State Penitentiary administration ever tallied all the sentences and wondered why Mitchell had only ever served a total of four years behind bars for so much larceny.

In the entire file of particulars on Patrick Michael Mitchell, the only detail that of acute interest to prison authorities was missing. There wasn't a single word of warning that he was also an escape artist.

***

On June 14, 1985, the model prisoner with no apparent propensity for escape was transferred out of the maximum-security dungeon at Central to the South Unit, a separate facility at the far corner of the windswept acreage. In one year and one week Paddy Mitchell had sweet-talked his way into medium-security. Plan B was right on schedule.

South Unit was a summer camp compared to life in the maximum-security Central Unit. It still had its share of stabbings and beatings and other unpleasantness expected of nasty types locked up in a cage. But most of the psychopaths were too old and broken by stints in CB-6 to be bothered killing anyone. Even the Aryan, Black, and Hispanic gangs could usually manage a few innings of baseball without clubbing each other to death.

Mitchell was moved into one of the unit's seventy-two-man dormitories, each located in a separate one-story building in early-concentration-camp motif. There were no cells—the dorm doors into the yard were simply opened at dawn and locked again at dusk. The accommodation was a far cry from the Biltmore, but it was still five stars better than the rat haven back at Central.

Mitchell studied every inch of the place. He quickly ruled out going over the high chain-link fences studded with watch towers and topped with razor wire. One hapless con who did try to make a break for it was shot the instant both feet touched the fence. Within two hours the administration had completed an "institutional investigation" and issued letters of commendation to all three guards involved. The folks at Arizona State pen didn't fuck around.

Another faked heart attack would only get Mitchell a fast ride to the prison hospital at Central. Anything that couldn't be treated there probably wouldn't be treated. Just another suicide.

Cutting through the fences or even building another Millhaven tunnel was equally futile. Even if successful, there was nowhere to run—just miles of flat, barren high desert. And a lot of those ominous guards Mitchell had seen on horseback were professional trackers who could follow a mouse across marble. Human footprints in the sand would be child's play.

The only part of the entire prison perimeter that wasn't fence or watch towers was the one-story administration building. There was no way to go over it—the roof was covered in razor wire and exposed to the nearby guard tower. There was no way under it. And there was no way to get through its series of steel doors and iron grates without a bulldozer.

Then one day he spotted it. He had been sweeping a patio area where the main perimeter fence met the wall of the administration building. A repairman in an air-conditioning company van pulled up about fifteen feet away and disappeared through an exterior steel door. It was not locked.

Mitchell quickly ascertained that the repairman had gone into the main utility area housing the electrical panels and air-conditioning units for the administration building. The room was essentially a cement-block bunker accessible only from the parking lot outside the fences, a feature that allowed external contractors to get to the equipment without passing through security. There was no access to the room from inside the prison—at least nothing official.

But where there's an air conditioner, there's a duct. All Paddy Mitchell had to do was get inside the administration building without winning a free trip to CB-6.

Plan B was definitely dangerous, but rolling nonetheless.

South Unit's deputy warden, Joe C. Martinez, had snakeskin cowboy boots, a thick southern drawl, cigars in his desktop pen holder, and twenty-odd years of dealing with cons. He would always remember Paddy Mitchell.

"I sure hate to admit it, but Mitchell was almost the perfect inmate. He was always very personable, real nice to staff. He was always so darn polite... He was real good with everyone. So I guess that's why everyone trusted him..."

Even Jim Gallagher, the head honcho guard known as the Major, described Mitchell as "your model inmate. Truly respectful. Real clean cut... At first, he worked on the outside maintenance crew, raking and chopping weed and stuff. But then he moved on into the visiting room. He seemed to like that a lot. By himself most of the time. But he was a good worker. Ya know, he wasn't the kind of guy ya gotta go out and find to do some job somewhere. This guy Mitchell was always there to work..."

In less than twenty months of an eighteen-year sentence of hard time, the affable bandit had managed to wangle his way down from one of the tightest lockups in America, to the medium-security unit, and now to the area closest to freedom without walking out of the place.

Cleaning the ground-floor visiting area was definitely the plum job at the pen, the one reserved for "model inmates" like Paddy Mitchell.

The room could have been any cafeteria without a food counter—some vending machines and thirty round tables, each with four plastic chairs. It was bright and spacious, and surrounded by windows with no bars.

Visitors came into the front lobby from the parking lot, checked in at the plexiglass guard station, and were then locked through a series of sliding steel grates and doors. The inmates had their own door behind the guard post. Access was controlled electronically.

On a typical day, the guards simply locked Mitchell into the visitors' area alone and left him to clean the place. That suited him just fine, a peaceful respite from all the craziness—and crazies—of prison life.

It also gave him plenty of time to climb on top of the pop machine, push up a few acoustic tiles, and check out the ductwork leading back to that air-conditioning unit in the outside utility room. It was all exactly as he had figured—except for the four thick steel bars blocking the escape route.

The duct also ran right over the guard station and straight across the ceiling of the warden's office.

Cecil Thurman Kinkade was ten years younger than Mitchell, appeared twenty years older, and usually looked as if he had just fallen off a freight train. He was also a bit of a sore loser. Apparently dropped ten grand in a poker game one night, marched the lucky winner into the desert, and blew the fellow's head off. Kinkade always claimed it was a friend who pulled the trigger, but the judge didn't care—gave them both life sentences.

Ordinarily, the ruddy-faced, former carpet salesman would not have been Paddy Mitchell's first choice for enchanting company. But the two were next-door neighbors in the hell-hole at Central, and Paddy logically concluded that someone like Killer would make a better friend than enemy. Besides, the two of them were talking the same language—namely, escape. Kinkade didn't have much to lose; he was either going to die in the place or be killed trying to get out of it.

Shortly after Mitchell was transferred out of Central, Kinkade convinced his jailers that he was sufficiently rehabilitated to spend the rest of his life in medium security. The two would-be escapees were reunited in the yard at South Unit. Mitchell explained that he could not be cleaning the visiting room carpets and sawing bars in the ceiling at the same time without the guards noticing something amiss. He needed a partner.

Not long thereafter, Kinkade just happened to mention to the Major that there seemed to be a lot of gum on the carpets in the visiting room, and since he used to be in the carpet business and had nothing much else to do for the rest of his life, well, gee, he'd sure appreciate a chance to contribute something constructive to prison life. The administration was so thrilled by his offer that Kinkade was allowed into the visiting room pretty much whenever he liked. Sometimes they didn't even know he was there.

Over the next few months, Kinkade sawed in the duct while Mitchell watched for guards. Paddy wasn't stupid—if they got caught, Killer would go to CB-6 for attempting to escape. Mitchell was just dusting.

The work was painfully slow. It took two weeks to fashion a drill just to start the hole in the duct. It took another three weeks to get a piece of broken hacksaw-blade smuggled out of the welding shop. It took another month to make a pair of metal shears from two broken knife blades (there were plenty of those around the pen), a bolt, and a couple of chunks of garden hose for rubber grips. (They would one day be especially thankful for the rubber grips.)

Then came the hard part. Mitchell would go about his cleaning chores while Kinkade climbed into the ceiling, crawled into the ductwork, and began sawing the bars almost directly over the warden's head. Butter was smeared on the blade to dampen the noise of steel ripping steel. Three strokes. Butter. Three more strokes. More butter.

Paddy kept watch with his small portable radio turned up, partly to drown out the sawing overhead, but mainly so Kinkade could hear it. If the radio was turned off, it meant the guards were coming. It also meant Killer was stranded in the ceiling until they left.

By late April, almost five months since they had begun their dangerous game of hide-and-saw, Kinkade had already cut the bars out of one duct, only to discover the tin tunnel narrowed to almost nothing before reaching the boiler room. Now he was almost finished his handiwork in a parallel duct. In a matter of days they would be ready to attempt their final crawl to freedom—or straight to CB-6.

Suddenly, the radio went dead.

Kinkade slithered backward in the duct and peered down through the holes in the ceiling tiles. He could almost breathe on the top of the guard's head. A priest had come into the visiting room to bestow his blessing on a troubled inmate. Right under Killer Kinkade.

The guard told Paddy Mitchell to leave.

Killer checked his watch. At 3:00 p.m. sharp he would be expected back at his dormitory for the daily headcount. It was already 1:45.

The next seventy minutes were the longest of his life, as he lay in the duct above the priest's head, sweating, shaking, knowing that any small movement would cause the tinwork to crinkle—and send him and Paddy Mitchell to CB-6 for a very long time.

At 2:55, Mitchell lined up for the headcount, clutching a towel soaked in his own facial perspiration. If God had a message for anyone that day, Paddy prayed it would be for His long-winded man of the cloth. Just a short message: for chrissakes, *leave!*

At 3:01, Cecil Thurman Kinkade came striding across the prison yard, cursing the wristwatch that had made him late for headcount.

The plan was unfolding perfectly, at least as far as it went. Unfortunately that was only as far as the door of the utility room. From there, escaping into the desert without a getaway car was like slipping out of Alcatraz without a boat. Kinkade was from the region and knew all kinds of people with cars, but Paddy figured that most trustworthy folk wouldn't have given Killer a lift to his execution. Mitchell weighed the risks of sharing the big secret with another player. He had no choice.

Johnny Salazar Stuart was a happy-go-lucky black kid who had split most of his life between the wrong side of the tracks and the nearest jail. Despite his twenty-five years of hard knocks, the handsome thief was always full of laughs and pranks and even flashed a big smile for his prison mug shot. The warden would always be baffled about how Paddy and Johnny ever connected. "For someone like Mitchell, a real outsider from out of state, to trust one of them Phoenix blacks was rather unique...And it's hard to trust a joker, ya know."

But Mitchell liked Stuart for his good humor and gentle disposition, rare commodities in the Arizona State pen. For his part, Johnny came to like Paddy as he had never liked a white boy before—he would have followed Mitchell down the heating duct to hell.

Stuart had a plan, and her name was Lori. She was young and sweet and lonely. She was also over two hundred pounds and not very bright. Easily confused.

Lori was visiting a relative in the South Unit when, by no coincidence, she was introduced to the handsome thief with the friendly smile and seductive eyes. It wasn't often anyone gave her a second glance, much less seemed interested in her, much less a good-looking dude like Johnny. She was smitten.

Over the next two months, while Kinkade sawed and Mitchell watched, Johnny Stuart wrote love letters to Lori, held her hand during prison visits, and generally romanced the girl off her feet. She would do anything for him.

Paddy Mitchell declared Plan B ready to go.

Shortly before ten o'clock on the night of Thursday, May 8, 1986, the Major went in search of Johnny Salazar Stuart and handed him an urgent telephone message. It read: "Your father has had a heart attack. Call the hospital immediately."

Everything was going exactly to plan. Stuart knew there was no way he would be allowed out of his locked dormitory at that hour, even to make an emergency phone call to the hospital. The inmate phones monitored by the administration were turned off overnight and not reactivated until 8:00 a.m. That suited him just fine.

At 6:30 the next morning, a harried-looking Johnny Stuart knocked on the door of the guard hut in the prison yard.

"Excuse me, sir," Stuart said anxiously to one of the guards. "Like, I'm truly sorry to be botherin' you, but the Major gave me this message late last night to say that my daddy has had a heart attack and, like, I know our phones aren't activated until eight o'clock and I was just wonderin' if by some miracle of the Lord you would allow me to use your phone so I might talk to my daddy one last time before he dies. The Major told me last night it would be okay."

The guard read the message signed by the Major, his boss. It didn't say anything about letting Johnny Stuart use an unmonitored administration telephone. But what the hell? He showed the convict to the phone and left the room.

Johnny called Lori in Phoenix and said he had a special three-day pass and he just wanted to spend every wonderful moment of it with her. Lori was almost crying with joy as Johnny gave her explicit instructions. She was to pick him up in her car at South Unit at precisely 9:00 a.m. Park by the fence next to the administration building. South Unit. Don't be late.

Lori was so excited that Stuart had to repeat the message four times. He hoped she got it straight.

While Stuart was on the phone to Lori, Paddy Mitchell was addressing a quick note to Stephen Reid, who was by then only weeks away from a Canadian parole hearing.

Hoping this letter finds you in wonderful spirits as you prepare to re-enter society as a thoroughly rehabilitated and respectable human being. Bon chance...Everything is going just fine at this end. I'm in terrific shape...and look forward to getting out of here myself. Won't be long now. Take care, my friend. God bless...

CHAPTER THIRTY-ONE

Arizona State Penitentiary, Friday, May 9, 1986

7:25 a.m. Paddy Mitchell drops his cryptic letter to Stephen Reid in the mail bag and walks to the administration building for his daily cleaning duties. He is being even more diligent than usual; he's a half hour early. He tells the guard on duty he didn't sleep a wink. Darn back pains are driving him crazy. But not to worry—he'll have the visiting room spotless by the time the folks arrive at one o'clock for the regular Friday inmate visits.The electronic door lock thwacks open. The guards neglect to snap it shut again.

8:10 a.m. Cecil Kinkade wanders into the administration building and asks the guard if he can get a Coke from the visiting room vending machine. The jailer nods and goes back to reading his book.

8:20 a.m. Johnny Stuart tiptoes past the guard station unnoticed. Must be a good book.

The guard at his station faces straight into the main lobby. He cannot see into the visiting area to his immediate right. But there's no need to worry. It's only Mitchell and that other disheveled character. The two of them clean in there together all the time. No one ever watches them.

Mitchell really hasn't slept. Too jumpy. So many months of planning and work and risks. So many years of hard time in CB-6 if they get caught.

The perpetual smile on the face of Johnny Salazar Stuart is wider and brighter than usual as he joins the other two in the visiting room. In forty minutes he has a date with a fat girl named Lori. Nine o'clock, sharp. He repeated it four times on the phone. He hopes she understood.

Lori got the message, all right. She couldn't wait to see her dashing prince charming. In fact, she has arrived early and is nervously standing around outside in the parking lot. Talking to the warden.

8:25 a.m. Warden Joe C. Martinez parks his car in the spot with his name on it and looks over at the fat girl and her young nephew who is playing with the pay phone not ten feet away. It all seems a might strange for a Friday morning. It's hours too early for the inmate visits, and there's no other reason for anyone to hang around South Unit. All the shipping and receiving of prisoners on temporary passes is conducted through Central.

"Can I help ya some way?" the warden asks. "You folks waitin' on somethin' perhaps?"

"We's gittin' my Johnny," Lori says shyly, staring at her feet. "He says come to South. Furlough today. This South?"

"Well now, this here's South Unit, all right, but I'm afraid y'all come to the wrong place," the warden says pleasantly. "Anyone on furlough's goin' to be leavin' from Central."

"No, no, South," Lori insists meekly, shaking her head. "He say South, I knows he did. South. Don't be late."

"Well, there musta been some mistake then," the warden says patiently, as though talking to someone the young nephew's age. "Anyone goin' home leaves from Central."

"No, South," Lori says pleadingly, eyes on the ground. "Johnny say South."

"Well, why don't you take a drive around to Central anyway and check?" the warden suggests. "Be glad to point the way, and I'm sure you'll find him over there."

The warden gives her directions to the ugly yellow complex a half mile down the road. Lori and her nephew get into the blue Mercury and drive away.

8:40 a.m. Mitchell turns on the vacuum cleaner and attacks the carpet area by the vistors' entrance where he can see anyone leaving the guard station. He gives the signal.

Go!

Johnny Stuart is the first onto the stack of chairs. He slides the large ceiling tile back and tears away the fiberglass insulation hiding their gaping hole into the ventilation duct. He wriggles into the duct and disappears.

Cecil Kinkade crawls into the duct behind Stuart. Mitchell runs back to his vacuum cleaner. The guard is still at his station. Still reading. Paddy scrambles onto the stacked chairs, crosses himself, and follows the other two into the ventilation duct.

Mitchell has the entire operation planned to the minute: they will have to move slowly and carefully in the duct, since they will be crawling right over the heads of the guard at his station and the warden in his office. One crinkle of the tin, one cough, and it's all over but the homecoming festivities at CB-6. Still, the trip shouldn't take any more than three to five minutes. Then they will have to pull the ductwork apart to get out at the other end and drop into the outside utility room. He has allowed fifteen minutes there, just in case they have to cut their way out of the air shaft with the homemade shears, the ones with the rubber garden-hose handles.

That should put them into the utility room at nine o'clock. One minute to pull off their blue prison garb, leaving them all in the street clothes they are wearing underneath, then they can saunter over to Lori's waiting car, looking just like three ordinary guys.

The plan assumes everything will go smoothly. They have no time to waste—at any moment the guard could find the visiting room empty.

The plan also assumes there will be a getaway car for them to walk to.

After a few wrong turns, Lori has found her way to Central. Unlike the unimpeded traffic flow at the South Unit, anyone entering or leaving the maximum-security complex has to pass through barricades manned by guards. Lori is stopped.

"I knows he say South," she keeps saying.

"Well, I already told you, lady, this is Central," the guard snaps impatiently. "That's South over there."

"I knows dat," Lori says almost in tears. "We's jest come from dere."

"So if ya want South, what are ya doin' at Central?" the guard asks angrily.

"Cuz da man o'er dere tells me to come o'er here for South," Lori says.

"Well, I'm tellin' ya to go back over there, cuz that's South and this ain't."

"South?" she repeats. "I knows Johnny says South."

The guard snaps the window shut and turns his back.

It is nine o'clock.

The three escapees in the air duct are right on schedule as they slither towards the utility room. First Stuart pulls himself forward a few inches, the ventilating air blowing in his face. He stops. Listens. Then Kinkade, then Mitchell. Never more than one at a time. Always stopping. Always listening.

At first, they hear a couple of guards chatting at their station.

Then the warden on the phone.

Stuart is no more than fifteen feet from the end of the duct. The warden says something to his secretary. They stop. The warden is back on the phone. Mitchell inches forward, the tension sending a torrent of sweat down his cheeks.

They crawl past the bars that took months to saw. In the dim light filtering through a room vent, Mitchell can see the a dangling coil of wire near the end of the duct. They had seen it before. Nothing serious. Just a piece of scrap.

Almost there. Stuart reaches up with the shears to cut the nuisance wire out of the way. There is a loud crack and a flash of orange fire in the duct. The air conditioning shuts down.

For an instant, they are frozen. Maybe it's an alarm. Maybe it's there to electrocute anyone getting past the bars they have removed. Stuart thanks the Lord for the rubber garden-hose handles on the shears.

By Stuart's own description, the terrified escapees then "proceeded to exit out of the duct in a backward direction at a considerably high rate of speed."

Mitchell reaches the end of the duct, loses his balance, and crashes backwards through the ceiling, landing in a heap eight feet below. He thinks of CB-6 and wishes the fall had killed him.

Lori's encounter at the Central Unit barricades has left her thoroughly bewildered.

She is sure Johnny said South. Nine o'clock. Sharp. Don't be late. She had been early. But then that man at South had said Central was South. Then the man at Central said South was South and no one was going anywhere from Central. She was sure Johnny had said Friday. A three-day furlough. Pick him up at South.

It's all so confusing. And now she's late. What to do? Where to go next?

Maybe go back and talk to that nice man at South.

9:10 a.m. The three escapees are hopping around the visiting room in a panic. The retreat was all for nothing—the ominous coil of wire was simply a low-voltage air cleaner that wouldn't have caused more than a tingle through their clothes, if they hadn't cut it. They could have been on the road to Phoenix by now. Had they known. But they didn't.

They wait for the guards to barge in on them, but no one comes. What to do next? They can't give up, not now. There's a four-foot hole in the ceiling where Paddy's fall broke through the ceiling tiles. They have to do something. And fast.

As they were retreating, Mitchell had caught a glimpse of a room below one of the vents. He is convinced it is the boiler room. Must be. Maybe they can get out that way.

The others are not so sure, but they have no better ideas. All three climb back on to the stacked chairs and into the duct again. This time, Killer is first with the shears. He reaches the vent and begins cutting. The area he can see through the vent slats doesn't look like a boiler room. But it doesn't matter. It's too late to turn back.

The tin crinkles with the first gnawing cut of the shears. Kinkade stops. They all listen. The guards are talking at their station. The warden is saying something to the Major. There is no mention of the escape in progress over their heads. Now there is another voice in the office below. Something is said about a problem with the air conditioning.

Frantic hand signals are exchanged in the ventilation shaft. Mitchell wants Killer to cut faster.

They are all thinking the same thing.

Lori.

It is almost 9:20.

A wall of windows gives Deputy Warden Joe C. Martinez a panoramic view of the parking lot into which is returning the blue Mercury and the confused fat girl with the young boy. He watches her park and walk to the pay phone. Obviously she's got things all mixed up. But it figures. You'd have to be a little confused to fall in love with a con at Arizona State pen. The warden goes back to his paperwork and pays her no further heed.

Lori calls the prison not twenty feet from where she is standing.

"South Unit," the voice on the other end of the line says.

"Is this South?" Lori asks plaintively.

"What can I do for you?" the voice asks.

"Johnny say come to South, so I's come to South. Where's my Johnny?" Lori whimpers.

"Sorry, ma'am, visiting hours don't start till one o'clock."

"Is this South?"

"Yes it is," the voice snaps. "And you can't see anyone before one o'clock."

"But Johnny say *South*."

Click.

Lori hangs up the dead phone and walks towards the front doors of the South Unit administration building. That nice man who sent her over to Central. He'll find her Johnny.

Kinkade completes his delicate sheet-metal work before he announces the bad news. The area below isn't the boiler room, after all. It's the administrative depot, stacked high with boxes of files and office supplies.

They drop from the duct into the room. Mitchell is bigger than the other two and can barely wriggle through Kinkade's hole. The jagged tin rips a six-inch gash out of his forearm. Blood spurts through the tear in his shirt. Stuart pulls the tattered sleeve apart and wraps Paddy's arm tightly to slow the bleeding.

They stare around them at the cement-block walls. The one with the door leads into the photocopying and secretarial area. The wall behind them must be the parole-board interview room—the last time any of them will be close to that for a long time, one way or another. A wall almost covered in filing shelves probably separates them from the warden's office. The duct runs over the other wall; the far side of it is probably the boiler room. Probably.

The three convicts are doing a panic jig in the file room. Mitchell grabs them both by their arms. "Everyone just stay calm," he whispers, the sweat pouring down his own cheeks. "Here's what we're going to do. Get up there in the corner and push the ceiling tile back. That should put us past that electrical thing. Then we cut back into the duct and we're outta here. Okay?"

The others nod.

Mitchell and Stuart help Kinkade climb up the shelving. It teeters, then stabilizes. Killer pushes back one of the large ceiling tiles, looks around in the attic, then pushes another tile back and looks around some more. He climbs back down.

The look on his face says it all.

"We're toast," he whispers. "We're fucking finished, man. I can see the electrical cable going into the duct, but it's past the cement wall. We can't get at it. We're dead meat."

"Everyone stay cool," Mitchell pleads in a whisper. "I'll think of something."

Then they hear them. Faint at first. Then louder.

Footsteps. Coming straight towards the door.

While Mitchell is trying to salvage a miracle from disaster, so is Lori. Her blue Mercury is still in the parking lot. But she's not in it.

Lori is at the guard station in the front lobby.

Mitchell is shaking and sweating so badly he can barely breathe. Even his faked heart attack was less painful than this marathon anxiety attack. The footsteps stop right outside the door. They hear the secretary's voice, then the whirring of the photocopier, then the footsteps retreating again.

Kinkade wants to make a run for it. Just burst through the filing room door, down the corridor to the front lobby, and out the visitors' entrance. But Mitchell knows better—they'd all be shot dead in the parking lot. He scrambles onto the file shelves and pushes back another ceiling tile. For a long minute, he just studies the situation. Thinking. There has to be a way.

He reaches up and pulls away a wad of pink fiberglass insulation next to the duct. He can feel a sheet of tin on the other side of the hole the size of a cement block. The next brick down has no mortar on the top or on the side next to the ventilation shaft.

Mitchell scrambles down the shelves: "We're out of here," he says to the other two in an excited whisper. "The boiler room's on the other side of that wall. It has to be."

Stuart and Kinkade hope the mastermind has got it right this time. If they're wrong, they will chisel their way right into the warden's office.

***

The guard at the station in the front lobby of South Unit is almost as puzzled as Lori.

"Gotta see Johnny," Lori says. "Johnny said South. This South?"

"Yeah, this is South," the guard says. "But ya ain't seein' nobody before one o'clock."

"Johnny he says nine o'clock. This South?"

"Johnny who?" the guard asks, the first time the question has been posed by anyone all morning. "What's Johnny's last name?"

"Johnny Stuart. You get Johnny?"

"Your Johnny's busy right now," the guard says, pointing to the visiting room through the two steel grates. "If you come back at one o'clock he'll be right in that room."

Lori looks through the grates.

"Don't see no one…"

11:05 a.m. Ordinarily, the warden's assistant and other administrative staff would be in and out of the storeroom at least a half-dozen times in a morning.

But on this day the footsteps have gone no further than the photo-copying machine immediately outside the door. It has already happened four times since they cut their way into the room. Each time, Paddy Mitchell has braced himself for the worst—a hostage taking; a hostage killing; the horseback hunters from Central bursting into the room with shotguns and an itch to use them.

Mitchell at least got it right this time. He found probably the only structural defect in the entire fortress—a piece of tin slapped over a hole where there should have been a cement block. The shears make fast work of the thin metal obstruction. Now he can hear the whirring of machinery. He pokes his face into the hole and finds himself staring into the next room. The boiler room.

That leaves one cement block between them and freedom, the one with mortar on just two sides. Luckily for them, the storeroom comes equipped with a set of screwdrivers otherwise kept under lock and key, for obvious reasons. Mitchell takes one and grinds the steel blade into the mortar. Poke and turn. Poke and turn. The cement slowly falls away in a fine dust. Slowly. Too slowly. But he has no choice—he can hardly just grab a hammer and chisel the stuff ten feet from the warden's ear. Poke and turn. Poke and turn. Mitchell's shaking fingers can barely hang on to the screwdriver grinding the cement. It has been two and a half hours since they first crawled into the ventilation shaft. Remarkably, no one has noticed them missing from the visiting room. No one heard them sawing through the ductwork. So far, no one has noticed their demolition of the concrete-block wall.

Mitchell knows their luck is about to run out any minute. But he is no longer thinking about getting caught or killed. He just wants out of there, to crawl through that hole in the wall, change his clothes, and walk to the blue Mercury.

The one that just pulled out of the parking lot.

The guard in the front-lobby control station apparently didn't take Lori's astute observation that there was no one in the visiting room too seriously.

"If you want to see Johnny, come back at one o'clock," he had growled. "I told you, he's busy right now."

Flustered and thoroughly confused, Lori shuffled back to her car, started the engine, and pulled out of the parking lot for the fifty-mile journey back to Phoenix.

Her heart is broken. She had never been so excited about anything in her life. Ever since Johnny mentioned something about a possible furlough a week ago, she had been redecorating her room for the promised romantic weekend with her dream lover. And then he called to say come and get me, sweetheart.

And then she was at South and he wasn't. Or maybe he was at South and she wasn't. It was all just too confusing.

11:13 a.m. At first it seems to move ever so slightly. Then it won't budge. Mitchell finally braces himself on a pile of boxes, and grabs the edge of the block with both hands. If all those years of fitness fanaticism have done anything at all, every ounce of it is going into one desperate yank on a hunk of cement.

The mortar crumbles. The pathway to freedom is finally clear. They squeeze through the opening and tumble into the utility room.

Mitchell tries the door. It is unlocked. He opens it a crack and sees only a guard in the nearby tower. Sunlight and the shooting gallery. The view of the parking lot is obscured by a low brick wall. Mitchell prays the blue Mercury is on the other side of it. He closes the door and announces optimistically that they are all free men.

They scramble to tear off their prison garb covered in soot from the dirty duct. Their dress shirts and pants underneath are blotched in sweat. Otherwise, they look like just three normal guys. Euphoric hand-shakes and backslapping all round.

Suddenly the door flies open. "Hey!" a man's voice booms. "What are you guys doin' in here?"

Lori is ten miles away from the Arizona State pen on her way back home to Phoenix when she pulls over to the side of the road and starts to cry.

How is this possible? she sobs. Go to South, her Johnny had said. Don't be late. She went to South early, and then to that other South, where they sent her back to the first South. But no Johnny. And then everyone kept telling her to come back at one o'clock. Then she could see her Johnny.

She checks her watch.

The three would-be escapees are rigid with fear. Their mouths hang open as they stare at the air conditioning repairman in the boiler room doorway.

"You guys ain't supposed to be in here," the burly serviceman growls.

Johnny Stuart takes a few steps towards the man. If life on the street has taught the wily black kid anything, it is how to think on his feet, especially when lying to authority.

"Yeah, yeah, okay, we were all just leaving," Stuart sputters. "We're all just lookin' for the visitation area, and it's very fortunate on our part that you happened upon us at this time, because it would appear we are not in fact in the visitation area. You mind tellin' us where we might find the visitation area of which I am speaking?"

The man looks at the three men in street clothes and concludes they couldn't be convicts. He doesn't notice the pile of sooty blue prison garb in the corner. Or the hole in the concrete block wall. Not yet.

"The visitation room is inside the main front doors of this building," the serviceman says sourly. "Now get the hell outta here and don't let me catch yuz 'round here again."

"Promise," Paddy Mitchell says as the three brush past the repairman and walk out the door.

The three men in street clothes hop the low brick wall and land in the parking lot. They stop and look around.

No car. No Lori.

Nothing ahead of them but CB-6. A one-way ticket to hell.

"There," Mitchell finally whispers. The blue Mercury is parked beside the pay phone. Lori has returned to sit in the parking lot and wait for the regular one o'clock visits to start.

The guard in the tower has been watching it all. He looks at their clothes and thinks they must be with the air conditioning repairman.

The three men are walking faster. Across the parking lot. Away from the boiler room. Away from the repair truck.

The guard calls the warden on the direct emergency line.

The warden picks up the phone as the three men reach the car outside his office window.

"Where da heck you been, Johnny?" Lori asks, tears of joy now streaking down her face.

"You wouldn't believe me if I told you, sweetheart," Johnny laughs.

Suddenly, her voice turns cold. She wants to know why two white guys are getting into her car.

Johnny Stuart is laughing. "Just giving these two dudes a lift to town, honey."

The guard in the tower is hesitant on the phone: "It's probably nothin', warden, but three males in street clothes just got into that blue Mercury that's been comin' and goin' all mornin'."

There are only two roads from Arizona State pen to the freeway. Even the shorter one is more than ten miles. That's why the street clothes had been so important. They needed to be able to slip away unnoticed. They needed a good fifteen-minute headstart, or a pair of state police cruisers could hem them in completely.

One suddenly very anxious warden was watching them pull out of the parking lot. Lori is terrified. Mitchell is in the back seat with a map on his lap and panic in his voice.

"Faster! Get moving! Turn left at the next road!" he shouts. "Now! Turn left, I said. Left! Dammit! Left! Faster!"

Mitchell has never met Lori before. Luckily he doesn't ask her to go South.

Now he is twisting his head around like a radar scanner gone berserk—look at the map, check the rear window, then the front, then the sides, then back at the map.

In the distance ahead, two vehicles are heading towards the highway from intersecting side roads. One on the left. The other from the right.

Mitchell can tell from their dust trails that both are converging at high speed.

"Faster!" he yells at Lori who is already convinced she is about to be shot and dumped in the desert. "I said, faster! Move it! Now! Go!"

"Johnny, tell him to stop yelling at me," Lori begs.

But Johnny Salazar Stuart just throws his head back and roars with laughter.

Mitchell checks his map. There is nothing between them and the two converging dust-trails.

Arizona just happens to be one of the few states in America that maintains a full-time fugitive squad. Not that they have more escapees than anywhere else. It's just that the kind of folks sent to Arizona State pen are best not left on their own too long.

A quick call from the pen to the police switchboard automatically triggers a well-rehearsed emergency plan. While the prison's tactical squad gives chase from that end, state cruisers converge on the area from all other directions. Helicopters are available if necessary. Usually, they aren't. There's just nowhere to go from Arizona State pen. Just two roads and a lot of flat desert.

The warden hangs up on the tower guard and rushes out to the parking lot. The door to the utility room is open. Inside, he finds three sets of soiled prison clothes and a hole in the cement wall.

The trackers at Central are alerted immediately: "A possible Code Two Hundred. Three of them."

A "possible" escape. Not a certain escape in progress. No one ever escapes from Arizona State pen. It has been five minutes since the blue Mercury pulled out of the parking lot. No one has called the state police.

The Mercury reaches Interstate 10. The two converging dust trails belonged to an ordinary pickup truck and a four-by-four. Mitchell orders Lori onto the freeway heading to Phoenix. Four lanes are harder to roadblock than two, but the getaway car is easier to spot.

Mitchell is screaming at Lori to do what she is told. First he wanted her to speed up. Now he wants her to slow down; no way he wants a speeding ticket to CB-6. Johnny Stuart is laughing in the front seat. Killer Kinkade just stares at the passing landscape.

A few miles down the freeway, Mitchell orders Lori to take the next exit.

"Oh, no, Johnny!" she pleads, now certain she is about to be taken into the desert, murdered, and left for the buzzards. "Tell him to stop. Tell him, no, Johnny."

"Just shut up and do what he says," Johnny barks. He laughs some more.

The exit leads to a parallel side road that eventually leads back onto the freeway. They take another exit, another side road, get onto the freeway, get off the freeway. Mitchell has every inch of the route planned.

Finally, the car exits the Interstate for the last time at Williams Field Road leading into suburban Chandler. Kinkade wants to stop at a pay phone. Mitchell doesn't want to stop for anything.

No one argues with Killer.

Kinkade makes his call and jumps back in the car. Lori hears him talking about his wife having everything set up. He doesn't have a wife, but that doesn't matter. He says the plane is waiting for them.

Someone else has wired some money to a Western Union office. At least that's what they're saying. Thousands of dollars. They have to get to the Western Union office.

Mitchell hopes Lori will pass everything along to police. If she doesn't get confused and tell them something else.

The car pulls away from the curb. Lori is terrified. Mitchell is barking directions. Straight towards Sky Harbor International Airport.

There are sirens in the distance. They're getting closer.

The prison trackers in high leather boots, spurs, and Stetsons have abandoned their horses for cars and are now racing towards the Phoenix airport—just in case the "possible" escape turns out to be the real thing.

Meanwhile the warden has ordered an immediate roundup and head count of all six hundred inmates. The process takes almost forty minutes to complete.

Yep. No doubt about it. Three missin', all right.

It is noon, forty-five minutes after the blue Mercury disappeared down the road. Someone finally calls the state police.

***

Mitchell orders Lori to turn onto a side road at the northeast corner of the airport and stop.

He scans the landscape one last time. There are railway tracks, a field, then the parking lot of Sky Harbor International Airport. He opens the door. There are no sirens, just the screams of jets taking off.

The three fugitives scramble out of the car. Lori is crying.

"Johnny! Johnny! Hey Johnny, where ya goin? Johnny! Johnny! Come back Johnny!"

The emergency plan of the state police fugitive detail is activated the moment the pen's call for help reaches the switchboard.

"Patrick Michael Mitchell...CONSIDERED EXTREMELY DAN-GEROUS!!!" Always three exclamation marks.

The prison trackers aren't far from the airport now. In a matter of minutes they will be stomping through the main passenger terminal in their boots, spurs, and Stetsons.

Paddy Mitchell slams the car door and yells something over his shoulder.

It sounds like: "God bless..."

EPILOGUE

Stephen Reid received Mitchell's cryptic going-away letter and laughed for days—only Paddy would write from prison to say he was about to escape.

Reid eventually found his own way to freedom. But it was a long time coming.

On May 6, 1983, Reid was transferred from the United States back to Joyceville medium-security prison from which he and Mitchell had escaped four years before. An hour after his arrival, he was put back in the paddywagon and shipped off to the super-maximum-security wing of Millhaven, the reason typed in triplicate: "More suitable training facilities."

His homecoming back at the Mill was no joyous occasion. "They put me in a cell at the far end of the range and said, 'Just sit there, Reid. Don't ask for anything. Don't ask to make any phone calls. Don't ask for any favors. Don't get sick. Just sit there. We'll call *you*.' "

It was during that time that Reid began to write, mainly to kill the black depressions and monotony of his days. He completed ninety pages of a fictional account of life on the lam, but wouldn't show them to anyone. He threw it all in a drawer where it stayed for several years.

Eventually, he sent the partial manuscript to a university criminologist writing an academic book on bank bandits. The professor was so excited with what he read that he passed it along to Susan Musgrave, one of the country's best-known writers and poets.

Musgrave fell in love with the work, and within a month, Stephen Reid had his first legitimate employment since he was seventeen—a book contract.

As it happened, Susan Musgrave also fell in love with the novel's main character. On October 12, 1986, the poet and the bandit Stephen Reid were married in the chapel of the maximum-security Kent prison in British Columbia.

351

That same year, Reid again applied for parole, a day pass, anything. The Parole Board all but laughed him out of the room.

Reid's book, *Jackrabbit Parole*, was a huge success, but it was certainly no ticket to freedom. In fact, when Paddy Mitchell escaped from Arizona State pen that same year, officials considered putting Reid in the super-max isolation unit at Kent to prevent a possible Stopwatch Gang reunion.

One day about a year later, Reid got a message out of the blue: the Parole Board wanted to see him again. "They just said I was out of there in thirty days. See you later. I was stunned."

On June 1, 1987, one of America's most prolific bank robbers was led to the prison gate, handed $130, and told to be a good boy for at least the next decade while he would be on parole.

For the first time in his life of crime and prison escapes, Stephen Douglas Reid walked to freedom. Tucked in the pocket of his lucky Levis was a postcard he had received that morning from somewhere in the United States. It wished him well on the outside, and asked to be remembered. It was signed, "Mikey."

At forty-two, Stephen Reid now leads a peaceful existence with Susan Musgrave and their two children in a pretty seaside cottage on Vancouver Island. When he isn't playing dad, husband, housekeeper, and the occasional game of hockey, the former desperado has writer's celebrity status on the guest lists of posh gatherings with judges, lawyers, and police chiefs. He also likes to ask his bank manager if his money is safe.

Reid was appointed to the high-profile Citizens' Forum on National Unity (the Spicer Commission) to conduct public hearings and advise the federal government on the future of the nation.

"I'm having a lot of fun," he says, already well into his next book project. "I can't unlive my past, and why would I bother to try? That period is over."

The former member of the Stopwatch Gang smiles and shakes his head: "When the sign at the grocery store says, Please Use Other Door—I do."

Lionel James Wright was transferred from United States federal prison in Leavenworth, Kansas, to Millhaven in 1984. He has since been moved to medium security at Joyceville where he is the clerk in the inmate canteen. By all reports, he keeps meticulous books and the cash is never a penny short. Since he has been behind bars, he has caused no problems of any kind. Prison officials report: "Lionel pretty well keeps to himself."

Wright has been eligible to apply for early release since 1988, but he only appeared before the National Parole Board once. They asked him a lot of questions, but didn't seem to get a lot of answers. His application was denied. He has refused to reapply, and is sitting out his lengthy sentence.

He is due for release in 1994.

The Stopwatch Gang touched hundreds of lives over the years, the experience etched in vivid memories that seem to engender everything from fondness and laughter to anxiety and bitterness. One way or the other, no one was ever quite the same.

In Canada:

Paddy Mitchell's wife works as a senior civil servant and continues to write songs. By mutual agreement, she served her husband with divorce papers at Arizona State Penitentiary in 1986. The documents were discovered unsigned in his cell two days later, the afternoon following his escape. She was finally granted a divorce in his absence in 1990. "I feel sorry for him," she says. "Money and good times are great, but they won't buy the things that really matter to him. He can never see his son again, nor any of his family. He has lost everything."

Mitchell's son, now thirty-one, is happily married with a new baby, a good job, and no criminal record. He says simply: "I still miss my dad."

Reid's former girl friend JoAnne eventually found her white picket fence. She is married to a wealthy businessman, has a child, and lives in a large suburban home.

Fat Boy was serving a minor jail sentence in Montreal in 1984 when he ran up a prison drug debt he couldn't pay. He agreed to turn prosecution witness in return for protection. He subsequently confessed to so many bank robberies (more than a hundred) that police stopped driving him to the crime scenes, and instead supplied him with city maps and stick pins. He is currently serving a lengthy sentence in protective custody for multiple counts of armed robbery. While his testimony also put a dozen other felons behind bars, he never turned state's evidence against any member of the Stopwatch Gang.

Detective Robert ("Archie") Archambault, who first busted the gang for the Great Gold Robbery, married the daughter of former billionaire developer Robert Campeau and left the police department.

Gary ("the Winch") Wincherook, Archie's sidekick in the gold investigation, also left the force for a safer job with the federal government.

Police Chief Kenneth Duncan retired amid controversy over his management of the force.

Tommy Harrigan, the drug importer who disappeared with partner Chris Clarkson in the middle of the cocaine-suitcase trial and was subsequently sentenced to twenty years in absentia, remained on the Wanted list for thirteen years. In fall 1989, Harrigan was arrested in New York State and deported to Canada to begin serving his twenty-year sentence. However, the appeals court ruled the original judge had no authority to try and sentence anyone in absentia. A new trial was ordered, but never held. It seems the RCMP had long since destroyed the evidence. The Crown, however, successfully appealed the appeal, and Tommy Harrigan is now serving a fifteen-year sentence.

Christopher Clarkson fled to the United States with Harrigan and has never been found. Sources say Clarkson assumed a new identity, got a law degree from a highly respected university, and is now an upstanding member of the bar with a wife and three children.

Justice Frank Donnelley, who sentenced Clarkson and Harrigan in absentia, and then sent Paddy Mitchell and Lionel Wright away for seventeen years, found himself in a bit of hot water after the trial. It seems the official court transcripts edited by the judge did not match those originally prepared by the court reporter.

The two judges who originally exonerated Paddy Mitchell on the drug conspiracy charges before the federal Justice Minister intervened found themselves in a whole lot of hot water. One subsequently resigned and the other was tossed off the bench after they were found in the company of prostitutes.

Gary Robert Coutanche, the Air Canada inside-man for the gold robbery who later turned informant, refused a police offer of relocation and a new identity. Instead, he went back to school and continues to live in the capital where he works for the post office.

In Florida:

Janet Lynn Rush, Paddy Mitchell's girlfriend at the time of his arrest in Florida in 1983, finally found a boyfriend not on anyone's Most Wanted list. She later told a reporter: "I didn't go out with anybody for a long time after [Mitchell]. It has taken quite a while to let myself love somebody again. Looking back, he could have been anything if he weren't so lazy. He could have gone into politics and really made it."

Chuck Hogan, Paddy's Florida friend whose motel harbored the gang after their respective Canadian jail breaks, became a wealthy land developer. Other than being the mysterious Gil Minski who bailed Mitchell out of the slammer in Phoenix, he denies all other involvement with the gangster—or his capture. He has never been charged with anything.

In Sedona, Arizona:

Jack Seeley continues to run the Sedona Flying School. He and his wife Judy didn't stop liking Stephen Reid when they discovered he was really a member of the notorious bank-robbing Stopwatch Gang. They have kept in touch over the years and, says Judy Seeley, "He remains one of the nicest, sweetest guys we have ever met. He would be welcome in our home any day."

Beckie, Mitchell's girlfriend of Sedona days, traveled around Europe for a while until she had a skiing accident, at which point she returned to her native Ohio.

In San Diego:

Loomis armored-truck guard Harlen Lee Hudson couldn't bring himself to go near the Pacific Beach branch of the Bank of America for almost six years after the Stopwatch heist. In the meantime, he was robbed again and accidentally ran his armored truck off a two-hundred-foot cliff. After seven months of recovering from his injuries, he returned to his job and was robbed again. His company gave him an official commendation for not shooting the bandit. Hudson maintains a small library of everything ever written or filmed on the Stopwatch Gang. And he hates them all. "Reid owes me," he says.

Special agent Norman A. Zigrossi, boss and mouthpiece of the FBI in San Diego during the Stopwatch era, subsequently quit policing to become Inspector General of the Tennessee Valley Power Authority in Kentucky, the largest power corporation in North America. In 1992, he was promoted to president.

Michael Aguirre, Wright's defense attorney with political ambitions, eventually ran for Congress and lost.

Reid's second lawyer, Michael McCabe, remains one of the top defense attorneys in San Diego, having recently represented Robert Harris, the first person to be executed in California in almost two decades.

Barton Sheela III, Mitchell's defense attorney who tried in vain to keep his favorite client away from Arizona State pen, was delighted by the news that Paddy had escaped: "I thought, great. Good for him. I hope he's back in Canada, and I hope he's near his mom." Sheela is a member of the state ethics committee.

Big Sam Stone, the prime suspect in the money-switch and theft of the gang's stolen loot, walked free for almost three years after the incident. In 1983, he was sentenced to twenty years in federal penitentiary for crimes unrelated to the Stopwatch story.

In Phoenix:

Police Detective Jim Thomas, who spent two years tracking Mitchell across America, was taken aback by the news of Paddy's subsequent escape from Arizona State pen. "I thought, naw, it can't be. That's not possible. It had to be someone with the same name." Thomas says his only regret is that he never got a chance to talk to the affable bandit again before he escaped. "He's a fascinating guy, and I've always thought it would be fun to just sit and chat with him for a while...I hope they find him before I retire."

Phoenix Detective George Edward Harden, who chased and finally arrested Paddy Mitchell in the parking lot of Diamond's Department Store, retired from the force in 1986 with a disability pension and another medal of valor (they spelled his name wrong on the plaque). He admits he wanted to kill Mitchell during the robbery. But the master bandit's escape from prison three years later doesn't seem to bother Harden. "Frankly, I don't give a shit whether he's caught again or not. He's smart. He hasn't killed anybody. And he hasn't done anything that would make me upset enough to want him killed. I'd like to see him caught because he should be caught. But I don't care...And more power to him if he doesn't get caught. Who cares? There are a lot worse guys out there. Rapists and child molesters, those are the guys I want in jail...[The Stopwatch Gang] were good at what they did, and you gotta give the devil his due. If those guys hadn't been bank robbers, they probably would have been cops...

And what of Paddy Mitchell?

Minutes after Mitchell and his two co-escapees jumped out of Lori's car at the Phoenix airport, the prison trackers descended on the terminal in their boots, spurs, and Stetsons. But the trio was not to be found.

Over the next few days, the Arizona State Police fugitive squad manned a special command post around the clock to coordinate the dragnet for the three fugitives. All-points-bulletins and Most Wanted posters were issued to police departments across the United States: "CONSIDERED ARMED AND EXTREMELY DANGEROUS!!! Always three exclamation marks.

The police had no trouble finding Lori from the license number on the getaway car—she was in tears, frightened, and still very confused. They interviewed a couple of Killer Kinkade's associates, who apparently said they'd be only too happy to help the police put him back behind bars. And they talked to Johnny Stuart's folks who said, nope, Johnny hadn't been home in quite some time.

The police had almost nothing to help them in their search for Paddy Mitchell. They contacted police in Canada who staked out the homes of Mitchell's mother, wife, and son, but the fugitive didn't come knocking. They contacted detective Jim Thomas at the Phoenix PD, who had plenty of information in his file from his own previous hunt for Richard Joseph Landry, a.k.a. Patrick Michael Mitchell, but it all got them nowhere.

Actually, the three fugitives never boarded a plane—no flying for Paddy, ever. Instead, they took separate cabs and checked into the hotel closest to the Phoenix police headquarters. Cash and clothes were delivered to them there. The next morning, three rather odd-looking types boarded a sightseeing bus for a tour of the Grand Canyon. Mitchell was impersonating an invalid with a pale powdered face, thick spectacles, and a checkered polyester suit. He claimed to have paralysis in his left arm and leg. Cecil Kinkade had a shaved head, sun glasses, and expensive duds—he was supposed to be Paddy's rich uncle. Johnny Salazar Stuart was dressed up to look like Mitchell's nurse.

Somewhere along the rim of the Grand Canyon, the invalid, his rich uncle, and the nurse ditched the sightseeing tour and caught a limo to Vegas.

Over the next few months, the three stayed on the run across the southern states until finally their friendship wore thin. One morning, Kinkade invited Mitchell to step out of the car and fight like a man. Paddy calmly rolled up the window and drove off with Stuart, leaving Killer on a street corner in a small town in Mississippi.

Eventually, the white mastermind and black street kid made their way to Florida. Mitchell found himself a sprawling ocean-front home and took up with the stunning young daughter of a millionaire with a string of seafood restaurants. Johnny Stuart later told authorities, "The guy used to pat Paddy on the back as though he was his son. I mean, this guy was big-time. And Paddy was always just the perfect gentleman. People with all this wealth and power used to want to be around Paddy all the time. Me too."

A file of photographs later recovered by police showed Mitchell having a swell time, all right—dancing with beauties, sipping drinks on the beach, cooking some gourmet extravaganza at his beach-front mansion.

In October 1987, seventeen months after his escape, Cecil Thurman Kinkade was arrested in Georgia, and returned to Arizona State Penitentiary where he continues to serve his time in CB-8, the only place in the pen—and maybe on the planet—worse than CB-6.

The FBI, meanwhile, had known Mitchell was back on the lam from the day he escaped from prison in Arizona. They also began to notice a familiar pattern of bank heists across the southern states—each one well-planned and executed with "military-like precision." No one ever hurt. Unusually polite for gangsters. Then they'd just vanish. Stopwatch-style.

And what had the federal force done about it all? Waited for the necessary paperwork, of course, for one of those troublesome UFAP warrants. In fact, they waited nineteen months for it. They waited a bit too long.

On the morning of December 14, 1987, in Gainsville, Florida, two men watched an armored truck making its first deliveries of the day before the banks were open for business. Shortly after 8:00 a.m., an anonymous male called the local police switchboard to say a bomb had been placed in a highschool twenty-three blocks away from the Merchants and Southern Bank. Every available cruiser was dispatched to the scene.

Ten minutes later, an armored truck made its delivery to the Merchants Bank and left.

One minute after that, two men wearing Ronald Reagan masks smashed the locked glass doors of the bank with a sledgehammer and demanded the money just dropped off by the armored truck service. On their way out the door, one of the bandits threw a shaving kit on a table. "This is a bomb," he yelled. "If anyone tries to follow us, it will go off."

They fled with more than $300,000 in cash, bigger than even the record-setting Brinks job in San Diego.

Three days later, Paddy Mitchell bid Johnny Stuart a final and teary "God bless," and disappeared.

Johnny Stuart headed for Bowling Green, Kentucky, where he was arrested by the FBI the day after he arrived. He was returned to Arizona State pen and tossed into CB-8 where he remains, serving an additional twenty-five years for the Gainsville bank robbery.

Larry Troutt, who headed the Arizona state police hunt for the fugitives, recalls, "Johnny Stuart returned to prison a whole different person than when he left. He had watched Paddy cavorting with all these people of wealth and power, and that's what Stuart wanted to become. Here was this eastside Phoenix street kid who came back full of self-confidence and talking about all the finer things in life—cigars, wines, good books. Paddy had a profound effect on the kid."

Following the Gainsville bank heist, and almost two years after Paddy Mitchell had escaped from prison, the FBI finally contacted the Arizona state police to obtain a UFAP warrant giving the federal force proper authority to start looking for the fugitive once on their own Ten-Most-Wanted list.

As usual, the FBI had been given a tip as to Mitchell's whereabouts. And as usual, they were too late.

Since then, the hunt for the elusive gentleman bandit Patrick Michael Mitchell has become something of an obsession for FBI agents across America.

In 1991, the FBI finally turned to the media for help. On four separate occasions, Paddy Mitchell was featured on the popular television shows *America's Most Wanted* and *Unsolved Mysteries*. The result was more than 600 leads—most of them led nowhere; a few led to a pot still boiling on the stove and an open door. Paddy Mitchell was last officially seen driving off into the sunset in a gold Cadillac with a trunkful of cookbooks.

The Arizona fugitive squad's Larry Troutt has worked closely with the FBI on the case. He concedes that Mitchell isn't exactly a serial killer.

So why all the fuss? "Let's face it: he's hurting us, especially the FBI. It's embarrassing. The guy has beaten us. And he has beaten the best we've got to offer. It's not like we haven't given it our best shot. We damn sure have. We've used about every tool available to us. And he's beaten all of it. Ask anyone at the FBI about him and they'll just roll their eyes."

Special agent Chenoweth of the FBI says: "There is a good chance that had Mitchell escaped from Arizona State and not done anything else, he would never have come to our attention again. There is even a possibility we might never have obtained a UFAP on him."

So why does the FBI want him so much? "He's not like other bank robbers. He's smart. He's careful. He's very good at what he does. He's a professional. And we want him…The crimes he has committed probably mean he will spend the rest of his life in prison."

Chenoweth rolls his eyes: "If we can ever get him back."

In the middle of the night on Saturday, December 1, 1990, a Brinks twin-engine execu-jet laden with $31 million in cash, gold, jewelry, and securities touched down at Montreal's Dorval Airport on its routine armed-transport courier run from New York.

Suddenly, at the far end of the airport, a bomb blew up an empty construction shack. Police on duty at the airport rushed to the scene of the blast. It was an odd thing—a month before, another bomb had blown up a parked car in the same area of the airport. Police had been baffled by that one. There had been no apparent motive, no explanations of any kind. But minutes after the construction shack was reduced to kindling, the earlier incident suddenly made sense.

As the airport police investigated the latest bombing, the jet and its precious cargo taxied to a stop on the tarmac almost a mile from the blast. At that moment, a stolen garbage truck crashed through the high wire security fence.

Seconds later, two Econoline vans sped through the hole in the fence and pulled to a stop beside the Brinks aircraft. The side door of the plane was yanked open.

The pilot, co-pilot, and guard on board the aircraft were expecting armored vans to retrieve the payload. Instead, they were staring down the barrel of a submachine gun. As another bandit stood guard on the tarmac, three others unloaded the plane.

A hundred and eighty seconds later, the bandits vanished with booty worth $16 million, including thirty-one gold bricks valued at $6.1 million.

The Dream Score.

The last Stephen Reid heard from his old partner-in-crime was a letter from Paddy Mitchell somewhere on the lam:

> Hi Stephen,
> Just a short note to let you know that I am well and hope my letter finds you as good.
> Sorry that I haven't written before now, but as you can imagine things have been quite hectic...
> I miss you, brother, and wish there was more I could say and do. You're not just my brother, but my best friend. I will always love you.
> Your Big Brother,
> Mike

Enclosed with the letter were two one-hundred-dollar bills.

Paddy Mitchell remains at large.